Writers of Italy

The New Italian Novel

Writers of Italy

edited by
LINO PERTILE
and
PETER BRAND

The New Italian Novel

edited by
ZYGMUNT G. BARAŃSKI
and
LINO PERTILE

EDINBURGH UNIVERSITY PRESS

© Edinburgh University Press, 1993

Edinburgh University Press Ltd
22 George Square, Edinburgh

Typeset in Linotron Bembo
by Koinonia Ltd, Bury,
and printed and bound in Great Britain by
The University Press, Cambridge

A CIP record for this book is
available from the British Library

ISBN 0 7486 0414 6

Contents

Foreword   vii

Introduction   The Italian Novel Today: Politics, Language, Literature
LINO PERTILE   1

Chapter 1   Gesualdo Bufalino: Baroque to the Future
PETER HAINSWORTH   20

Chapter 2   Aldo Busi: Writer, Jester and Moral Historian
MASSIMO BACIGALUPO   35

Chapter 3   Gianni Celati: 'Fictions to Believe in'
ROBERT LUMLEY   43

Chapter 4   Vincenzo Consolo: Metaphors and False History
JOSEPH FARRELL   59

Chapter 5   Andrea De Carlo: The Surface of Consciousness
MARTIN MCLAUGHLIN   75

Chapter 6   Daniele Del Giudice: Planimetry of Sight/Vision in
Three Books
ANNA DOLFI   89

Chapter 7   Francesca Duranti: Reflections and Inventions
SHIRLEY W. VINALL   99

Chapter 8   Rosetta Loy: The Paradox of the Past
SHARON WOOD   121

Chapter 9   Giuliana Morandini: Outer and Inner Frontiers
ELVIO GUAGNINI   139

Chapter 10   Roberto Pazzi: Dialogues of History and Fantasy
PHILIP COOKE   151

Chapter 11   Fabrizia Ramondino: The Muse of Memory
JONATHAN USHER   166

Chapter 12 Francesca Sanvitale: Investigating the Self and the World
ANN HALLAMORE CAESAR 184

Chapter 13 Antonio Tabucchi: Splinters of Existence
ANNA LAURA LEPSCHY 200

Chapter 14 Pier Vittorio Tondelli: The Calm After the Storm
DIEGO ZANCANI 219

Chapter 15 Sebastiano Vassalli: Literary Lives
ZYGMUNT G. BARAŃSKI 239

Note on Editors and Contributors 258

Index 259

Foreword

This book was originally conceived in 1988. It immediately received the warm encouragement of Martin Spencer, thanks to whose good offices it was accepted for publication by Edinburgh University Press. We are sad that his untimely death has prevented him from seeing our project in print.

We should like to thank Paul Barnaby, Peter Brand, Olive House and Jon Usher for their help with some of the tasks involved in preparing the final typescript.

Earlier drafts of a number of the chapters were presented and discussed at a conference organized by the Department of Italian at the University of Edinburgh in October 1990 and at the 1991 Symposium of the Society for Italian Studies.

Unless otherwise indicated, translations from the Italian are by the authors of the individual chapters.

ZGB & LP

The Italian Novel Today
Politics, Language, Literature

LINO PERTILE

> Were I to choose an auspicious image for the new millen-
> nium, I would choose that one: the sudden agile leap of the
> poet-philosopher who raises himself above the weight of the
> world, showing that with all his gravity he has the secret of
> lightness, and that what many consider to be the vitality of the
> times – noisy, aggressive, revving and roaring – belongs to the
> realm of death, like a cemetery for rusty old cars.
>
> Italo Calvino, *Six Memos for the Next Millennium*

THE REVIVAL OF THE ITALIAN NOVEL: AN INDUSTRIAL FICTION?

Italian fiction has recently been enjoying considerable popularity and critical
acclaim in France and Germany. At the 1988 Frankfurt *Buchmesse*, coinciding
with the launch of Umberto Eco's second novel, *Il Pendolo di Foucault*, a whole
pavilion was devoted to Italian writing. Britain, however, continues to remain
largely indifferent to the revival of fiction that has been taking place in Italy
during the 1980s. It is true that never before have so many new Italian writers
been translated into English, but these translations generally pass unnoticed and
unread in Britain, except by specialists. National newspapers, on the rare
occasions when they review Italian titles, tend to squeeze them into their least
conspicuous spaces, and reviewers seldom seem to be impressed by what they
read. Is this odd state of affairs the result of a long-standing prejudice, or does it
indicate the objective merits of current Italian writing?

This is one of the questions this book will attempt to answer. First, however,
it is necessary to dispel a doubt as to the nature of the phenomenon itself: is the
revival of the Italian novel a natural development, the result of a new generation
of young writers replacing old ones – the generations of Moravia (1907–90) and
Calvino (1923–85) – or is it largely induced by an ever more powerful
publishing industry? Traditionally, new writers have not been viewed in Italy as
a sound commercial investment. In the 1970s in particular, when even Italian
essays, criticism, philosophical and sociological works were on the whole more
marketable than indigenous fiction, major publishers tended to back established

authors. To the persistent demand for new fiction, they responded by flooding the market with translations, especially from Latin America and other new, hitherto untapped, traditions, such as the Mitteleuropean and the Japanese. On the other hand, small, provincial publishers were more ready to experiment with unknown authors, but were unable to mount the kind of promotional campaigns that would make a bestseller.

This state of affairs was dramatically altered by Italo Calvino's *Se una notte d'inverno un viaggiatore* (1979, English translation, 1981) and by Umberto Eco's *Il nome della rosa* (1980, English translation, 1983). The two books enjoyed a sensational success in Italy and then in the rest of the world, a success which generated enough money to persuade Italian publishers that the time had come for a radical change in their marketing procedures and outlook. Meanwhile the political and social situation had changed too. Terrorism seemed over. The militant revolutionaries of the 1970s had turned into the *pentiti* of the 1980s. The economy was picking up, indeed the country was enjoying a new mini-boom. Despite the apparent intractability of old and new problems, such as the North–South divide, urban poverty, drug addiction and rampant criminality, a new air of confidence was sweeping the peninsula, and the publishing industry was busily feeding it and feeding off it. While Feltrinelli, a publisher traditionally more open to new authors and more sensitive to the demands of the young, published *Altri libertini* (1980) by Pier Vittorio Tondelli (born 1949), Calvino at Einaudi backed *Treno di panna* (1981) by Andrea De Carlo (born 1952) and *Lo stadio di Wimbledon* (1983) by Daniele Del Giudice (born 1949). Suddenly, 'Italian' was beautiful in Italy too: encouraged by Eco's and Calvino's success abroad, Italian publishers turned their attention and marketing skills on the young or, at least, on the new. Adelphi launched Aldo Busi (born 1948); Marietti bet on, and won with, Roberto Pazzi (born 1946). On the other hand, Sellerio – putting their money on the *new*, rather than on the *young* – discovered the sixty-year-old Gesualdo Bufalino and published his first stunning novel, *Diceria dell'untore*, in 1981.

However, once they had achieved success, the small publishers were unable to keep their champions. So Busi moved to Mondadori, Pazzi to Garzanti, Bufalino to Bompiani. In addition, a number of excellent, roughly middle-aged writers, who in the 1970s had been confined to the second or third division, were now rediscovered and skilfully promoted. Gianni Celati, Vincenzo Consolo, Antonio Tabucchi and Sebastiano Vassalli belong to this group, which also includes, for the first time in the history of Italian letters, an impressive number of women writers: Ginevra Bompiani, Francesca Duranti, Gina Lagorio, Rosetta Loy, Dacia Maraini, Giuliana Morandini, Fabrizia Ramondino, Francesca Sanvitale, Marisa Volpi and others. These too were soon to be followed by yet another wave of new, young, women writers: Paola Capriolo, Marta Morazzoni, Elisabetta Rasy – and the list could continue.

This frantic publishing activity was strongly supported by the media and by a multitude of literary awards, which were now orchestrated by powerful financial conglomerates. There were prizes for all: the Strega, the Campiello, the Viareggio, the Bagutta, the Rapallo, the Bancarella, the Prato, the Grinzane-Cavour, and so forth – all well plugged in advance, discussed in the press and on the radio, debated live on television, with the awarding ceremonies fully televised on national networks at peak time. Novelists, young and old, became pundits, lecturing everywhere, writing columns in dailies and appearing on the small screen at all hours of the day and night, to give their opinions on literary matters, but preferably on topical issues: political, social, religious and sexual.

Obviously, something remarkable was happening. Novel-writing, which in the 1970s had been accepted with condescension or dismissed with scorn, was more alive than ever; furthermore, it was regarded once again as a respectable activity. The best way of capturing the attention of the consumer was now to describe any book as *romanzo*, regardless of its content. Biographies, memoirs, diaries, historical investigations, travel reports, social documentaries, philosophical musings were all described as 'novels', or at least as 'narrative'. Thus such disparate works as Vincenzo Consolo's *Lunaria* (Einaudi, 1985), Claudio Magris' *Danubio* (Garzanti, 1986), Luigi Meneghello's *Bau-sète* (Rizzoli, 1988) were all sold as 'novels' or 'tales'; and even a collection of essays such as *Diario di un uomo a disagio* (Mondadori, 1990) by Giampaolo Rugarli, another recently discovered writer, was presented in the blurb as 'a sort of unconscious novel' or, better still, a 'non-novel'.

Already by 1986 the phenomenon had acquired enough momentum to justify Pier Vittorio Tondelli's initiative in instigating and editing *Under 25*, an anthology of writing by young authors, three volumes of which were published within two years: *Giovani blues, Belli & perversi* and *Paper Gang*. As if there were not enough novels on the market, the publishing industry, hunting for 'the revelation of the year', stimulated production by publicly inviting teenagers to send in their manuscripts. Thus Mondadori 'discovered' the nineteen-year-old Lara Cardella whose autobiographical novel, *Volevo i pantaloni* (1989), aided and abetted by a huge promotional campaign, was instantly turned into a popular success, surpassing even Eco's *Il Pendolo di Foucault* in the weekly bestseller lists. Other publishers started new collections, devoting them entirely to young authors. In ten years the average age of the Italian writer had been more than halved. By the end of the decade a full-blown anthology of young writers appeared in the popular Oscar Mondadori paperback series, containing no less than twenty-four new authors, most of them born around 1955 and still unknown in 1985. Its title is highly significant: *Italiana: Antologia dei nuovi narratori* (edited by Ferruccio Parazzoli and Antonio Franchini, 1991). Exactly fifty years earlier Elio Vittorini (1908–66) had published *Americana*, an anthology of new American literature which was meant to send shockwaves through the old Italian literary establishment and was indeed censored by the fascist regime. Now Italy had its own homespun *Italiana*: the myth of America had been replaced by the myth of Italy; or rather, the suggestion was that the myth of America had come true in Italy. No wonder the country's publishing machine played the part of protagonist at the *Buchmesse* of 1988: by the mid-1980s, book production and marketing were proclaimed and perceived in Italy as a sure sign of the country's newly acquired wealth and international status. The *sorpasso* – the disputed fact that Italian *per capita* income was higher than in the UK – was not only a glowing economic statistic, it was a cultural reality of which the whole country could be proud: money was thus redeemed by literature, and literature redeemed by money.

Clearly, however, in a situation in which the culture industry seemed to monopolize both the production and the marketing of literature, success in terms of exposure, awards, national and international sales no longer acts as a reliable indicator of solid artistic merits. On the other hand, just because literary .works are backed by incisive marketing – a state of affairs with which the critic must learn to live everywhere – it does not necessarily follow that they are unworthy of serious critical attention in specifically literary terms. This is why it has seemed interesting and useful to consider the recent revival of Italian narrative from the outside, and in particular from a point of view which, whilst taking full account of the country's literary tradition and linguistic history, is not vitiated by any vested interest or prejudice.

The collection of writers discussed in this volume is not meant to be exhaustive, but it aims to be representative of the complexity, variety and richness of Italian narrative today. Not all readers will be satisfied by it. The criterion for inclusion or exclusion has been dictated by a combination of contingent factors, as well as by personal taste. The project achieved its consolidated form in 1988–9 and most of the chapters were written in the following year. This accounts for the absence of some new writers who have come to prominence in the late 1980s, such as Paola Capriolo, Claudio Piersanti, Giampaolo Rugarli, Enrico Palandri and Marco Lodoli; or for the absence of Dacia Maraini who, though very active throughout the 1970s and 1980s, produced her best novel, to date, in 1990. The exclusion of Eco and Calvino was due to their over-exposure: it seemed more useful to look at the literary world from which they emerged, than to insist on their works as though they were oases in a literary desert. On the other hand, there is a long list of established writers who would well deserve a volume of studies of their own, even if, because of their age, language or themes, they were never promoted in the 1980s as either *young* or *new*. Ferdinando Camon, Giorgio Manganelli, Luigi Meneghello, Anna Maria Ortese, Goffredo Parise, Carlo Sgorlon, Fulvio Tomizza, Paolo Volponi and many others can be said to belong to this category. Although profiting from the growing demand for Italian narrative, they have undoubtedly lost out as a result of the emergent and more marketable new wave. Therefore, this volume could not, and does not, pretend to be a comprehensive history of Italian narrative today. It is rather an attempt to explore the distinctive features of contemporary writing in Italy – within the limits of some of its most significant manifestations – as well as to identify whatever links there may be, historically, between it and the past tradition and, geographically, between national and international production. My intention in this chapter is to sketch out the historical and cultural context within which the present revival came about, focusing on the changes that have occurred in Italian society, and on the different ways these have affected the production and consumption of literature. A work of this kind may offer some points of reference for those who wish to see an updating of Italian reading lists, wherever Italian literature is taught, but it may also offer, albeit indirectly, a much-needed insight into the actual life of a country which the English-speaking world insists on viewing, despite all statistical data, as charmingly pre-modern.

THE TRADITION OF THE ITALIAN NOVEL

What has been said so far may have given the impression that the field of the Italian post-war novel is vast and, if anything, still growing. This impression is correct. However, the tradition of the novel in Italy is still relatively young. The great masters of Italian literature – Dante, Petrarch, Ariosto, Tasso, Leopardi, Montale – are all poets, not novelists. Boccaccio's Decameron played a seminal role in the rise and development of the European short story; but when other national literatures evolved from the short story to the novel, Italy was unable, unwilling and unprepared to follow suit. Its socio-political situation (in particular, the absence until a century ago of a sizeable and educated reading middle-class), the elitist and literary nature of its national language, and its dependence and reliance on its classical heritage ensured that in literature it remained faithful to poetry, considering prose – except perhaps in its 'high' form of prosa d'arte – as an inferior and 'popular' medium. The century of the European novel produced in Italy only one major contribution – Alessandro Manzoni's I promessi sposi – a historical novel, the formal models of which had to be sought abroad, and the language to be 'rinsed in the waters of the river Arno', that is brought closer to canonical Florentine usage, before its Milanese author felt confident enough to publish it in its definitive version (1840). There certainly were other major novelists in nineteenth-century Italy, from Giovanni Verga to Italo Svevo, but the genre on the whole failed to establish a narrative koinè that commanded the kind of respect and prestige given to poetry.

This lack of a narrative tradition is parallelled by the absence of professional writers. Even in the first half of the twentieth century there were very few professional fiction writers in Italy, perhaps less than a dozen or so. As the parallel processes of industrialization and universal schooling, and the gradual formation of a solid middle class got under way after the Unification, the increasing demand for fiction was satisfied by translations from French, English, German, Russian and other languages. Italian publishers acted mainly as importers of foreign literature, and in this sense played a vital role in the process of cultural modernization of the country. Many Italian writers lived, and still live, on the meagre proceeds of translations. Even now the Italian public seems to favour the non-professional anomalous writer: the scientist, teacher or university professor, lawyer, engineer, who writes in his or her spare time and hesitates between poetry and the novel. Posthumous publication is often a key to success, especially if the author has committed suicide. A case in point is that of Guido Morselli (1912–73) who has now achieved the status of 'a modern classic of Italian literature' (to quote the blurb in his *Diario*, Adelphi, 1988) thanks to his eight novels and diary, all published since his suicide.

This state of affairs has meant until recently that no Italian writer could start writing without first asking a number of basic questions that in other European traditions were taken for granted: why write? who for? in what language? Manzoni's work as novelist highlights in its starkest terms the knot of intractable problems that face a writer without a tradition: in a nutshell, the twofold problem of the relation between a writer, history and society, and between a writer and language. Indeed, if Manzoni wrote only one novel, admittedly a masterpiece, that was because its writing raised more problems than it solved. And in effect this has continued to be the case until now. The historical conditions in which Italian writers have operated since the heyday of Romanticism have been such that a narrative tradition could not be established, or a narrative language consolidated, until fundamental changes had occurred in Italian society.

The moment of change seemed to have come at the end of the Second World War. Suddenly, though foreign novels were to continue to dominate the market for many years, indigenous fiction too was accepted as a respectable literary product. The novel saw its readership and practitioners increase enormously, while poetry became the preserve of a small and exclusive circle of initiates. The new situation was the result of the extraordinary socio-political changes that had taken place in the country since its unification, from liberal monarchy through fascism to democratic republicanism. In the aftermath of the war there was an irrepressible eagerness to tell 'true' stories. Cinema and the novel became the favourite vehicles for the immediate communication of 'truths' that fascism had kept hidden for twenty years. Even if the models were the ideologically conservative – albeit linguistically innovative – Verga of the late nineteenth century and the American writers of the 1930s, fiction-writing in the so-called 'neorealist' mode was regarded as a statement of socialist belief. The writer's first aim was to sow among the people the seeds of a historical and social awareness which in turn, it was thought, would bring about a radical renewal of society. *Impegno* – commitment – was the order of the day; *andare al popolo* – to move towards the people was the password, and cinema and the novel were considered the best means to go about doing this.

However, this movement was largely the preserve of writers and intellectuals whose primary allegiance was not to literature, but to social change. The theoretical and ideological implications of realist language – that is, of a language supposedly based on *things* (meaning, reality) rather than *words* (meaning, literature) – were at first generally ignored. What mattered was that, with the realist novel, writers felt they were responding to the urgent needs of the nation. Rather than labouring under the weight of a secular, literary and highly compromised tradition, they were starting afresh, establishing their own rule even as they wrote. The purpose of literature was to convey and illustrate in the most convincing and accessible way a 'truth' that lay elsewhere, outside literature. As we shall see later, in all this there was a great deal of youthful enthusiasm and wishful thinking, but little logic. Writing was supposed to bring about social change, but social change was a pre-condition for writing to achieve its practical aims.

The publication amid heated polemics of Giuseppe Tomasi di Lampedusa's *Il Gattopardo* in 1958, the first Italian novel to achieve international acclaim this century, signalled that things were actually changing, though not in the direction forecast some ten years earlier. The country was in the middle of a remarkable economic boom, and the momentum gathered by the left in the immediate postwar years was clearly petering out – a process considerably speeded up by the Soviet intervention in Hungary in 1956. At the same time, the neorealist novel was losing its position of pre-eminence, as other non-political themes (the psychological, the existential, the fantastic, the sentimental) were gaining ground once more. It is not by chance that *La ragazza di Bube* by Carlo Cassola (1917–87) came out in 1959. This was in many ways an excellent novel in which, however, the faith in the inevitable progress of History, that was at the heart of neorealist writing and communist ideology, was viewed as a complete and dangerous mystification. Less polemical, though hardly less bleak, was the condition of individual isolation so sensitively depicted in Giorgio Bassani's compelling books *Gli occhiali d'oro* (1958) and *Il giardino dei Finzi-Contini* (1962), two other novels that captured effectively the sense of disillusionment of the period.

The neorealist novel was attacked not only from the right, but also, and more vehemently, from the left. By the end of the 1950s it was clear that the opposition between bourgeois and socialist cultures could not be resolved in the crude terms in which it had been posed in the immediate postwar period. A new generation of intellectuals, armed with a new and more sophisticated philosophical baggage – sociology, structuralism, phenomenology, neopositivism, psychoanalysis – began to denounce the neorealist novel on grounds of both literary form and ideological substance. On the one hand, the most radical of literary critics accused the neorealist writers of populism, that is, of indulging in a literature that was 'consolatory' rather than revolutionary. On the other, the *neo-avanguardia* questioned the cognitive powers of a language so deeply enmeshed in the ideology of the ruling classes that it could only perpetuate their perception and representation of reality. For them, the content of literature was its language, and innovation was possible only in so far as it subverted the conventional codes of artistic representation. This made for a great deal of sophisticated linguistic and structural experimentation, in poetry perhaps more than in prose, but did not do much for the novel itself. The 'anti-novel' was hardly the kind of narrative likely to attract many readers, except from among the *addetti ai lavori* ('experts'). By 1968 the Italian novel lay in tatters, with nothing to replace it. The growing mass of Italian readers could only turn to a staple diet of fairly conventional foreign translations and more or less respectable home-produced fiction: Alberto Moravia, Carlo Cassola, Italo Calvino, Giorgio Bassani, Natalia Ginzburg and many others, not to mention Cesare Pavese who, having committed suicide in 1950, remained throughout the 1960s and 1970s one of the writers most loved by Italian youth.

Despite the intense theoretical debates of the 1960s and the excommunication, if not of literature, of the committed novel, the notion, albeit confused, of a relationship between literature and politics, of the writer as the country's social and moral conscience, remained central to Italian culture throughout the 1960s and well into the 1970s. A current of realistic fiction developed in the late 1950s, focusing on the alienated condition of industrial workers in the society of 'the economic miracle', and producing novels that attracted a great deal of critical interest and, in some cases, popular attention, too: for example, *Il calzolaio di Vigevano* (1959) by Lucio Mastronardi, *Tempi stretti* (1957) and *Donnarumma all'assalto* (1959) by Ottiero Ottieri, *Memoriale* (1962) and *La macchina mondiale* (1965) by Paolo Volponi, *Il Padrone* (1956) by Goffredo Parise, and so on. Even in the 1970s when the Italian novel seemed incapable of responding imaginatively to the political and moral crisis that swept the country, there were writers, such as Paolo Volponi (*Il sipario ducale*, 1975), Vincenzo Consolo (*Il sorriso dell'ignoto marinaio*, 1976) and especially Leonardo Sciascia (*I pugnalatori*, 1977; *Candido*, 1977; *L'affaire Moro*, 1978), who participated convincingly in the ideological debate with their fictional writing as well as with essays, articles and documentary investigations. Moreover, Italian writers, conscious of the recent fundamental changes in Western culture and society, discovered wider concerns, for instance for the ecology of the planet. The so-called 'apocalyptic' theme was inspired not only by the writers' gloomy outlook on Italian life, but also by a genuine preoccupation with issues of a planetary dimension, as can be seen in novels such as the posthumously published *Dissipatio H. G.* by Guido Morselli (1977), *Il pianeta irritabile* by Volponi (1978), *Il re del magazzino* by

Antonio Porta (1978), *L'uomo e il cane* (1978) and *Il superstite* (1978) by Cassola, and others. And even the sudden blossoming of a neohistorical genre (utterly zany in Luciano Malerba's masterly pastiche *Il pataffio* (1978); more serious, but ordinary, in Giuseppe Pederiali's *Le città del diluvio* (1978) and *Il tesoro del Bigatto* (1980), Italo A. Chiusano's *L'ordalia* (1979) and Gian Luigi Piccioli's *Sveva* (1979)), which anticipated Eco's spectacular success, was a reflection of the writers' concern for a country that seemed on the brink of a new age of darkness.

Yet there were also clear signs that other elements, besides writers and readers, were taking an increasingly decisive role in the literary equation. In particular the publishing industry was extending its powers and altering its marketing strategies. With the deregulation of radio and television in the mid-1970s, large conglomerates were formed, capable of controlling traditionally separate media and institutions: literary awards, daily newspapers, weekly and monthly magazines, radio stations, television networks and film production. At the same time dozens of new small publishers were entering the market, catering for specialized demand, from feminists to political extremists, as well as from a host of unknown poets and novelists who were being rejected by the big firms. What all publishers seemed to learn quickly and effectively was the art of orchestrating *casi letterari*.

I shall offer four examples of this phenomenon from the 1970s, which was to become a regular feature of every literary 'season' in the 1980s. First, the case of Guido Morselli, whose entire *œuvre* was published by Adelphi only after his suicide in 1973. Morselli was a very talented writer who could not be 'discovered' any earlier for two fundamental reasons: first, politically, his work did not exhibit any definite ideological leanings except away from communism; second, linguistically, he was a writer who did not draw attention to his language, except in so far as it was neutral, clean, clear and effective. These features, which in the past twenty years had been considered as faults, began in the 1970s to be seen as positive qualities: Morselli's suicide in 1973 drew attention to them, and his success was guaranteed. The second example is Elsa Morante's *La storia*, published in 1974 by Einaudi directly in paperback. Formally, the novel was rather conventional, using a third-person narrator and a language that, if anything, had strong literary connotations. As for its content, it was History as suffered by the most innocent and helpless of its victims, as 'a scandal which has lasted ten thousand years' – on either count not a recipe to please the critics. However, the book, assisted by Einaudi's skilful marketing, quickly became a bestseller with nearly one million copies sold within one year of its publication. My third example is *Horcynus Orca* by Stefano D'Arrigo (Mondadori, 1975). In this case too all the odds seemed to be against the novel. It was inordinately long (nearly 1,300 pages), written by an unknown author over many years, in a difficult, idiosyncratic mix of italianized Sicilian and literary Italian, and having as its subject, ostensibly, a soldier's mythical short journey home from Calabria to Sicily after the September 1943 armistice. Yet the publisher was clever enough to stand all these apparent handicaps on their heads, turning them into natural ingredients for a *caso letterario*: the result was a memorable success. Finally, a harbinger of things to come, *Porci con le ali* (Savelli, 1976), a bestseller by Rocco and Antonia, two fictitious fifteen-year-old authors behind whom were Marco Lombardo Radice and Lidia Ravera, both actually in their late twenties. What is especially interesting about this book is that it is one of the very few novels that focused on the themes of *contestazione* (as the 1968–9 'revolution' is known in Italy) and certainly the only one which, albeit for the wrong reasons as we shall see, achieved mass circulation.

In Italy 1968 did not produce the kind of literary waves that one might justifiably have expected in view of the ideological elaboration that had preceded it. There were a few novels, directly inspired by the *neo-avanguardia* (for instance, Nanni Balestrini's *Vogliamo tutto*, Feltrinelli, 1971, and Renzo Paris' *Cani sciolti*, Guaraldi, 1973), in which ideological commitment was sustained by linguistic experimentation, but they did not reach a significant audience. The only exception was *Porci con le ali*. This was a love story of sorts, set in the midst of the 1968 student and feminist struggles, and published by a firm of impeccable, though recent, left-wing pedigree. However, what ensured its sensational circulation was its superficial anticonformism, in particular the boldness of its language, drawn mainly from fashionable media and students' jargon, and the uninhibited depiction of sex. To be true, these ingredients were cleverly mingled with the ritual homage to the 1968 trinity of Marx-Lenin-Mao, but the new religion was in no way related – very much like the old one – to the private lives of the two young lovers. Indeed the odd mixture of sex and politics was clearly calibrated to pander to the reader's lowest expectations: far from questioning conventional values, it served only to corroborate them, thus effectively undermining the ideological foundations of the youth movement the book purported to represent.

What have these four 'cases' in common? And what have they in common with what was to be the next 'case' – Umberto Eco's *Il nome della rosa*? The signs are contradictory. The only fact that consistently emerges is that there is now a sizeable public for Italian narrative, whose response however is largely determined by the culture industry. This industry pursues its commercial interests, but it does not necessarily sacrifice quality in favour of quantity. Indeed three of our cases are, undoubtedly, quality work, and they are all published by established firms; it is, interestingly, the 'progressive' publisher of the fourth that cashes in on scandal and sensation. Thus, now more than ever the responsibility lies with the individual writer. With the demise of the *neo-avanguardia* and the collapse of ideologies, literary schools and movements no longer exist, nor are there political parties with which the writer can identify. The writer is alone, and he or she cannot act any more as a vehicle for the transmission of fixed truths. Even the literary critic has now been made redundant or irrelevant. It is a time of *riflusso*, we are told, but for the writer there is no 'flowing back' for the simple reason that what has been left behind is no longer usable. It is also the time of a great new opportunity for the Italian writer. A narrative tradition may not be in place yet, but at least the debates, experiments and mistakes of the past years have definitely shown what the best Italian writers knew all along: that the writer has no other responsibility except to literature.

ITALIAN LANGUAGE AND THE NOVEL

While writers and critics were busily arguing about the relationship between reader and writer, politics and literature, reality and fiction, another irresistible process was taking place up and down the country. Language, that other problematic focus of Italian literature, was changing irreversibly – not, however, the language of the novel, but that of its readers; and the change was so radical that, if Manzoni started writing nowadays, he could do so unhesitatingly from Milan, and count not on the twenty-five readers he ironically claimed, but on millions.

Fifty years ago Italian was a language that an overwhelming majority of Italians either did not know, or knew, after a fashion, only because they had learnt it at school. For most people their mother tongue and only accessible language was their regional, or more precisely local, dialect, and the country offered almost an infinite variety of dialects, all incompatible – except perhaps the Tuscan and Roman varieties – with the official national language. Communication for most Italians was possible only within limited geographical areas: a Venetian *gondoliere* could not understand a Milanese worker, let alone a Neapolitan *scugnizzo* ('street urchin') or a Sicilian *picciotto* ('young man'). Nor could they easily read an Italian novel, except in the unlikely event that they had been at school for a good number of years. How did they communicate then? The answer is simple: there was no communication, for the simple reason that they never met, except perhaps during compulsory military service, which in any case did not involve the female population. The majority of Italians lived and worked on the land where they were born, and they spoke only the dialect of that land. They did not read. Only the educated middle classes – the *signori*, meaning at once both the 'gentlefolk' and the 'wealthy' – could speak Italian and read books and newspapers. Italian was perceived in Italy as the language of the affluent, dominant class, whereas dialect was associated with a socially subordinate and inferior condition. The acquisition of Italian implied a major change in the social status of the speaker, and as such was quite unthinkable in the society of the 1920s and 1930s. However, it began to seem possible soon after the Second World War. The single and most momentous discovery that a large majority of Italians made in the 1950s, at the time of their remarkable economic transformation, was that they wanted to 'speak Italian', and if they could not do it themselves for all sorts of reasons – age, habit, lack of schooling – they desired it at least for their children.

Language was also the fundamental problem the neorealist writer had to contend with. The neorealist novel, bound by the rules of verisimilitude and conceived with the explicit purpose of raising the political consciousness of the people, could not be written in the language of the people and could not be read by them, no matter how much its author struggled to devise forms that seemed to be closer to any spoken variety. All efforts in this direction were doomed to result in artificial constructs, lacking the legitimacy of either the national language or of any of the spoken dialects. Only other literati could understand and appreciate these efforts. As for the rest of the reading public – the literate middle classes – they soon grew weary of the same diet, and turned to the variety and excitement of foreign products, which were translated into standard Italian, indeed an Italian from which any idiosyncrasy that might have been present in the original text was erased or largely ironed out.

If neorealist fiction was condemned for linguistic reasons to fall short of its ideal target, it was also doomed, for the same reasons, to date very quickly. In the extremely mobile society of postwar Italy any attempt at mimicking the language of the people in any one of its ephemeral stages was bound to become quickly obsolescent. The language of Pasolini's Roman novels (*Ragazzi di vita*, 1955, *Una vita violenta*, 1959), precisely because it was modelled on that of the Roman *lumpenproletariat* of the 1950s, sounds now incredibly dated. On the contrary, the neutral Italian of Calvino's trilogy (*Il visconte dimezzato*, 1952, *Il barone rampante*, 1957, *Il cavaliere inesistente*, 1959), free of regionalisms, jargon and special effects to the point of seeming translated, is as sparklingly new today as it was forty years ago. What is disconcerting to realize with hindsight now is that the political project implicit in the writings of so many committed Italian writers of the 1940s and 1950s, regardless of the consensus they found among the critics, was fundamentally at odds with what turned out to be the actual aspirations of the people for whom they were writing. And something similar could be argued with regard to the much more sophisticated language the *neo-avanguardia* experimented with in the late 1950s and 1960s.

In fact, all artistic experimentation, conducted in order either to mimic or to subvert people's language, pales into insignificance when compared with the experimentation that was, and still is, going on in the living language. Literature and life were moving in two completely separate worlds. Linguistic experiments were essential to clarify the writer's position *vis-à-vis* literature, but they were impotent to influence the choices the country was making. Language was indeed changing, but only as part and parcel of what Pasolini in the early 1970s used to call, recoiling in horror, 'the anthropological mutation' of the Italian people; to put it in less dramatic terms, language has changed as part of the cultural transformation that has redrawn forever the map of Italian society.

The result of this process is that almost all Italians can now understand and read Italian; most of them, except perhaps the very old, can also express themselves in a variety of Italian that can be understood all over the country. This is to say that, although the dialects remain and are still vigorous, there are now perhaps as many varieties of 'popular' Italian as there are dialects, but these varieties, unlike the dialects, are all mutually compatible and, what is more, they are growing closer. In addition to regional 'popular' Italian, there is an average, everyday level of Italian, informal and semi-formal, that is both spoken – even if with different local accents – and written everywhere. Finally there is standard, formal Italian that is mainly written but also, in specific circumstances, spoken. Thus, where fifty years ago there were only dialects and formal Italian in stark opposition, there is now, in addition to dialects, a wide range of levels of Italian which are all mutually compatible. The level of expression will depend on the speaker's education and on the context of communication, but this will be a matter of choice, rather than one of necessity.

The mainspring of this transformation has been social and psychological; the means that have contributed to bringing it about have been education and the media. Television in particular has been instrumental in the spreading at national level of both standard, and regional and foreign forms that characterize, at least on the surface, 'medium usage' Italian (*italiano medio*). All teenagers now say 'uau' ('*wow*') and all Italians, including the President of the Republic, say 'OK'. This is perhaps why this level of Italian is the one towards which all other levels seem to be converging. This Italian is often accused of being flat, colourless and homogenized. However, if one looks systematically at it in its written form the impression one gets is certainly of less rigidity and formality, but also of substantial continuity between the past and the present. If Italian has changed in the past fifty years, and the gap between high (meaning, 'formal and literary') and low (meaning, 'informal and private') varieties has narrowed toward the lower end of the scale, this is not necessarily a sign of decay. Indeed it shows that now, as people of all backgrounds begin to know the language, or to know it a little better, Italian is being slowly modified for the simple reason that for the first time in its history it has come truly alive on a national scale. The important point is that social connotations have all but disappeared from the spoken language – which does not mean, of course, that social problems and anxieties have disappeared; only that they now find different channels of expression.

What does all this mean for the Italian writer today? Thirty years ago one could presume, or hope, that with the process of mass education then well under way – the compulsory schooling period was extended then from five to eight years – the conditions could be created in Italy for the development of a broad national culture similar in kind to that which existed in other industrially advanced European nations, with professional writers who could count on a stable or growing readership. Italian literature too could then have gradually overcome its traditional isolation and elitism. This however has not happened. The country's rapid development from an agricultural to an industrial and now a service economy has ensured in effect that this phase in its cultural evolution has been largely missed out. The written word had not managed to establish itself as an integral part of popular culture before it was overtaken and replaced by audio-visual communication. As a consequence, the 'serious' Italian writer, despite the totally different social and cultural context, is still writing for a relatively small and initiated minority, and even successful books find an audience that is modest compared to that of a *telenovela*. While in the past the masses were kept away from books for social reasons, now that they can read they prefer – as is the case everywhere else in the developed world – to do something else, like watch television or go to discos. Hence, professional writers in Italy are still very rare.

This is not all bad. Whilst half a century ago neorealist writers pitched their language at a low level in order to *andare al popolo*, the writers of the 1980s pitch it high to avoid the trap of uniformity and indistinctiveness set by the media. In certain cases they will seek models as distant as possible from current usage, and in so doing they will attempt to re-establish between spoken and written forms a tension which the postwar writer tried so desperately to abolish. This means that the average quality of Italian writing is high. No doubt, a sort of 'linguistic 1968' has taken place in Italy, but if the Italian employed by the fifteen writers studied in this collection is anything to go by, it seems hardly possible to argue that, as a consequence, the language has lost much of its expressive qualities. The authors included in this volume come from many regions of Italy: Piedmont, Lombardy, Veneto and Trieste, Emilia-Romagna, Rome, Naples, Sicily; only one, Tabucchi, comes from Tuscany – the traditional home of 'good' Italian – and he hardly displays any of the features typical of his region of origin. The loss of literary supremacy by Tuscany dates from the immediate postwar period; however, now Tuscany has clearly lost its linguistic hegemony, too. It simply no longer matters where one comes from. No writer now would even dream of going to 'rinse' his or her books in the River Arno, as Manzoni did 150 years ago. The consensus is for a 'modern' language that does not reside anywhere in particular, a language that is supple, precise, clear, and without local or social inflexions. Most of our writers, Celati, De Carlo, Del Giudice, Duranti, Sanvitale, Tabucchi, even Vassalli, all use today a language of this kind, that is close to the traditional norm and often also very elegant. Of course there are exceptions. For instance Bufalino and Consolo (both, perhaps significantly, from Sicily) seem to favour a refined, mannered, hyperliterary idiom. On the other extreme, there are writers, such as Busi, who delight in special effects, in the irreverent and baroque parody of all registers; or others, such as the Vassalli of the late 1970s and early 1980s, who mimic the jargon of a specific subculture in order to make a point about it. Only Tondelli, and not in all his works, attempts to reproduce faithfully the 'low' language of his characters, with effects that, to say the least, are ambivalent. However, the expressive effectiveness of all deviations can now be gauged by measuring them against an average everyday model that exists and is known, even if only passively, to every reader. In short the question of the language is no longer a socio-political question, but one of style.

PLURILINGUALISM AND POSTMODERNISM

In this context something needs to be said about 'plurilingualism' and the twentieth-century Italian writer who is regularly associated with it – Carlo Emilio Gadda. Plurilingualism, in the broadest terms, is that style which achieves its quintessential form through the conscious and systematic deformation of, or deviation from, the accepted norm of writing. This is done first, by incorporating into the text a multitude of different idioms (Latin, foreign languages, dialects, invented forms), and second, by violently mixing levels and registers. Its purpose is not to mimic reality, but to achieve intensity of expression. By its very nature this style is self-reflexive, it draws attention to language itself rather than to the contents language is supposed to communicate. Among European classics Rabelais and Joyce are often invoked as superb examples of this style. In Italy the plurilingual tradition is said to go back as far as Dante's major poem, whose odd title itself, *The Comedy*, is thought by many influential critics to refer specifically to the extraordinary range and diversity of its linguistic mix. The other writer to whom the tag is universally applied is the novelist Carlo Emilio Gadda (1893–1973). The hallmark of Gadda's narrative language is a wholly idiosyncratic mix of archaic, dialectal, and scientific forms – some already existing, some coined by the author himself – which have the coherence, compactness and inner necessity of a real linguistic system. It is a language that constantly predicates its own centrality and yet refuses to take itself seriously, a language that explodes any degree of confidence the reader might have in the representational power of the narrative, let alone in his or her own ability to know reality. Gadda's language was to some extent a reaction. It challenged on the one hand the artificial prose of formal, official and bureaucratic Italian, and on the other the realistic pretences and illusions of the socially committed writers. As such, it was an eminently literary construct, though its survival well after the demise of both its antagonists is proof enough of its unique qualities.

Now it has become customary in much Italian literary criticism to speak approvingly of plurilingualism and to mention regularly Gadda's influence every time a piece of narrative seems to deviate from the norm at the lexical, syntactical or rhetorical level. But what sort of plurilingualism is possible in a situation in which neither a formal norm exists, nor a socially connotated construct is any longer viable? A situation in which plurilingualism is effectively the stuff of everyday Italian? Obviously, what is possible are only the systematic, precious and entirely artificial – hence timeless – constructs of Bufalino and Consolo, that bear no resemblance whatsoever to the spoken language. Oddly enough, however, and in spite of Gadda's undoubted achievement, it is precisely in 'monolingualism' – that is, in standard Italian – that the only viable alternative to the babble of everyday discourse lies. Indeed even the 'low', parodic plurilingualism of a Vassalli, let alone Tondelli's mimetic variety, is bound to undergo rapid obsolescence. This realization of what in a different culture may seem obvious is a 'discovery' Italian writers have made only recently, and it may well turn out to be their most positive contribution towards the consolidation of a national narrative tradition.

Here perhaps is also the reason why Italian high culture, normally so quick in assimilating ideas from abroad, is so reluctant to accept the notion of postmodernism. 'Plurilingual', 'kitsch', 'baroque', 'experimental', 'pastiche', 'metanarrative' or 'metaliterary' are all interchangeable tags that often emerge from reviews of Italian narrative. They are employed in Italy rather loosely in preference to the postmodernist label that would be used in similar cases, no less loosely, outside Italy. It is true that postmodernist discourse makes little sense in a literature that has never, or hardly ever, spoken of modernism. However, there may be a more profound reason for this reluctance. In Italy there still is, by and large, an unquestioning faith in the eminence and dignity of literature. Despite the fact that Italians seem to accept wholeheartedly the homogenized diet that is administered to them daily by the media, they still believe in the traditional nexus between culture, books and education. What distinguishes Italy from the other highly advanced nations is the coexistence of a whole series of different, even contradictory, phases in its development from a pre-modern to a post-modern culture. The Italian workers of today, despite being surrounded and bombarded by postmodern disorder, still aim to send their children to university in the hope of seeing them one day become rightful members of a highly educated minority: the only difference with twenty or thirty years ago is that now they will want not only their sons, but also their daughters, to be involved in this process of social promotion. In such a 'modern' context, while the notions of *riflusso* and 'weak thought' may have epistemological value, that of postmodernism seems to be of little use.

BACK, OR FORWARD, TO THE MODERN?

Thus we come full circle. After the political novel of the 1940s and 1950s, and the experimental novel of the 1960s and 1970s, we return to the monolingual, literary novel of the 1980s. Though one would be hard put to find a negative review in a literary supplement, magazine, or journal, the terms most commonly employed by Italian critics to describe as a whole the literary world they live in are hardly flattering: *riflusso, vuoto* ('emptiness'), *babele* ('chaos'). In my view these terms, rather than signifying anything objective about the state of literature today, are indicative of the disarray in which Italian critics find themselves. While literature seems to have gained much from the collapse of ideologies, criticism on the contrary, deprived of extraliterary terms of reference, is all but lost. The problem is that the unexpected ways in which Italian society has evolved since 1968 have called into question the very foundations of contemporary literary historiography, with the consequence that the literary universe appears now fragmented, confused, contradictory and empty.

Literature, however, is alive and well with more producers and more consumers than ever before in Italian history. The contemporary novel is often accused of helplessly mirroring the decay, emptiness and chaos of Italian society with a retreat at the thematic level into *il privato*: psychological themes, introspection, autobiography, personal memories and obsessions, a contraction of all horizons to the sphere of an individual and usually private self, caught in the web of insignificant and everyday events. 'Minimalism' is a term that keeps recurring in connection with several of our authors. The term is borrowed from American criticism, but needs qualification when it is applied to Italian literature. Italy has its own indigenous tradition of minimalist writing. Its most recent and accomplished representative this century was perhaps Carlo Cassola, the already mentioned author of *La ragazza di Bube*. Cassola remained throughout the 1960s one of the most popular Italian writers producing novels – *Un cuore arido* (1961), *Il cacciatore* (1964), *Ferrovia locale* (1968), just to mention a few – in which the social and political dimensions of experience were utterly rejected in favour of the calligraphic description of a banal, humble, and insignificant domesticity. In the 1960s this kind of writing was branded as ideologically unsound, its connotations judged to be all negative, suggesting hopelessness, weakness, withdrawal, renunciation, disenchantment. Now, however, associated since the early 1980s with the young writers and legitimated by American parallels, the 'minimalist' tag conveys meanings that may differ widely according to the critic's expectations. Its use in an Italian context may be confusing. When Andrea De Carlo in 1981 published his first novel, *Treno di panna*, Italian critics greeted it as a breath of fresh air. In his blurb for the book Calvino could not use the term 'minimalism'; he wrote instead of 'the surface of consciousness which brushes against a world which is all surface'. The description was apt and helpful because it did not pigeonhole the new book into a pre-existing scheme, nor imply a value judgement based on extraliterary assumptions. Something similar could be said of Celati, Del Giudice and Tabucchi: their 'worlds of surfaces' lead the reader to look and see well beyond external appearances.

The retreat into the *privato* as the only safe area for the novel to explore is undoubtedly symptomatic of a profound disillusionment with public life, radicalism and what used to be called History. However, it cannot by itself be either good or bad. Or, rather, it is bad only if one expects of literature the sort of answers that history, politics and society refuse to give. The question is not *where* but *how* the writer goes. On the other hand, it must also be said that the writers' retreat – much lamented in Italy – is far from total. Fabrizia Ramondino's ostensibly private memoirs offer an analysis of the 1968–9 crisis that is more 'true' to life and certainly more compelling than any ideologically driven social inquiry. Rosetta Loy's lyrical immersion in her ancestral Piedmont makes each one of us painfully aware of what with the passing of time we have irrevocably lost and continue to lose. Sebastiano Vassalli's bleak reconstruction of a seventeenth-century witch trial is more powerful than any political pamphlet of the 1960s: as he appears to recognize in despair the futility of any attempt to change a world that is rotten to the core, he makes you feel that you want, must and can change it. These are only a few examples, and there are many more: not bad going for a literature that is said to be empty.

The contemporary literary scene in Italy is rather exciting precisely because the writer no longer feels bound for a destination that has been fixed in advance by someone else. Now that the linguistic divide between writer and reader has been all but bridged, the writer's allegiance and responsibility need only be to literature. This awareness is limiting, but it is also liberating. In terms of both themes and structures the Italian novel of the 1980s looks distinctly modern, whatever postmodern ingredients one might find in it. Equally, despite the oft proclaimed death of the author, there seems to be an inexhaustible reservoir of young and not-so-young men and women ready to prove that they are alive and passionately eager to write and to be read. Our fifteen writers do not belong to any literary school or movement. What they have in common is a belief in literature not any more perhaps as a means of changing the world, but as a still valid means of knowing it. In their best work there is, I think, a lightness that contrasts sharply with the struggling ponderousness of the past. Whether this lightness is, as Calvino put it, that of the poet-philosopher who rises above the heaviness of the world or that of the kingdom of death, is a question that the essays in this collection will attempt to answer. Be this as it may, there is no reason to despair that the secret of lightness will never be found. The quest has just begun.

BIBLIOGRAPHY

Barań ski, Z. G. and Lumley, R. (eds), *Culture and Conflict in Postwar Italy* (Basingstoke: Macmillan, 1990).

Caesar, M. and Hainsworth, P. (eds), *Writers and Society in Contemporary Italy* (Leamington Spa: Berg, 1984) pp. 1–34.

Caesar, M., 'Italian Fiction in the Nineteen-Eighties', in Smith, E. J. (ed.), *Postmodernism and Contemporary Fiction* (London: Batsford, 1991) pp. 74–89.

Calvino, I., 'Usi politici giusti e sbagliati della letteratura', in Calvino, I., *Una pietra sopra. Discorsi di letteratura e società* (Turin: Einaudi, 1980) pp. 286–92.

Calvino, I., *Lezioni americane* (Milan: Garzanti, 1988); translated by P. Creagh as *Six Memos for the Next Millennium* (Cambridge, Mass: Harvard University Press, 1988).

Cannon, J. A., 'Italian Postmodernism and Calvino's *Lezioni americane*', in Cervigni, D. S., op. cit., pp. 198–211.

Carravetta, P., 'Postmodern Chronicles', in Cervigni, D. S., op. cit., pp. 32–55.

Cervigni, D. S. (ed.), *Italy 1991: The Modern and the Postmodern. Annali d'Italianistica* 9 (1991).

Coletti, V., *Italiano d'autore. Saggi di lingua e letteratura del Novecento* (Genoa: Marietti, 1989) pp. 11–18.

De Michelis, C., *Fiori di carta* (Milan: Bompiani, 1990) pp. ix–xv.

Forgacs, D., *Italian Culture in the Industrial Era 1880–1990* (Manchester and New York: Manchester University Press, 1990).

Lepschy, G., 'How Popular is Italian?', in Barań ski, Z. G. and Lumley, R., op. cit., pp 63–75.

Manacorda, G., *Letteratura italiana d'oggi 1965–1985*, (Rome: Editori Riuniti, 1987).

Raponi, L. and Lepschy, G., 'Il movimento della norma nell'italiano contemporaneo', *Comunità* 189–90 (1988), 364–79.

Tani, S., *Il romanzo di ritorno* (Milan: Mursia, 1990) pp. 129–50.

Tondelli, P. V., *Un weekend postmoderno. Cronache degli anni ottanta* (Milan: Bompiani, 1990).

Gesualdo Bufalino
Baroque to the Future

PETER HAINSWORTH

Bufalino's is a remarkable case of late flowering. Whilst, on his own account, he has written stories and poems since his youth, he had turned sixty when he published his first novel. This was *Diceria dell'untore*, first drafted in the immediate postwar years, but kept back and intermittently reworked until the Palermo publisher, Elvira Sellerio, persuaded him to draw a line and to go public in 1981. Since then he has published two further novels, a collection of short stories, a book of poems, and various collections of short prose pieces. As he himself put it with his usual irony, *omertà* has been succeeded by logorrhoea (*Saldi d'autunno*, p. 251).

In some ways he has so far written what we might expect from a retired Sicilian schoolteacher with most of his life behind him. The first two novels are autobiographical: *Diceria dell'untore* looks back to the immediate postwar period, *Argo il cieco ovvero I sogni della memoria* to the summer of 1951. Much of the non-fiction is concerned with the now disappearing culture of Comiso and its region, where Bufalino has spent almost all of his life and which was more or less unknown to the world at large until it became the main Italian base for cruise-missiles in the early 1980s. Bufalino writes about what it has been like to live in Cruisetown (as he calls it), but he also draws affectionate charts of the vanishing local culture and the people of his youth. Only with his two most recent works of fiction has he stepped outside the limits of personal experience, ranging through the ages in the stories of *L'uomo invaso e altre invenzioni* and setting *Le menzogne della notte* in the nineteenth century. In all his books, and especially in these last two, he chooses to write in a highly literary form of Italian, which he knowingly and ironically cultivates. As he says in an essay entitled 'In difesa del congiuntivo' (*Cere perse*, pp. 29–32), literariness is a barrier against the false certainties of the conversational, no-nonsense language which modern media and habits of mind both prefer. Probably Bufalino's idiom could only have been formed away from the metropolitan centres of Italy or even of Sicily itself. As with certain contemporary poets – say, Philip Larkin in England or Andrea Zanzotto in Italy – the apparently backward province seems to stimulate the making of an individual style which owes much to past traditions and little to modern orthodoxies.

Still, contemporary Sicilian fiction as a whole has tended to be rather formal, even elaborate in expression. It has also tended to give pride of place to a tragic vision of Sicilian history. Broadly speaking, Sicilian writers have seen Sicily as oppressed from without and corrupted from within, any prospect of change for the better being doomed from its inception. Bufalino is much concerned with the Sicilian character, and is quite aware of past and present criminality. But he has no vision of history, no grand myth of the island which he projects in his novels, and he has little to say about organized crime. In his non-fictional writings he does discuss Sicily but from a perspective which prefers to note particular events or features, to attempt to characterize certain landscapes, to take stock, ruefully and nostalgically, of the radical changes which have taken place in his lifetime. Rather than the unchangingness which others have stressed it is the mutability of things Sicilian which impresses him.

Such an impression is not only of things Sicilian. Bufalino is obsessively aware of the instability and the insubstantiality of human life, the meaning of which is beyond us (if it exists) and the main fact of which is death. These are familiar concerns, perhaps universal ones, though Bufalino finds them particularly prevalent amongst Sicilians. In his fiction he faces the issues abstractly and explicitly, especially as they present themselves to a man whose life must come to an end sooner rather than later, and also creates images, situations, characters in which the general awareness takes on a brilliantly specific form.

He has no solutions, no creed. And yet reading him is not depressing, at least only depressing for the very faint-hearted. One reason for this is the thoroughness of his scepticism. The writer who knows for sure that he doubts has made a kind of Archimedean point from which he may, at least in principle, force the world (and the reader) to submit to his gloomy dominance. Bufalino doubts whether we can know even that we doubt. He is constantly drawn to paradox, to contradiction, to disavowals of authority or superior vision. Any one way of putting things, even negatively, is partial, inadequate, likely to be overturned because something unforeseen happens or because there is always another perspective. It is in fact a danger (though it may be passionately desired) to round things off, to declare some aspect of human life resolved and ordered. The only terminal point is death. Life, and with it any literature that attempts to find metaphors and representations which correspond at all to life, means openness, irresolution, multiplicity, and also comedy. Partly because, even more than Pirandello, he sees the absurdity of what is also tragic (and, of course, vice versa), Bufalino makes his readers laugh.

Unlike Pirandello, Bufalino has no confidence in the transcendental power of art, nor has he elaborated any other sort of theoretic edifice to sustain his own operations as a writer of literature. Words are suspect. When he tries, half-playfully, to explain the reasons for writing ('Le ragioni dello scrivere', *Cere perse*, pp. 15–18) the best he can do is list all the negative and positive reasons he can think of, from guilt and/or childish pleasure to a desire for illusory immortality or even a desire for death. In practice the status of the fiction itself is constantly undermined or changed or thrown open. The tone is ironic, unbelieving, dissonant, unstable in spite of classicizing features in his prose, the dominant impression is of excess: Bufalino often uses several formulations where a more sober writer would prefer one, or manufactures elaborate, sometimes deliberately tasteless metaphors which seem to announce their artificiality and their emptiness rather than their power of illumination, or suddenly and wilfully switches from exalted matters and perspectives to ones which are vulgarly comic and trivial.

There is then something transgressive in a good deal of Bufalino, something which invites the reader to enjoy suspect pleasures without really authorizing them, without the reassurance that all is justified through its being art. But the machinery of high literature, the display of traditional, literary skills, the delight in rhetorical excess, the flaunting of artifice – all this baroque virtuosity suggests that this really is Art. Though the suspicion is also artfully stimulated that what is being read may after all be a parody, a schoolboy's, or a schoolmaster's, charade.

All in all the reader is put in a difficult, though enjoyable, position the more so if he or she then has recourse to literary categories. Bufalino is obviously not a provincial realist of a familiar sort: his traditionalism stops him from being a modernist. Though he would certainly dislike the idea, in a way he is a postmodernist, a writer who plays ambiguously with tradition but who is conscious always of the void beneath his elaborate constructions. Or perhaps he is a postmodern realist, since he does find an accord with reality after all, but only if reality is to be seen either as unknowable or as nothing more than unstable simulacra vanishing into each other or superimposing themselves on each other.

Perhaps we can also see reasons, beyond natural reticence, why Bufalino did not publish until late in life. He has said that the neorealist 'ice-age' (*glaciazione*) was an unpropitious time in which to bring out *Diceria dell'untore*, and one can see why. The absence of a political stance and of a historical vision of any sort, let alone of left-oriented *impegno* as it was understood in the 1940s and 1950s, the refusal to imitate the spoken language, preferably the language of the *popolo*, must inevitably have marked the book as reactionary, indeed as unacceptable in the cultural climate of the time. But it is also a book which runs counter to the avantgardism of the 1960s and 1970s: Bufalino has no truck with revolutionary theories of literature or with the structuralist and post-structuralist currents that inform the later work of, say, Calvino. In many ways he is a writer whose time is indeed the 1980s and the present, who, thanks to cultural developments which he cannot possibly have foreseen or calculated, finds himself voicing attitudes which chime with those of much younger contemporaries, whilst, of course, still maintaining his distance and his distinctiveness.

Autobiographical novels about youth usually concern themselves with the emergence of the protagonist into maturity. To be schematic, two perspectives on growing up suggest themselves. Childhood may be a privileged state, whose loss is infinitely regretted but to some degree compensated for by the act of remembering, or it may be a time of distress and underprivilegedness, from which the protagonist manages somehow to escape. In the first case (*À la recherche du temps perdu* is the canonical example) maturity is barren and the remembered past is of value. In the second case (*David Copperfield*, for instance) the terms are almost inverted. *Diceria dell'untore* manages to combine both perspectives and at the same time to nullify both, as if neither are at all adequate ways of looking at the appalling and yet rich experience which the protagonist undergoes. Like Thomas Mann's *Magic Mountain*, to which it owes a certain amount, the novel is set in a tuberculosis clinic which forms a world to itself and from which human life is seen in a different, in some ways clearer, perspective than that which we normally have. But, unlike Mann, Bufalino thrusts death into the foreground from the very beginning and keeps it there to the last page, never losing sight of the unpleasant physical aspects of disease, nor hazarding any philosophical or religious consolation or justification for its brutality and mystery. All the main characters know that they are condemned. All die, except for the protagonist (whom I shall call Gesualdo to distinguish him from the novelist). For the greater part of the novel he, too, believes that he is doomed. That he survives is due not to any virtue or resourcefulness on his part or on the part of the doctors, but merely to chance. For some reason he gets better and the others do not. Thus, for him, youth is neither idyllic nor imbued with promise: it is a time of death, and its main privilege, shared with his companions, is precisely that awful one of looking at death in life in a way that is denied to those who are healthy. And the survival which is granted to him and which common sense might well think of as a much more real privilege on an everyday level, becomes a source of unease and guilt, as if to survive were a betrayal, much as it has been felt to be by survivors of the concentration camps, who also have often found it impossible to answer the question, 'Why me? Why not the others?'

It is in this light that we can begin to appreciate the force of the title. Bufalino provides partial definitions of *diceria* and *untore* as a kind of epigraph. Let us take the second first. The *untori*, who are best known in literature from the plague chapters of Manzoni's *I promessi sposi*, were reputed to be responsible for the spread of the plague in seventeenth-century Italy through infected ointments which they smeared on doors and walls and which were then touched by the unwary. Bufalino cites some trial proceedings which characterize an *untore* as: 'Dispensatore et fabbricatore delli onti pestiferi, sparsi per questa Città, ad estinzione del popolo ...' ('A dispenser and manufacturer of the pestilential ointments, smeared about this city, to cause death amongst the people...'). The young Gesualdo is infected and infectious physically: he remarks that he felt tempted in the early stages to bring his life to a rapid end out in the world at large, were it not for the fear that he would 'lasciarmi dietro a ogni passo le mie lumacature e polluzioni d'untore' (*Diceria dell'untore* p. 34) ('leave behind at every step my smearer's slime and pollution'). But the overstatement alerts us to his self-punishing sense that his pollution is deeper. Like the others, he feels himself to be corrupted in his innermost being, even if he is also the more or less innocent victim of disease. And in some ways rightly: for, again like the others, he finds himself behaving towards his fellows in a ruthless, almost perverted way, in spite of his sense of community with them, destroying rather than supporting, looking for and finding what satisfaction of the senses he can. In this extreme situation selfishness is the norm and what usually passes for altruism collapses, as if it were indeed a charade.

In this then the message? Is Bufalino the writer also an *untore*, his pollution now become verbal, as the phrasing of the title implies? Perhaps. Certainly there is no hint that the guilt has been assuaged or that his guilt or the desperation of the human condition is to be resolved through writing about it. The most positive thing that the novel can say comes at the very end when, reflecting once again on his being spared, Bufalino puts to himself this possibility: 'Per questo forse m'era stato concesso l'esonero: per questo io solo m'ero salvato, e nessun altro, dalla falcidia: per rendere testimonianza, se non delazione, d'una retorica e d'una pietà', p. 196) ('Perhaps I was granted exemption for this purpose: for this I alone and no other was saved from the slaughter: to be a witness, if not an informer, regarding a form of rhetoric and a form of suffering.') But things may be better – or, perhaps, from the point of view of our understanding the reality of the situation, worse. The *untori* were of course a fabrication, a desperate, prejudiced attempt to find an explanation for the spread of the plague and someone to blame for it. The psychological reality of guilt may therefore be unquestioned, but the verbal *untore* is no more (and no less) responsible for the way things are than anyone else.

This brings us to the first part of the title. Bufalino's definition of *diceria*, taken from the Tommaseo-Bellini dictionary, runs as follows;

> Discorso per lo più non breve, detto di viva voce; poi anche scritto e stampato ... Di qualsiasi lungo dire, sia con troppo artifizio, sia con troppa poca arte ... Il troppo discorrere intorno a persona o cosa ...

> A discourse, commonly not brief, spoken aloud; then also of one written down and printed ... Used of any lengthy discourse, whether over-elaborate or not elaborate enough ... Excessive discoursing about someone or something ...

The implications are important. What we are reading is either deficient or excessive: it does not and cannot speak of things as they really were: it is not a narrative of the familiar sort, in which the sequence of events has economy and order and gives economy and order to the novel as a whole. The *diceria* may, knowingly, deviate away from narrative into reflection or lyricism, or into apparently tangential incidents or episodes, or conversely it may omit matters that an ostensibly more balanced narrative would include (such as the pre-history of some of the characters or their actual deaths). And throughout there may be complex verbal structures, a deliberately artificial metaphorical play, but the rhetoric constantly undermines itself, as well as being constantly indulged by an author who simultaneously enjoys and sees through artifice.

For all these baroque features there is a firm, even dramatic momentum. If we are aware from the beginning of death and disease, it is only as the novel moves forwards and eventually reaches its moving climax that the full force of these themes and these words becomes apparent. The opening words are abrupt and mysterious: 'O quando tutte le notti – per pigrizia, per avarizia – ritornavo a sognare lo stesso sogno ...' (*Diceria dell'untore*, p. 13) ('Or when, every night – out of laziness or meanness – I dreamed the same dream again ...'). The formulation suggests that one option among many has been arbitrarily chosen by the narrator, and at the same time takes us directly into the crucial theme of a visitation of the realms of death. The writer, we soon gather, is a kind of Orpheus, who, like the mythical Greek poet, loses his Eurydice and the company of the other dead and is forced back into life, though it may also be that he has played at dying, as if the visit to the underworld has been a game. This prelude, which anticipates much of what is to follow, leads into the narrative proper, with the evocation of the hospital of *la Rocca*, to which the sick Gesualdo comes in the year after the end of the war, having like many others made his way from war-torn northern Italy back to Sicily, only in his case with the expectation not of beginning again but of dying. This antechamber of death, full of sunlight and colour seems itself almost unreal, theatrical, its tormented and despairing inhabitants like actors on a stage who are drawn to play parts which are overwritten and melodramatic.

Three of these are of particular importance. One is the doctor, Mariano Grifeo Cardona di Canicarao. Whether he is as nobly born as his name suggests or not, he is known by the less aristocratic sobriquet of *Il Gran Magro* ('The Great Thin One' – as opposed to *Il Gran Mago*, 'The Great Magician'). He too will die, as we gather from the beginning, although there are moments when it seems that he might recover. *Il Gran Magro* is the first of the characters, apart from Gesualdo, to emerge with any definition, largely through his own hyper-bolic and elaborate speeches, with their unusual literary and scientific terms and their insistent rhythms which, in distorted and distorting form, present the blackly comic vision of human life which he shares with Bufalino himself:

'No, ragadi siamo, ragadi sopra il grugnocolo di Dio, caccole di una talpa

enorme quanto tutto, carni crescenti, pustole, scrofole, malignerie che
finiscono in oma, glaucomi, fibromi, blastomi ...' (*Diceria dell'untore,* p. 24).

'No, we are sores, sores on the snout of God, droppings from a mole as big as
the universe, excrescences of meat, pustules, scrofula, malignant growths
ending in – oma, glaucomas, fibromas, blastomas ... '

Il Gran Magro will continue in the same vein to the end, joking viciously, or
trying to, philosophizing, quoting, parodying (including an effective, though
tasteless, adaptation of Catullus VIII (p. 141)), riddling, his most telling riddle
being the story of the three prisoners and the five hats (pp. 144–8), the point of
which is the analogy between Gesualdo's reprieve and the way in which the
third prisoner saves himself – at the cost of the lives of the other two.

The second, who appears soon after *Il Gran Magro* but is the first of the three
to die, is the military chaplain, Padre Vittorio, the voice of Christianity, which,
we gather from poems published in *L'amaro miele* in 1982, but written during
the immediate postwar years, was not easily abandoned by Bufalino. Traces still
persist in all his writing, and not solely in the form of linguistic desecration. It is
an indication of the force of what has been intellectually rejected that it is in his
relations with the chaplain that the novel most fiercely represents Gesualdo as
untore, helping to undermine a faith which is already being tested. But as always
the issue is left unresolved. In his very loss of a sense of God's presence Padre
Vittorio may be continuing on the Christian path, in so far as he refuses to
surrender to the temptation to complete despair. Whether that is so or not, the
final dialogue between the two of them, itself marked by uncertainty and
falsehood (p. 72), signals the end of any possibility of Christian consolation or
understanding for Gesualdo and the others. There is from now on no way out.
What is left is the sense that something or someone unknown is manipulating us
like puppets, the full force of this image being made clear towards the end of the
novel (pp. 169–71).

It is in this climate that the third and most important of the three figures
comes to occupy the centre of the stage. She is Marta, Gesualdo's Eurydice,
whom he first sees at a grotesque *soirée*, apparently organized by *Il Gran Magro*,
acting a scene from *Romeo and Juliet* and then dancing, the flush of blood
beneath her pale skin causing *Il Magro* to break into Dantesque poetry – 'Come
di lume dietro ad alabastro ... Così sono i serafini' (*Diceria dell'untore*, p. 57) ('As
of a light behind alabaster ... So are the seraphims') – in a way that Gesualdo
finds odious, but which suggests something of the seraphic qualities which
Marta has in addition to the sexual appeal of her decaying body. She may or may
not have been a dancer, a call-girl, a collaborator who sees her lover shot by the
partisans and has her head shaved, may or may not be Jewish: everything about
her is ambiguous, perhaps a pretence, but it is in her that the tragic energies of
the novel are most concentrated. Gesualdo's tortuous affair with her is a
representation of young love *sub specie mortis*: it is complete with rejections,

moonings, flights and it has moments which are almost idyllic, but it constantly turns into a parody of itself, the only real matter of importance being premature, inexplicable death.

Marta's death is the climax of the novel: it occurs in a cheap hotel by the sea, to which they have escaped from *la Rocca*, Gesualdo knowing by this stage that he will recover and that Marta will not. It is the first death actually to be described, and in some way it is as if we, the readers, are now at last exposed to the reality which has been threatening but has so far remained hidden.

> Mi levai, accorsi accanto a lei, non sapevo che fare. Era chiaro dai suoi occhi atterriti, dalla plumbea tinta del viso, che qualcosa era imminente, stava bussando dietro un muro. Una paratia sottile, oh quanto sottile, resisteva ancora, lo vedevo, dentro di lei a una pressura di nascosta alluvione. Ma non c'era speranza che non cedesse da un momento all'altro. Intanto l'affanno cresceva, gli sputi sanguinosi si facevano più ricchi e frequenti. Finché mi trovai a reggerle il capo, come nelle sfide di carnevale alle matricole ubbriache di triple-sec, mentre lei si sentiva salire alle labbra un irrefrenabile zampillo di rossa schiuma e di morte. Un sangue immenso, seminato di bollicine rotonde, le irruppe dal petto e allagò le lenzuola, enfatico, esclamativo. (*Diceria dell'untore*, p. 177)

> I got up and ran to her side, not knowing what to do. It was plain from her terrified eyes, from the leaden colour of her face, that something was imminent, was knocking behind a wall. A thin partition – oh, how thin it was – still held up, I could see, against the pressure of a hidden flood. But there was no hope that it would not yield at any moment. Meanwhile her breathing was becoming more difficult and she was spitting blood more frequently and more thickly. At a certain moment I found myself supporting her head, as if she were a freshman who had got drunk on champagne in a carnival drinking challenge whilst she felt the red foam of death gush up unstoppably towards her lips. A great wave of blood, speckled with small round bubbles, burst from her chest and flooded over the sheets with emphatic, exclamatory force.

It is a powerful moment, but also a piece of literary virtuosity. Deliberate overwriting undermines the tragic tone, as does even more the strident comparison with drunken students. Bufalino has not lifted the verbal veil: we are still, however moved or disgusted, in the area of theatre and performance.

The remaining pages will stress the note of defeat, though it is by now plain that there has also been, in some sense, a success, in so far as falseness which acknowledges its falseness has a measure of truth. Departure from the paradoxically rich world of *la Rocca* into colourless normality coincides with the ending of the novel. Writing (now located in these last pages in 1971) provides neither catharsis nor clarification: neither do normality and not writing. But, as with Samuel Beckett, who confronts similar dilemmas in a minimalist vein, a sense of liberation rather than despair may emerge from the conceptual impasse, to a large extent because the language, the very substance, of Bufalino's writing has such vitality in *Diceria dell'untore*, but also because ultimately there is no pretence here, or none which is not implicitly unmasked.

Diceria dell'untore is Bufalino's most compelling novel to date, and the book which establishes the stylistic and thematic parameters for his subsequent fiction. There are particularly strong links with his second novel, *Argo il cieco ovvero I sogni della memoria*, written in the early 1980s and published in 1984, which in many ways is a variation on it – lighter in tone, less tormented by incurable guilt, more willing to expose, or to pretend to expose, the narrator as he is now at the time of narration, but returning with increasing intensity, and in accents which are recognizable from the first novel, to the same sense of vanity, incomprehension and mortality.

Bufalino – and he explicitly names himself as narrator and protagonist – is now looking back to the summer of 1951, when he was twenty-nine and completing a year as a teacher of Italian literature in a girls' school in Modica on the southern coast of Sicily. Modica, like *la Rocca*, provides the tonal as well as the geographic setting, with its heat, its isolation, its more or less peculiar inhabitants. These are largely Sicilian stereotypes – the impoverished old aristocrat (Don Alvise), the feckless young aristocrat (Rosario Trubia), the sexually available and demanding widow, now past her best (Madama Amalia), and so on – all of whom, individually and collectively, seem to be playing for themselves and for others parts which, in Pirandellian fashion, they are not completely convinced are worth playing. The explicit theatricality again echoes *Diceria dell'untore*, as does the inclusion of a friend and colleague, Pietro Jaccarino, who, like *Il Gran Magro* voices tasteless parody and sacrilegious despair.

But the focus is now on the erotic, on an excitement of the senses and the imagination, stimulated by youth, summer, and the presence of so many coquettish girls, almost all seeming desirable at one moment or another. Bufalino represents himself as responding almost indiscriminately to these erotic stimuli, but also as in love, or deluding himself that he is in love. The object of his affections is Maria Venera, whose name suggests an impossible combination of the Virgin and the goddess of love. Gesualdo is disdained and finds himself a bit-player in a sordid, provincial comedy of elopement and abortion. The obsession with Maria Venera runs through the novel, but it is interrupted, just over half-way, by a brief affair with another, older woman, Cecilia, who is passed to Gesualdo apparently on the spur of the moment, by the rich Don Nitto, who likes to change his women every six months. From this squalid beginning comes one of the most overtly poetic episodes in the novel, though its termination is as coarse as its beginning, being marked by Gesualdo's discovery of his landlady, Amalia, and his friend, Jaccarino, *in flagrante*. The beautiful Cecilia, now nearly forty and showing signs of imminent decay, with an undivulged life of suffering and abuse behind her, appears in Gesualdo's life and in his story like the mysterious Isola Giulia which emerged suddenly out of the sea off Modica and then after a short while disappeared again. But the comparison is also made with Persephone, the goddess of the underworld. Once again passing erotic delight is associated with death.

From now on death, which of course had not been ignored from the very beginning, will invade more and more of the novel. Again it will provide the climax. The culmination of the summer and of the whole experience of Modica is a ball, the description of which echoes and parodies other sumptuous literary balls (such as those of Lampedusa and Proust). Here the erotic seems more than ever fantasmagoric. When Maria Venera unexpectedly appears, it is to go through a violent public row with her cousin, which, even more disturbingly, leaves no impression on the company. Everything seems now transient, ultimately insignificant, already haunted by death. The actual death, which brings the ball to an end and ushers in the end of the summer and departure from Modica, is that of old Don Alvise, who collapses whilst directing quadrilles. But by now the illusion of love is fading too. The last sexual references in the novel are to mercenary encounters with prostitutes.

Chapter I opens: 'I was young and happy one summer, in 1951.' ('Fui giovane e felice un'estate, nel cinquant'uno.', p. 13). But, though we temporarily forget it, we are told from the beginning that this is a fiction. Before Chapter I comes a brief Chapter 0, in which Bufalino evokes the image of himself as an unhappy writer who

> decide di curarsi scrivendo un libro felice ... Sennonché, più il racconto va avanti, e si trucca di fiabe, e formicola di luminarie, più lascia varchi fra le righe al soffio del nero presente. Non resta allo scrittore che differire sine die la salute, pago di aver cavato dall'avventura qualche momentanea lusinga ad amare l'inverosimile vita. (*Argo il cieco ovvero I sogni della memoria*, p. 11)

> decides to treat his condition by writing a happy book ... But, the more the story progresses and decks itself out with fables and sparkles and glitter, the more it leaves gaps between the lines for the black present to blow through. There is nothing the writer can do except postpone health indefinitely, content that he has extracted from the adventure some passing enticement to love life in its implausibility.

The intention, then, real or imagined, was to write an account of the delusions of youth, interwoven with a representation of the now elderly author, though the actual point of departure is the failure of the project. In the earlier parts of the novel it is the past which dominates, though the present keeps on intruding, particularly in the chapters numbered III *bis*, VIII *bis*, and so on, in which, in eighteenth-century fashion, the author addresses the reader and comments, usually adversely, on how the story is going. Already in chapter XII *bis* he dismisses the opening to Chapter I as completely false (p. 146). As he goes on, the present makes itself felt more and more, the *bis* chapters depicting an old and sick Gesualdo Bufalino, sleepless in an unappealing hotel in Rome where he has come to see a specialist, and all too aware that sex is even more squalid than it comes to seem to his younger self. The representation of present miseries and fears of the author merges with more and more pessimistic assessments of the account of his youth, which seems increasingly a construction whose mechanisms are to be exposed. And, as Chapter 0 had said would happen, the whole project of writing a happy novel which will somehow make up for present unhappiness is thus called into question. The last *bis* chapter (XVII) marks its complete collapse: if writer and reader have been temporarily distracted, the dead who were to be exorcised refuse to die. Words have run away with themselves (Bufalino provides a whole list of ones that he claims were waiting to be used on p. 201 and on the next page speaks of a further, unused chapter that had appeared of its own accord). The fiction has been a mockery, even as fiction. 'Scrivere è stato per me solamente un simulacro del vivere, una pròtesi del vivere. E ogni tropo ripeteva, ripete un tafferuglio di mercenari, un vizio da consumare nel segreto di un gabinetto' *(Argo il cieco,* p. 205) ('For me writing has been only a pale copy of living, an artificial substitute for living. And every trope repeated and repeats a set-to between mercenary forces, a vice to be practised in the secrecy of the lavatory'). But, as always with Bufalino's calculatedly violent and elaborate overstatements, that is not the whole truth, as he admits in the next paragraph. The brief conclusion to the whole book, chapter XVII *ter,* leaves the issues unresolved: all that can be known is the transience of life and the desire, to which writing is a response, that, in spite of everything, it should not simply vanish.

Argo il cieco is a remarkable *tour-de-force*, in which the artist attempts to reveal himself as fully and as crudely as possible failing at the act of writing and yet continuing (successfully) to write. He has an ironic awareness that every formulation, whether about the past or the present, falsifies or fictionalizes, but, being mindful of mortality and vanity, he cannot surrender to the game of fiction with any innocence. All that he can do is to make the most of his story-within-a-story system in order to create multiple perspectives, any and all of which, like the eyes of the keen-sighted Argus of his title, may in fact be blind.

It is difficult to see how Bufalino could have given further twists to self-conscious autobiographical writing after *Argo il cieco*. In any event, he changes direction in his next two books of fiction, *L'uomo invaso e altre invenzioni* (1986) and *Le menzogne della notte* (1988). Not that the thematic orientation or the cast of mind undergo any substantial alteration. It is rather that theatrical self-display is largely eliminated. The ironies created by sudden shifts of tone or register are also made more subdued: deliberately false notes are still there, though the underlying falseness is that created by a style which has been made more unremittingly literary, more patently artificial. The overall result is a loss of urgency and tension, though there is gain in range and a greater distance from the narrated events. At some cost Bufalino has become more classical, even if his baroque qualities are still very evident.

The twenty-two stories, none of them more than a few pages long, that make up *L'uomo invaso* might seem like the superficially disparate results of a trawl through European literature. One after another we encounter Eurydice, Noah, the sophist Gorgias, Baudelaire, the Bourbon king Ferdinand I, a pathetic vagabond who might have appeared in Verga or Pirandello, a monk on Mount Athos in a post-apocalyptic future, a Kafkaesque private detective, as much the object as the subject of investigation, and so on. All this diversity, however, revolves around certain concerns which are exemplified in the title-story, the first in the collection. An apparently normal man feels that he is haunted by another being: mysterious sores are appearing on his back which could be the beginnings of wings and he sees signs of what appear to be supernatural activities in him and around him. Perhaps he has been taken over by an angel or else, as he increasingly suspects, by a devil, though he could simply be suffering from physical sickness and psychological delusions. No resolution is offered. Bufalino concentrates rather on the ambiguous change which causes the protagonist to see his life and the world in a different light from any he had previously entertained, indeed makes him feel that he has no substantial reality as an individual at all and that it is something or someone else who is living or manipulating his existence.

This sense of an interaction between two or more levels of reality, or illusion, frequently of a literary or culturally saturated sort, with problematic religious implications, appears in story after story, frequently comically, though not always. In some stories the paradox is basically simple, though elaborately presented. 'Il ritorno di Euridice', for example, is a serio-comic evocation of a classical underworld centred on Eurydice's gradual realization that Orpheus deliberately turned and lost her in order to be able to compose his song of loss. 'L'ultima cavalcata di Don Chisciotte' which is equally elaborate and lugubrious in its atmospherics, has the old Don Quijote being the one who sees through the illusions which have given him his adventures and his life, whilst Sancho Panza finally surrenders to the power of words. Others are more like the title-story in being disturbingly open-ended. 'Ciaciò e i pupi', for example, mixes the world of crude sexual desire (reality?) with that of the dream world (but is it?) of the puppets representing fabulous medieval knights, with their courtliness of behaviour and language. Or there is the exaggerated formality of the letter, written to his bishop by a nineteenth-century country priest, which comprises 'Il ladro di ricordi' and which tells of a man, deprived of all memory of his own past thanks to a fall, who, through furious concentration, has come to be able to steal the memories, and thus the very selves, of others, including, it appears, those of the priest.

As with the first two novels, we always know that what appears to be revealed is either another story or the emptiness of knowledge beyond knowing that the one sure reality is death. This particular emphasis in Bufalino's writing achieves its most baroque realization to date in *Le menzogne della notte*, a novel which, in a tradition stretching back to Boccaccio, is also a collection of stories, but which, unlike the *Decameron*, creates dramatic interaction between the framing story and the stories within the frame.

The setting is the south of Italy sometime in the years when agitation for unification had begun but before there was any real sign that the Bourbon kingdom would collapse as rapidly as it did. We might expect from this that Bufalino would use the novel to put forward an interpretation of an important moment – some would say the important moment – in modern Sicilian history, along the lines of Lampedusa's *Il Gattopardo* or Consolo's more recent *Il sorriso déll'ignoto marinaio*. Instead Bufalino suggests no vision of history other than to take it for granted, as he had already done in *Diceria dell'untore*, that history means violence, suffering, abuse, deceit. Perhaps, in broad terms, he aligns himself with the opposition to Bourbon absolutism, but his interest focuses less on the political significance of the *Risorgimento* than on the literary and meta-physical issues that concern him elsewhere. As in *L'uomo invaso*, he uses the historical mode mainly to produce an effect of distance, almost of fable, perhaps with moral implications of a characteristically bleak sort. In his dustjacket note he suggests that he has written an 'historical fantasy, a metaphysical detective-story, a legendary morality-tale' ('fantasia storica, giallo metafisico, moralità leggendaria'), though he adds that 'l'autore non esclude che, a sua saputa o insaputa, taluna emozione pubblica o metafora dell'odierno o parabola possa essersi insinuata fra le sue fiabe' ('the author does not exclude that, with or without his knowledge, some widely-felt emotion or contemporary metaphor or parable may have crept into his fables').

The precise setting has analogies with *la Rocca* of *Diceria dell'untore*: it is an island-prison, evoked with loving gloom and horror in Bufalino's ornate prose, to which four members of an activist political group (terrorists? freedom-fighters?) are brought for execution. The prison-governor offers reprieve if one of them will disclose the name of the leader of the group who so far has evaded capture and who is known as the 'Padreterno'. The novel is principally the account of their last night which they pass by each in turn telling a story about himself. The idea is first suggested by a mysterious fifth prisoner, a religiously-minded but blodthirsty bandit, Frate Cirillo, who has been put into their cell and who, with knowing implausibility, Bufalino depicts as having once read the *Decameron*. But instead of his weak proposal that the stories should be about moments of happiness, it is the much more Bufalinian formulation of one of the four, the baron, which is accepted:

> 'Dunque raccontiamola pure, o inventiamola, la nostra ora più memorabile.
> Ma più ancora vorrei che dal raccontarsi venisse un senso al nostro destino. E
> deducessimo perché moriamo e concludessimo con un'ipotesi, almeno
> riguardo al mistero ch'è stato lo spettacolo delle cose dintorno a noi; e che

trovassimo una scusa a discarico o di Dio o di noi, prima che l'alba si levi. Ché se poi questo senso non si scopre, né il senso del nostro morire, ebbene per paradosso ti dico,' e qui si volse al ragazzo, 'che noi vorremmo ugualmente morire, ma tu avresti il diritto di dirlo quel nome e salvarti ...' (*Le menzogne della notte*, pp. 40–1)

'So let us indeed recount, or invent, stories of our most memorable moments. But I would wish still more that our storytelling should give a sense to our destiny. That we should deduce why we are dying and should conclude with some hypothesis, at least regarding the mystery which has constituted the spectacle of things which surround us, and that we should find an excuse that would mitigate the responsibility of God and ourselves, before dawn rises. For if that sense is not revealed after all, nor the sense of our deaths, well then I tell you, paradoxically,' and here he turned to the boy, 'that we would wish equally to die, but you would have the right to speak that name and to save yourself...'

It is in this ambiguous light that the four – the young man, the baron, the soldier, and the poet – tell their curious, somewhat inconsequential stories, each of which, it is suggested well before confirmation is given at the end of the novel (p. 150), is more false than true, and none of which seems to yield in any way the justification which the baron thought they might find for their lives and deaths. As in *Argo il cieco* but with darker implications, story-telling seems to collapse into insignificance, to be a rickety device for eluding the all too pressing thought of imminent death. But here the paradoxes are taken a stage further. Frate Cirillo's part resembles that of Bufalino in the earlier novel: for he sees himself as the author and manipulator of the night's entertainments (p. 138), even though from the beginning they have taken a turn which he did not anticipate. His own story, which is the last, is incomplete: after a savagely formulated version of Bufalino's pessimistic views on the shifting masks which are all we are, it evolves into a conversation with the young man, from which there does at last come the revelation of the identity of the 'Padreterno', quickly followed by the disclosure of the real identity of the friar. But this whole episode has a disconcertingly theatrical, indeed unconvincing air to it which, I think, is deliberately engin-eered, much as was the failure of the novel in *Argo il cieco*. The last chapter is an undelivered letter, sent by the prison-governor after the execution of the prisoners (whom the disclosure had naturally not helped) just before his own suicide. This was provoked partly by age and illness, but more by the strong suspicion that he had in fact been manipulated, and that the stories and the final disclosure of a name had been used by the prisoners as a way of continuing their campaign of subversion through false incrimination. He who had apparently won has apparently lost: the 'author' has become the victim and the stories, far from being distractions whose function it is to entertain or distract (as the stories of the *Decameron* might be thought to do), have become agents of death. But of course there are no real winners or losers, since all the main characters must die, the victims of a 'Padreterno' who has never disclosed even so much as his name, and may be nothing more than a fiction. *Le menzogne della notte* is Bufalino's most overtly artificial construction to date. Some readers may feel happier with the earlier fiction, and also with the collections of occasional pieces, especially *Cere perse* (1985) and *La luce e il lutto* (1988) with their more familiar, more personal, though still literary, tone. One book, which stands somewhat apart from these and from the fiction too, deserves a mention in conclusion. *Museo d'ombre* (1982) is a collection of short prose pieces recalling the world of Bufalino's youth through evocations of trades, places, people, dialect phrases, all of which have disappeared and of which the book is the shadowy museum. Many of these pieces are almost prose poems on the topos of 'Where are they now?' Some are almost embryonic stories. Here we find a relatively relaxed Bufalino, more melancholic than melodramatic, more elegiac than paradoxical. The baroque novelist is daringly and often successfully ambitious: this quieter writing is perhaps more touching, though less exciting.

BIBLIOGRAPHY

Main works

Fiction

Diceria dell'untore (Palermo: Sellerio, 1981).
Argo il cieco ovvero I sogni della memoria (Palermo: Sellerio, 1984).
L'uomo invaso e altre invenzioni (Milan: Fabbri, 1986).
Le menzogne della notte (Milan: Bompiani, 1988).
Since this chapter was completed, Bufalino has published two more works of narrative: *Calende greche* (Milan: Bompiani, 1990), and *Qui pro quo* (Milan: Bompiani, 1991).

Poems

L'amaro miele (Turin: Einaudi, 1982, revised and expanded edition, 1989).

Other Prose

Museo d'ombre (Palermo: Sellerio, 1982).
Cere perse (Palermo: Sellerio, 1985).
Il malpensante. Lunario dell'anno che fu (Milan: Bompiani, 1987).
La luce e il lutto (Palermo: Sellerio, 1988).
Saldi d'autunno (Milan: Bompiani, 1990).
Bufalino has also published a play, *La panchina*, in *Trittico: Bufalino Consolo Sciascia*, edited by Antonio di Grado and Giuseppe Lazzaro Danzuso (Catania: Domenico Sanfilippo, 1989); an anthology, *Dizionario dei personaggi del romanzo* (Milan: Il Saggiatore, 1982); and translations of Giraudoux, Madame de la Fayette, P.-J. Toulet, Renan, Baudelaire, Victor Hugo and Terence.

Critical Works

Amoroso, G., 'Gesualdo Bufalino', in Mariani, G. and Petrucciani, M. (eds), *La realtà e il sogno. Narratori italiani del Novecento* (Rome: Lucarini, 1987) Vol. 1, pp. 95–106.
Zago, N. *Gesualdo Bufalino: la figura e l'opera* (Messina: Pungitopo, 1987).

Chapter 2

Aldo Busi
Writer, Jester and Moral Historian

MASSIMO BACIGALUPO

Aldo Busi, born in a small town near Brescia in 1948, has published four novels between 1984 and 1988. These were accompanied by a number of translations, the most notable of which are John Ashbury's *Selfportrait in a Convex Mirror* and Lewis Carroll's *Alice's Adventures in Wonderland*. These were followed, in 1989, by a book of occasional writing, mostly travel. More recently, he completed a 'translation' of the *Decameron*, and brought out a book plus cassette, called *Pazza* (cant for 'gay').

During this period Busi made himself into a public figure, largely thanks to several television talk-shows, and by intentionally getting into tight corners: a trial for obscenity concerning his provocatively titled *Sodomie in corpo 11*, an arrest in England for objectionable behaviour in a London lavatory, and a much advertised failure to pass the written test for journalists. He is also given to a grandiosity of the Gertrude Stein sort, claiming to be the greatest living Italian or European writer and making adverse remarks about most of the challengers for this title. So there is room for the sociologist as well as for the literary critic. One would like to keep the extremely scrupulous writer, a notable stylist, distinct from the jester who features often on the front-pages; but this is hardly possible, there being little demarcation between his public figure and his writer's identity. Only, the writer is more interesting, both less and more exposed in his various strengths and weaknesses, than the notorious Busi, whose *bragadoccio* confirms an essential shyness and possibly an insecurity about his homosexuality – which is more likely to be disparaged in peasant Montichiari from which he has come than in the publishers' office in which he has found money money money (another compulsive subject). And it is the values of Montichiari that his fiction mostly underwrites, values notable for an honesty and frankness (about certain fundamental dishonesties, among other things) that are not easily found among more astute practitioners of the craft.

Busi's best books are his earliest, written before he was taken up by the commercial hullabaloo. They are, as all of his work except for the third novel, autobiographical fictions, in which a young male homosexual narrator is drawn into a dangerous novelistic situation out of which he happily emerges intact, a hero-observer who cannot but succeed and whom everyone, male or female, loves at first sight. Nobody can ever have enough of the Busi-hero and within the frame of the two novels this may well apply to the reader.

Seminario sulla gioventù is a playful title related to university sit-ins, in which students conducted 'seminars' on whatever they fancied. Busi was not at university in the 1960s, but, belatedly, in the late 1970s, the 'years of lead', when the various theories of liberation of the 1960s petered out, and disenchantment followed. Busi's hardboiled cynicism is very much a child of this age. But in Italian *seminario* is also a seminary for priests, and Busi has grotesque passages about the local seminary, the underwear of its students, the washerwoman who took it to the river to be cleaned and commented on the evidence of sexual activity she found there: 'Ah, la gioventù l'è prope un gran seminare' (p. 41) ('Youth is all of it a good deal of sowing'). So within the title we move from the aseptic and engagé conference room to the river-bed of an archaic peasant culture, whose humour is largely sexual. This is in fact the span taken in by Busi's writing: the high culture of Writing with a capital W, writing as a complicated game of Rimbaud-like *Illuminations* and prose-poems, and the vernacular which serves as a measure of the other. The result is notably rich and invigorating.

Seminario begins with a third-person revisitation of the narrator's childhood, spent in his parents' shop, where peasants come for food and drink, on the background of the Po flatland, and its dusty road. This section, with its stories of sexual initiation and childhood rivalries, with its hate of the father and brothers and love (though never so named) of the mother and sister, and chiefly with its landscape of memory drawn with control, is an impressive opening. The rest of the novel is largely set in Paris, with the exception of Chapter 4, 'Diary of a Bar-Boy', and Chapter 7, 'More Swamps', which take us back to Italy. Here the narrative is in the first person. Young Barbino has become a male prostitute of sorts and eventually a student in Paris. Slowly the central situation of the novel unfolds: Barbino's ambiguous relation with his hostess Arlette, one of three elegant women who have taken him up as a poor deserving student. Arlette is an unhappy single woman who would only be too willing to have an affair with him. Barbino, however, is not interested, and plays with the reader's expectations by insisting on his ingénue's attractions, while playfully commenting that breasts are disgusting to him. What we get is a life in the homosexual underworld, and in contrast to this a respectable ménage which however cannot but hide unspeakable secrets. It is only at the end of the novel that we discover indirectly that Geneviève, the undisputed leader of the tercet, is 'really' a man who keeps Arlette and Suzanne in some sort of bondage. The construction of the whole episode is interestingly novelistic, even Jamesian one could say, because of the amount of attention given to a single fact: as in Henry James, the attention itself enlarges the event and convinces the reader of its momentousness. He or she is going to share in some secret, and it is a breach of discretion to tell the story in a couple of sentences.

Chapter 4, the bar-boy's diary, is a foretaste of Busi's debunking of the monumental. If, later, as a correspondent at the Venice Film Festival, he announces his boredom with Peter Brook's *Mahabharata*, and, on another occasion, writes of his distaste for museums (he visits them he says, only to find suitable covers for his books), the earlier Busi is content with a vision from below of the great and mellifluous Eugenio Montale, Italy's major twentieth-century poet, who predictably exhibits many human weaknesses and is culpably unaware that the cultivated bar-boy who occasionally accompanies him on his strolls is a budding genius. The writing sparkles, as the bar-boy manages to gate-crash a party and meets many people whom he has served in his professional capacity: these find his face familiar, and think they have seen him at La Scala, Cortina, or Forte dei Marmi. Busi is a fine comic writer.

Vita standard di un venditore provvisorio di collant and *La delfina bizantina*, Busi's second and third novels, are best approached as exercises in the comic, the former conspicuously successful, the latter less so. *Vita standard* is the story of a student, Angelo Bazarovi, whose name is clearly reminiscent of the student Aldo Busi. He is the fortunate recipient of a monthly cheque from a philanthropic lady, but in order to make ends meet also takes on odd jobs, mainly as interpreter for Celestino Lometto, a local producer of pantyhose or *collant*, with international ambitions and a somewhat psychotic family. Aldo, that is to say Angelo, alternates hilarious trips abroad with Lometto, a sort of Busian Leopold Bloom with all the vices of the blatant parvenu, with exams in the Verona Faculty of Letters, whose lady professors he despises for their tea-party method of conducting examinations, kindly asking his opinion on this and that writer. The novel is a brilliantly constructed story of fifteen days in eleven chapters and three books – we have a unity of action in the present and a series of flashbacks to reconstruct Angelo's background. As in *Seminario*, the plot thickens when Lometto apparently arranges for a handicapped child of his to be done away with in a New York hospital and Angelo finds himself sent there to oversee the affair. A woman *à la* James Bond also puts in an appearance, inevitably falls for the homosexual hero, and in the close strips for his and our benefit. But the fun and success of the book is in the Falstaffian power of Lometto, who is absolutely exasperating and despicable and delightful in his out-and-out baseness. Here Busi reveals himself as the loving satirist of the acquisitive Italian middle class, and shows his essential respect for the self-made man of initiative, however much a charlatan. He also reveals himself as a sentimental moralist, the knight without sin who goes off to set the world to rights, and somehow pulls it off.

As in *Seminario*, much is made of gay jargon and shop-talk, and the narrator's attitude is again hard to pin down. One theme is that the exception is the norm, that everyone everywhere is homosexual, and that even Lometto would be willing to join the party, though he is always making fun of Angelo and vaunting his virility. On the other hand, Angelo barely tolerates the goings-on of the gay underworld, though he parades them at great length. He does not care for the queens along the shore of Lake Garda, and even less for closet homosexuals. In fact, he only approves of his own sexual behaviour, and even reserves the right to look at a girl, certain as he is that he will be irresistible to all attractive males and females.

Busi is good at epigrams, at hitting the nail on the head with an apt turn of phrase, though it is usually he who gets the benefit of being brilliant in a world made of odious slobs.

> 'Sintesi. Stringere,' e Angelo faceva così col pugno. Non gli disse che 'sintesi' era anche la qualità di dire con diecimila parole entusiasmando quanto gli altrí dicevano con dieci facendo sbadigliare. (*Vita standard di un venditore provvisorio di collant*, p. 284)

> 'Synthesis. Condense' – and Angelo held up his clenched fist. He didn't say that 'synthesis' was also the quality of saying with ten thousand words that made for excitement what others said with ten words that made for yawns.

In its paradoxical identification of fiction with 'the real thing', this is again a rather Jamesian statement. It is also a defence of the inordinate length of his books, which reviewers have often complained about. But *Vita standard* is a memorable picture of a culture where everything is fake and a pretence, and where one survives by mere gumption, as Angelo and Celestino do. The book offers a hilarious and sobering image of the Italy of the 1970s but goes beyond the local in its heartless depiction of the fight for survival in the modern world.

With *La delfina bizantina* (1986), his third book, Busi rewrote *Vita standard* in the third person thickening his plot around certain improbable grotesques in the neighbourhood of 'Byzantine' Ravenna. In *Vita standard* there is the suggestion that the ravenous Lometto family is given to cannibalistic practices, and this theme recurs in *La delfina bizantina*. 'Mysterious Happenings in the Village', could well be the book's subtitle. Given a house with a sinister fame, the village wags will embroider endlessly, until Anastasia and her daughter, the monumental 'dowager' Teodora, aged seventeen, become absolute monsters. Once again multi-national industrial and armament concerns loom in the background of the innnocuous-looking camp site on the Adriatic that Anastasia runs. The book is Busi's most overtly novelistic exercise, and this appears to be the reason for its weakness: it lacks an ego, a centre of interest. Busi cannot tell us how brilliant and naughty he is, so we do not quite know what to think of the characters who appear in it. The writing becomes an end in itself, exhibitionistic, and we soon tire of pretending to be amused and outraged, as Busi expects us to be. This is not to say that the book is without its rewards: there are truly savage episodes like that of the dogcatcher. An overextended joke, experimental in structure and even typography, it is Busi's *Finnegans Wake*, or *Gravity's Rainbow*, though a closer model may be Carlo Emilio Gadda's masterpiece, *Quer pasticciaccio brutto de via Merulana*, with its gargantuan excess of language.

After *La delfina bizantina*, Busi returned to first-person narratives. In fact, he began writing in his own persona. *Sodomie in corpo 11* (a pun on the human and the typographical 'body') is subtitled *'non viaggio, non sesso e scrittura'*. So if the book is about non-travel and non-sex, it is still Writing with a big W. *Sodomie*, however, has the makings of a novel, for Busi wrote it to please himself and to please his publisher, as a unit; whereas *Altri abusi* is largely made up of occasional writings that have appeared in the weekly magazine, *Epoca*. Homosexual paradises and infernos are very much at the centre of *Sodomie*, and Busi the charmer is his old self. The book opens with a powerful sex-scene in the parking area off a motorway: Busi picking up a young boy who anxiously asks for a second meeting but is pitilessly refused by the narrator, a sort of *auteur fatal*. The boy will return to his anonymous and uneventful life, whilst our hero pursues his excesses, his controlled *dérèglement de tous les sens*.

So it is no surprise that in *Altri abusi* (another punning title, playing on A. Busi and 'abuse') we find him writing about Arthur Rimbaud with great admiration, as if he still needed discovering and defending, and travelling to Charleroi and to the abandoned granary where *Une saison à l'enfer* was composed. In a review of *Seminario*, I suggested that Busi's prose-poems were reminiscent of René Char, but Aldo quickly set me straight: he would never dream of being influenced by such a literary nonentity as Char! The truth is that both Char and Busi have one source in common – Rimbaud. Another possible precedent for Busi and in particular for *Sodomie* is Henry Miller and his beatnik followers. However, in this case one should take away a good deal of mysticism and add the irony that Miller often lacks (though Busi can be equally lacking in self-irony). In the Milan circles in which young Busi the translator and aspiring novelist moved he would have been subjected to the myth of writing, a Jamesian–Proustian concoction, to which he added the accursedness of the outlaw, and his peasant good sense and laughter.

In *Altri abusi* the occasional travel reports are excellently written, and have clearly been expanded from their original journalistic form. Besides, Busi has inserted between one feature and the next (there are no chapter divisions) his by now familiar prose-poems and sketches. One may be tempted to skip these to get to the meaty conversations with Oscar Niemeyer or the President of Iceland, who, as other fine women, falls for Aldo when he tells her about Mrs Sterlino's strange doings (in *Delfina*). Yet they are worth reading, and in some cases debate the central issues of Busi's vocation and his spendthrift attitude:

> Una frase batte alle tempie di domenica sera: 'Qualcosa di struggente' ... Entra scuotendosi di dosso la neve il mio fratello maggiore: come è rimasto impercettibilmente lo stesso da decenni a questa parte e mi scoppia nella

memoria tutto quanto mi lega a lui, un'altra frase, che lui disse fissandomi con cattiveria: 'Perché andare di qui e di là come te? E poi, avrai vissuto tutto quanto e troppo alla svelta.' (*Altri abusi*, p. 188)

A phrase dully beating in his forehead on Sunday evening: 'Something touching' ... My older brother comes in shaking off the snow. How he's remained imperceptibly the same for decades and everything that binds me to him explodes in my memory – another sentence, which he said looking at me spitefully: 'Why run around as you do? In the end, you will have experienced everything, and everything too quickly'.

In another fine passage Busi writes about himself from the viewpoint of his young niece, whom he spoils and adores. Busi is a poseur without conviction, and his verbal fireworks very often offer genuine insights into social and human relations. He has proved himself a very able writer – 'a great writer', as one reviewer maliciously put it, 'who writes bad books'. Busi speaks of a fourth and final novel, *Casanova di se stessi*, but appears to have found a more congenial form in the first-person reportage, where he can play at being Aldo Busi, perilously taking for granted that he has become a public figure, and that success can only snowball.

This is the game he plays in *L'amore è una budella gentile: Flirt con Liala,* a slim volume of 1991 which repeats in miniature form the structure of *Seminario*, with the notable difference that Barbino is no longer a penniless student whom only a small coterie has the fortune to know, but a celebrity whose wit and wisdom is available to everyone. In both cases, however, he is begging the question of his irresistible charm, and this suggests that the happy-go-lucky speaker is no stranger to anxiety about his true status.

Like *Seminario, L'amore è una budella gentile* begins with Busi's young manhood in Montichiari, but the tone is more affectionate. The reader is introduced to a group of girls who, in the bar run by Busi in lieu of his father, conducted their affairs with the aviators from a nearby airfield, and found consolation in the countless sentimental novels of Liala (pen-name of Liana Negretti, born Como 1897) – novels in which love always wins the day against convention (and which are still selling well). This opening section occupies one half of *L'amore è una budella gentile* and contains some of Busi's most relaxed and attractive writing, with fine descriptions of the humorous goings-on at the Bar Fiat and of the Edenic landscape of poppies, daisies, streams with frogs: 'C'erano giorni d'estate che a causa della distesa di soffioni sembrava di avere un piede nella fabbrica della nebbia.' (p. 12) ('On some summer days because of the stretches of dandelions one seemed to have one's feet in a factory of mists'). The second part of this peculiar novelette goes on to the *Flirt con Liala*, whom Busi visits as an interviewer. Liala's role may be compared with Montale's in *Seminario*: though at opposite extremes of the literary ladder, they represent success, a name that has become a trademark – a process that Busi never tires of wondering at. Liala, in her nineties, lives with her daughter Primavera and with her bossy servant Tilla. Busi plays his usual cards and elicits boundless admiration from all three women, who cannot account for the fact that he is still a bachelor, are enchanted by his talk, and compliment him on his physique. Again, in a minor key, this is a replay of the tercet of mysterious women in *Seminario*, who were so taken with the speaker (one of them, Arlette, even managed to seduce him). But in *L'amore è una budella gentile* the situation is more comic and realistic, and Liala brings in her memories of past greatness: it was no less than Gabriele D'Annunzio who suggested her pen-name, telling her 'I will give you a Wing', in other words an *ala* – hence the change from Liana to Liala. The veteran sentimental novelist also likes to reminisce about Italy's former royal family. Busi's instinct enables him to detect a continuity between the multifarious levels of Italy's society, culture and history – Liala and Montale, Busi and D'Annunzio. Liala is a gargoyle whom he can use as a butt, but he has some genuine affection for her naive professionalism, her novels built according to formula, and her dedication to 'love'. Perhaps this Lady Wing *à la* D'Annunzio who has so much to say to the boys and girls of Montichiari, may be taken as a figure of Italy itself, a raffish old lady whom Busi never tires of courting and mocking.

Liala's nanny had told her that if she pricked her finger while sewing, blood would spill, and with it the *budella gentile*, but she had never explained what this 'gentle gut' was. (It is in fact a rarely-used idiom for the rectum.) So, as he exits from Liala's house in Varese, Busi asks her if she ever found out what her nanny meant. Liala does not know, or has forgotten, and in the moment of her uncertainty Busi flashes back in somewhat experimental fashion to the flowering young girls (so unlike Proust's) of Montichiari. When Liala answers that she does not know, he gives himself the final line: 'Nor have I ever known what love is'.

The suggestion is that he does not quite care, but he is also close to confessing his own unsatisfied love to the enchanter of generations of teenagers. And the reader may wonder, is not Busi's revisitation of Montichiari, and of his absurd predecessor, a labour of love? Here the opening paragraph of *L'amore è una budella gentile* is telling, for in it Busi is seen sitting up into the night at his old typewriter and beginning to fit together the words of his monologue. If the purpose of his writing is to evoke attention, sympathy, admiration, and finally love, by taking for granted that he already enjoys all the prizes, here Busi admits that lifting oneself by one's bootstraps does not really work.

Though neurosis and hysteria are never too distant in the background of Busi's books, his writing expresses at best an attitude of affectionate and humorous superiority to the world he observes. A self-taught craftsman, he occasionally makes the mistake of being too literary, of enjoying his wordplay too much, and so loses his reader's interest, as well as the control of his syntax. Equally obsessive, and tiresome at times, is his depiction of homosexuality. At best, as in *Seminario, Sodomie* and *L'amore*, he is a masterful writer of unusual fictions, detached and sympathetic, surprisingly sane under the cover of his raucous humour, with a view of things and of himself much more sober and controlled than he is usually given credit for.

BIBLIOGRAPHY

Works

Seminario sulla gioventù (Milan: Adelphi, 1984); reprinted with a foreword by Piero Bertolucci and an Afterword by Massimo Bacigalupo (Milan: Mondadori, 1988). Translated by Stuart Hood as *Seminar on Youth* (Manchester: Carcanet, 1988; London: Faber, 1989).

Vita standard di un venditore provvisorio di collant (Milan: Mondadori, 1985). Translated by Raymond Rosenthal as *The Standard Life of a Temporary Pantyhose Salesman* (New York: FSG, 1988; London: Faber, 1990).

La delfina bizantina (Milan: Mondadori, 1986).

Sodomie in corpo 11: non viaggio, non sesso e scrittura (Milan: Mondadori, 1988); reprinted with an Afterword by Massimo Bacigalupo, and with documents relating to the trial collected by Carmen Covito (Milan: Mondadori, 1992). Translated by Stuart Hood as *Sodomies in Elevenpoint* (London: Faber, 1992).

Altri abusi. Viaggi, sonnambulismi e giri dell'oca (Milan: Leonardo, 1989).

Pâté d'homme (with Carmen Covito and artwork by Dario Cioli) (Milan: Mondadori, 1989).

Decamerone: da un italiano all'altro, 2 volumes (Milan: Rizzoli, 1990–1).

L'amore è una budella gentile. Flirt con Liala (Milan: Leonardo, 1991).

Since this chapter was completed Busi has published two more books: *Sentire le donne* (Milan: Bompiani, 1991) and *Le persone normali (La dieta di Uscio)* (Milan: Mondadori, 1992).

Interviews

Enrico Ragazzoni, 'C'è un romanzo nella tazza di caffè', *L'Europeo*, 7 April 1984.

Maria Luisa Agnese, 'Io stramaledico gli inglesi', *Panorama*, 27 September 1987, 122–8.

Mino Monicelli, 'Io, Aldo Busi, intellettuale brigante alla François Villon', *Millelibri* 35 (October 1990), 44–8.

Massimo Bacigalupo, 'Uscio, la dieta di Busi diventa un romanzo', *Secolo XIX*, 9 June 1991, 9.

Chapter 3

Gianni Celati
'Fictions to Believe in'

ROBERT LUMLEY

Crediamo che tutto ciò che la gente fa dalla mattina alla sera sia uno sforzo per trovare un possibile racconto dell'esterno, che sia almeno un po' vivibile. Pensiamo che anche questa sia una finzione, ma una finzione a cui è necessario credere.

We believe that everything people do from morning to night is an effort to come up with a credible account of the outside world, one that will make it bearable at least to some extent. We think that this too is a fiction, but a fiction in which it is necessary to believe.

Gianni Celati, 'Finzioni a cui credere'

Gianni Celati is a writer of fiction who also writes literary criticism and translations. His work has come out in book form but also in reviews and newspapers. He has written accompanying texts for exhibitions of photographs, done radio programmes and produced a piece for television, set in the Po Valley, *Strada provinciale delle anime* (1991). Not least, Celati has encouraged others to write and has brought to public attention writers who would probably otherwise have remained little known to an Italian readership.

Ideally, a chapter like this would look at the full range of Celati's work. His work as a translator, for instance, is extensive – authors translated include Céline, Barthes, Swift, Twain, London and Melville. Can this be regarded as 'his' writing as well as 'theirs'? How has translating served as an ongoing apprenticeship for Celati's other writing? It is significant in this respect that Einaudi publishes a series entitled Writers Translated by Writers (which includes Celati's translation of Jack London's *Call of the Wild*), and that a contemporary author should have commented with reference to Celati: 'It could be that from now on the language which we must draw on if we want to write – the writer's lingua franca – can only be the language of translation' (Rasy, 'Gianni Celati', p. 125). Another set of questions might well be asked of his essays: Can they too be seen as fiction as well as a commentary on fiction? Guido Fink, for example, has spoken of the importance for him of *Finzioni occidentali* in the following terms: 'It remains one of the few "theoretical" books of that period to retain some value both as a recapitulation of things said and thought and (by others) vaguely felt, and as a survival manual for anyone still interested in telling stories or listening to them' (Fink, 'Da dove vengono tutte le storie', p. 68).

My piece is less ambitious and starts with an acceptance of the conventional genre distinctions. It will focus on what can be called Celati's fiction (novels, stories, *novelle*): *Comiche* (1971), *Le avventure di Guizzardi* (1973), *La banda dei sospiri* (1976), *La bottega dei mimi* (1976), *Lunario del paradiso* (1978), *Narratori delle pianure* (1985), *Quattro novelle sulle apparenze* (1987), and *Verso la foce* (1989). (Three of the novels from the 1970s were republished with some revisions in one volume entitled *Parlamenti buffi* (1989).) However, Celati's *Finzioni occidentali* (1975) and other essays will be read alongside the fiction as a kind of parallel text constituting as they do explorations of areas between anthropology and literature that 'accompanied (indeed had as their nucleus) his creative activity as a novelist' (Calvino, 'Da Buster Keaton a Peter Handke', p. 95).

Although relatively little has been written on Celati, he has been well served by reviewers and has himself provided useful pointers to understanding his work in interviews. In fact, Celati's articulateness about writing has encouraged others to read him in his own terms. What is more difficult to grasp is his development as a writer in relation to contemporary literature and literary tradition.

Celati has tended recently to stress his debt to Italian writers. *Parlamenti buffi*, which is dedicated to Italo Calvino, has a preface naming those he particularly admires − 'our fine *novellatore* Masuccio Salernitano', 'our great comic poet Teofilo Folengo' and 'our Angelo Beolco, otherwise known as Ruzzante' (*Parlamenti buffi*, p. 7). Yet he participated in the avant-garde of the 1960s and shared its enthusiasm for foreign modernist rather than Italian writers, doing a *tesi di laurea* on Joyce and going on to teach Anglo-American literature. Even as someone who rejects the provincialism of those Italians who despise the provinces in the name of cosmopolitanism, there remains a profound ambiguity in Celati's relationship to his own country and its culture: 'In questo paese gli uomini sono diventati così sospettosi, timorosissimi che qualcuno possa scavalcarli, che non esiste più un luogo dove qualcuno potrebbe sentirsi al proprio agio' (*Parlamenti buffi*, p. 8) ('in this country people have become so suspicious, so fearful that someone might supplant them, that there is no longer a place where one can feel at one's ease').

A further complication in placing Celati's writing in a context is what he sees as his engagement with non-literary language. Much of his writing is unusual for its extraordinary closeness to forms of spoken Italian. Coming from a working-class (artisan) background, Celati's rendering of popular speech has a liveliness and veracity not attributable to pure study. Moreover, curiosity has drawn him to non-literary texts − the historical enquiries of Carlo Ginzburg, the socio-linguistics of Dell Hymes, the ethnomethodology of Irving Goffman, and Danilo Montaldi's collection of life-stories. Tellingly, Celati writes of the life-story of Orlando P.: 'it attains an epic-lyric grandeur without parallel in official literature' ('L'angelo del racconto'). An adequate account would also need to reconstruct the microcosm of a Bologna where the author taught (at the university) and lived – for example, the network of friendship and collaboration which is alluded to in acknowledgements written into the story of Giovanni in *Lunario del paradiso* and the political movements active there in the dacade after 1968 (*Lunario*, pp. 8–10).

However, instead of attempting to be comprehensive, my aim in this chapter is to examine Celati's fiction under two headings; the body, and the landscape. The body with particular attention to the earlier writings, and the landscape with reference mostly to his later work.

Discourses about the body were at the centre of discussion in the 1970s, notably in relation to the work of Foucault and Bakhtin, and are very much in evidence in both Celati's fiction and essays. A systematic play on and subversion of dichotomies and dualisms (mind/body, inner/outer, high/low) runs through all his writings. Landscape, on the other hand, seems to have been a discovery of the later period. Certainly Celati's own statements as well as commentaries suggest a radical transformation in his fiction in which landscape stands as a metaphor for a turning outwards toward the world ('Finzioni a cui credere'; Calvino, 'Da Buster Keaton'). It ceases to be a background. Whereas the Celatian body is constituted by humours, his landscape is an endless combination and dispersal of elements (earth, air and water) which are shown to constitute the preconditions for human existence in more than a simple physiological sense. Again, Celati's writing participates in a wider cultural shift (this time associated with ecological thinking), but its power and fascination lie in prompting the reader to look and listen anew to landscape, that embodiment of the taken-for-granted. We are asked to rediscover a sense of wonder that we have lost to our peril.

> Mi ha spiegato quel mistero: non si resiste all'illuminazione, tutto esce, evapora, si scioglie, il corpo s'innalza, ah sapessi come si sentiva lui nel corpo! Si sentiva come se il corpo gli volasse, una libellula, lui massiccio sergente, una farfalla si sentiva, una nuvola del cielo, dopo le scoregge.
>
> E la mente? Non potevo immaginarmi cosa aveva visto nella sua mente mentre s'illumina. Beate visioni del cielo, altroché. (*Lunario del paradiso*, p. 107)

> He explained this mystery to me: one can't resist the illumination, everything comes out, evaporates, melts, the body rises up, ah if only I knew how he felt in his body. He felt as if his body was flying, a butterfly, he the massive sergeant, felt a butterfly in flight, a cloud in the sky, after farting.
>
> And the mind? I couldn't imagine what he'd seen in his mind when it was illuminated. Beatific visions of heaven, nothing less!

In this episode, 'Ciofanni', the narrator, is invited by the German father of his Beatrice to admire his fantastic house of lamps designed to illuminate the mind.

The juxtaposition of the ethereal and the grossly corporeal, the light and the heavy, the expression of fantasy and the emission of farts is typical of this period of Celati's writing. A sentence that begins with the body floating upwards and concludes with an act of deflation ('dopo le scoregge') demonstrates that wind originates in the lower regions. In the novels of the 1970s the body provides the author/narrator with ingredients for his fiction. The body as vector of action and thought not entirely belonging to or controlled by the individual, the body as repertory of gestures, as matter and the material world, as the obvious and the unknown. Characters make repeated attempts (sometimes successful, sometimes not) to defy the law of gravity and escape from the constraints of the body, especially on the final page. In *Comiche* there is a magical bicycle ride into the sky, in *La banda* an acrobatic leap onto the roof of a moving tram, in *Quattro novelle* a flight by plane and a climb toward mountain-tops.

As anyone who has watched a child learn to crawl, walk, talk, and 'act proper' will know, coordinating limbs with intentions is a painful and comic apprenticeship. Indeed, it is too easy to forget, as adults, the complex process that makes it possible to put one foot in front of the other, shake someone's hand, smile, laugh, or cry at the appropriate moment. The illusion is acquired that the mind is somehow independent of (but in control of) the body and that everyday gestures are natural as well as normal. For Celati, however, these assumptions are problems to explore, not facts to be accepted. In his writings, characters display a continuity between the physical and the mental which is absolutely contrary to a psychologically-centred type of characterization in which inner and outer are separated. Moreover, normality is continually disturbed. Hence the importance in Celati's fiction of people who would otherwise be labelled deviants and marginals who do not want to or cannot conform, and those, like autodidacts and immigrants, who try hard to master conventions not their own, thereby drawing attention to the unspoken rules governing social interaction. But their role, especially in *Narratori* and *Quattro novelle*, is also to show that normality itself is a fiction that everyone is busy sustaining.

The narrator-protagonists of Celati's novels of the 1970s are all 'immature'. Garabaldi in *La Banda* is a child becoming an adolescent, Giovanni in *Lunario* is a student, and Guizzardi in *Avventure* is a young man of indeterminate age. Later the author changes perspective so that the son in 'Scomparsa d'un uomo lodevole' in *Quattro novelle* is viewed by the narrator-father as an indecipherable appendage, whilst in *Verso la foce* youths appear as a race apart. However, in the work of the younger Celati the world is seen through the eyes of the sons.

In *Comiche*, a schoolteacher inside an institution, which could be an asylum, a holiday home or a school, is put in the position of an inmate or pupil and notes down his experiences of correction in a delirious paranoid prose. Everyone is against him. In *Avventure*, Guizzardi behaves like a difficult and noisy child, showing constant verbal and physical aggression (kicks and punches) and an inability to enter adult society due to lack of control over his appearance and movements. At one point in his picaresque wanderings a captor dresses him as a woman; at another, he is imprisoned in a pigsty to be fattened up and married off to two daughters. On top of it all, the protagonist is unsure of what he is called (is his name Guizzardi or Danci or something else?), who he is, and who the others are (especially signora Frizzi, also known as Tofanetto) (Caesar, 'Caratteri del comico nelle *Avventure di Guizzardi*').

If *Avventure* is the infernal world of the infantile and *Lunario* the paradise of the young lover, *Banda* is the purgatory of adolescence in which Garibaldi 'lives out his idea of sexuality – an admixture of delirious ravings and infantilism – in a family busy falling apart' (Marcoaldi, 'Le virgole di Celati'). Halfway through the novel, he wakes up one morning and sees himself in the mirror:

> Vedo che mi è spuntata una bocca larga come un forno, se la aprivo o ridevo. Io l'ho aperta e mi sono preso spavento, chiudendola in fretta. Tornavo a guardarmi allo specchio in punta di piedi per vedere se c'è un errore [...] una faccia che prima era bella e seria, e una mattina è diventata scandalosa per via di quella bocca che si apre. (*La banda dei sospiri*, p. 140)

> I see I've grown a mouth as big as an oven, whenever I opened it or laughed. I opened it and got a shock, shutting it in a hurry. I went back and looked at myself in the mirror on tiptoe to see if there's some mistake [...] a face once handsome and dignified, and one morning it's become an outrage thanks to that mouth that keeps opening.

Shortly afterwards, he feels himself longer in the body:

> Adesso ero un ragazzo lungo che tutti mi dicevano: com'è allungato quel ragazzo. Anche avevo una faccia tutta lunga con la bocca larga. Anche le gambe erano lunghe più di quanto io mi immaginavo a trovarmele attaccate. Che dunque facevo molti sbagli perchè non hanno abitudine a quella lunghezza e inzuccavano le ginocchia dappertutto. Però qui c'è la novità di dire che finalmente i vestiti ereditati da Federico Barbarossa cominciavano ad andargli bene a Garibaldi, come vestiti fatti su misura per lui dal sarto. (*La banda dei sospiri*, p. 152)

> Now I was a tall boy so everyone'd say to me: how that boy's stretched. What's more I had a long face with a wide mouth. Then my legs were much longer than I imagined when I found them sticking onto me. I kept getting things wrong as they weren't in the habit of being so long and my knees banged into everything. But that brings me to something new 'cos the clothes handed down by Frederick Barbarossa at last began to fit Garibaldi, like clothes made to measure by a tailor.

Limbs and organs have a life of their own and go in directions of their own choosing. They have to fit the clothes, not the clothes them. Their owner feels himself at their mercy and sees those who surround him as equally defined by their physical features and appetites: uncles who are thin and fat, gargantuan aunts, a brother who lives in a world of fiction yet hungers for sex. In a dream

Garibaldi imagines Donna Cannone, the wife of the schoolmaster: 'nel sogno era come se fosse piccolo come me e pelato, e lei lo teneva per le gambe come fosse un bastone che si tiene in mano' (*La banda*, p. 52) ('in the dream it was as if he was small like me but bald, and she held him by the legs like a broom that you hold in your hand'). While uncles carry on a furious war over property, father and brother lay siege to Veronica Lake, the blond seamstress in the mother's employ. Bodies collide in a hectic series of fights and chases.

This is writing that makes you laugh, that demands a physical response (which may be embarrassing if you are on the London underground or in a public library – is this man mad?). As Calvino noted of *Comiche*, 'Celati's poetics is based on "physiological reactivity", the response that it calls for from the reader is not articulated in discourse but in the instinctive reflexes of convulsive laughter' (Calvino, 'Gianni Celati *Comiche*'). As comedy it does not ask to be taken seriously, to be analysed. However, pointing to the devices and models can invite further readings that do not have to detract from the pleasure. We can visit the author's *La bottega dei mimi* and learn a few tricks (Muzzioli, 'Celati e i segreti dell'arte tomatica').

In fact, Celati makes no secret of his masters and presents the writer's work as a Craft rather than as Art. In his essays of the early and mid-1970s, he explains what Laurel and Hardy, Buster Keaton and the Marx Brothers have to teach a writer. From *Comiche* onwards, Celati aspired to mimic the tics of his screen heroes in verbal forms, finding in Beckett someone who had already invented such correspondences (*Finzioni occidentali*, pp. 155–85). With *La banda* it is possible to see a convergence or interpenetration of his reflections on silent film comedy and on Bakhtin's *Rabelais and His World*, especially in relation to the essay 'Il corpo comico nello spazio'.

In this essay, Celati, following Merleau Ponty, distinguishes between two types of bodily movement – the abstract one manifested in the act of display, and the concrete, tactile act of grasping. He then postulates correspondences between the prevalence of a type of movement and forms of theatre and comedy. Thus, the theatre of ideas is described as a 'utopia of the virtual', whereas music-hall, vaudeville, and Artaud's theatre (with its 'kicks up the bum, punches, chases and thieving') celebrate the physical. Whilst, at one extreme, Keaton ('the great philosopher') substitutes abstract for concrete movements, the Marx Brothers, at the other, create 'the utopia of an elementary condition in which there is no room for ideas and feelings, and there is only touching, catching, grabbing and the invasion of space' ('Il corpo', p. 22). In *La banda*, the 'disgraziato fratello', who refuses to eat, lolling on divans smoking and fantasizing about a world populated by fictional characters at his command, is a Keatonian figure. Garibaldi, by contrast, gives an account of family and neighbourhood life evocative of Marx Brothers films. Films, which for Celati, have Rabelaisian features:

Solo considerando il mio corpo come sorgente e canale di flussi, i flussi di cibo e flussi escrementali, posso arrivare a pensare uno spazio dove gli incontri e tutte le mistioni sono possibili, ma soprattutto dove la società funziona come corpo unico, come il corpo del gigante che incarna il Carnevale ... Questa è un'utopia che può spiegarsi solo escludendo l'individualità separata, e pensando ad una comicità interamente collettiva. ('Il corpo comico nello spazio', p. 28)

Only by considering my body as a source and channel of motions, motions of food and excremental motions, can I come to conceive of a space where encounters and all mixtures are possible, especially in cases where society functions as a single body, like the body of the giant that incarnates Carnival ... This is a utopia that can only be explained by leaving out separate individuality and thinking in terms of a wholly collective comic spirit.

The comedy of *La banda* can be seen as containing such carnival. Religion is turned on its head quite literally when little Garibaldi does a somersault from his bicycle:

Da acrobata inverosimile facendo salti nei fossi e una volta anche in un letamaio a testa in giù [...] è così che ho avuto la cresima io invece di andare in chiesa [...] le uniche preghiere che so sarebbero le sfilze di bestemmie che il padre pronunciava alla mattina digiuno appena sveglio' (*La banda dei sospiri*, p. 20)

Like an amazing acrobat leaping into ditches and on one occasion into a dung-heap head first ... and that's how I got to be confirmed instead of having it done in church ... the only prayers I know are the string of swear words uttered by my father every morning from the moment he woke up.

Classical music provokes stomach ache and even diarrhoea, painting and painters are stripped of their aura and literature mocked, to say nothing of school-teachers and politicians.

The language is 'vulgar' and 'plebeian', full of the corporeal imagery of 'the area called the Lower Quarters'. The pleonasms and ellipses of the narration are those of spoken language. Grammatical 'errors' abound, though there is not the insane 'verbigerazione' of the previous novels. At the same time miniature cosmologies are created which bring to mind the expressions of Montaldi's Orlando P.: 'È questa la dura legge della vita, che i quattrini fanno ballare i burattini, e nessuno dà niente per niente, e chi ne ha spende e chi non ne ha si pulisce la bocca', says the father (*La banda*, p. 178) ('And that's the hard law of life, money pulls the puppet strings, nobody gives you something for nothing, and whoever's got it spends it, and whoever's got nothing wipes his mouth'). For the mother: 'ognuno ha un destino così quando si nasce disgraziati e bisogna tirar la carretta per tutta la vita' (*La banda*, p. 90) ('that's your fate if you're born poor and got to pull the cart for the rest of your life').

An attentive reader of his work, Giuliano Gramigna, has written of the 'corporality of Celati's fiction' in which 'talk unavoidably means action'. He cites as typical a sentence in *Lunario* describing what happens after the phantom cyclist has struck Giovanni with his pump: 'Sono rimasto fermo nell'erba del fosso disteso, a riposarmi dalla fatica di prendere botte' ('I stayed put in the grass in the ditch stretched out, resting from the hard work of getting hit'). Gramigna observes: 'In fact the last sentence has no logical sense; it is simply the incorporation in gesture of a fate befitting a comic character (the person appointed to the task of getting hit, passivity turned into connotative activity)' (Gramigna, 'Serio, serissimo, del tutto comico', p. 12).

This 'corporalità' is also evident in the insistent signs whereby the narrator draws attention to the writing process and the materiality of words. In *Comiche* the sheets of the notebook that fall out of the suitcase together with the unwashed underwear as the protagonist ascends on his bicycle are 'anch'essi sporchi né meno anzi di più pieni di macchie cancellate grossi errori indecenze sentite e riportate certo non da mostrare a qualcuno' (*Comiche*, p. 147) ('dirty too not less but more covered with rubbed out stains gross errors indecencies heard and recorded and on no account to be shown to anyone'). In *Lunario* a view becomes a series of punctuation marks, a virtuoso piece:

> Da un lato del lago la spiavo in distanza la grande città che si profila laggiù; vedo le guglie delle chiese; vedo un ponte tipo circonflesso; una serie di trattini sono le macchine; i puntini sono passanti; virgolette che virgolano nell'aria e questi sono i gabbiani che volano laggiù sopra l'estremo lato della città. (*Lunario del paradiso*, p. 32)

> On one side of the lake I picked out in the distance the big city in outline; I can see church spires, I see a circumflex bridge; a series of hyphens are cars; the dots are pedestrians; inverted commas comma in the air and they're the seagulls flying way above the far side of the city.

At various moments, especially when visions multiply, we are reminded by the narrator that it isn't even he who is doing the writing: 'Guardate che io lascio andare avanti questa macchina da scrivere color smeraldo, che ci pensi lei a dirmi le cose della vita' (*Lunario*, p. 108) ('Look, I'm letting this emerald coloured typewriter carry on, so it's up to it to tell me what's going on in life').

In the new edition of *Lunario*, published in 1989 with *Avventure* and *Banda* under the title *Parlamenti buffi*, these interpellations have been excised. The previous ending, 'Caro pensatore, dacci un taglio di fare il cretino prova anche tu a farti delle storie e vedrai che è la sputtanata verità' ('Dear thinker, stop being a fool and try making up your own stories and you'll see it's the bloody truth') is no more. Ten years after writing that, Celati has commented: 'It's been a slow process of liberation from the mannerist obsession with the act of writing' (Marcoaldi, 'Le virgole di Celati'). However, there remain continuities between the earlier and later writings which perhaps include this obsession too.

In the novels of the 1970s we are invited inside the head of the narrator and see the world through his eyes. In the next decade Celati's writing undergoes a radical transformation. There is a shift away from dialogue, the construction of character and the attempt to create a strong visual language, and a move towards minimalism (Terrone, 'Le favole del reale', p. 103). After *Lunario*, Celati felt unable to write for several years until some photographers involved him in a project on 'the new Italian landscape'. Out of this collaboration came exhibitions and also *Il profilo delle nuvole*, in which Celati's text is read alongside photographs by Luigi Ghirri. But other works draw on the experiences of wandering 'alla deriva' in the plains of the Po and learning from the photographers. This is most evident in *Verso la foce*, which Celati calls 'racconti d'osservazione', but *Narratori delle pianure* and *Quattro novelle sulle apparenze* are equally results of a discovery of landscape. It is indicative that all the book-covers use photographs (by Ghirri), and that in two of them the figures have their backs to the camera (and reader) so that one looks beyond them at the landscape.

Working with the photographers seems to have been of seminal importance for learning how to look. Ghirri, in particular, is acknowledged for teaching Celati to look at buildings and places as they 'ask to be looked at' – adopting a position of humility and openness, not projecting the self onto everything (Turnaturi, 'Il collezionista', p. 93); 'Ghirri dice che di solito non vediamo quello che è diffuso ai lati dello sguardo, non spiamo da un angolo ridotto. Siamo sempre dentro a qualcosa che è come un abbraccio avvolgente e dobbiamo usare la visione periferica' (*Il profilo delle nuvole*, 12 May) ('Ghirri says that we don't usually see what is spread out to either side of the look, nor do we restrict our view to a narrow angle. We are always within something that is like an all-encompassing embrace, and we must use our peripheral vision'). As for analogies between writing and taking photographs, these can be seen in the treatment of perspective (and of what enables us to see in the first place), and in the objective of shifting the viewer's/reader's look ('dislocare lo sguardo').

Perspective implies a position of knowledge and hence of power or power-lessness. It also implies relativity. However, as Celati notes, this idea has become so banal that it is difficult to reproduce the effect of it in writing (Celati, 'Per rompere'). All the more remarkable, therefore, is the *faux naif* 'Traversata delle pianure' in *Narratori*. In this tale the moment of agnition for the reader coincides with that for the characters – immigrants from the countryside, who after many months of residence finally discover that the sun sets on the horizon even in cities. Perspective is a point of view informed by knowledge. In this case, there is an incredible credulity that leads on arrival to taking the words of the customs official 'il sole non riesce mai ad andar giù dall'orizzonte' ('the sun never sets on the horizon') quite literally. Perspective is also built into much of the environment: 'uno dei paesaggi più architettati del mondo' ('one of the most architected landscapes in the world'), writes Celati elsewhere (*Il profilo delle nuvole*), but this has to be learnt, internalized, by the outsider.

Looking at things the way they ask to be looked at suggests a consonance between people and their surroundings, which is rare. Very occasionally on his nomadic walks of *Verso la foce* the author comes across a harmony between people and place: 'questi abitano il luogo' (*Verso*, p. 64) ('these people live the place'); 'come entrare in casa d'altri e sentire un andamento benefico delle abitudini' (*Verso*, p. 56) ('like entering other people's houses and feeling the beneficent flow of habit'). Otherwise, Celati's landscape is populated by people and things that no longer belong: the man who feels most at home in airports where passengers, like him, 'come lui già sottomessi al loro destino di viaggiatori o turisti perpetui' (*Verso*, p. 79), 'were already resigned to their fate as eternal travellers or tourists'; the cypress trees out of place in the plains, like so many displaced persons ('dispersi'). As Carlo Ginzburg has commented, *Narratori* seems to deal with a world 'after a catastrophe of which nobody has heard anything said', namely 'the irreparable degradation of the landscape brought about by Man' (Torrealta, 'Ecologia della parola'). Yet Celati is fascinated as well as appalled. There are recurrent scenes, here and in the other works, where the detritus and abandoned objects of industrial society induce a sense of *pietas*, recognition of a shared lot, and an urge to find out what has happened.

Perspective for the painter of fairground panels and landscapes, Emanuele Menini, is about whether one can see the 'nube' that envelops the plains, and how to find places where objects are immobile in the light and not in a continual state of reverberation.

> Aveva pensato che per vedere la nube bisogna trovarsi in punti speciali, come ad esempio al di qua di quel cavalcavia. Ma anche nei punti speciali le cose erano due: o si sta dietro al tremore o si guarda. E in quelle periferie guardare e vedere qualcosa era quasi impossibile.
>
> 'Perché?', si è chiesto. E ci ha spiegato il perché: perché uno guarda e pensa di aver visto qualcosa, ma il tremore nell'aria porta via subito il pensiero di quello che ha visto. Così c'è solo il pensiero di muoversi nella luce scoppiata, e bisogna muoversi e basta nell'affaccendamento di ogni giorno. (*Quattro novelle sulle apparenze*, p. 43)

> He had thought that to see the cloud one had to be at special points – for instance on this side of the bridge. But even at these special points there was a choice of two things: either you follow the tremor or you look at it. And in these outskirts to look at and see something was almost impossible.
>
> 'Why?' he asked himself. And he explained to us why – because you look and you think you have seen something but the tremor in the air immediately carries off the thought of what you have seen. So there is only the thought of moving in this exploded light and you have to move yourself and that is all there is to it in this everyday bustle.

Menini finds that many regard him with disbelief when he explains his ideas for they cannot see the 'nube'. Seeing then, in 'Condizioni di luce sulla via Emilia' (*Quattro novelle*), ultimately concerns an awareness of mortality when, in Celati's words, it is 'as if the entropy of our world could be seen from the outside' (Celati, 'Per rompere'). In the story, Menini discovers a place where all is still in the middle of the snow-covered landscape, and dies there.

Landscape in Celati's fiction is about learning to look but just as important is learning to listen. In the opening story of *Narratori*, the island off the Scottish coast is described over the airwaves to the radio hams in Gallarate before they go there and see it for themselves. Even then, their contact, Archie, is only known to them through the stories he himself recounts, leaving a question mark over whether Archie is two people or one. As Celati says in 'Finzioni a cui credere': 'siamo già da sempre nella rappresentazione' ('we are already and have always been within representation') (West, 'Lo spazio nei *Narratori delle pianure*', p. 69). And for 'homo fabulans', that is all of us, the most significant representations take the form of stories.

The relationship between stories (and language more generally) and place or landscape is central to *Narratori* where it constitutes an 'implicit frame' similar to those of Fellini films (Lumley, 'The Novella and the New Italian Landscape', p. 42). It is 'geography' that brings the *novelle* together, as indicated by the map of the plains at the beginning of the book. While the 'narratori' for the most part remain nameless, place-names recur as in a litany. Yet their relationship to one another is hard to track down. Sometimes it appears arbitrary, as with the chance contact of the radio hams or in 'The Japanese Girl' where the protagonist's moves from New York to Los Angeles to Milan are dictated by an 'astrological adviser'. More often, a loss or separation has occurred of which the characters (including the character of the author himself) are dimly or painfully aware. The man at home in airports 'without a language of his own in which to speak and write' used to find solace in 'the accents and intonations he heard in bars' but these are now a memory; the uncle who discovers the existence of foreign languages only does so (too late) when he returns to France to find his son spoke so differently from himself that 'gli è venuto in mente un mare pieno di nebbia che non si può traversare' (*Narratori*, p. 103) ('so that he pictured in his mind a fog-bound sea that was impossible to cross').

The loss is frequently a loss of particularity, of uniqueness, in which the colonization by the architecture of uniformity has its parallel in the language of experts and advertising. Why, asks the printer in 'What Makes the World Go On', had the number of words to be read everywhere been continuously growing? 'Something must have happened'. He never learns. Meanwhile the landscape fills up with hoardings, and everything becomes a sign interpellating the passer-by. In another story, the women said to be conversing with the dead in a cemetery must, the editors say, be actually shown to speak by the photographer so that the readers of the magazine can see for themselves. The absurdity of the assignment is patent but at stake is the sanctity of silence and respect for a sense of place.

The mouth of the Po, Celati writes, is 'fotograficamente quasi inavvicinabile, perché dove c'è solo cielo e orizzonte la fotografia si trova a disagio') ('almost impossible for photography to approach because where there is only sky and horizon photography feels ill at ease') (*Il profilo delle nuvole*). But for the writer too there is the difficulty of how to render a landscape so apparently featureless. To see how this is achieved by Celati it is necessary to *listen* to the rhythm and metre of his prose, to gather the sense of the words from the accumulation of sounds rather than from their individual meanings.

Take the story 'Time Passing' in *Narratori*. A woman drives to work every day and on her return journey 'she starts to listen to time passing'. It could be said that nothing happens except what always happens. At the same place every evening, the woman is struck by the strange silence she always finds in the countryside and she speculates on what constitutes this 'silenzio residenziale' ('residential silence') so different from that found in open spaces. A spiral of repetition beginning with the title concludes with a sigh of 'abbandono': 'Più nessuna voglia di giudicare niente, che passi tutto, che vada dove deve andare; in fondo, dice, è solo tempo che passa' (*Narratori*, p. 49) ('Not the slightest desire to judge anything anymore – let it all pass by, go wherever it has to go: after all, she says, it's only time passing').

It is a story, like many others, without a climax, made up of impassive observations on a landscape in which 'the lines of the landscape stretch out evenly all the way to the low horizon in the distance'. The incantatory writing evokes the flatness of the plains yet without monotony, seeming to 'abbassare la soglia d'intensità del suo racconto, fino al punto da poter eliminare ogni richiamo all'insolito e insieme all'attualità' ('Finzioni a cui credere') ('lower the threshold of intensity to the point where it is possible to eliminate every reference to the unusual or to the immediate').

Antonio Tabucchi has written of *Narratori*: 'Celati puts himself forward first as listener and then as storyteller ... he knows how to turn himself into a medium and the secret of his implosive writing comes from this hard-to-achieve openness.' (Tabucchi, 'Voci sperdute fatte racconto'). If in the novels of the 1970s the writer (the act of writing) is an insistent presence, with *Narratori* and *Quattro novelle* he has become a listener in the background or a storyteller on the same level as his characters.

Listening (or not listening), like looking (or not looking), becomes a metaphor for an attitude of openness or closure towards the world. The story of Baratto in *Quattro novelle*, who listens but does not talk and who gives up shutting the doors to his flat, is exemplary. Baratto has regularly been likened to *Bartleby the Scrivener*, the obvious model for his mute refusal of the social obligation to speak. However, Melville's tale is ultimately tragic in that the scrivener dies closed within himself, whereas Celati's is comic and the gym-teacher is cured of his aphasia. Baratto's silence is equally impenetrable to others but it also involves a salutary emptying of the mind of its thoughts. Others talk and he listens, and the day comes when 'oramai sta guarendo e comincia a pensare solo i pensieri degli altri' (*Quattro novelle*, p. 29) ('now he is recovering and is beginning to think only the thoughts of others'). When he talks for the first time it is during a séance and his words are taken to come from the dead. When soon afterwards he makes the appropriate gestures to show that he has woken up, they hear him say 'Oh, mi è tornato male al menisco' (*Quattro novelle*, p. 36) ('Oh, my meniscus is hurting again').

The banality of this last remark is deliberate, and a (typically Celatian) reference to the body brings everything down to earth. Baratto does not keep to that silence which some thinkers have seen as the ultimate resistance to coercion, nor does he shout 'Eureka!'. He is reconciled to everyday reality, whether this is constituted by the thought 'dawn' with reference to the sun's reflections on a distant building, or whether it arises from phatic exchanges with neighbours – all express ideas circulating like the air people breathe, and this is the nature of language (Lumley, 'The Novella and the New Italian Landscape', pp. 49–51). By a curious paradox, the disruption of normality leads not to its rejection as such but to a recognition of the intrinsically social nature of human existence. As Celati writes, 'obviousness is our vertiginous link with others', and the task of writing is not to change the world but 'to get closer to the outside world and to the things we have in front of us' (Pomilio, 'Ovvietà, l'ultima rivelazione', p. 15).

With Baratto we can see Celati revisiting preoccupations that appear in earlier writings. Gestures, movements and pure physicality realize the 'arte tomatica' ('tomatic art' – a pun on 'auto-matic') celebrated in *La bottega dei mimi* where it is asked: 'Ma cos'è un corpo? Uno di noi spiega a quell'altro che è una cosa con muscoli e cartilagini, cervello e cervelletto, pelle e palle, ma chi ne ha mai visto uno?' (*La bottega dei mimi*, p. 9) ('But what is a body? One of us explains to the other that it's a thing with muscles and cartilages, brains and cerebellum, skin and balls, but whoever's seen one?'). In fact, there is an allusion to the world of mime when Baratto stops at the roadside to look at something: 'Chiude un occhio per osservarlo meglio. Solleva una gamba, grattandosi col piede il polpaccio dell'altra gamba, e resta così in bilico a vacillare con aria meditativa e un occhio chiuso' (*Quattro novelle*, p. 15) ('He raises one leg, scratching the calf of the other leg with his foot, and stays poised like that swaying with a meditative air and one eye closed'). Then, Baratto's trances, when he 'goes into a state of apnoea', brings to mind Giovanni's 'emptying of the brain' – a condition of self-forgetting akin to bliss in Celati's fiction in that the division between inside and outside, body and mind is momentarily annulled. Lastly, there is an anarchic implication in the gym-teacher's refusal to speak ('non è mica legale che a scuola uno non parli': 'It simply isn't legal for someone not to speak in school', p. 15) that is again in keeping with an earlier rebellion against the tyranny of norms and rules.

However, in Celati's writings of the 1980s the celebratory materialism has receded. Meditations on mortality have come to the fore. Whereas before, notions of spirituality were the stuff of comedy, terms such as 'ecstasy', 'spirit' and 'soul' are being openly reinstated in an article of 1989. They are now seen as conceptions referring to human experiences that modernity has refused to acknowledge to the point of banishing words from the acceptable vocabulary. Above all, the recognition of death, says Celati, is something contemporary society cannot countenance because of its inflated ideas of subjectivity ('Sciamani d'amore').

Nowhere, for Celati, is this more evident than in contemporary literature with its obsessions with 'the author' and the pursuit of immortality. In 'The Readers of books are always more false' in *Quattro novelle*, the pretensions of the literary world are mercilessly depicted before the protagonists, who are its dupes, finally come to some conclusions about mortality and books. A student of literature sets out to discover 'what books mean', attending university lectures where the lecturers 'do not talk to boast about what is written in the books but merely to boast about themselves for having understood them', before becoming an encyclopedia salesman, a newspaper critic, and, lastly, himself an author.

It is when he is a critic that the student meets again a woman he had known earlier who has in the interim gone in search to establish 'what is so fascinating about books'. The woman (like many of Celati's female characters) has already had intimations which anticipate the student's later reflections. She talks of the effect of words on her:

> È come quando da bambini certe parole vogliono dire per noi chissà cosa. Oppure certe strade, una casa, anche un'ombra vogliono dire per noi chissà cosa. Non può essere che tutte queste cose ci danno trepidazione proprio perché non sono niente? (*Quattro novelle sulle apparenze*, p. 84)

> It's like when we are children and certain words mean something or other to us. Or certain streets, a house, even a shadow, mean something. May it not be that all these things cause trepidation precisely because they are nothing at all?

To which the student replies: 'What – they are nothing? What has got into your head?' But later he comes to write that writing is already dust from the moment the words are on the page, and yet: 'noi chiediamo di poter celebrare questo insostanziale, e il vuoto, l'ombra, l'erba secca, le pietre dei muri che crollano e la polvere che respiriamo' (*Quattro novelle*, p. 95) ('We ask to be able to celebrate this insubstantial something and the void, the shadow, the dry grass, the stones of crumbling walls and the dust we breathe').

It is not that writing should be abandoned (though Celati did give it up for seven years) but that it should free itself of the literary aura, accepting its own mortality and ordinariness. Asked during one of his explorations of the Po whether he was a writer, Celati's character hesitated and then replied: 'I'm someone who writes'. The distinction is not new, echoing that made earlier between artist and craftsman, but now a link is being made between writing and the transitoriness of both human and natural phenomena.

There is a mystical dimension to the writing in that transport, losing oneself (one's way, one's self-possession) is presented as a path to wisdom, so that it does not come as a surprise to discover that Celati considers himself a devotee of St Francis. For the woman in 'I lettori di libri' it takes the form of the 'trepidazione' that comes over her when she reads; for Emanuele Menini it is wonder at the sight of the great cedar tree against the light that makes him think of God; for Baratto it is the light falling on metal waste in the distance that makes him stop and look. And for the writer in *Verso la foce*: 'Come una tendenza naturale che ci assorbe, ogni osservazione intensa del mondo esterno forse ci porta più vicini alla nostra morte: ossia, ci porta ad essere meno separati da noi stessi' (*Verso*, p. 10) ('Like a natural tendency that absorbs us, every intense observation of the outside world perhaps draws us a little nearer to our deaths: draws us, that is, to being less separated from ourselves').

The movement towards death is as ineluctable as the movement of the great river whose presence unites this trilogy of books, but there is no ulterior destination: 'we wait but nothing waits for us, neither a spaceship nor a destiny'. Many of the lessons in living that can be drawn from Celati's writings seem indebted to religious sources – the need for humility, awareness of the finitude of human existence, awe before nature and the cosmos, doubt about the claims of science, exaltation of ecstatic experience. The modern world, by contrast, is seen as regulated according to rules that are the very negation of these ideas. However, the recognition of death's companionship does not necessarily entail religious belief in God. Humans need to believe, and life consists of constructing believable fictions that get us through the day. But the searches and researches made by the restless characters of Celati's fiction are never concluded. The pursuit continues in the expectation that an answer will be found one day, or else there is a reconciliation to the idea that carrying on is all that is left. A scepticism about the limits of fiction forestalls any satisfactory ending or resolution to life's problems.

BIBLIOGRAPHY

Works

Fiction

Comiche (Turin: Einaudi, 1971).
Le avventure di Guizzardi (Turin: Einaudi, 1973).
La banda dei sospiri (Turin: Einaudi, 1976).
La bottega dei mimi, Nuovi argomenti, 50 (1976), pp. 9–20.
Lunario del paradiso (Turin: Einaudi, 1978).
Narratori delle pianure (Milan: Feltrinelli, 1985). Translated by Robert Lumley as *Voices from the Plains* (London: Serpents Tail, 1989).

Quattro novelle sulle apparenze (Milan: Feltrinelli, 1987). Translated by Stuart Hood as
   Appearances (London, Serpents Tail, 1991).
Verso la foce (Milan: Feltrinelli, 1989).
Parlamenti buffi (Milan: Feltrinelli, 1989).

Other Writings

Finzioni occidentali (Turin: Einaudi, 1975).
'Il corpo comico nello spazio', *Il Verri*, 3 (1976), 23–32.
'Finzioni a cui credere', *Alfabeta*, 69 (1984), 9.
'Per rompere il mutismo dell'ovvietà', *Il manifesto*, 20 September 1985.
'L'angelo del racconto', *Il manifesto*, 30 October 1988.
'Lo stregone quotidiano. L'estasi e il Sabba', *Il manifesto*, 23 April 1989.
'Sciamani d'amore. Il libro di Carlo Ginzburg', *Il manifesto*, 30 April 1989.
'Una richiesta d'amore', *Il manifesto*, 11 February 1990.
'I confini dell'oasi', *Il manifesto*, 17 September 1990.
Il profilo delle nuvole (with L. Ghirri) (Milan: Feltrinelli, 1989).

Critical Works and Reviews

Bakhtin, M. *Rabelais and His World*, (translated by H. Iswolsky) (Bloomington: Indiana
   University Press, 1984).
Caesar, M. 'Caratteri del comico nelle *Avventure di Guizzardi*', *Nuova corrente*, 97
   (1986), 33–46.
Calvino, I. 'Gianni Celati *Comiche*', in Celati, G., *Comiche* (Turin: Einaudi, 1971).
Calvino, I. 'Da Buster Keaton a Peter Handke', *L'Espresso*, 30 June 1985.
Fink, G. 'Da dove vengono tutte le storie', *Paragone*, 426 (August 1985), 67–73.
Gramigna, G. 'Serio, serissimo del tutto comico', *Il Giorno*, 3 December 1978.
Lumley, R. 'The Novella and the New Italian Landscape: An Interview with Gianni
   Celati', *Edinburgh Review*, 83 (1990), 40–51.
Marcoaldi, F. 'Le virgole di Celati', *La Repubblica*, 11 September 1989.
Montaldi, D. *Autobiografie della leggera* (Turin: Einaudi, 1961).
Muzzioli, F. 'Celati e i segreti dell'arte tomatica', *Nuova corrente*, 97 (1986), 47–64.
Pomilio, T. 'Ovvietà, l'ultima rivelazione', *L'indice* (April 1989), 15.
Rasy, E. 'Gianni Celati: *Verso la foce*', *Nuovi argomenti*, 32, (October–December 1989),
   123–5.
Tabucchi, A. 'Voci sperdute fatte racconto. Il nuovo libro di Gianni Celati', *Il
   manifesto*, 22 June 1985.
Terrone, G. 'Le favole del reale. Il percorso espressivo di Celati', *Nuova corrente*, 97
   (1986), 89–106.
Torrealta, L. 'Ecologia della parola. Benni, Fink, Ginzburg su Celati', *Il manifesto*, 3
   July 1985.
Turnaturi, G. 'Il collezionista', *L'Espresso*, 30 June 1985, 93–7.
West, R. 'Lo spazio nei *Narratori delle pianure*', *Nuova corrente*, 97 (1986), 65–74.

Chapter 4

Vincenzo Consolo
Metaphors and False History

JOSEPH FARRELL

It has often been said that one of the main characteristics of the modern – or modernist – novel is its self-reflexive quality, its conscious eye turned in on itself making it ironically absorbed in the act of writing itself, and sceptical about its ability to portray external reality. On the other hand, one of the essential, identifying characteristics of the Sicilian tradition of fiction has been its exclusive absorption in Sicily itself, in the social, cultural and historical ills afflicting the island through the ages. The judgement that was once given of the Russian novel – that frequently the principal character was Mother Russia herself – could be made of many Sicilian novels.

It is clear that there is, at the very least, the potential for conflict between these two visions. Can history form the subject matter for the novel at a time when the prevailing belief is that the novel can only portray itself and its own imaginary sphere? These two contrasting notions are in permanent tension and it is from this tension that much of the richness and depth of the work of the novelist Vincenzo Consolo derives. In many ways he represents a synthesis of the two tendencies: the attitudes, the doubts, the ironical self-awareness he brings to his writing are those of his contemporaries elsewhere, while his novels display the moral and (occasionally) political passion, as well as the exclusive fascination with the island's history which link him with earlier Sicilian writers.

In one of his interviews, Consolo made a distinction between writers he calls 'orizzontali' and those he terms 'verticali'. The distinction is as fundamental to his approach to writing as was the celebrated division Pirandello made, in his introduction to *Six Characters In Search Of An Author*, between philosophical and historical writers. For Consolo the 'orizzontali' (horizontal) are the great cosmo-politan writers such as Graham Greene and Hemingway, the nomads of the world of letters, who could find the subjects for their fiction in any country they visited. On the other hand, he went on:

> Quelli verticali siamo noi, i Napoletani, i Sudamericani connotati da una realtà troppo forte per non affondare la scrittura in quelle radici. Maggiore è

l'infelicità sociale di una terra, piú i suoi scrittori sono 'verticali' per il bisogno di spiegare il proprio dolore, di capirne il perché. (*Europeo*, 31 October 1987, p. 123).

The vertical writers are people like us, like the Neapolitans or the South Americans, all marked by conditions of life so strong as to compel us to root our writing in them. The greater the social unhappiness of a country the more its writers are made 'vertical', by a need to explain their own pain and to understand its origins.

Vincenzo Consolo was born in the village of Sant'Agata di Militello in eastern Sicily in 1931, but has lived in Milan for most of his adult life. Initially he worked as a teacher, but for several years has made his living as a full-time writer. His fictional output is relatively limited, but he contributes frequently to the Italian press. In his own terms, he is a 'vertical' writer, whose subject is Sicily, and by preference the Sicily of the past, whether recent or more distant. Perhaps for that reason several contemporary Italian critics have labelled him a 'scrittore inattuale', a writer who shuns the present. There seems to be a reproach implicit in the words, as though he were failing in the duty of the novelist to confront his own times directly. As a judgement, it is ludicrously inadequate, not least because his fictional recreation of other times can be viewed as an approach to the present condition of Sicily by another route. The use of history as the *materia prima* of his novels was a very conscious choice.

La letteratura siciliana è una letteratura periferica con una fisionomia precisa, di tema storico e sociale, quasi mai intimistico. Anche Verga e Pirandello pagarono un loro tributo storico. Questo aspetto storico è piu marcato nella parte occidentale dell'isola. Io sono nato in una zona anodina, a metà strada fra la provincia di Messina e quella di Palermo. Ho scelto la seconda, ho scelto la storia (*Grazia*, 30 October 1988, p. 97)

Sicilian literature is a peripherical literature, with a precise physiognomy made up of themes which are social or historical but scarcely ever personal. Even Verga and Pirandello paid their dues to history. This historical aspect is more marked in the west of the island. I was born in an anodyne zone, halfway between the provinces of Messina and Palermo. I made a choice of the latter; I chose history.

His choice of historical period in the novels indicates a preference for those moments when human will could have intervened to effect change in the dynamic of Sicilian history, when different courses could have been followed, when alternative forces could have come to the fore. The first postwar election, the invasion of Sicily by Garibaldi with the wave of inchoate optimism it brought in its wake, the liberation of the island from Fascism in 1943, that eighteenth century of Reason and Enlightenment which has become the golden dream of Sicilian writers of this century – all represent in different ways and to differing degrees decisive points in the formation of the moral-political culture which holds sway in the island. It is not by chance that they provide either the background or the central subject matter of Consolo's fiction.

The title of his first novel, *La ferita dell'aprile* (The Wound of April), is allusive and emblematic but never fully explained in the course of the book itself. It may refer to the elections of April 1948 when the Catholic Church, afraid of a communist victory, mobilized behind the Christian Democratic Party inflicting a wound on the hopes of reformers, or it may refer to the sensibilities of youth wounded by contact with an alien, uncomprehending adult world which it is on the point of entering. When it was first published in 1963, the few who took serious note of it at the time classified it as a late neorealist work, but while Consolo does maintain in it the objective, unobtrusive approach compellingly reminiscent of his Sicilian Verist predecessors, he had already moved beyond that tradition most especially in his linguistic experimentation. The structure is fractured and episodic, with each chapter recounting an autonomous incident only loosely linked to the preceding and successive events. The linkage is provided by the continuity of character.

In the novel, an adult narrator recalls the final year of his education, spent in a college run by a religious order in a village in Sicily. This particular year is presented as a break with the recent past, as the end of a turbulent, unsettled period following the death of his father. In retrospect, the other years appear to him no more than a blur, but his memory singles out that year as the one when he matured from boy to man and when the course of Sicilian politics was set. His memory will not, however, provide the means for a rigorous self-analysis. Whilst other novels about adolescence, from Kipling's *Kim* to Salinger's *Catcher in the Rye*, concentrate on the inner experiences – the private traumas of the rumbustious joys of those years – Consolo limits himself to the outer event. His is a novel of incident. The characters, including the narrator Scavone, are drawn on a very flat surface, and even granted the contemporary disfavour into which the psychological realism of many nineteenth-century writers has fallen, few novels can be so consistently behaviourist in their approach.

The two levels – of personal maturing and political decision – are not forced into some artificial synthesis or counterpoint, nor are the boys endowed with a consciousness or vision beyond their years. They may be the new generation, the inheritors of the post-fascist, postwar order in whom so many hopes are placed, but the gulf between them and the generation which followed Mussolini and fought in the war is not primarily political. It is the gap in perception and in the quality of hope which exists between young and old at any time. The events in the outside world intrude only to the extent to which the boys have some awareness of them. The principal focus is always on college life, with its attendant tensions, disappointments and cheerful camaraderie. Consolo is a story-teller, for whom the coherence and consistency of the fictional world he portrays is of paramount importance. In the novel, any tendency towards pamphleteering is kept at bay.

Since it is a religious institution, many of the outstanding events are those of the ecclesiastical calendar. Christmas, Holy Week and Easter, as well as the annual play performed by the pupils in the presence of the dignitaries of the locality, may be minor events in comparison with choices facing society at large in that uncertain time, but they are the prime focus of the novel. Consolo never permits himself any level of knowing or superior irony over the life he depicts. The play, for instance, may be a visible exercise in sentimental piety, featuring a missionary coaxing a native tribe out of devotion to their own gods and into acceptance of the Christian way, but it is recounted without overt mockery or satire. It is simply one of the highlights of the school year, to be chronicled as such.

Interspersed with routine experiences, are the first encounters of the narrator with those deeper realities, with those forces – the equivalent of T. S. Eliot's trilogy of birth, copulation and death – which are decisive in the formation of the individual person. Scavone encounters death when the father of one of his friends dies, and sex when Fillipo Mustica introduces him, immediately after the funeral, to the blind girl who is his lover. Scavone is the follower, the shy introvert who requires to be initiated by his more brash or worldly-wise companions, principally Filippo Mustica, but he remains something of an 'outsider' figure, whose feelings are a puzzle to his contemporaries. His own, delicately drawn, relationship with Caterina will falter because of his awkwardness and hesitation.

The college is not totally isolated from the dramatic events occurring in Sicily at that period, but such events are filtered through the boys' immature perception. History unravels outside the gates of the institute, in the world of the adults, in a dimension separate from the enclosed, quasi-monastic routine of college life. Only Filippo Mustica whose father is a communist, has any wider, deeper awareness, but the others register what happens with the naivety of immature minds. They see in Don Sergio, the ex-army chaplain, who arrives in the college fresh from the experiences of the Russian campaign, not a representative of the fascist army but a figure enveloped in his individual aura of mystery and adventure. In the event, his impact is immediately diminished during his first sermon by the fact that he is unable to clear his throat properly.

In spite of this early mishap, Don Sergio emerges as the principal adult figure, the authority figure whom the boys find most sympathetic. Himself a fanatical anti-communist, his support of the Christian Democratic party, his willingness to propagate their cause and to denounce all that smacks of Marxism are unswerving. The other, more directly political figures, such as Schiacchitano, the Christian Democrat candidate, remain distant shadows. Political disputes intrude almost by chance, through glimpses of election posters or of writings on the walls, or through names, such as that of the celebrated bandit, Salvatore Giuliano, overheard at random. Scavone has one encounter with a brigand gang when returning with his uncle from a commercial trip to Etna, but at that point they seem to the boy romantic figures from the pages of Dumas. Giuliano is not afforded any such spurious glamour. One faction may glorify him on an election hoarding as a killer of communists, another may recall him as the man who gulled the police but finally he is denounced, in the only passage of unequivocal authorial passion in the work, for the slaughter of the peasants who gathered at Portella Della Ginestra for the annual May Day celebrations. The event is recalled by the narrator in a stream of consciousness passage when, after attending his mother's second marriage, he sets to wondering about the relations of strength between the landless poor in the plains and the wealthy with their estates in the hills. When the peasant class assembled for their celebrations with their red banners and slogans of protest, they were savagely gunned down by Giuliano and his men from the heights above them.

> Girarono come pazzi in cerca di riparo ma li buttò buttò buttò riversi sulle pietre una rosa maligna nel petto e nella tempia: negli occhi un sole giallo di ginestra, un sole verde, un sole nero di polvere di lava, di deserto. (*La ferita dell'aprile*, p. 120)

> They ran around like madmen in search of shelter but an evil rose in the breast and temple hurled hurled hurled them on their backs on the stones; in their eyes a broom-yellow sun, a lava-black sun, a green sun, a desert sun.

This passage occurs towards the end of the year, when, having seen his mother and uncle marry, having watched his friends mature and make decisions for their futures, having absorbed the influences of the teachers and fellow pupils, the narrator is no longer the ingenuous boy who had been admitted twelve months earlier. Of his immediate circle, Mustica has been expelled as a 'spreader of poisons', Seminara, who had earlier imposed pious torture on himself by tying a leather belt round his waist so tightly that he fainted, leaves to follow a vocation as a priest, but Scavone comes to realize that his way will be different. This novel is also its own *Portrait of the Artist as a Young Man*. It is totally without the aesthetic passion or fervour for pure art that distinguish Joyce's masterpiece, but by the time he is ready to join the adult world, the narrator is clear that he will be a writer. Instead of the exultant, artistic certainties displayed by Stephen Dedalus in his discourses over the nature of beauty in St Thomas, the narrator expresses self-conscious doubts over writing and its value, but he is sure that this is the path he will follow. In a lyrical passage, the narrator recalls, and does not dismiss, the scorn of his uncle over his choice:

> Uno che pensa, uno che riflette e vuol capire questo mare grande e pauroso, viene preso per il culo e fatto fesso. E questa storia che m'intestardo a scrivere, questo fermarmi a pensare, a ricordare non è segno di babbìa, a cangio di saltare da bravo i muri che mi restano davanti? Diceva zio: È uomo l'uomo che butta un soldo in aria e ne raccoglie due: lo sparginchiostro non è di quella razza. (*La ferita dell'aprile*, p. 103)

Anyone who thinks, who reflects and tries to fathom out this great, fearful sea is just a prick, waiting to be conned. This story I'm determined to write, this pausing to think and remember instead of vaulting the walls which stand in my way, could this not be just a sign of idiocy? Uncle used to say: A real man tosses one coin in the air and catches two: your penpusher is not up to that.

This novel was of an altogether different quality from the standard apprentice work, and many of the notions expressed in it recur later. Consolo always returns in a quizzically ironic vein to the question of writing, to what it could achieve and to what its ultimate purpose is. The obsession with language itself first surfaced in Scavone, who found himself scorned for the rustic dialect he spoke, but it was to become a standard feature of all Consolo's work. He intertwined Sicilian usages with standard Italian terms, not from a cult of novelty for its own sake or from any narrowly aesthetic considerations, but from a concern to give dignity to a dialect – or language – which had for long been considered uncouth, fit only for the illiterate or uneducated. In every country, the language of the centre acquires a special privilege by being the daily currency of people who wield power. Consolo can be regarded as a linguistic radical, who extends his political radicalism, his feeling for the underdog, his identification with Sicily into the sphere of writing. He chooses to make use of Sicilian words and phrases in his writing so as to give them, and the people who use them, a status conventionally denied them. Not all Sicilian writers made this choice. Others chose the compromise path, once employed in similar circumstances by Sir Walter Scott, of using local terms for direct speech but of maintaining standard forms and terms for narrative passages. Leonardo Sciascia himself drew attention to the fact that Sicilian usages were progressively eliminated from his own lexicon, while Consolo's contemporary, Gesualdo Bufalino, prefers to adopt only a vocabulary dignified by national acceptance.

Consolo's fullest historical novel, and the book which brought him to public attention, was *Il sorriso dell'ignoto marinaio* (The Smile of the Unknown Sailor), published in 1976. The title refers to a portrait by the early Renaissance Sicilian artist Antonello da Messina, and the period, the Sicilian Risorgimento following Garibaldi's landing at Marsala in 1860, has held an irresistible fascination for Sicilian writers. Such classic works as De Roberto's nineteenth-century saga *I Vicerè*, Lampedusa's *Il Gattopardo*, and Pirandello's only historical novel *I vecchi e i giovani* all deal with the same moment. The island was torn between Liberal adherents of the new order and conservative supporters of the *ancien régime*, and Garibaldi offered the hope, or threat, of change. Consolo chooses a different focus from his predecessors. De Roberto and Lampedusa are at home with the ousted patrician caste, the former depicting the cynical manoeuvrings of the noble Uzeda family to maintain power and privilege, and the latter the Prince's aristocratic conviction that nothing will really change; Pirandello, writing of the period immediately after Unification, describes the power games of the new élite. Consolo, on the other hand, features those denied a voice in the works of his predecessors, and excluded from power under both systems. He deals with the conditions and aspirations of ordinary people.

The historian Mack Smith has written that Cavour's aim was to secure a 'conservative revolution', that is, a change of the political system which would not unleash social unrest and demands for redistribution of property. However, dreams of Italian national unity were of little concern to the peasantry of Sicily, who looked to the Risorgimento forces to implement exactly that social revolution which Cavour so feared. They took matters into their own hands with a series of risings, of which the most famous was in Bronte (described in Verga's short story, *Libertà*), and another in Alcara Li Fusi, which is the subject of Consolo's novel. The novel is a complex, multi-layered piece of work, with constantly shifting focus, and with a stronger claim to being viewed as the 'anti-Leopard', than *The Council of Egypt*, a historical novel by Sciascia published a decade earlier. Consolo brings the peasants, who have no significant role in Lampedusa, to the centre stage. His novel is imbued with a deeper sense of history than Lampedusa's work, and is free from all suggestion that there exists an eternal, mythical Sicily outside history and impervious to change. He espouses, as did Lampedusa, the views of those revisionist historians who had been systematically dismantling the myths of the glorious, heroic Risorgimento, but at the same time he displays a robust, contemporary scepticism over the concept of history itself.

In a review of the book, Sciascia defended Consolo from the charge that the novel was 'constructed'. The line of defence was not that the accusation was unfounded, but that all great novels were, in the last analysis, 'constructed', or put together according to a more or less visible scheme. The novel lacks all conventional flow and continuity of plot, partly because the author is operating on boundaries where history and fiction overlap and blur, and partly because linearity is eschewed. Narrative chapters are interspersed with appendices containing extracts from letters or documents composed at the time; since the main characters are taken from history and played a prominent part in public affairs, many of their writings are extant. The invented minor characters, on the other hand, come into the novel for brief periods of time, then fade out. Further, Consolo seems almost to be commenting on known events rather than narrating, and is happy to allow his readers to play an active part in making good gaps in his narrative. The reader, as Umberto Eco postulated, must be an alert participant in the act of storytelling. Consolo gives no first-hand description of the riots in Alcara Li Fusi, events which would have constituted the dramatic core of a more conventional novel. From an account of the peasants listening to their leaders inciting them to take to the streets the following day, the focus switches immediately to a letter written by Baron Mandralisca interceding for the now defeated and imprisoned rebels. The construction is like the layout of a museum. Each chapter is an exhibit in itself, none ultimately of supreme importance.

The novel is founded on series of dualities, with the varying strands intertwining, and every image or character juxtaposed to an equal and countervailing one. The principal contrast is between two men, Baron Mandralisca and Giovanni Interdonato, both of whom are characters from history. Mandralisca was a renowned student of malacology as well as a discriminating collector of works of art. His most celebrated acquisition was the portrait of the Unknown Sailor by Antonello da Messina which gives the novel its title. The ironic, sardonic, superior yet compassionate and intelligent smile – strangely reminiscent of La Gioconda – acts as a leitmotiv throughout the novel.

The two men are united in their dedication to the Liberal cause and to the unification of Italy but they represent clashing values and codes of conduct. Mandralisca is an intellectual, pursuing a range of solitary and private interests, Interdonato the monomaniac revolutionary activist. In tandem with their open, articulately verbalized dispute over the right to personal fulfilment as against the obligation to pursue the collective good, a series of opposing images – some recurrent, some specific – indicate subtler, subterranean conflicts. The enigmatic smile on the portrait is throughout pitted against the image of the snail shell, whereas at a dinner party in Mandralisca's house, the image of a classically tranquil, newly excavated statue of the goddess Korē is paired with that of the seemingly formless orange tree in a tapestry sewn by Interdonato's fiancée Catena, where both represent contrasting visions of a future Italy. At all times the individual, especially if an 'intellectual', poses to himself unresolvable dilemmas about the nature of what would be called, in the age of Consolo and not of his creations, 'commitment'. The final dialectic is, as Lukacs insisted must be the case with a historical novel, between the time of writing and the time of the action, between the nineteenth and twentieth century, for if the narrative recounts the events of the Risorgimento, the underlying ethical and political questions had more urgency at the time of the novel's appearance than in the age of its fictional setting.

Mandralisca may not dominate the action of the work in the way Fabrizio, Prince of Salina, dominates *Il Gattopardo*, but he is the conscience of the piece. His dedication to all Risorgimento ideals, both to national reunification and to reform, is not in doubt. That combination was rare in the Sicilian aristocracy, and certainly was beyond the grasp of Fabrizio or of the Uzeda dynasty in De Roberto's work. Mandralisca suffers the indignity of expulsion from Naples, he allows his house to be used for clandestine meetings of the revolutionaries but later, once Garibaldi's Red Shirts impose their own brand of order, it is he who breaks ranks with the newly rampant Liberals and with his own class to plead for the lives of the Alcara rebels. In spite of these convictions and gestures, he will not march in the front line; indeed he will not march. His driving, inner passion is all for the collection and cataloguing of Sicilian snails and molluscs; he is the man of science in the quintessential Victorian mould, the cousin germane of Darwin and Huxley, and clearly such a cast of mind holds no charms for his friend, comrade, foil and rival, Interdonato.

Interdonato is every inch the man of action, all ardour and self-abnegating dedication. As a fully committed revolutionist, he had been on the barricades in 1848, had suffered exile in Paris, had given himself to clandestinity and to unceasing activity for the patriotic cause. The two may esteem each other, but there can never be a meeting of minds. When they meet in Mandralisca's salon after Interdonato had delivered the Antonello portrait, Interdonato upbraids Mandralisca for his half-hearted-commitment, leaving Mandralisca incapable of finding words to justify or even explain his choices. His appeal to his earlier promise to himself to prepare the most exhaustive study ever made of Sicilian malacology leaves Mandralisca himself unconvinced. He can distance himself from his fellow aristos, from Maniforti with his unquestioning loyalty to the *ancien régime* on the one hand, or from Manca with his exclusive devotion to science on the other, but his own anxiety over his debt to society, his uncertainty over the obligations he owes his fellow humans in general and fellow Sicilians in particular remain. In his own person, he dramatizes the postwar, Sartrean dilemma over *engagement* and the autonomy of the intellectual, over the nature of the contribution to society owed by creative individuals who by preference work in their own way. It was a debate which lay at the heart of the polemics between the Sicilian writer Elio Vittorini and the Italian communist leader Palmiro Togliatti.

After the riots, the roles are reversed, since Interdonato now has assumed judicial responsibilities and it is Mandralisca who begs him to 'agire' — to abandon inertia and spur himself into action on behalf of the condemned rebels. Mandralisca had been holed up in the mountains above Alcara at the time of the uprising, even if, typically, he had not been there out of any desire to back the uprising, but simply because he had chosen that time and place to continue his researches into snail life. His is both an impassioned appeal for pity and a heterodox view of how the landing of Garibaldi and the high words spoken at that time had been interpreted by the peasantry. When the rebels had gathered in the town the night before the uprising, the bourgeois leader had suggested 'Viva l'Italia!' as the most appropriate code word to call the people onto the streets, but the peasant leader insisted on 'Giustizia!' ('Justice!'). The gulf was deep. For the higher orders, the aim of the Risorgimento was to unite Italy while leaving everything else as it was; for the peasantry, the goal was the attainment of social justice, which meant the redistribution of land and property. Garibaldi had come to be viewed by them as a liberator, not from the Bourbons, but from hunger and poverty. Anything else was a futile game which did not concern them. Mandralisca's letter reports the bitter cry of one of the condemned peasants in self-explanation and self-exculpation: 'C'è la terra, vera, materiale e eterna!' (*Il sorriso*, p. 97) ('There's only land, real, material and eternal!'). The purpose of his letter is to speak for the peasants and convey the concrete nature of their demands as against the more ethereal hopes of the aristocratic Liberals, who may have supported the cause of Unification, but not at the price of loss of status and privilege.

The contact with the peasants and his identification with their sense of injustice causes Mandralisca to revise the most basic tenets of his own life and activity. What had previously been the mainstay of his existence now seems to him the most arid and futile of all occupations. He writes to Interdonato:

> Confesso: dopo i fatti d'Alcara ho detto addio alla mia pazza idea dello studio sopra la generale malacologia fluviatile e terrestre di Sicilia; ho dato fuoco a carte, a preziosi libri e rari, fatto saltare dal terrazzo il microscopio ... (*Il sorriso dell'ignoto marinaio*, pp. 98–9)

> I confess: after the events of Alcara, I have said good-bye to my insane idea of a general study of the land and river malacology of Sicily. I have set fire to papers, to rare precious books, I have hurled my microscope from the terrace ...

In this letter, the aesthetic and moral climax of the book, the scattered images of the narrative are, with deft finesse, woven into one. They give the work a deeper imaginative dimension and a tantalizing ambiguity. From the very outset, Interdonato had appeared to him in the guise of the nameless sailor of Antonello's portrait. Mandralisca, when bringing the portrait to his home, was struck by a resemblance between the nameless figure on the canvas and a sailor on board who turns out to be Interdonato in disguise. Later, however, when Interdonato attempts to cajole or coerce Mandralisca into a higher level of involvement, Mandralisca found all the justification he needed for his own reserve in that enigmatic smile with which Antonello endowed the subject. Its detached irony, its implication that all activity is futile and that the superior mind must withdraw into its own sphere, enabled him to continue disregarding developments in society around him. Cataloguing snails by species and shell pattern seemed to him an adequately rewarding activity, and one which repaid any debt he owed himself and society.

The *chiocciola* itself, the snail shell, provides the other dominant image in the work, but, in a reversal of perceptions after the riots, Mandralisca comes to view the shell, with its intricate patterns, as a meaningless form, and therefore his dedication to that branch of science as futile. For the reader, the shell becomes a variation on a Borgesian labyrinth, circling, twisting, curving but aimless and directionless. The Italian word has a second meaning, spiral staircase, and it is with dismay that Mandralisca discovers that the rebels are imprisoned in a Chiocciola in the castle of his fellow nobleman, Maniforti. The shell might be a kind of intellectual prison or cul de sac. Plainly any attempt at too literal unravelling of such poetic metaphors risks being clumsily pedestrian, but a quotation, worked into the text, from Pascal, who also used snail shells as an image, implies to the reader that the dedication to forms and patterns without meaning is an inexcusable divertissement, inadequate in any scale of values. For Mandralisca, under the impact of his encounter with the prisoners, the images of the *chiocciola* and of the Unknown Sailor's smile merge. 'Ho capito: lumaca, lumaca è anche quel sorriso!' (*Il sorriso*, p. 101) ('I understand: that smile too is a snail!'). Detachment is not enough.

This overturning of attitudes is more than moral and political, for it expresses itself in a radical scepticism about history and about writing. The imprisoned peasants are not just people who suffer injustice but people who have been denied a voice in history. His willingness to speak on their behalf is inadequate, for the intervention of the observer-narrator is an inevitably distorting factor, made all the greater when the narrator has unconscious interests of his own to protect. What has history been until now, wonders Mandralisca? 'Una scrittura continua di privilegiati' (*Il sorriso*, p. 96) ('a chronicle invariably written by the privileged'), he writes in reply to his own question. In his altered state of mind, he is tormented by the contradiction between his need to write, to set down his testimony to what has occurred and the impossibility of doing so without betrayal. He himself, for all his enlightened beliefs, belongs to the class of the privileged, to those who have a command and control of language denied the poor and illiterate. History itself is a hollow enigma, an empty sack waiting to be filled with ideological lumber, and the powerful have always undertaken that task. Writing itself is part of the problem, rather than a resolution of it. This approach is new in Sicilian literature. Sciascia would have inveighed against political power and the corruption of the few, but Consolo's concern is not just that, in Simone Weill's phrase, truth is always the refugee from the victor's camp, but also that linguistic and social relationships mirror each other. 'Language is a power', in the words of Roland Barthes. Consolo is now far from being the invisible author. He is present asserting his own credo.

To escape from this impasse, to give a voice to the dispossessed, Mandralisca, like a good nineteenth-century liberal, expresses his confidence in the value of education, but also gives voice to that linguistic radicalism which is, in Consolo, the indispensable accompaniment of any political radicalism. After the rising, he had overheard peasants like Peppe Smirna, express themselves with fluency and confidence in their native idiom, but incapable of such mastery in using the national language which does not belong to them. The powerful command social status, ownership of land, economic privilege, the advantages given by a habit of deference, but their hegemony also extends to language and culture. Consolo dismantles that dominance in every field. He himself in his own writing, in his choice of registers and vocabulary subverts the language codes which maintain authority, while recounting the attempts of peasants from the past to act in the same way over the land question.

In his narration, Consolo extends his linguistic experimentation. His aspirations are toward poetry, or at least toward a poetic diction, with images woven into his writing not as incidental embellishment but as the means of conveying the structure of his thought and for advancing the narrative. Language is a *materia prima* of his work, never merely an expressive means, and has a richness frequently characterized by Italian critics as baroque – a term invariably employed for Sicilian writers – and 'Gaddian'. The comparison with Carlo Emilio Gadda is only partially helpful, since Gadda was much more of a pasticheur who, in works like *Quer pasticciaccio brutto* employs, like Joyce, a language of his own, involving archaisms, dialect usages, new coinages and purely fanciful inventions. Consolo is infinitely more fastidious. His distaste for modern usages is profound, and while his vocabulary may have at times an archaic ring, it is never self-created but invariably has roots in popular speech. He aims to combine a language which reflects a tradition normally dismissed as uncouth or vulgarly dialectal with a distinctively literary idiom.

The self-interrogation on the nature of writing was to become more insistent and more central in his subsequent books, but no reader of the savage events outlined in *Sorriso dell'ignoto marinaio* could have anticipated that the following works would be closer to fantasy, and would portray a dream-like, idealized, idyllic Sicily. Some such schizophrenic duality, between the depiction of Sicily as a satanic land or as an El Dorado, has been apparent all through the course of Sicilian writing. Literature has produced its own version of the two Sicilies. The first, drawn in stark, uncompromising terms, is the savage land of violence and injustice, the victim of successive waves of invaders, the home of the mafia and of men who prey on each other in the name of 'honour': its history was once described by Sciascia as the 'unending defeat of reason'. Side by side with this tradition there exists the myth of the magic, enchanted, sensual, fabled and perhaps metaphorical and metaphysical Sicily. This paradise-Sicily is most obviously the creation of travellers, engaged on a quest for the abode of the old gods, but several local writers surrendered, at times quite unconsciously, to the same pull. One of the most startling and paradoxical cases was that of Elio Vittorini in his novel *Conversazione in Sicilia*.

Consolo's contribution to this myth is plainly ironic. His next work *Lunaria* carries a suitably delphic dedication to *Lucio Piccolo, first inspiration with his 'The Moon's Funeral.' To lunar poets. To poets.* Cast in the form of a play, the work is an adult fairy tale set in the Palermo of the eighteenth century where an unfortunate and unhappy Spanish viceroy has to contend with a city and a people for whom he has little love. He dreams of the moon falling to earth, and this dream seems to come true when a group of peasants come to announce that the moon has fallen, and shattered, in their village. Fable though it may be, some of Consolo's deeper concerns shine through. The Viceroy is concerned with the degradation of the city and of the civilization behind the elegant baroque façades, while the language spoken by the peasants has a direct, dialect pithiness and force which is in contrast with the stylized idiom employed at court.

The same fabled Sicily is the setting for *Retablo*, a work which combines the charm of *Alice's Adventures in Wonderland* with an insistent, if veiled and allegorical, probe into the history and condition of the island. In different ways, and at different levels, Consolo's book is a travelogue, an extended mataphor, a love story or a cluster of criss-crossing love stories, a pseudo-Enlightenment pastiche, an unravelling of Sicilian history, a venture in storytelling while being also a wholly contemporary, slightly ironic, self-deprecating meditation on art and on the nature of fiction.

As is always the case with Consolo, the title has an emblematic function. A *retablo* is, in Spanish, a triptych or a series of painted panels recounting episodes of one continuing story, and the novel itself, divided into three sections, entitled *Oratorio*, *Peregrinazione* and *Veritas*, has a comparable form. Each fragment covers the same, or at least contiguous, ground but is told from the perspective of a different character. There is no absolute truth to be had, only the accumulation of various points of view.

The central character, Fabrizio Clerici is, in life, a twentieth-century artist who, in the fiction, is converted into a Milanese antiquarian from the Age of the Enlightenment who sets out to travel in Sicily. In part his motivation is to overcome an unhappy love affair with Teresa Blasco who, both in history and in the fiction, married Cesare Beccaria. Another purpose of the journey is to sketch classical ruins. The yearning to find, and take refuge in, a dimension separate from the contemporary is a constant one for Consolo's characters, but Clerici's evasion is totally conscious from the outset, and has a different context from Mandralisca's. All attempt at pseudo-factual reconstruction is abandoned in favour of overt myth, fable or poetry. Any realism has a magical overlay. The climate is deliberately 'artificial'.

Clerici engages as his servant for his journey one Isidoro, an ex-monk whose unfortunate love affair with Rosalia, together with his consequent expulsion from the monastery and imprisonment, had been the subject of the opening – *Oratorio* – section of the book. En route, they are initially robbed, then subsequently befriended, by Don Vito, a brigand and an ex-monk, passionately in love with a woman also called Rosalia. Behind these two identically named women stands the mystical figure of Saint Rosalia, the patron saint of Palermo. The first – assuming that these are distinct figures – gives her account of the relationship between herself and Isidoro in the closing section, entitled *Veritas*. At various times, the three male lovers recognize their ladies in an identical portrait, and indeed their only approach to them is through representation, through the representation that is art. When Clerici absentmindedly sketches a pen portrait of Teresa, both Isidoro and Don Vito see in her their own Rosalia. The being of this woman, or these women, or perhaps of Woman, is evanescent and fragile, whilst the very borders between illusion and reality, between invention and nature, between what is created and what is given are precarious. At one point, Isidoro falls into a delirium in front of a statue, allegorically (and ironically) entitled *Truth*, for he believes he recognizes in the model who had posed for the work his own Rosalia – now a singer and kept woman of an operatic castrato. In this flux, art provides the only point of contact between Isidoro and Rosalia, but art is itself a dignified fraud and the connection between art and its object is distant, uncertain and unsatisfactory. It may even be, as the castrato singer concludes, that all who seek to represent this world in whatever style are in some sense castrati:

> il musico, il poeta, il cantore, il pintore ... siamo ai margini, ai bordi della strada, guardiamo, esprimiamo e talvolta, con invidia, con nostalgia struggente, allunghiamo la mano per toccare la vita che ci scorre davanti. (*Retablo*, p. 158)

> The musician, the poet, the singer, the painter ... we exist on the margins, by the side of the street, watching, expressing and sometimes, with envy or poignant nostalgia, stretching out our hands towards this life which flows in front of our eyes.

Through the *retablo* image, Consolo questions traditional notions of art, literature or originality. His travellers encounter, at a fairground, a charlatan sculptor and poet who displays a *retablo* and goads the crowds into accepting the fiction to the point where they would willingly tear each other apart. Clerici muses that however unedifying the spectacle of such gullibility, it may also represent the nature of all art, which can never be more than acts of deceit or shadows like those which fooled Don Quixote or misled Plato's men in the cave. It may also be that all 'creation' is essentially an act of copying, or of construction on the basis of previously manufactured structures. This thought occurs to Clerici when, for lack of fresh paper, he finds himself obliged to scribble his diary notes on the back of used paper obtained by theft from the monastery. By chance, these sheets turn out to be a confession written by Rosalia, containing details of the misdemeanours of her then lover, Don Vito. The circle is complete, and totally closed; the narrative is created on the back of the original events, themselves recreated in written form. Further, this diary, the basis of the central part of the book, is similar to the upper part of a *retablo* in that it too 'poggia su una predella o base già dipinta, sopra la memoria vera, vale a dire, e originale scritta da una ragazza di nome Rosalia.' (*Retablo*, p. 89) ('It rests on a platform or previously painted base, in other words on the true and original memoir written by a girl named Rosalia.').

The *retablo* has become a subversive metaphor for the act of writing. All literature restates and recycles previously written literature, and has an insecure and pluri-mediated relationship with external reality. *Retablo*, with its deliberately incredible coincidences and tone of fantasy never itself seeks any willing suspension of disbelief; the reader is continually and forcibly reminded that this is not life, and not a 'realistic' portrayal of life. The examples of the reaction of the mob in the fairground or of Isidoro before the statue are there to demonstrate the limits of such a view of art.

Nevertheless, there is a deeply felt tension between this rejection of the idea of fiction as image of society and reality, and a lingering desire to treat and comment on history. Consolo continues to give the impression of being a frustrated realist. Travel and exploration may provide him with the materials for a pliable metaphor on grand themes such as life and art, but the book also chronicles a journey, as allegorical as Bunyan's, through Sicilian life and history. It is not so much that Clerici is compelled, almost *malgré lui*, to notice the prison which overlooks his port of arrival, to record the brutal facts of hunger and poverty, and to observe that even someone intent on nothing more than sketching antiquity cannot avoid being struck by 'immagini attuali, di vita bruta, dolente e indecorosa' (*Retablo*, p. 58) ('raw, present-day images of life, in all its indecorous pain'), as that the various characters he encounters and places where he stops represent the peoples who have dominated Sicily down the centuries. Clerici has a letter of introduction to a Soldano, whose castle is plainly Arab, he makes his way to the temple at Selinunte which is Greek, he finds himself near a Norman church, he spends time rooting among Phoenician and Carthaginian ruins before ending up in the bustle of eighteenth-century Trapani with a merchant in love with his own native place. The experience of contemplating the ruins allows him to give vent to mock Enlightenment polemic with Montesquieu over the supposed conquest of barbarism in history, while his lords in the Arab castle host a debate among Academicians over whether the written language of Sicily should be pure Tuscan or should admit some elements of Sicilian. The idyll of his time in Trapani is destroyed by an apocalyptic earthquake which forces the travellers to flee to Palermo, where the encounter with the Rosalia statue awaits them. In whatever fabled colours this Sicily is now sketched, it is still Sicily; however magical the realism may be, there is a reality behind it.

Of all Consolo's works, *Retablo* is his most idiosyncratic and his most accomplished. He has found a style and an approach which combine the playfulness of the pastiche with the underlying seriousness of a writer who feels driven to confront the history of his own land. Nevertheless, the tension between the will to treat history and the doubts over whether fiction can be an apt instrument for establishing a relationship with social and political reality can only be brought into a provisional balance. Fiction allows him to express both sides of the dialectic. His most recent work *Le pietre di Pantalica* is a series of Borgesian pieces operating on the frontier between fiction and the essay. An essay on Sciascia has the outlines of a short story, while the tale of the arrival of the Americans at the Liberation is a mixture of invention and recreation. No one else, not even Sciascia, has so successfully made the Sicilian novel European. And no one else, in attempting that, has written with such panache and verve.

BIBLIOGRAPHY

Works

La ferita dell'aprile (Milan: Mondadori, 1963 and 1989).
Il sorriso dell'ignoto marinaio (Turin: Einaudi, 1976).
Lunaria (Turin: Einaudi, 1985).
Retablo (Palermo: Sellerio, 1987).
Le pietre di Pantalica (Milan: Mondadori, 1988).
Since this chapter was completed Consolo has published a new novel, *Nottetempo, casa per casa* (Milan: Mondadori, 1992).

Chapter 5

Andrea De Carlo
The Surface of Consciousness

MARTIN McLAUGHLIN

Andrea De Carlo first appeared on the Italian literary scene as a youthful protégé of Italo Calvino. His debut novel, *Treno di panna*, written at the age of twenty-nine, was published by Einaudi in March 1981 with a blurb on the back cover penned by Calvino himself. The book, which went on to win the Premio Comisso later that year, narrates the successful breakthrough into the film world of a young Italian in Los Angeles. According to Calvino, the novelty of De Carlo's achievement is his method of narrating the entire story through his protagonist's eyes, which, like a telephoto lens, concentrate exclusively on the surface of things. Calvino must have seen the similarity with his own *Palomar*, which he was writing at this time, since he highlighted this novel's narrative centre as 'la superficie della coscienza che sfiora un mondo tutto in superficie' ('the surface of a consciousness which brushes against a world which is all surface'). Yet despite these affinities he felt De Carlo's work had no obvious literary models; unlike other young authors, he concentrated exclusively on externals and surface, not on internal, existential content, and the only discernible influences were his previous training as a photographer and certain aspects of American 'hyper-realist' painting.

De Carlo's literary career, then, opened with considerable success. *Treno di panna* earned him a reputation for youthful originality and for links with the visual concerns of the 'école du regard' (the Italian designation for the *nouveau roman*) and of the later works of Calvino. His second novel, with the catchy title of *Uccelli da gabbia e da voliera*, was published the following year, 1982, and to a certain extent confirmed the promise shown in his first book. Again there is a young, aboulic protagonist, who registers in minute detail the surface feelings that wash over him as he tries to cope with the grimness of Italy in the 1980s, and to make some success of his personal life.

The two novels that followed, *Macno* in 1984, and *Yucatan* in 1986, were both published by Bompiani, and although it is difficult to say whether this change of publisher was cause or effect, they were more down-market, more closely related to popular genres than the Einaudi novels. De Carlo's literary

abilities were now called into question and critics began to wonder if success had
come too soon for an author who was still only thirty-four when his fourth
major novel was published. Fortunately for De Carlo, he rehabilitated his
reputation towards the end of the decade with *Due di due*, published in 1989 by
Mondadori.

De Carlo's literary career, with its five novels spanning the years 1981 to
1989, fits neatly into the decade of the 1980s, but in no sense can he be regarded
as paradigmatic of the so-called 'giovani narratori'. His style, as Calvino observed, has links with American rather than Italian fiction, and even the two
novels that are set in Italy (*Uccelli da gabbia* and *Due di due*) are constantly looking
beyond the boundaries of the peninsula for cultural models.

So what is the essence of De Carlo's fiction? The common thematic focus is
the youth culture of the 1960s, 1970s, and 1980s with its emphasis on rock
music and soft drugs, and with its aspiration towards easy sexual relationships, as
well as a life-style more in harmony with nature. The protagonists are regularly
unmotivated youths in their twenties, trying to give some shape to their
destinies, experimenting in their relationships with each other, attending to the
outward manifestations of their sentiments rather than to their inner echoes, and
engaged in a constant polemic against the alienating cities in which they live,
whether these be Los Angeles, London, or Milan. Despite this rather hackneyed
thematic, De Carlo in his best work avoids the dangers of clichéd writing by his
attention to visual detail and his ironic detachment in narrating.

The literary style which De Carlo deploys in the novels is totally suited to this
fictional world: straightforward, terse narration, often confined to the present
tense, and cinematic in technique; a kind of neo-Hemingwayesque style, both
in its short or at most paratactic sentences and in its largely macho viewpoint.
Occasionally the anglicisms border on the excessive, perhaps carrying to extremes that tradition of mixing English and Italian evident in writers such as
Fenoglio and Meneghello. But on the whole De Carlo's prose is not without
metaphorical depths and a sensitivity towards varieties of prose style. Although
the setting is often exotic, the problems are those dear to the hearts of young
Italians living in the 1980s: the squalor of the urban environment, the political
stagnation despite the threats posed by terrorism and kidnapping, and the
vacuity of most personal and social relationships.

Despite treating predictable topics, De Carlo's fiction exudes a freshness and
relevance that perhaps is lacking in some of the older, more established Italian
novelists; but conversely, it is also susceptible to the limitations of its contemporary content, exposed to the charge of being superficial, plastic, and eventually
dated. Nevertheless De Carlo would argue, as he does in *Due di due*, that the
evolution of the city, from being a source of pride in the Middle Ages and
Renaissance, to its present problematical status is neither a superficial nor dated
topic, but one that is central to our very survival.

Treno di panna is the story, narrated in the first person of Giovanni Maimeri, a twenty-five-year-old Italian photographer, who comes to Los Angeles, initially to stay with friends, but who eventually settles there and breaks through into the world of Beverley Hills actresses and directors. But it is an ironic rather than straightforward success-story, with sharp observations on the alienating urban environment and on the obsession with breaking through into the cinema world: 'sfondare' is the universal ambition. The narrative, which consists of eight chapters of varying length, opens with Giovanni landing at Los Angeles airport from Honolulu and cleverly stealing one of the many crates of pineapples from the baggage reclaim in order to give it to his hosts, Ron and Tracy. The following three chapters represent a flashback to their first meeting on holiday in Ibiza, to Tracy's letter inviting him to visit them in California, and to Ron's stream-of-consciousness letter also inviting him to stay, but clearly written in a state of euphoria induced by cocaine and Californian Riesling:

> giovanni ciao le macchine passano sopra la mia testa in una catena senza fine di movimento & scuotono la casa & le girano attorno in anelli di energia che si trasmette dalle pareti della casa alla mia schiena & poi lungo il mio braccio fino alla punta della mano che tiene questa penna con cui ti sto scrivendo (*Treno di panna*, p. 18)

> ciao giovanni the automobiles are shooting overhead in an endless chain of motion & shaking the house & encircling it in energy rings which are transmitted from the house walls to my back & then down my arm right down to the fingertips of my hand with which i'm holding the pen i'm using to write to you.

This is one of the few examples of hypotaxis in the novel: a virtuoso display of De Carlo's master of American rhythms even when writing in Italian. By contrast Tracy's letters, Giovani's narration, and the rest of the dialogue consists of simple, short clauses.

There follow two more short chapters on the tensions of living with Ron and Tracy. But the tension is eased in one of the comic sequences when Tracy, to earn some money from the local health-food store, dresses as a macrobiotic chocolate-chip cookie and cycles round the block on a tandem with Giovanni amidst the lethal Los Angeles traffic (pp. 26–33). In another comic set-piece, Giovanni takes a job in an Italian restaurant, staffed by downtrodden but mean Mexican waiters (pp. 35–50).

The last two chapters are the longest in the book, recounting Giovanni's teaching jobs at two language schools, one in Santa Monica, the other in Beverley Hills. At the latter he discovers that his pupil is one of his favourite actresses, the improbably named Marsha Mellows, the star of *Treno di panna*, which had been shot in Venice in 1971. Thus it is Giovanni, not Ron or Tracy, who breaks through: he teaches Marsha at her home and is invited to a party there where he shines briefly in conversation with film people. In the last chapter Marsha takes Giovanni to a party in Beverley Hills where they and other stars swim naked in the swimming pool. The novel ends with Giovanni nearly stepping on the head of the famous Tim Howards:

> Così ho pensato che alla fine ero al centro del mondo; che quando avevo dodici anni tenevo un manifesto di Tim Howards appeso in camera da letto, e adesso avrei potuto mettergli un piede in testa per far ridere Marsha Mellows; che la notte era solo a metà. (*Treno di panna*, p. 209)

> So I reflected that finally I was at the world's centre; that when I was twelve I had a Tim Howards poster stuck up in my bedroom and now I could have put my foot on his head to make Marsha Mellows laugh; that the night was only half done.

Consistent with these themes of survival and the cinema, the two main strands of imagery in the novel derive from the animal and photographic world. The animal images function well in this desperate environment where everyone is struggling to survive: Ron and Tracy are described as 'due giovani squali insicuri, rissosi' (*Treno di panna*, p. 209) ('two young sharks, insecure, quarrelsome') as they await the telephone call which will announce their breakthrough into a well-paid job; by contrast, in an effective mixture of metaphors, Marsha's film director/husband is 'un grosso animale da preda, uno squalo da freeway' (*Treno di panna*, p. 162) ('a large predator, a freeway shark'); while the famous guests at the party at the end are fittingly described as 'come cani a una esposizione' (*Treno di panna*, p. 200) ('like dogs at a dog show').

But if the animal metaphors, though effective, are rather predictable, the photographic imagery is original and appropriate. In the mornings after working in the restaurant Giovanni remembers half-gestures of the customers of the evening before more clearly than the rest of the preceding day: 'Questi dettagli perdevano proporzione durante la notte, si ingrandivano come fotografie' (*Treno di panna*, pp. 88–9') ('These details would lose their true dimensions during the night, becoming magnified like photographic enlargements'); when he is first introduced to Marsha Mellows he sees the meeting as through a series of filters, and watches her as though seeing a series of photographs of the filmstar (pp. 130–1); and in an interesting variation on this lens imagery he contrasts his desires with his actual achievements in these terms:

> La sfera di quello che avrei voluto essere e fare diventava spessa e stagna; lontanissima da quella che conteneva invece la mia vita. Il vetro delle due sfere diventava così denso e opaco da schermare del tutto la luce. (*Treno di panna*, p. 148)

> The sphere relating to what I wanted to be and do became solid, watertight; a world away from the one which actually contained my life. The glass constituting each of the two spheres was growing so thick and opaque as to screen out the light completely.

The image of glass spheres persists when he is introduced to guests at the party at

Marsha's house: 'Mi sembrava di essere precipitato al centro delle cose ...
Cercavo di demolire il vetro delle sfere alla svelta; metter in contatto la mia vita
con la vita vera' (*Treno di panna*, p. 166) ('I felt I had suddenly precipitated into
the centre of things ... I tried to smash those glass spheres quickly; to bring my
life into contact with real life'). Appropriately the final two images merge these
two lines of metaphor, both the animal and the visual: at the final party
Giovanni smokes marijuana and seems to observe the room 'da un punto di vista
di rettile: in scie di sensazioni strascicate, filanti' (*Treno di panna*, p. 205)
('through a reptile's eye: in streaks of trailing sensations, spun out'); and as he
stares through the kitchen window at the guests making love in the room next
door, he describes it as 'come guardare un acquario, o terrario forse, dove non è
chiaro se chi osserva è a sua volta osservato' (*Treno di panna*, p. 206) ('like
looking at an aquarium, or perhaps a terrarium, where it is not clear whether the
viewer is also being viewed').

The aptness of this imagery is underscored by the fact that the whole novel is
enclosed between two verbs of seeing: at the beginning Giovanni is on the
airplane 'guardavo Los Angeles dall'alto: il reticolo infinito di punti luminosi'
(*Treno di panna*, p. 3) ('looking down on Los Angeles: an endless mesh of bright
points'); in the final paragraph of the book he is again looking down on the city,
but this time from the successful heights of the Beverley Hills party:

> Ho guardato in basso, e di colpo c'era la città, come un immenso lago nero
> pieno di plancton luminoso, esteso fino ai margini dell'orizzonte. Ho guardato
> i punti di luce che vibravano nella distanza. (*Trena di panna*, p. 209)

> I looked below me, and suddenly, there was the town, like an immense black
> lake full of luminous plankton, stretching as far as the horizon's edge. I looked
> at the points of light that glimmered in the distance.

This understated conclusion is typical of the novel's tone, and on the whole De
Carlo's first book represents a considerable achievement, a deft mixture of
youthful content, detailed but detached observation, and stylistic consistency.

Uccelli da gabbia e da voliera (1982) opens with a remarkable paragraph which
sets the tone for the rest of the book:

> Alle tre di pomeriggio sto guidando la mia MG bianca lungo Goldfinch Avenue
> verso le colline, con una cassetta dei Rolling Stones a tutto volume sullo stereo,
> e salto uno stop senza accorgermene. Vedo una Chevette verde chiaro che mi
> arriva da destra, scivola verso me come un piccolo cetaceo sott'onda. Non cerco
> di frenare, o di girare il volante, o. Guardo il verde chiaro che si avvicina, senza
> togliere il piede dall'acceleratore. (*Uccelli da gabbia e da voliera*, p. 3)

> At three in the afternoon I'm driving my white MG along Goldfinch Avenue
> towards the hills, with a cassette of the Rolling Stones playing full blast on the
> car-stereo, and I go through a stop sign without noticing. I see a pale green
> Chevette coming from my right, it slides towards me like a small cetacean
> under the sea. I don't try to brake, or to turn the steering-wheel, or. I watch
> the pale green coming closer, without taking my foot off the accelerator.

As this passage demonstrates, De Carlo retains a number of the successful features of his debut novel: the young first-person narrator, who even after this crash continues to coast aimlessly through life, the flat narrative, now even more direct by being narrated entirely in the present tense, and the metaphorical depth supplied by the marine and animal similes. There is also the strand of cinematic and technological imagery which had been present in the first book: thus when Fiodor and Malaidina feel drawn to each other for the first time, he tells us that 'l'involucro sottile che delimita i nostri campi magnetici si tende e si tende finché di colpo si lacera come una pellicola trasparente' (*Uccelli da gabbia*, p. 54) ('the thin membrane which delimits our magnetic fields stretches and stretches until it suddenly splits like a transparent film'); or when he sees Malaidina after a long absence, he describes the sensation as seeing the original after months of looking at an overexposed photocopy (p. 161).

Structurally, however, there is a difference between the two novels in that the 220 pages are divided not into 8 uneven chapters but into 25 chapters each roughly the same length. In terms of location there is a shift from the exotic, transalantic setting of California, Costa Rica, and New York in the first three chapters to Milan and its hinterland for the rest of the novel. Nevertheless there is still the same playing around with elliptical narration: if the description of the few seconds of the car crash lasts nearly two pages, the end of the opening chapter when Fiodor leaves Maggie in Santa Barbara, summoned by his father, is in complete contrast:

> Maggie deve essere in cucina o da qualche parte, perché quando esco c'è solo la sdraio vuota sul prato.
> Volo da Santa Barbara a Los Angeles.
> Volo da Los Angeles a San José di Costa Rica. (*Uccelli da gabbia e da voliera*, p. 8)

> Maggie must be in the kitchen or somewhere, because when I leave there is only the empty deckchair on the lawn.
> I fly from Santa Barbara to Los Angeles.
> I fly from Los Angeles to San José in Costa Rica.

Later, when he is making love to his boss's wife in the mountains North of Milan, the scene shifts with equal rapidity:

> Siamo in piedi di fianco al tavolo, con le labbra quasi a contatto.
> Siamo seduti sul bordo del divano, con le labbra a contatto e i polpastrelli umidi.
> Siamo per terra di fianco al divano, con le mani sotto le reciproche camicie.
> (*Uccelli da gabbia e da voliera*, p. 136)

> We are standing beside the table, with our lips almost touching.
> We are sitting on the edge of the sofa, with our lips touching and our fingertips clammy.
> We are lying on the ground beside the sofa, with our hands under each other's shirt.

In the end Fiodor Barna's listless existence acquires direction when he decides finally to emigrate to Australia with his girlfriend and some other friends, a decisive act of will certainly, but one to which he is driven more by his obsession for the mysterious Malaidina than for any political or ecological motive.

There are a number of other significant differences between the two novels. *Uccelli da gabbia* is a more serious book, lacking the humour of the American location of the first novel, and being forced to deal with the problems of contemporary Italy more directly. Sue, the wife of Fiodor's boss in Italy, elaborates on the exasperation of living in Milan, coping with the traffic, the strikes, the perennial fear of kidnapping and terrorism. She also mentions the earthquake (presumably that of 1980) and the money which had been lent by her husband's firm only to be channelled into the pockets of the local mafia, but Fiodor is indifferent. Only when his love, the Italian Malaidina, provides her outline of Italy's overeducated but indolent youth and its corrupt government ministers, abetted by supine interviewers, does Fiodor begin to contemplate escaping the stricken country.

Another major divergence from *Treno di panna* resides in De Carlo's more consistent exploitation of the imagery of his elegant title, in particular the contrast between cages and aviaries. In Chapter 2 Fiodor visits his father's Costa Rican home with its exotic birds in their carefully constructed aviaries and this is clearly contrasted with his return to Milan at the start of Chapter 4, and the description of the enormous cupola of grey smog that merely envelops layers and layers of more grey smog. The idea of Milan as a huge prison-cage is developed when Malaidina first comes to his flat and criticizes all Milanese housing as 'delle vere gabbie di energia' (*Uccelli da gabbia*, p. 53) ('real energy cages'), and at the end when Fiodor's friends decide to emigrate to Australia to raise exotic birds and they describe Milan as 'una specie di galera, più che una città' (*Uccelli da gabbia*, p. 196) ('a kind of prison rather than a city'). Although the contrast between *gabbia* and *voliera* may not always be clear-cut, since even the 'voliera' is still a cage of a kind, the imagery does hold a certain coherence: at a moment of delirium, when Fiodor is making love to Malaidina, he imagines himself in three other ecstatic activities, building a complex aviary, painting, or constructing or playing a musical instrument; but the next instant he finds words inadequate to convey his euphoria and condemns them as 'rigide e limitate come piccole gabbie' (*Uccelli da gabbia*, p. 175) ('stiff and limited like little cages').

Another reason for the difference of tone is that the lightness of touch in the previous book is here replaced by a more insistent romantic interest which also at times is combined with elements of the thriller, including both a pursuit of a terrorist on foot and a car-chase. In the end, *Uccelli da gabbia* remains too close to the 'romanzo giallo' (the thriller) and to the 'romanzo rosa' (the love story), as well as too faithful to a realistic description of Italian city-life for the ironic and humorous touches that undercut any serious pretensions in *Treno di panna*.

Perhaps this difficulty of depicting contemporary Italian reality encouraged De Carlo to resort once more in his next novel to an exotic location. *Macno* (1984) is set in an imaginary, but not very convincing Latin American dictatorship ruled by the eponymous hero of the novel, an ex-rock star turned investigative television journalist and then politico. It remains De Carlo's weakest novel, despite retaining a number of the techniques successfully deployed in the others. Like its immediate predecessor, it is narrated entirely in the present, but in the third person this time, and with a female protagonist.

But De Carlo, like Calvino, seems unable to narrate convincingly from the female point of view: indeed characterization as a whole is one of the major flaws in the novel. Liza, the protagonist, has no depth as a character, there is no lead up to her infatuation with Macno, so that her affair with the superstar/dictator makes her as much a female stereotype as he is a male one: 'Lui la stringe tra braccia forti, lei perde il senso dei propri contorni ... ' (*Macno* p. 79) ('He takes her between his strong arms, she loses all sense of her contours ...'). The rest of the characters are similarly stereotyped: the naive American cameraman, the English botanist Durrell, the American gossip-columnist Gloria Hedges, and so on. Macno's eulogy to Liza of the ancient, pre-Christian civilizations founded on water (p. 106) is so banal that initially one might think it is a parody; except that there are other instances of tired dialogue, notably when Liza is explaining to Ottavio the electrifying effect Macno has on people (p. 182).

But apart from characterization and dialogue, the setting is also unconvincing, since this Central American dictatorship clearly has many Italian characteristics: before Macno took over, the country had spiralling inflation, a corrupt central and local government, and everything was carved up amongst the main political parties; and Tarminelli, the politician who had been in every cabinet since the 1940s, is a clear cipher for Andreotti.

The language of the novel is another source of critical dissatisfaction. There is the by now familiar marine imagery, but here it seems tired and mechanical: Macno talks of 'quanti squali ci sono sul fondo torbido con le mandibole aperte' (*Macno*, p. 96) ('how many sharks there are on the muddy bottom with their jaws open'), and at one point, before diving into his pool, he and Liza strip off their clothes 'mossi da un'ansia marina' (*Macno*, p. 127) ('driven by a marine anxiety')! The other linguistic defect is that the excessive anglicisms seem to denaturize the Italian, and they lack point since the setting of *Macno* is not the California of the first novel.

Yucatan (1986), however, is located mostly in California but interspersed by two trips to Mexico. Like the previous two books, it is narrated entirely in the present tense; the principal narrator is Dave Hollis, the young apprentice filmmaker to the Yugoslav director Dru Resnik, but in seven out of the twenty-three chapters Resnik's own thoughts are conveyed in italics. The plot is fairly thin:

Resnik and Hollis go to California to shoot a film based on a novel by the Latin American author Astor Camado, called *Incontro con il vuoto*. A series of anonymous notes forces the two film-makers to go on an abortive trip to Mexico looking for locations. When they return, more anonymous letters induce them to go back to Mexico in order to lose their 'negatività' and to regain harmony in ancient Aztec sites. Back in Los Angeles, they are manipulated toward a final, anticlimactic meeting with the Voice who has been sending the messages.

Apart from its weak conclusion, this novel marks in most respects an improvement on the banalities of *Macno*. In the Californian setting De Carlo rediscovers some of the verve and humour of his first book, notably in the portrayal of the cinema world's eccentric inhabitants. There is also some fine writing in his description of the Arizona desert landscape on the way to Mexico (pp. 61–3), and the Aztec temple sites, which contrast well with the decadent scenes in the Los Angeles strip-club and the crater-like multi-story hotel in Mexico. The metaphors are not all automatically drawn from the animal world; some images have an appropriate apocalyptic dimension, as in this description of the deserted site of the Aztec temple:

> Adesso sembra davvero un immenso campo da baseball dove siano atterrate delle astronavi minacciose e scomparse le tribune e il pubblico scappato via tranne qualche disperso che si aggira instupidito dallo shock senza rendersi conto di cosa è successo. (*Yucatan*, p. 123)

> Now it seems really like a huge baseball pitch on which some menacing spaceships have landed and the stands have disappeared and the spectators all dispersed except for the odd straggler still wandering around in a state of shock unable to understand what has happened.

Also on the positive side is the fact that Camado's *Incontro con il vuoto* reacts to a certain extent intertextually both with the film Dresnik is trying to shoot, and with De Carlo's novel. Camado himself must be a fictional version of Carlos Castaneda since his story is of a young New York musicologist who goes to Mexico for research only to encounter an Indian wizard who draws him into a web of voodoo practices, which eventually transport him into another or parallel world. What fascinates Dresnik (and De Carlo) is the American mixture of empirical rationality with the cult of the paranormal, and his description of the Latin American book is clearly an echo of *Yucatan* itself:

> C'è il suo allontanamento progressivo dalla razionalità scientifica dietro cui si riparava all'inizio, e questi paesaggi fatti di luci e minerali allo stato puro, questi personaggi strani e difficili da decifrare come raffigurazioni precolombiane. È una storia di stati emotivi, di spostamenti, più che di fatti. (*Yucatan*, p. 12)

> There is his progressive distancing from scientific rationality, behind which he used to shelter at the beginning, and there are these landscapes made of lights and minerals in their pure state, these strange characters who are as difficult to decipher as pre-Colombian paintings. It is more a story of emotional states, and movements, than of events.

De Carlo's novel, of course, turns out to be concerned more with Dru's emotional states and movement than with actual events.

The seven chapters where Dru's thoughts are recounted in the first person are thus as important as the events narrated in the other chapters. At times Dave seems to be a cinematic version of De Carlo himself, notably when Dru talks of Dave's 'attenzione implacabile per lo scorrere della superficie e la definizione dei dettagli' (*Yucatan*, p. 25) ('relentless attention to surface flow and the pinning down of details'). But on other occasions, it is Resnik who reflects the author's position, notably when one of the anonymous letters articulates criticisms that seem directed at the author of *Macno* as much as at Dru: 'Il tuo lavoro è una ripetizione fredda di motivi a cui hai dato intensità in passato, e che ora usi come ingredienti di una ricetta' (*Yucatan*, p. 93) ('Your work is a cold repetition of motifs to which you gave some intensity in the past, but which you now use just like the ingredients of a recipe'). Similarly, although Dru declares that he is not a director with a mission to propagate a message (p. 144), at the end of the book he finds himself articulating the message about pollution and materialism which the anonymous notes and manipulations have been trying to communicate all along.

This seems to be the one common strand of thought that unites the disparate output of De Carlo up to this point. Although set in America, De Carlo in this novel considers urban pollution a universal problem, and at one point Dru specifically mentions Italy as a 'paese ... talmente squarciato e intaccato e fatto a pezzi ormai, le radiazioni ti trapanano', (*Yucatan*, p. 70) ('country ... which is now totally ripped apart, corroded and ruined, the radiation levels go through you'), and describes the destruction of the landscape by cement buildings, supermarkets and factories. It is this ecological theme which comes to the forefront in his final novel of the decade.

Due di due, although published in 1989, was begun as early as 1984, and indeed is mentioned in *Yucatan* (p. 97) as a European novel which is being made into an American film. This long gestation period of five years is not surprising when one considers both the bulk of the novel and the literary ambitions which subtend it: twice the length of his previous works, this book sets out to chart the significance of the two decades from 1968 to 1988 for De Carlo's generation. Here the narrative is wholly centred on Italy, dealing with the youth and maturity of Mario, the narrator, and his friend Guido, as they grow up in the years of student revolt and political unrest in Italy. The title derives from the similarity and difference of their lives, which Mario articulates about halfway through the novel: 'Pensavo a quanto le nostre vite erano state diverse in questi anni, e anche simili in fondo, due di due possibili percorsi iniziati dallo stesso bivio' (*Due di due,* p. 209) ('I thought about how different our lives had been in all these years, and also how similar in the end: the two of us had travelled along two of two possible paths which had started at the same intersection').

The novel is divided into two halves, each of 26 chapters, the first part dealing with the period from the mid-1960s until 1973, the second half covering the years from 1973 to 1986. There is thus greater attention devoted to the adolescence of the two boys and De Carlo effectively conveys the heady atmosphere of the days of protest in the schools and universities. He is also convincing in his narration of the two protagonists' private lives, particularly their early sexual encounters, which often end with embarrassing interruptions:

> Sono sceso con la mano alle sue ginocchia, al sottile velo crespatello delle calze; risalito cauto verso la pella nuda e tenera dove le calze finivano. Ero così confuso che non riuscivo più a distinguere i miei gesti dalle mie pure intenzioni, ed è suonato un campanello. (*Due di due*, p. 34)

> I put my hand down to her knees, to the sheer, crinkly transparency of her stockings; then I felt cautiously up to the tender, naked skin where her stockings ended. I was so confused that I could no longer distinguish my physical actions from my mere intentions, and then a bell rang.

There is also some memorable writing about a liberating holiday in Greece, where Mario and Guido meet Canadian, French, and Scottish students in an atmosphere which allows them to feel that they are escaping the provincial barriers of Italy, as they discuss the music of the Rolling Stones, and *The Great Gatsby*. The holiday in Greece is a turning point, as it allows Mario to see the staleness of his relationship with his Italian girlfriend; and it encourages Guido to leave Italy and go off to live in London, Boston, and San Francisco. In his absence Mario, who has always been in awe of Guido, drifts through his first two years at university, and at the end of the first half of the novel he has a nervous breakdown from which he seems reluctant to recover until his mother arrives to tell him that her husband has died.

In the second half Mario turns from contemplation to action. With the money his stepfather had left him, he buys land near Gubbio, builds his own farmhouse, and becomes self-sufficient. He meets a similarly ecologically-minded girl, Martina, who comes to live with him and eventually bears him twins. Now it is Guido who drifts and starts to envy Mario's stability. After a period in Australia, he returns to Italy, develops a relationship with Martina's sister, Chiara, and in a period of rare calm he completes his first novel, which eventually becomes a 'caso letterario'. In 1980 Guido and Chiara tire of the rural existence, and go off to live in Milan. But in the end Guido leaves her, becomes an alcoholic and dies in a car crash on his way to Milan to visit Chiara and his child. After the funeral Mario and Marina plunge themselves into their autumnal labours on the farm, but remain undecided about what to do with the other house which Mario had built for Guido beside his own, but which Guido had never lived in. In a rather unconvincing but symbolic finale, Mario impulsively douses the house with petrol and sets fire to it. Next morning they plant the area with rosemary and lavender. The final low-key paragraph has a touch of Pavese about it, not only in its evocation of the hillside landscape after the bonfire, but also in its elegiac understatement:

> Quando abbiamo finito sono andato a fare una passeggiata da solo, fino alla collina che anni prima in un giorno di neve io e Guido avevamo risalito per contemplare il paesaggio. Ho cercato il punto preciso in cui ci eravamo fermati e ho guardato in basso come avevamo fatto allora, ed era strano vedere una casa sola dove ce n'erano state due. (*Due di due*, p. 385)

> When we finished, I went for a walk on my own, up as far as the hill which years before in a day of snow Guido and I had climbed to view the landscape. I looked for the precise spot where we had stopped and I gazed down as we had done then, and it was strange to see just one house where previously there had been two.

Due di due exploits the by now familiar twin strands of De Carlo's imagery: metaphors from the animal world and from the world of technology, particularly the cinema. These areas of imagery appropriately embody the two poles of this novel's dialectic: nature versus technology. But often De Carlo falls back on hackneyed animal metaphors, especially when portraying the negative characters. Thus the attendant in the *manicomio* where Guido escapes military service has a 'faccia scimmiesca' (*Due di due,* p. 122) ('face like a monkey'); and the military doctor who examines Guido is described as 'un ratto di fogna gonfio di veleno' (p. 128) ('a sewer-rat bloated with *poison*').

More subtle, though again not very original, is the glass imagery. Guido first invokes it when he urges Mario to summon the courage to talk to the girl he likes, comparing his existence to living behind glass and encouraging him to break it, not thinking of the pain it may cause, but mindful of avoiding an old age full of regrets (p. 24). It is a lesson that Mario remembers: 'la tecnica della rottura del vetro' (*Due di due,* p. 104) ('the technique of glass-breaking') also works in each of his successive encounters with women. The glass clearly acts as a screen between the private world of desire and the reality on the other side: but it is also a screen that can be broken in less positive circumstances, as when Maria's mother comes to the clinic to tell him that her husband is dead.

> E ho visto un'incrinatura formarsi nell'involucro trasparente che mi avvolgeva, correre in diagonale e lacerarlo in una frazione di secondo: di colpo ero esposto senza alcuna protezione, senza il minimo filtro tra me e lo stridio frenetico di sensazioni che mi assalivano da tutti i lati. (*Due di due*, p. 180)

> And in the transparent film which enclosed me I saw a crack form, run diagonally and split it in a fraction of a second: suddenly I was exposed without any protection, without the slightest filter between myself and the frenetic clamouring of sensations which assailed me from all sides.

But more than for its imagery, *Due di due* will be remembered for its content, for its attack on modern society and the city in general, as well as on contemporary Italy in particular. Always in the background to this novel there lurks the pollution and inhumanity of Milan. Mario's move from the scene of student revolt to a peaceful, 'alternative' existence in the country seems paradigmatic of the general movement of *riflusso* experienced by many young Italians in the 1980s. The critique of other aspects of Italian life embraces a number of familiar targets. Italy's antiquated education system is compared to 'una vecchia nave decrepita che affonda lentamente in acque basse' (*Due di due*, p. 45) ('an old, decrepit ship, slowly sinking in shallow waters'). For the protagonists foreign writers like Stendhal, Kafka, and Fitzgerald seem much more 'relevant'; and in musical terms America and rock music are at the centre, while Italy is merely on the periphery. Hence the book is studded with refrains from songs by Bob Dylan and allusions to the Rolling Stones. Italy is criticized as 'un paese di parole' (*Due di due,* p. 185) ('a land of words'), in which the newspapers, even when read abroad after an absence of some years, seem a morass of stale political gossip and false moralism, described in words that are only chosen for their sound (p. 211). Italian television likewise has the same powers of distortion as the press, reducing the sharp angles of Guido's polemical book to a flat plane of bland homogeneity (p. 300).

Due di due will probably remain an important fictionalized account of these fundamental decades in Italian history. As Calvino's generation felt the need for THE novel of the Resistance, so the generation that was born in the 1950s would like to see THE novel about the protest years and their legacy. De Carlo's last work of the 1980s makes a reasonable claim to be that novel, though as in the case of the Resistance novel, there will probably never be unanimity about this.

Looking back over Andrea De Carlo's literary career, one can immediately pick out the positive features: the refreshingly youthful viewpoint, the rejection of anything other than a flat, terse narrative, the attempt to expand Italian fiction beyond its peninsular confines, and the foregrounding of important, almost committed, themes such as the environment and political stagnation. Indeed his output in the 1980s has evolved away from the light, American superficiality of his earlier novels toward a much more serious and weighty concentration on the ills that continue to afflict Italian society. The writing has acquired weight, but in so doing it has lost its ironic humour and its concern with surface details and externals, in order to deal with themes that require that inner, almost existential dimension which Calvino highlighted as being absent in his protégé debut. De Carlo still tries to remain faithful to certain of Calvino's ideals, his attempt to write simple prose, for instance:

> Anche in *Due di due* ho cercato una scrittura semplice. Non ho mai pensato che la complicazione della forma sia indispensabile per esprimere la complessità di ciò che si vuole narrare. Italo Calvino insegna: la forma cristallina del suo stile era in realtà tormentatissima, i suoi manoscritti un tessuto unico di cancellature per arrivare alla difficile semplicità della leggerezza (*Panorama*, 8 October 1989, p. 143)

Even in *Due di due* I aimed at a simple style of writing. I have never believed that a complicated form was essential to express the complexity of what one wants to narrate. Italo Calvino provides a lesson for all of us: the crystalline form of his writing belied a tortuous struggle, his manuscripts were an endless tissue of rubbings out necessary to attain the difficult simplicity of lightness.

But although De Carlo here returns the compliment paid by Calvino at the beginning of the decade, there are too many other areas in which he clearly does not follow his master for him to be considered part of a hypothetical 'Calvino school'. The lightness of touch and the registration of the external surface of reality are apparent only in his first novel. In the later novels the visual obsession disappears or rather transfers from the level of content to that of imagery. By the end of the 1980s De Carlo has returned to a 'heavy', existential subject matter, in which he denounces the ills of contemporary reality but often finds it difficult to avoid clichéd writing. The referentiality of words or texts is never once called into question, so that De Carlo diverges from Calvino most of all in his continued pursuit of an unproblematical, lengthy realism which is found only in the early writings of his master, and which remains totally untouched by the literary, although not by the political, polemics of the 1960s and 1970s.

BIBLIOGRAPHY

Works

Fiction

Treno di panna (Turin: Einaudi, 1981). Translated by John Gatt as *The Cream Train* (London: Olive Press, 1987).
Uccelli da gabbia e da voliera (Turin: Einaudi, 1982).
Macno (Milan: Bompiani, 1984).
Yucatan (Milan: Bompiani, 1986).
Due di due (Milan: Mondadori, 1989).
Since this chapter was completed De Carlo has published a new novel *Tecniche di seduzione*, (Milan: Mondadori, 1991).

Films

Treno di panna (1988).

New German – 3A

Chapter 6

Daniele del Giudice
Planimetry of Sight/Vision in Three Books

ANNA DOLFI

In his *Art of the Novel* Kundera stated that implicit in every novelist's work is his or her own view of the history of the novel, and that whether he talks about himself or about other writers a novelist always provides a sort of 'practitioner's confession' of what lies concealed beneath the tension of his own act of writing. One gets the impression from reading some of Daniele Del Giudice's recent comments on Italo Calvino that the delicate thread of Ariadne to which Kundera refers is suddenly exposed, and that in defining Calvino's writing Del Giudice at the same time provides us with an intimate portrait (significantly Calvino is said to be 'a point of reference for other novelists, indeed the only one, even though Calvino himself was not aware of this'; 'he had opened up the only real area of *diversité* in the Italian narrative tradition of the second half of the century' ('Un écrivain diurne')); and indeed if we consider the three fundamental characteristics that Del Giudice attributes to Calvino – his being a *diurno*, mannerist, non-novelesque writer – none of them seems to be irrelevant to the work of the younger novelist.

Del Giudice explains his notion of *diurno* as follows:

> The *diurno* writer is one characterised by measure and control of his material, one who does not deny the beast within him, perhaps allows it to roar, but he uses that roar to create and set in opposition to it other imaginary monsters, which may be more beautiful or uglier, but which, just because they are fictitious creations, have also been tamed. He is someone who *thinks* his act of narration, his creation of form, like an act of moral craftsmanship, a continual effort to understand and to make connections and so to establish order, while knowing that order is always provisional, constantly gnawed away by Chaos, like sand-castles on the sea-shore. ('Un écrivain diurne')

Del Giudice, like Calvino, is a writer characterized by measure and control, a writer searching for a way of recreating the world around us according to a mathematical/geometrical formula, using a language that is de-lyricized, exact, precise and a syntax that is perfectly articulated (based above all on variations of tense) set out in balanced, paratactical constructions which accentuate the semantic precision.

In Del Giudice's novels (which normally take the form of the short novel or long tale – *Nel museo di Reims* being the best example) his modernity is filtered, as in Calvino, through a kind of melancholy which is not made explicit but arises from the situations, the silences, the dialogues, from his intuition of a feeling of alienation, of the gap between words and things which makes it impossible to bring vision and reality together within physical or verbal bounds; in the desire for, and at the same time a sense of the absence of any true knowledge of reality or the ability to represent it. This leads to a sort of blowing of the mind so that it can grasp them both and project them in an act of personal re-reading. Here he comes closest to the late rather than the early Calvino, whose *Cosmicomiche* marks a change of direction which will reach a disturbing conclusion in *Palomar* – although we should bear in mind the significance for Del Giudice of Calvino's painful struggle in *Città invisibili*; and here it is possible to see something of the originality of Del Giudice's poetics, which he had outlined previously in the *Magazine littéraire*:

> I was quite sensitive to the limitations of the *diurno* element and of mannerism, and I should have liked to contaminate them with the magma of opposing traditions – my own existential urge was more direct or at least I thought that while ideas could not constitute the explicit theme of my narrative they must be respected and used rather like a subterranean source of sentimental and emotional energy. ('Un écrivain diurne')

Identifying the limitations of Calvino's narrative in its promotion of ideas as the themes of his stories, Del Giudice points out the dangers of what Kundera had considered the climax of the *modus narrandi*: the emergence of a novelist who *thinks* his or her story, superseding description and narrative (albeit with an overall loss of effect). Whilst certainly a product of Calvino's illuminism, but also of Conrad's obscurity, Kafka's irrationality and Handke's anti-realism, Del Giudice tries to replace ideas (which he has lost faith in) with a subtler, more intimate dynamic, bringing into play delicately shaded horizons of desire and expectation and of the unknown, all of which are hidden within ideas but which can be tapped and exploited by the writer as a force driving the narrative, not explicit but concealed and self-contained (like Calvino's impregnable fortress or the star-shaped fortress of Del Giudice's own military stories). This force exerts itself not so much upon the characters as upon the objects which the protagonists (who are so conscious of the modern, technological world they live in) are struggling to grapple with and which they tensely scrutinize, trying desperately to understand their inner structure – a structure that includes time, though time has now escaped human consciousness. Whilst there is no sign in Del Giudice's work of the claims of play and dream (if we still keep in mind the typologies proposed in Kundera's *Art of the Novel*) the claims of thought and of time do appear, in combination, mutually correcting each other – time integrated with thought and thought with the sense of time. Then the relationship between internal and external becomes more complex, and only when they coincide can the truth hope to appear, just as an object appears when exposed to the multiple vision of perspective or to the focusing of one's gaze by collimation (a compound of vision and blindness). The structure of objects, the physical properties which make up their form, are always on a razor-edge between coherence and disintegration, poised at a point where time can suddenly overflow and form is seen to collapse, making way for an act of vision which unites subjective and objective time.

So Del Giudice sets off in pursuit of this cognitive process (that is the acquisition of physical knowledge as opposed to the ontological knowledge of ancient philosophy and to psychological-existential knowledge – in fact he offers us a modern semantic theory quite different from those earlier systems) and he attempts in his three novels to formulate different situations and with them to explore new horizons of feeling – to investigate potential forces, or forms of propulsive energy which can stretch out beyond ideas, beyond form, to what can only be reached with great precision, lightness of touch and lucidity. And so, with this more direct, neo-existential search for the subterranean springs of emotion, the feeling we have for things, for life and art, Del Giudice attempts the difficult and elusive task of constructing a diagram of human sensibility, using first-person narrators who are surprisingly fragile but at the same time have the strength and the power to see beyond vision, beyond the bounds of visibility. Vision as an organ, an instrument, a metaphorical object or theme recurs as a dominant element in his novels, almost to the exclusion of any other – combined with the complementary topos of lack of knowledge, invisibility. So his characters elude us (like Bobi Bazlen in *Lo stadio di Wimbledon*) or they seek each other out and communicate with each other in a desperate attempt to give substance to what is only movement and light (for example, the two protagonists in *Atlante occidentale*, especially those pages providing a parallel reading of the fireworks on Lake Geneva, where the narrative metaphor creates images of movement whereas the author's technical skill had evoked a dream of moving images). For these characters knowledge can only be intermittent, emotional and nocturnal, because we cannot see the hidden form of things which is only visible to those willing to read it independently of any other distracting form or substance. In *Nel museo di Reims* the near blindness of the protagonist is coincidental with his will, his refusal to give form to what is beyond his knowledge: Barnaba, who cannot see exterior forms, will be able to go beyond the frames of the pictures that escape his vision, beyond the figures he cannot see or can only partially see or of which he can only see the colour; he will be able to reach out and grasp the secret *energeia*, the colour-metaphor, the colour-feeling. In the play between internal and external Del Giudice challenges us to reverse the relationship, and so will speak of pictures that come from outside us and move inside, and which cause an intersection of vision and time in respect of external and internal. The close-up view which the young man in the Rheims museum is obliged to take in order to see things with his eyes prevents him from seeing the whole, because it separates matter into segments making it appear fragmented, reduced to atoms, to tonality. His act of vision is not directed at the object, it does not perhaps come from within himself but from the outer edge of his pupil, from that delicate point where the body touches and grasps the void.

If what counts for Del Giudice and his characters is the internal dimension (the emotional resonance), the external may not even exist: formless colours will be the greatest concession to form (in this connection the decision to associate Nereo Rotelli's sixteen paintings with the story is extremely pertinent): they are a new source of energy creating further bodies, figures, landscapes whose existence depends on a new balance between order and invention. In the brief note appended to his reproduction of the pictures Del Giudice spoke quite deliberately of the fascination of narratives 'di cui si potesse parlare così, dall'interno, senza correre ai significati, che molto spesso non ci sono' (*Nel museo di Reims*, p. 82) ('that can be discussed from the inside without recourse to meanings that often do not exist'), and he insisted on the hidden element of chance that had given birth to his own story – an exemplary one in many ways in the corpus of narrative experiments which Del Giudice has published, with its alternation of first- and third-person narrators apparently merging the techniques tried out by the first-person traveller in *Lo stadio di Wimbledon* and the third-person narrators in *Atlante occidentale*. Shut in as he is in his encroaching blindness and deprived inevitably of the outside world, Barnaba starts to wonder whether he really cares about those paintings (that is the external world) or just his own 'journey of exploration' in search of colours, lights, feelings including those covert feelings about death in the key picture in the museum, David's *Marat assassiné*. The identification of the protagonist with the hero of the picture leads, via the discussion of colours, light, settings and perspective to the theme of vision (Marat the doctor and physician treating blindness), and at the same time it raises the question of the relationship between objective truth and lie (using the character of Anne, the young woman who goes with Barnaba and describes the pictures to him, but lies to him and creates a non-existent reality or at least one only true to her own fantasy). If everything 'nella realtà è staccato, disunito, non messo lì per assomigliare a qualche cosa' (*Nel museo di Reims*, p. 82) ('in reality is detached, separate, not intended to resemble anything'), if the only things that matter are just tones, shades, colours, then perhaps these things are truer than the concrete comparisons which Barnaba uses in his attempt to remember colours, the sentimental abstractions evoked by Anne's memory, and perhaps she too is constrained by another sort of colour-blindness and forced to exist at the outer edge of her eyes, outside any 'point of truth' in the world of 'pure and formless colours'. It is not in the words themselves but in the aura emanating from them, the glimmerings of meaning behind them (the link between physical reality and geometry, between things and their atomic constitution) that we can trace those nodules of nostalgia, tenderness and modesty, which determine the relations between the characters (in *Nel museo di Reims* and in *Atlante occidentale*) – a particular smile for example, a mixture of affection and modesty – will create points of contact and establish a second layer of discourse, perhaps the true one, distinct from the objective reality of the actual words – sight that extends beyond sight; words that reach out beyond words, taking advantage of that elusive chart of sensibility which words create without managing to define it, except when they become colour and vision themselves.

In this sense Pietro Rahe and Ira Epsteim, the young physicist and the old writer in *Atlante occidentale*, are complementary characters each mirroring the other ('allowing the eye no escape route'), each bound by the same precision and the same gentleness of approach. Both are trying to see beyond mere form, in the one case into those regions of artificial space where matter is absent (in experiments using the particle accelerator the function of which is to disintegrate matter into infinitesimally small pieces), in the other in the creation/vision of what does not exist, on the borderline between things and non-things. Both are visionaries whose vision embraces both what exists and what exists yet at the same time does not exist, and to which nonetheless they feel obliged to give a form, a word so that it can be an object of knowledge and communication. Concerned as they are with the extreme limits of vision they reduce everything to a sense of form, to energy that outstrips action and perception that goes beyond knowledge. The references to the fluorescent light under the eyes of certain species of fish, and to the outline of various pieces of antique furniture left by the light on the walls of certain rooms in an old castle are not fortuitous – and it is no accident that the two protagonists are used to flying over places at a great height, to seeing things as tiny points (atoms, lines), and it is no accident that the peak of communication and comprehension occurs at night (the night-shifts in the CERN laboratories, and the fireworks), at a time when one can exist outside of time and stretch out beyond the present into the future. In the labyrinth of a Geneva divided geometrically by streets named after great physicists, in the elusiveness of an international city which seems to force people 'to be more in play', the customary dimension of space and time are changed and we witness an imposition of mind on space, of physical reality on time that is typical of Del Giudice's characters. In the disturbance of our normal coordinates, of our usual boundaries, we can enjoy an almost continual reduction of everything (time included) to a unique spatial order, and our attention is focused on those points where internal and external are separated, which is always apparent when people deliberately slow down their actions or exaggerate them physically, or when they slow down their words and deliberately enunciate them as though on the very tip of their tongue. We can focus on the 'allure' (the total effect of our bearing including our psychological make-up) which corresponds to a sort of mental image, an auto- and hetero-projection of the individual to others and to himself. Ira Epsteim will criticize Brahe for his way of moving his hands, of touching space, for his ability to create objects by means of movements, for his ability to see things with his eyes closed, including himself, and for his attempt, analogous to his own, to unite figure and background in a relationship of equal dignity.

If 'when looking one only sees the background', and 'when thinking one only thinks of the figure', never 'the two things together' Del Giudice's aim will be to unite sight and thought, physical reality and words in an attempt 'to link persons with objects, and objects with experience and feelings, with perception of self, with ideas' and create a new kind of time which pierces through the present and genuinely stretches out towards the future. Emotional time is the time-world of the aura or halo and at the same time the world of precise, exact vision. When Ira waits for his friend at the station he is able to see everything, past and present, in the shop-window/mirror which provides him with a representation of reality (the plastic model of Geneva and the trains) – and that occurs significantly after the night of the fireworks display, the same night when the scientific discovery was made and the Nobel prize awarded. Beyond the light and the darkness and the colour contained within the colour of the night is consciousness, feeling, desire for an atlas of uncontaminated light, of pure energy which transports one forwards and backwards at the same time, toward the future and the unknowable and back into the unfathomable depths of the past, to the point where the whole of life is obliterated and all that remains is the ineffability of what has happened in the modified time of physics and words:

> so che c'è un tempo delle emozioni che non va assolutamente con questo tempo, e senza emozioni mi pare che una cosa non sia intera, che non si fissi nella memoria, che non riuscirò a ricordarla […] le emozioni vanno più lente, si mettono in moto dopo e si fermano dopo, sono come spostate rispetto agli avvenimenti, attorno e a fianco, una specie di alone e di sfondo che non riesco a percepire bene, e certe volte ho l'impressione di prendere ogni cosa togliendola dal suo alone, dal suo fondo, e così non riuscirò mai più a ricordarla. (*Atlante occidentale*, pp. 46–7)

> I know that there is an emotional time which does not coincide exactly with ordinary time, and I don't think things are complete without emotions and they can't be fixed in the memory and I shan't manage to remember them […] emotions go more slowly, they start later and stop later; they are in a way displaced with respect to events, they exist around them and alongside them, like a halo or background which I don't manage to perceive clearly, and sometimes I have the feeling I am detaching everything from its halo, from its background, and that I shall never manage to remember it.

> piacerebbe anche a me parlare di un sentimento e del modo di produrlo […] una storia è fatta di avvenimenti, un avvenimento è fatto di frasi, una frase è

fatta di parole, una parola è fatta di lettere? [...] dietro la lettera c'è un'energia, una tensione che non è ancora forma, ma non è già più sentimento. (*Atlante occidentale*, p. 129)

I should like to talk about a feeling and how it is produced [...] is a story made up of events, an event of sentences, a sentence of words, a word of letters? [...] behind letters there is an energy, a tension which does not yet have form but which isn't feeling any longer.

This (emotional) time is also nostalgia, if it is true that a 'desperate longing' for others and a nostalgia for what is equally past, present and future controls our double sight, our double image of things, that very intuition and energy that are essential tools of sight and memory. Such are the means used by the protagonist of the first novel in his long journey through a city, the detailed and abstract topography of which really corresponded to a topography of the mind made up piecemeal like a mosaic of successive items. Beyond the journey which the protagionist undertakes to trace Bazlen's last contacts there is perhaps only the 'intermittence between probability and improbability'; the attempt to capture that difficult, intangible point of motivation which affects all beings, things, choices, and the connection between imagination and action, between desire and achievement. As he makes his way with his exasperating visual sense in a sort of artificial and deliberate blindness the narrating first person will find that all is revealed to him in its symbolic meaning, and gradually his journey becomes one into both vision and invisibility. The insistence on verbs of sight (I see, I look) is balanced by verbs of vision (I imagine), by the hybrid mixing of seeing and non-seeing ('almost without seeing', as of Ljuba in London who confesses that she can see very little). This reflects back on the protagonist's impotence to see the photographs which would document the elements of reality he is searching for, and concentrates instead on the fuzziness around things. In holding the photograph further away, like long-sighted people do, the young protagionist will look at 'un punto astratto, fuori della cornice' ('an abstract point, outside the frame'); he will engage in the game of bringing the image into focus and changing it – a complementary feature of his search for the truth. Lateral time seems to him increasingly essential to the fulfilment of his mission, and so does lateral space which opens up other possibilities beyond the virtues/limitations of his gaze. If what interests him is 'un punto, in cui forse si intrecciano il saper essere e il saper scrivere' ('a point where the art of being and of writing coincide') then once again it will not matter to him not being able to see properly and he will attach increasing importance to the complementary function of invisibility. In the creation of reality thought will take the place of the camera found at Wimbledon. He will be searching again for something beyond form, in the subtle diagram that underlies form and is constructed out of the elusive signals that make up human relationships.

However, in order to see, with or without one's eyes, one must be ready (as at the moment of waking up on the train at the beginning of the novel), one must be tense and alert, not so much to objects as to relationships, to degrees, experienced consciously as forces of a moral order. One must see in perspective, not just in normal vision (as again in *Atlante occidentale* and *Nel museo di Reims*) how to undertake that parallel journey through books and through life – significantly reported as the title of a volume found in an old bookshop in Trieste. The first-person narrator will find himself making this parallel journey, out of place in each of the two changed realities, intent on imagining things before actually experiencing them and then verifying his images against reality, according to circumstances, in different proportions and degrees – coming closer to things in fact, gauging how far one is from them since the whole game is played out on the edge of one's iris, beyond which, within which, perhaps there is nothing. While outside reality, which only appears to be coherent, may appear or disappear before one's eyes or only appear in fragments or in bursts like Bazlen's non-existent writing. If reading and writing professionally only require the use of sight, Bobi (and with him the mimicking first-person narrator) tend to go beyond the act of reading, beyond the book, interchanging the two sides of the text at that elusive point where the two coincide – the limit of time/space where there are no books but only the possibility of writing them among so many other possibilities. You recognize reality by looking ' in a less automatic way', which means 'inverting the order of probabilities with respect to the act of reading', so that all the visual metaphors in the book can be turned upside down and interpreted to signify the total invisibility of everything that is close at hand. It was not by chance that Bobi Bazlen knocked twice into a glass window shortly before his death ('He didn't see it'), or that the protagonist finds himself increasingly surrounded by panes of glass in the course of his journey, or that he pays so much attention to the interiors of houses, to the lights and shadows evoked by old age and silence. The act of recomposition following the fragmentation to which sight subjects what is visible (remember the journey through the city, the geometry of which is always broken up; or, for example, the image of the old man 'Seduto lasciando le gambe sul marciapiede' ('sitting there sticking his legs out on the pavement') and then turning 'a 90 degree turn' and drawing them in), that act of recomposition is a consequence of the parcelling-out process we employ in methodical observation in order to form an integrated diagram, and goes further still in respect of non-concrete truths, which in this way suddenly surrender their secrets.

If 'nomi sono ciò che resta delle cose tolte tutte le correlazioni' ('names are what remains when things are deprived of all their correlations'), then one must proceed backwards from things in order to re-establish that subtle network on which their existence depends: a new mathematical alphabet made up of separate points (as in *Atlante occidentale*), perhaps similar only to the Braille system used by the blind woman to teach reading in *Lo stadio di Wimbledon*. Apart from the obsession with seeing and terms that paraphrase seeing and with different optical expressions which recur repeatedly ('point of view', keep an 'eye' on, give a 'glance', 'to focus'), and apart from his obsession with the impotence of his own sight ('l'ossessione di quello che gli altri saprebbero vedere, dove io, camminando e guardando, non vedo nulla': 'the obsession with what others could see where I, as I go about looking around me, can't see anything'), there arises the possibility of a juxtaposition in parallel; and this really favours the void, which is only slowly filled with the fuzzy purity of what surrounds it – just like the letters indicating the name of the aeroplane referred to by Ira in *Atlante occidentale* and which emerge from the stencils used by the workmen to paint them, the figure of Bazlen can only stand out as a result of the contrast and alternation of solid and blank, of word and silence, of light and shade, of life and work; it can only emerge in the empty shape of the pullover which the protagonist carries away with him, a unique and misfitting symbol of a search which has required a sharpening of perception, an overturning of the visual faculty in order to reach even a partial conclusion: a clause stressing the importance of 'the way of seeing', by a process of collimation and calculation, rather than the abstract seeing with which the protagonist had been obsessed from the beginning – see for example his vision of the ships, the repeated theme of blindness, the signals of real and model trains, which reappear in the later novels. All Del Giudice's characters in fact are sick, sick because of their lack of, and at the same time their craving for, a different kind of sight, that technique of collimation which would permit them 'di mettere a fuoco in una sola visione quello che è vicinissimo e quello che è lontano' ('to focus in a single vision what is close at hand and what is far away'), as in 'Dillon Bay', a remarkable military story written slightly before *Atlante occidentale*.

In the play between internal and external, inside and outside, space is displaced to the very edge of time, time is stretched to the point at which it becomes visible, while the deciphering of the secret signs of writing is also a significant factor in the operation 'Light knowledge' which is described in the star-fortress section of 'Dillon Bay' – I am thinking of the writing of Bobi Bazlen, the military maps, the physicist and the writer, the pictures which Barnaba is pursuing. But 'Light knowledge', those words remind us, could mean 'knowledge of the light', 'light of knowledge', 'luminous knowledge', 'light (not heavy) knowledge' in a mixture of pure meaning, ethereal, luminous, and weightless – perhaps the ultimate form beyond form, the diagram of feeling independent of event, the meaning behind things which Del Giudice is always straining for in the search for the elusive, almost impossible point of contact between writing and truth, between literature and life.

Translated by C. P. Brand

BIBLIOGRAPHY

Works

Lo stadio di Wimbledon (Turin: Einaudi, 1983).

Atlante occidentale (Turin: Einaudi, 1985). Translated by Norman MacAfee and Luigi Fontanella as *Lines of Light* (Harmondsworth: Viking Penguin, 1989).

'Dillon Bay, un racconto militare', in *La metropoli difesa*, edited by Amelio Fara, Rome 1985.

Nel museo di Reims, con sedici dipinti di Marco Nereo Rotelli, (Milan: Mondadori, 1988).

'Un écrivain diurne', *Magazine littéraire*, February 1990, pp. 26–9.

Interviews

'Il tempo del visibile nell'*Atlante occidentale* di Daniele Del Giudice', *Palomar. Quaderni di Porto Venere* 1 (1986), 66–96.

'Il volo dei sentimenti: a colloquio con Daniele Del Giudice', *Italienisch* 22 (1989), 2–19.

Chapter 7

Francesca Duranti
Reflections and Inventions

SHIRLEY W. VINALL

In the first decade of this century, Henry James concluded the Preface to his novel *The Ambassadors* by remarking that 'the Nóvel remains still, under the right persuasion, the most independent, most elastic, most prodigious of literary forms'. In 1984, over seventy years and much literary experimentation later, Giorgio Bassani's reading of *La casa sul lago della luna*, the third novel by the then little-known Francesca Duranti, encouraged him to reiterate his own faith in the continuing possibilities of the novel form: 'I have never believed,' he declared, 'in the crisis of the novel, the Italian novel included. [...] No possibilities of experimentation exist outside the bounds of the literary tradition.' (Bassani's review is quoted on the fly-leaf of the novel.) Duranti, a keen admirer of the work of Henry James, rejects the experimental novel of the 1960s and 1970s, as do many other Italian novelists who became successful during the 1980s. Whilst setting her novels firmly in the contemporary world, she works within a traditional framework: her books *tell stories*, the notion of character is not challenged, and the language is readily accessible. As her career advances, however, her narrative structures become increasingly inventive.

Duranti's aims are not conservative. She wishes rather to contribute to finding a way forward for the Italian novel, especially by helping to forge a language which will enable it to reach beyond its traditional charmed circle of intellectuals and appeal to a wider readership, like its modern English counterpart. Thus she bases her language on contemporary, educated spoken Italian, avoiding both the *recherché* and the banal, and endeavours to write in what she described in discussion at a Conference held in Edinburgh in October 1990 as a 'style which does not seem to be style', and which conceals its careful construction.

Given her particular admiration for the English novel, it is not surprising that such technical aims do not preclude social and moral considerations. Her books offer keenly, often ironically observed pictures of contemporary society, and in particular the world with which she herself is most familiar, that of the cultured classes of Tuscany and Milan. The plots set in this world are used to explore not only problems of contemporary relevance, but also more permanent human issues.

Perhaps inevitably, the contemporary social questions examined include that of women's position in the modern urban world. Woman's search for autonomy is a persistent theme, as the analyses of her individual novels will show. However, despite this, and despite the fact that several other themes and features of her writing occur frequently in that of other women, Duranti rejects as reductive the label of 'woman writer', and her stance is not a political or campaigning one.

Personal experience lies at the root of Duranti's writing. This is especially the case in her first two works, where her private world is explored most directly; however, it continues to be used, more indirectly, in her next four novels, as her canvas steadily broadens. Before achieving literary success with *La casa sul lago della luna* (1984), which won a number of literary prizes, and has now been widely translated, she had published *La Bambina* (1976) and *Piazza mia bella piazza* (1978), both under the imprint of La Tartaruga, a publisher of much women's writing.

The cover of the 1985 Rizzoli edition of *La Bambina* describes the book as a novel. Nevertheless, Duranti readily admits that its subject matter is autobiographical, and that no names of people or places have been changed. It traces the development of Francesca Rossi, the 'bambina' of the title (Rossi was the writer's maiden name) from early childhood to the threshold of adolescence and the beginnings of an awareness of society beyond the bounds of her restricted and privileged family environment. The child's development is set against the background of momentous public events – the outbreak of the Second World War, the German occupation, and the liberation of Italy. These events, however, are seen from the relative safety of a modern-day *locus amoenus*, the aristocratic Tuscan country estate where her Genoese family and their friends take refuge. Furthermore, such matters are explored only inasmuch as they impinge on Francesca's immediate, personal world. For instance, the activities of the author's father, Paolo Rossi, a distinguished lawyer and a prominent socialist, are presented only through what is perceived by the child – overheard conversations and, more importantly, the activities connected with the sheltering of Jews and other anti-fascists. Similarly, Paolo Rossi's role in the postwar Constituent Assembly is only briefly mentioned (p. 149), in relation to his young daughter's confused political views and her fears that because the Royal Family had been sent into exile, he was guilty of mortal sin.

By her own account, Duranti, when already in her late thirties, wrote this very striking and often moving first book very swiftly and spontaneously once she had rediscovered her childhood self through returning to her family home and found a means of shaping her autobiographical material into what is presented as a work of fiction: several features of the narrative technique will become characteristic of her more mature and self-conscious writing. She avoids the first-person confessional form of narration, presenting Francesca's story instead through an external narrator-focalizer who initially seems unpersonified, as in many traditional novels. Thus, in the opening sentence, the narrator portrays the focalized character from within, while expressing the young child's feelings in adult language:

> All'età di tre anni e mezzo Francesca si rese conto per la prima volta che, a parte le inadempienze alle leggi che regolavano la sua vita, c'erano altre cose sulle quali era opportuno mantenere il segreto. (*La Bambina*, p. 7)

> At the age of three and a half Francesca realized for the first time that, apart from the infractions of the laws which governed her life, there were other matters about which it was expedient to maintain secrecy.

Hints are soon given, however, which cause a revision of the reader's perception of the narrator. At times the narrator seems to be addressing the reader directly, as though to clarify matters, with remarks like 'Qui va detto che [...]' (*La Bambina*, p. 9) ('Here it should be said that...') or 'può sembrare strano che quest'ultima [la Bambina] fosse riuscita a liberarsi dal suo angelo custode' (*La Bambina*, p. 7) ('it may seem strange that the Little Girl had managed to escape from her guardian angel'). Such conversational touches then begin to be accompanied by the occasional use of the first-person form: 'quel bel giardino a terrazze di cui abbiamo parlato' (*La Bambina*, p. 12) ('that beautiful terraced garden which we've already talked about'). Nothing is revealed of the narrator, however, and the rare first-person interventions are limited to such linking passages as 'Ho già detto che [...]' (*La Bambina*, p. 23) ('I have already said that...') and 'come ho detto' (p. 148) ('As I have said').

No other character, apart from Francesca, is portrayed from within and no events are narrated which do not either form part of Francesca's direct experience or are told to her. For instance, her uncle's beating by fascist thugs many years before Francesca's birth is included in the narrative by means of a story frequently told to her by her grandmother (p. 18); information about the persecution of the Jews and the imminence of war is introduced through a conversation, at which Francesca is present, between her uncle and her grandparents; and, much later in the narrative, the German Lieutenant Wilkening's account of the battle of Cassino is overheard by the child (pp. 115–16).

The narrator's treatment of time is also revealing. In general, the narrative presents events chronologically, with each of the five chapters devoted to a stage in the child's life. However, the external focalization of Francesca can at times embrace a long period rather than a single moment, for example, 'aveva – ed ebbe fino ai cinque anni – una resistenza limitata alla lettura autonoma' (*La Bambina*, p. 8) ('she could only read to herself for limited periods – and this continued to be the case until she was five'). Furthermore, the narrator can move backwards and forwards in time. Not only does a remark like 'in quel periodo gli hippies non erano ancora di moda' (*La Bambina*, p. 16) ('at that time hippies were not yet in fashion') show that the act of narration is situated considerably later than the story itself; there are also several passages which reveal that the period of Francesca's life to which the narrator is privy extends well beyond the period covered in the text. There is a brief, elliptical reference to her childhood friends' marriage: 'Poi la Paola crebbe e fece sempre delle buone scelte, a cominciare da quella del marito' (*La Bambina*, p. 96) ('then Paola grew up and always made good choices, beginning with her choice of a husband'). Another flash-forward is occasioned by Francesca's hope that a particular boy will be attracted to her: 'ma questo non avvenne nè quella sera nè mai. [...] mai le capitò, prima o dopo di quei tempi, di essere così completamente ignorata da un uomo, grande o piccolo, su cui avesse messo gli occhi' (*La Bambina*, p. 75) ('but this didn't happen that evening or ever. [...] never, either before or after that period, was she ignored so completely by any man, old or young, who had caught her eye'). Even more interesting is the reference to the enduring sense of shame felt by Francesca and, apparently (though this is not stated with such certainty), by her childhood companions at the cruel games in which they had engaged at one time:

> Francesca, dopo, non poteva ripensarci senza sentirsi invadere da una cocente ondata di vergogna; ed anche la Paola, Ugo, la Puccia e Marina, evidentemente, non li ricordavano volentieri, perché nessuno, in seguito, accennò più a quel periodo, e tutti parevano volersene dimenticare. (*La Bambina*, p. 121)

> Afterwards Francesca could not think about those days without feeling overcome by a burning wave of shame; and obviously Paola, Ugo, Puccia and Marina were not keen to remember them either, for none of them subsequently referred to that period, and they all seemed to want to forget about it.

Most significant of all is the conclusion of the episode about Francesca's cousin's first communion, when the young children dared each other to say rude words to the guests: Francesca was punished by no longer being allowed to come into her parents' bed on a Sunday morning: 'Francesca non seppe mai se fu perdonata, e vorrebbe saperlo' (*La Bambina*, p. 25) ('Francesca never knew whether she was pardoned, and she would like to know'). The abrupt change from the past definite 'seppe' (knew) to the conditional 'vorrebbe' (she would like), which has its standpoint in the moment of narration, is dramatic.

All this evidence would seem to suggest that the reader should accept the narrating voice as that of Francesca's later self. Information about that later self, however, is virtually excluded so that the focus is on the understanding of the childhood world.

Memory, operating its own process of selection and emphasis, is the thread which holds the narrative together: 'Il periodo passato all'albergo Universo non lasciò molte tracce nella memoria di Francesca' (*La Bambina*, p. 37) ('the period which they spent at the Universe Hotel did not leave many traces in Francesca's memory'). Indeed, the narrator even admits to its unreliability:

> Forse, per dire la verità, quell'auto l'ebbe soltanto dopo la liberazione: ma è sicuro che in ogni periodo in cui Francesca lo vide per casa, egli le dette sempre un'impressione di gran spocchia. (*La Bambina*, pp. 94–5)

> Perhaps, to tell the truth, he [a young aristocrat called Lorenzo Guidozzi] only had that car after the Liberation: but it is certain that at whatever period Francesca saw him around the house he gave her the impression of being very conceited.

The untitled chapters, of varying length, are sub-divided into sections, also untitled, and each devoted to a single episode, or to a group of related episodes; the sections follow each other according to the logic of memory. For instance, the third section in Chapter 1 focuses on Francesca's happy memories of the conversations at her grandparents' home which contributed to her earliest impressions of politics. The theme of adult conversation links this to the next section, which opens by evoking the political conversations heard in her own home: however, because the most frequent occasion on which Francesca was able to hear such discussion was while she was in her parents' bed, the narrative soon moves on to the detailed account of the events leading to her exclusion from it.

Although Duranti chooses to depict the past in such a way as to minimize overtly retrospective judgement or explanations, different narrative voices are present in the text; and *La Bambina* derives much of its charm, and its characteristic blend of irony and nostalgia, from the shifts – which are sometimes almost imperceptible – between the voice of the adult narrator and that of the child. Extensive use is made of the device of presenting information through the child's limited perception and language. Sometimes this is achieved through the use of a kind of indirect free speech, as in the following passage, where the first sentence is in the 'voice' of the narrator, but the verb 'sapeva' ('she knew') introduces us into the child's thought processes. (Duranti's gentle irony is underlined by the choice of 'knew' rather than, for instance, 'thought', as it suggests certainty; whereas the reader swiftly becomes aware of the gap between the child's 'knowledge' and reality):

> Qui va detto che Francesca era molto pia ma anche molto confusa, riguardo alla religione. Per esempio sapeva che Dio era il padre di Gesù e che entrambi, soprattutto Dio, erano molto amici della Nane. Invece la Maria che stirava era amica della Madonna, moglie di Dio, ed andava ogni domenica a trovarla a Messa (*La Bambina*, p. 9)

> Here it should be said that Francesca was very pious but also very confused as far as religion was concerned. For instance she knew that God was the father of Jesus and that both of them, God especially, were very friendly with Nanny. On the other hand Maria who did the ironing was friendly with the Virgin Mary, God's mother, and she went to see her at Mass every Sunday

Elsewhere the narrating voice frequently enters into the child's perceptions without any such warning clues:

> Una mattina Francesca fu mandata a giocare sotto la sorveglianza della Nane nella terrazza più bassa del giardino [...] Mentre scendevano avevano visto arrivare lo zio Enzo, quello dottore, il dottor Corradi – che era il medico della Bambina ma che non la guardò neppure – e la signora Conci [che] aveva orecchie grandissime ed era un'imperatrice. (*La Bambina*, p. 31)

> One morning Francesca was sent to play, under Nanny's supervision, in the lowest terrace in the garden [...] While they were going down they had seen Uncle Enzo coming – the one who was a doctor – along with Dr Corradi, who was the Little Girl's doctor but who didn't even look at her, and Mrs Conci, who had huge ears and was an empress.

Only later does the reader discover, along with the young Francesca, that the reason for this mysterious and disturbing activity was the birth of her sister Marina, and that la signora Conci was not an empress ('un'imperatrice') but a midwife ('una levatrice')!

The same technique, together with an effective use of direct speech, again produces an indulgent smile on the part of the reader in the delightful account of how Fancesca, on her regular visits to her grandparents' house, would enjoy hiding from her uncle. When her grandmother told him that Francesca had not come that day, her uncle 'era proprio disperato' ('was really in despair') and would exclaim 'Oh che dispiacere, oh che rabbia!' ('Oh how sorry I am, oh how cross I am!'). Francesca's terrible yell when she eventually jumped out of her hiding-place 'spaventava a morte lo zio Enzo' (*La Bambina*, p. 19) ('frightened Uncle Enzo to death'). The reader perceives the gap between the child's understanding and reality, although this is not overtly stated. In the opening episode of the book, however, the reader is drawn so completely into the child's world that 'reality' is hard to distinguish. Francesca has apparently 'escaped' from the supervision of her nanny to read her comic on the lawn. Then, while playing trains with chairs in the loggia, she has a tremendous shock:

> Sembrava che il viaggio procedesse bene, ma quando girò lo sguardo per osservare la campagna che le fuggiva accanto, i suoi occhi colsero una visione orribile; la capra stava mangiando una pagina del Corrierino, e tutto il resto se ne stava sparso a pezzettini per il prato. (*La Bambina*, p. 9)

> It seemed as if the journey was going well, but when she looked round to watch the countryside slipping by alongside her a horrible vision met her gaze; the goat was eating a page from the *Children's Post*, and the rest of it was scattered in tiny pieces all over the lawn.

She prays fervently to the Virgin Mary for help (having prudently decided that, as she had been disobeying her nanny, her nanny's great friends Jesus and God would be less reliable!) and when she opens her eyes 'il giornalino era là, bello nuovo e piegato sull'erba, e la capra non lo guardava neppure' (*La Bambina*,

p. 10) ('the comic was there, as good as new, folded on the grass, and the goat wasn't even looking at it')! This 'miracle' is left unexplained, but it is probable that the phrases 'Sembrava' and 'una visione orribile' mean more than is suggested at a first reading.

As the passage about Francesca's game with her uncle illustrates, dialogue can express the child's limited awareness very effectively, while alerting the reader to the gap between the child's perception and reality, without overtly stating this. Such dialogue is used very frequently in *La Bambina*, not only for humorous effect, but also to create a sense of poignancy and sadness. When Francesca's mother is expecting Marina, Francesca, understanding only that her mother is ill, fears she will die. However, because she has been brought up to feel that she can please her mother by being a brave little girl, she does not know how to express her emotions. She tries instead to broach the subject of death casually:

> 'Quando sarai morta, potrò avere i tuoi gioielli?'
> La mamma rispose che sì, poteva averli.
> 'Saranno ancora lucidi?'
> 'Certamente.'
> Questo chiuse l'argomento. (*La Bambina*, p. 31)

> 'When you're dead, can I have your jewels?'
> Mother said yes, she could.
> 'Will they still be shiny?'
> 'Of course.'
> That was the end of the conversation.

Nothing is made explicit, but the reader perceives that Francesca's fears of her mother's imminent death are in no way allayed, and that the mother seems not to have understood the depth of her daughter's concern. Thus the use of direct speech paradoxically illustrates a lack of communication.

The difficulties in the relationship between mother and daughter could, in fact, be regarded as the novel's central theme. However, because she avoids retrospective judgements and the expression of the adult narrator's feelings, Duranti explores this problem through irony, understatement, and, indeed, by making the reader aware of what is *not* said. Almost all the episodes recounted are connected, explicitly or implicitly, with Francesca's feelings for her mother. Although the mother does not appear in the opening scene, when the child, at three-and-a-half, prays to the Virgin Mary to mend her comic, this absence is significant. Francesca is torn between the conflicting religious influences of her Swiss Protestant nanny and the Catholic maid: the mother has offered no guidance. The subsequent description of the family's huge house, where Francesca is familiar with only a few rooms, becomes an illustration of her parents' psychological as well as physical distance from her. The infrequency of her contacts with them is revealed – by omission – in a passage, presented through her perceptions, which shows her belief that her parents' interest in her (and particularly her mother's) depended on her various skills, like being clean and tidy, speaking German, and doing gymnastics:

> Forse per queste sue virtù o forse perchè abitava anche lei nella casa, a Francesca era permesso – prima di andare a letto – di entrare per un attimo nei salotti a salutare i grandi. (*La Bambina*, pp. 14–15)

> Perhaps because of these accomplishments of hers or perhaps because she also lived in the house Francesca was allowed, before she went to bed, to go into the drawing-room for a moment and say good-night to the grown-ups.

Francesca's unhappiness at this lack of attention emerges, by implication only, when she is struck by the fact that her cousins' parents eat with them, and in her comments on fictional families.

Later in the book, many of the descriptions of the Occupation focus really on Francesca's admiration for her mother's imperious presence and organizational capacities. In the memorable scene where the mother, using the child as an interpreter, orders some German soldiers to stop stealing the peasants' animals, the most important aspect is the 'solidarietà alla pari' ('solidarity between equals') which was established between her and her mother, 'un clima meraviglioso che riscaldava il cuore della Bambina e che non fu mai da lei dimenticato' (*La Bambina*, pp. 103–4) ('a marvellous atmosphere which warmed the Little Girl's heart and which she has never forgotten'). *La Bambina* ends, with pleasing symmetry, with another 'miracle', through which Francesca saves her sister's life. However, the final paragraphs show that the sub-text is still her relationship with her mother. Promised a reward for her actions, Francesca thinks for a long time and finally comes out with

> 'Voglio portare i capelli senza trecce e non voglio più avere il colletto bianco che spunta sotto il pullover.'
> Disse queste audaci parole tutte d'un fiato, piena di timore e di speranza.
> 'Neppure per sogno,' rispose la Mamma. (*La Bambina*, pp. 155–6)

> 'I don't want to have plaits any more and I don't want to have a white collar showing under my jumper.'
> She spoke these daring words all in one breath, full of fear and hope.
> 'Not under any circumstances,' Mother replied.

Dialogue, once again, reveals the distance between the two speakers.

The relationship between daughter and mother is a central theme in modern women's writing, both fictional and autobiographical: feminist theorists have stressed the significance and particular intensity of this bond, as the female self is not sexually differentiated from the mother. *La Bambina* exhibits several qualities often found in female autobiographies, such as understatement, humour, and an obliqueness of approach, but differs significantly from one of the earliest and most influential Italian feminist texts, Sibilla Aleramo's autobiography *Una donna* (1906). Duranti's autobiography focuses only on the world of childhood evoking this very successfully: this in itself is noteworthy as children have rarely appeared in Italian literature and have even more rarely been the centre of attention. Aleramo's protagonist, in contrast, becomes a mother as well as a daughter: thus the theme of motherhood is explored from two angles. The narrator of *Una donna* shows how, through her own experience of motherhood, she moved from a lack of sympathy for her mother to an understanding of the latter's suffering and self-sacrifice. This realization of their affinity, although too late for any successful communication between them, contributes to her decision to try to break what she sees as the 'chain' of maternal self-sacrifice and develop her own identity. In *La Bambina*, the very occasional insight into the perfectionism which seems to lie at the root of the mother's behaviour (pp. 47-8; 104–5), is presented as the *child's* understanding; and the lack of retrospective 'adult' analysis seems to correspond to the absence of an attempt to generalize from individual experience and present the mother-child relationship paradigmatically. Thus the apparently similar titles in fact point to different approaches; Aleramo's *Una donna* problematizes the word 'donna' and, with it, traditional notions of the female role, while Duranti's title, used throughout the text to evoke the intimate language of the family, seems instead to suggest only an individual, unique experience.

Unlike *La Bambina, Piazza mia bella piazza* has not been reissued, and Duranti herself now regards it as unsuccessful. Tracing as it does a woman's painful achievement of autonomy after two marriages and a series of affairs, its roots lie once more in Duranti's own life. The failure of the protagonist's second marriage, on which the novel focuses, results from the husband's resentment of her decision to become a writer: as Duranti told an interviewer from *Il Giorno*, Gabriele Moroni, on 4 December 1988, her own marriage broke up, after many years, because of her own desire to write, a desire fulfilled through the writing of *La Bambina*. However, the light touch and the distancing irony used to treat even the most painful of personal experiences in *La Bambina* are less evident here. The novel uses the third-person form of narration throughout, and although Paola, the protagonist, is sometimes portrayed from within, it is often not clear whether the narrator's position is one of unquestioning sympathy or critical irony. For instance, while the effects of family disruption on Paola's daughter, Eloisa, seem to be ignored for long portions of the text, the fact that a conversation towards the end of the novel, revealing Eloisa's difficulties at school, helps Paola to put her problems into perspective, suggests that the neglect could be interpreted not as the narrator's, but as a consequence of Paola's own self-absorption. Earlier in the narrative, though, this is far from obvious.

Indeed, the theme of motherhood again receives relatively little attention. Rather surprisingly perhaps, Paola's desire to become a writer is not presented as in conflict with her maternal responsibilities. The conflict arises instead from the resentment of her husband, Marco Francia, at what he perceives as the betrayal of their intense, exclusive relationship. Eloisa, depicted somewhat perfunctorily, is portrayed from within only in a passage seemingly designed to supply more information about Paola's character (*Piazza,* pp. 19–23).

The unsatisfactory relationship between Paola and her own mother, in contrast, is presented as a fundamental formative influence, similar to that described in *La Bambina.* This mother figure, however, not depicted through her child's admiration and longing, is portrayed far more negatively: for instance, her constant infidelity now appears as a factor in her child's distress; yet, when the grown-up Paola's marriage is in difficulty, her only concern is for a superficial 'respectability'. The young Paola's sense of imprisonment is presented as leading to her first, unsatisfactory marriage; while the desire to be liked, resulting from her unhappy childhood, is seen as contributing to the submissiveness which made her second marriage a further imprisonment.

Although this sense of being imprisoned is brought home vividly to Paola after a chance meeting with a feminist student, neither Paola, nor the narrator, tends to analyse her situation in terms of feminist theory. Instead, Paola compares her entrapment to that of the 'lepre pazza' (mad March hare) which, in the children's finger game recalled in the title, is caught by the fingers while in the 'piazza' of the hand. While explicitly not an anti-feminist (p. 29), Paola says she had thought little about sexual politics, and feels that feminists show an aggression which she lacks (p. 29). The subsequent flashbacks (pp. 31–42), describing Paola and Marco's early happiness, despite his unwillingness for her to have a career, are not presented as memories reinterpreted by a feminist consciousness. Although her later development is assisted by her friendship with other women in similar positions, this subject is not analysed theoretically either. The open conclusion leaves Paola in a tender but not stifling relationship with another man, and with no single aspect of her life obscuring all the others.

In *La casa sul lago della luna* Duranti breaks new ground. Whilst still drawing on her own experience, such as her cultivated Genoese background, her knowledge of German and her translation work, she distances herself from it by transferring these features to a male protagonist and using an invented plot. Furthermore, she goes beyond the bounds of the realist novel. She argued in a talk in Edinburgh in 1990 that novels should both convince and surprise: thus, in a much admired *tour de force*, this novel moves from its initial setting in the publishing world of contemporary Milan to a magical and mysterious one.

The thirty-eight-year old protagonist, Fabrizio Garrone, who is treated with a mixture of sympathy and irony, is portrayed as confusedly ill-at-ease in modern society. His traditional cultural values are out of fashion, and his family's wealth has disappeared. He earns a precarious living as a translator of German literary works, whilst, in contrast, his close friend Mario, born on Fabrizio's family estate, has become a successful publisher. Fabrizio's alienation is reflected not only in his failure to make his mark through intellectual achievements but also in his inability to establish any lasting and satisfactory sexual relationship. Then, his chance discovery of a reference by the critic Giorgio Pasquali (a real person) to a little-known novel entitled *Das Haus am Mondsee (The House on Moon Lake)* by a turn-of-the-century Austrian writer, Fritz Oberhofer, sends him to Austria in search of it, in the hope of translating it and making his name. This solitary quest is at the same time an attempt to prove – or find – himself.

However, although he finds the book and publishes both a successful translation and an even more successful biography of Oberhofer, he loses himself, by gradually becoming identified with the author, who had died at Fabrizio's age. Having failed to discover any historical facts about the woman who inspired this last, crucial novel, Fabrizio invents her character, creating his own complex ideal feminine figure. This creation, named Maria Lettner, gains an increasing hold over him, so that when he returns to Austria to visit Petra, who claims to be the granddaughter of his imagined Maria, reality and fantasy become increasingly intertwined, his hold on life becomes increasingly tenuous, and his energies slowly ebb away.

The Milanese sections of the novel include an ironic treatment of contempor-ary society, and the literary world in particular. For instance, Duranti satirizes the slavish following of intellectual fashions especially through the Maria Lettner craze which sweeps the periodical press, both popular and academic, even leading to the creation of a 'Maria Lettner look'. Before this success Fabrizio includes among his 'victorious adversaries' not only mediocre thinkers whose writings have become compulsory reading, but also 'rivoluzionari da salotto' ('drawing-room radicals') and 'femmine ribelli che discutevano le regole del gioco amoroso' ('rebellious women who questioned the rules of the game of love'), 'E ancora motociclisti rumorosi, inquinatori di fiumi, pubblici amministatori disonesti, delinquenti comuni e politici, fruttivendoli esosi, giovani maleducati e attoniti, trentenni maleducati e analfabeti' (*La casa*, p. 15) ('not to mention all the noisy motorcyclists, river-polluters, corrupt public officials, common criminals and political criminals, cutthroat greengrocers, rude and bewildered teenagers, rude and illiterate thirty-year-olds'). Since Duranti here portrays Fabrizio from within, through the free indirect discourse used so successfully in *La Bambina,* she is able to combine certain concerns such as the ecological one, which she appears to share, with others which humorously characterize Fabrizio's undiscriminating discontent.

The novel's main emphasis is, however, not on such social comedy but on the power of the past and the dead to haunt Fabrizio's imagination. Amongst the techniques used to achieve the subtle move from realism to the fantastic is the inclusion in the early chapters of passages whose full significance become obvious only later. The description of Fabrizio's thinness is also a premonition of his early death: 'il suo profilo asciutto, le sue membra scarne lo collocavano in quella categoria di persone destinate a ritornare alla polvere senza mai dover attraversare la fase in cui progressive convessità conferiscono l'aspetto solenne caratteristico dell'età matura' (*La casa*, p. 10) ('his gaunt face and fleshless limbs put him in the category of persons destined to turn back to dust without ever passing through the stage of life when increasing convexity lends the riper years an air of dignity'). The reference to Fabrizio's sense of powerlessness, as in a childhood nightmare, in the face of the hostile onrush of the 'orda vittoriosa' ('triumphant horde') described above not only suggests his immaturity but also prefigures a passage towards the end of the novel, when, exhausted and defeated, he is represented as being entirely overcome by a similar but more terrifyingly negative vision of the present (pp. 185–6). Again, even the early chapters hint that the young Fabrizio's escape into the literature of the past can be seen as a flight from life itself: 'Già da allora sembrava essergli impossibile stabilire con i vivi un legame altrettanto soddisfacente e profondo come con chi era morto, meglio se morto da un bel pezzo' (*La casa*, p. 20) ('At that age it already seemed impossible for him to establish relationships with the living as deep and gratifying as those he could have with the dead, especially the long dead'). A similar effect is created by the occasional flash-forward, as in this reference to his obsession with finding *Das Haus am Mondsee*, and his increasing secretiveness and paranoia:

> Furono quei fantasmi che lo strapparono, durante la vicenda che seguì, dal confronto quotidiano con i propri simili, segregandolo in un incubo solitario dove il reale, il possibile, l'immaginario giocano tra loro secondo leggi bizzarre e pericolose. (*La casa*, pp. 29–30)

> These same ghosts would tear him away from his fellow creatures during the events that followed, imprisoning him in a solitary nightmare where the real, the possible and the imaginary played games that followed strange and dangerous rules.

Echoes of earlier literature also contribute to taking the novel beyond the confines of realism. In some ways Fabrizio resembles the intellectuals of the late nineteenth-century Decadent movement who, feeling out-of-tune with the attitudes of contemporary society and uncertain of their own places in it, devoted themselves to the cult of a nebulous 'Ideal', attainable perhaps by escaping from reality through love, mysticism, art, or even death. The treatment of the female characters in the novel is particularly significant in this regard. Fabrizio's supportive and long-suffering girlfriend, the lively, capable, and well-balanced Fulvia, is in a sense a development of the character of Paola in *Piazza mia bella piazza*. Emotionally ready, after several years of widowhood, to embark on a new caring relationship, she is mature and in many ways self-sufficient, although, like Paola, she is not portrayed as a conventional feminist: her strong, confident step, while indicating profound independence, is 'non attutito dalla suola di para delle protofemministe' (*La casa*, p. 33) ('uncushioned by the rubber soles of the first feminists'). However, she is not the protagonist, and the novel's focus is not on women's social position. Rather, Fulvia is seen largely through Fabrizio's eyes, and she and the other two female figures, Maria and Petra, whose names provide the titles of the novel's three sections, correspond, like, for instance, the antithetical pair of female characters in D'Annunzio's novel *Il piacere* (1890), to different aspects of the male protagonist's sensibility, or different options open to him. As in that novel too, where Elena (as in Helen of Troy) embodies sensuality and Maria (as in the Virgin Mary) embodies the hero's aspirations towards purity and the ideal, the women's names suggest their significance. Fabrizio 'naturally' chooses the name 'Maria' for his unattainable ideal of femininity (p. 113). Fulvia and Petra represent the contrasting forces of reality and life, on the one hand, and fantasy and death on the other. Petra's name, which recalls Dante's 'donna petra', is explicitly 'tratto dalla fredda immobilità del regno minerale' (*La casa*, p. 173) ('drawn from the cold stillness of the mineral realm'), whilst Fulvia's, which derives from the Latin *fulvus*, the tawny colour of a lion's mane, can be seen as suggesting energy and vitality.

Fabrizio, happier with literature than with reality, swiftly converts the disturbing sight of a real girl who overtakes him coming out of the park into a quotation from Catullus (p. 22). In this he resembles the early twentieth-century poet Guido Gozzano who feeling 'exiled' from life like the Decadents, could relate to life (often symbolized by women) only through artistic representations and literary echoes, although, recognizing art and his other dreams as illusions, his characteristic tone is one of irony. Furthermore, the contrast between Fulvia, whose attitudes and appearance are very much of the 1980s, and Petra, 'una figura d'altri tempi' (*La casa*, p. 151) ('a figure from another age'), recalls that between the female figures who represent the 'two ways' in Gozzano's poem 'Le due strade', from *I colloqui* (1911) – the healthy young cyclist Graziella, a creature of the outdoors and the modern world, who represents the love, life and happiness which eludes the poet, and the older woman who is described in terms of artificiality and decay embodying perhaps the unhealthiness of the poet's illusions. Fulvia is also partly reminiscent of the good, homely Felicita in 'La signorina Felicita ovvero la Felicità', from the same collection: the intellectual narrator, 'stanco / delle donne fatte sui romanzi' believes that if he could marry her he could repudiate 'la fede letteraria / che fa la vita simile alla morte', but he is unable to make such a commitment. Gozzano's narrator's sense of repose at the 'cena /d'altri tempi' and in the kitchen of Felicita's home is echoed in Fabrizio's idealized view of the apparently simple and traditional life of Fulvia's family of country craftsmen: he singles out their Cantù furniture, linen sheets, and, above all, the aroma of the kitchen (p. 34).

The narrator in Gozzano's poem, 'Convito', who has not known love, is described as a 'fanciullo triste' who will take his 'gelido cuore' to the grave, for the magic powers of art will be of no avail. Similarly, Duranti often compares Fabrizio to a child: his physical appearance seems immature (p. 10); his attitude to Fulvia is like that of a child towards someone in authority who will protect him; and Mario feels the need to look after him (p. 34). To evoke Fabrizio's state of mind, therefore, Duranti makes frequent and very effective use of the imaginative world of childhood, as she had done in *La Bambina*. Thus the most significant and explicit echoes of earlier literature are the many references to the structural elements of the fairy tale. Fabrizio becomes fascinated with Fulvia after his visit to her home because, 'come un principe da fiaba aveva seguito la fanciulla forestiera fino alla dimora paterna e là, sopra l'alto portale, aveva trovato il motto inciso sullo stemma, la conferma del lignaggio' (*La casa,* p. 36) ('like a prince in a fable, he had followed the strange maiden to her father's abode and there, above the tall portal, he had seen the escutcheon with its inscribed motto, the proof of her lineage'). Later, in Fulvia's comforting presence, all the aspects of Fabrizio's situation which had seemed to him like a child's nightmare lose their power to frighten and become simply elements of a nursery rhyme or fairy tale: the heroes, 'l'intellettuale deluso e la ragazza leale e saggia' ('the disillusioned intellectual and his wise, loyal girlfriend'), will be able to defeat the villains, indifferent society and debased culture, with the help of the fairy godmother, Giorgio Pasquali, 'che dall'aldilà consegnava la mappa del tesoro' ('who from the beyond had provided the treasure map'), and Mario, the generous, trusty friend (*La casa*, p. 42). By means of many such references, Duranti gives Fabrizio's attempt to find the mysterious book, which he hopes will be the key to his happiness and good fortune, the character of a hero's fairy-tale quest to a distant land. But this is a fairy tale which becomes increasingly disturbing. To evoke Fabrizio's increasing terror and disorientation as he penetrates into a world where appearances are deceptive and there is a sense of impending disaster, Duranti draws not only on fairy tales and folk stories but also on other fantastic literature, especially that of the Gothic. Fabrizio's neglect of the living in favour of the search for his dead author is described as 'un patto diabolico con il mondo dei fantasmi' (*La casa*, p. 171) ('a diabolical pact with the world of ghosts'); he seems to have forgotten the lessons of German literature, for he should have known from his reading of fairy tales, Goethe's *Faust*, and Chamisso's *Peter Schlemihl's Remarkable Story* – the tale of a man who sold his shadow to the devil – that such a pact can only end in death. Maria Lettner, Fabrizio's own creation, seems to gain an independent existence which threatens to destroy him, like Frankenstein's monster. As soon as Fabrizio sees Petra's house and its apple trees (the house which *might* be the scene of the love of Oberhofer and Maria), it reminds him of a childhood fairy tale and seems to cast a spell over him: 'ma non sapeva dire se la casa che gli sembrava di riconoscere fosse quella della fata o quella della strega' (*La casa*, p. 142) ('But he could not tell whether the house that he seemed to recognize belonged to a fairy or a witch'). The woman who visits his bed at night – is it Petra or is it a ghost? – saps his vital energy like a succubus. Towards the end of the book the evil spell is nearly broken, as in fairy tales, by the visit of an external agent (in this case Fulvia); but the attempt fails, as Fabrizio can no longer see the problems of life in perspective, and, indeed, has lost the will to live. He imagines the aftermath of his death, and bequeaths Fulvia to Mario, his *alter ego* or double, who did know how to live – as the narrator in Gozzano's poem 'Il più atto' accepts death, handing over his life to his strong and healthy 'brother', his other self.

The combination of such disparate tones and atmospheres is very skilfully achieved. Dialogue is used extensively, to create a convincing illusion of contemporary reality in the Milanese sections, and later in the novel to present the enigma of Petra, the truth about whom neither Fabrizio nor the reader can penetrate. The other key element in Duranti's narrative technique, the frequent use of free indirect discourse, draws the reader gradually into Fabrizio's world, where fantasy and reality become indistinguishable.

Fairy tale elements reappear in *Lieto fine* (1987) but here irony is the dominant tone. The 'happy ending' of this comedy of manners of the idle rich in the late 1980s is itself very ironic. The humbly-born Aldo Rugani finally wins his 'princess' (p. 138), and thus the possibility of entrance into the family who have long fascinated him as symbols of success. However, the expected happiness eludes him because he has now become aware of the inauthenticity and falsity of their world. Although the members of the Santini family are concerned to keep up aristocratic appearances, the social situation on which such appearances depended no longer exists. Moreover, Aldo's own social persona is also revealed to be false: his reputation as an art critic and his wealth earned as an art collector and connoisseur are the results of his skill at faking ancient works of art. In achieving his ultimate ambition he really becomes a fake twice over ('il falso di un falso', p. 195). His hollow success is pointedly contrasted with a brief, much-idealised vision of lost alternative values, as epitomised in the country life of the Levi family, reminiscent of the description of Fulvia's home in the previous novel.

Duranti thus takes further the themes of social change and cultural decadence in postwar Italy, already touched on in *La Bambina* and *La casa*, and her satire of certain aspects of contemporary behaviour. For instance, Cynthia, the American daughter-in-law whose wealth now supports the Santini family, vaguely links her relatives' indifference to religion and to social politeness with the dirt and pollution of the nearby town: 'E inflazione, disoccupazione, bombe e colera' (*Lieto fine*, p. 126) ('And inflation, unemployment, bombs and cholera').

However, the author's main interest seems to lie in the theme of counterfeiting which was introduced in Fabrizio's creation of Maria. This subject fascinates Duranti. She described it in a radio interview as one of the most characteristic of twentieth-century fiction, especially as it suggests the artist's difficulty in coming to grips with reality directly and thus seeking artistic inspiration in art itself – a theme also present in *La casa*. Thus the Santini family are portrayed as though they were playing parts in a theatre – the 'theatre' on which Aldo gazes through his telescope – and this motif is repeatedly underlined by references to opera, especially that of Mozart, and to the musical. From being a spectator Aldo graduates to a supporting role like that of Leporello (p. 139) and finally reaches centre-stage (p. 203).

The novel focuses on the days leading up to this 'happy ending' and combines two narrative modes. One of these presents the consciousness of Aldo from the moment that he learns that Lavinia, whom he has loved unsuccessfully for years, is about to return to her mother-in-law's house: apart from the passages of memory, this mode uses the present tense. The chapters where Aldo's is the narrating voice, however, are intercut with others in the past definite, which use a non-personalized narrator to focus, in turn, on different members of the Santini family, presenting each of them where necessary, from within. In Chapter 19, however, when for the first time Aldo is incorporated into the complicated strategy which Violante, the *materfamilias*, is devising to solve her family's problems and ensure its survival, third-person and first-person narration are combined.

By such means Duranti explores the complex pattern of relationships within the family as change is brought about, though not in the way Violante plans. The uneasy equilibrium is disturbed, rather as in Pasolini's *Teorema*, by the unexpected arrival of a mysterious young man who does not belong to their world. A protean, sexually ambiguous figure, never portrayed from within, Marco may be a perfectly ordinary person, but to Lavinia, her brother-in-law and his wife he comes to embody a means of satisfying different erotic and emotional needs, which they are forced to confront. They are thus led to play different parts, so that when he leaves, the pattern of relationships within the family has changed. Lavinia, through her sexual encounter with Marco, para- doxically becomes able to put her relationship with her son Nicola, whom she had selfishly neglected, on a better footing. Violante at the same time comes to recognize that she had brought up Nicola, her grandson, partly out of selfishness and the need to compensate for the failure of her relationship with her own dead son. Through another sexually dubious relationship with Marco, Lavinia's sister-in-law Cynthia becomes aware of her desire for a child and consequently adopts a more mature sexual attitude towards her husband, Leopoldo.

The fairy-tale dimension is established at the outset, when Aldo compares the three houses whose inhabitants fascinate him, 'la grande, la media, la piccola' ('the big one, the middle-sized one and the little one'), to the houses of the Three Bears. 'Goldilocks,' he continues (the golden-haired Lavinia), 'will arrive tomorrow' (*Lieto fine*, p. 10). However, the emotions which will subsequently be uncovered will not be the stuff of a comforting sanitised Walt Disney world: when Leopoldo imagines his wife dreaming of 'un paradiso pieno di lanosi animaletti parlanti, ma senza serpenti e senza mele' (*Lieto fine*, p. 107) ('a paradise of little furry talking animals, without snakes or apples'), he is bitterly evoking Cynthia's immaturity. Unlike such fairy tales, traditional fantasy literature can hint at more disturbing emotions. Leopoldo sees his married life as the parody of a well-known fairy tale:

> se lui, il principe gentile in dorata armatura, avesse osato posare sulle labbra della sua principessa un bacio che fosse appena meno lieve del volo di una farfalla, all'istante si sarebbe trasformato agli occhi di lei in un immondo ranocchio. (*Lieto fine*, pp. 105-6)

> if he, the noble prince in shining armour, had dared to kiss his princess's lips with a touch just slightly lighter than that of a butterfly, he would have instantly been changed, in her eyes, into a foul frog.

Similarly, in further echoes of traditional story patterns, Aldo wonders what could constitute the 'magico filtro d'amore e di fertilità' ('magic potion of love and fertility') for Leopoldo and Cynthia, and how to bring about the 'agnizione' ('recognition') between Lavinia and Nicola which will restore their proper relationship (*Lieto fine*, p. 165). It is indeed through the almost mythic agency of the mysterious visitor that these matters are resolved.

Instead of the conventional closure of the fairy tale, however, the ending of the novel is left open. Like Violante, who was described earlier in the novel as 'troppo ragionevole per fare, per sé o per gli altri, progetti di felicità' (*Lieto fine*, p. 39) ('too reasonable to make plans for the happiness either of herself or others'), Aldo now understands that the attainment of something longed for does not bring the expected happiness. He makes no immediate decision about his and Lavinia's future: they will wait until winter, 'Poi si vedrà' (*Lieto fine*, p. 203) ('Then we shall see').

Duranti's highly-praised next novel, *Effetti personali* (1988), seems to develop and synthesize the most significant elements in her work. Returning to the use of a female protagonist, she revisits themes which were important in her early narrative and in much other women's writing – woman's search for autonomy, the position of the woman writer, and the mother-daughter relationship. However, she now explores these issues from a greater distance, through a plot which is no longer autobiographical. Furthermore, in the self-deprecating irony of the narrator-protagonist, a more sympathetic figure than the first-person narrator in *Lieto fine*, Duranti finds a particularly appropriate vehicle to treat these themes with a humour absent from *Piazza mia bella piazza*.

Social criticism, ranging from the satire of the literary world to a broader concern at cultural decadence, now has a more fully-developed and organic role in the narrative, and is cleverly integrated with these earlier themes. The title encapsulates this blend of the personal and the social: the novel raises the linked questions of whether one's individual identity is bound up with personal possessions, and, if so, whether there is any valid alternative to Western materialism and consumerism. Such far-reaching moral issues are explored through a plot which arouses suspense in the manner of a thriller and in which the theme of counterfeiting again plays a crucial part.

The narrator, Valentina Barbieri, has been abandoned by her husband, the go-getting Riccardo who has turned academic writing into a series of coffee-table money-spinners, exploiting Valentina's intellectual energies in the process. In the first chapter she humorously recalls the scene which sets the novel's action in motion – her discovery of Riccardo furtively unscrewing the name-plate – with *his* name on it – from the door of the flat they had shared. The loss of this object comes to encapsulate Valentina's sense of her own complete loss of identity: she is 'una scema senza più niente; nemmeno un nome sulla porta' (*Effetti personali*, p. 9) ('a fool without anything of her own, not even a name on the door'). In her ensuing attempt to redefine herself she resembles not only Paola in *Piazza,* but also Fabrizio in *La casa.* Her quest for the self, like his and that of many illustrious literary predecessors, takes the form of a journey to a previously unknown land, in this case an unspecified Eastern European country (before *perestroika* and the events of 1989), whose mysteries and contradictions recall both Kafka and *Alice through the Looking-Glass*: as in *La casa*, a convincing realistic Milanese setting gradually gives way to a mysterious, seemingly impenetrable one.

Again as in the case of Fabrizio, the quest for self is mediated through art. In her mother's home Valentina sees a copy of *La risposta*, the most recent novel by Milos Jarco, a writer who has achieved the apparently impossible by becoming successful on both sides of the Iron Curtain, but about whose private life little is known. As she has a good knowledge of Slavonic languages, she impetuously decides to try to obtain an interview with this elusive figure. She hopes thereby not only to establish herself as a journalist, and thus as an independent person, but also to find 'answers' to fundamental questions which trouble her, both about herself and about society. Her journey will become a quest for an equally elusive middle way, between Western consumerism and the communist denial of the importance of personal possessions, between a tolerance that denies moral standards and a rigid moralism, between an absorption in love which excludes all other areas of experience and a casual dismissal of its importance. From Chapter 2 onwards, the narrative consists of Valentina's account of her impressions and emotions, confided day by day to her tape-recorder.

In the course of the novel Valentina has an affair, in which the power-relationship is the complete antithesis to that which she had experienced with her husband. She emerges with a new self-confidence, having derived some happiness from this affair, but not being emotionally dependent on her lover. This specifically feminine dimension of Valentina's quest is explored not only through the contrast between Riccardo and Ante Radek, the writer who becomes her lover, but also through Valentina's relationship with her mother:

her development with respect to her mother and her husband, the two characters in relation to whom she needs to redefine herself, is traced through recalled
or imagined conversations with them. Although Valentina's loss of selfhood
derives largely from her marriage, her solutions are not presented as feminist
ones. Valentina belongs to a later generation than Paola in *Piazza*, who came
into contact with the organized feminism of the 1970s, although she did not
formally associate herself with it. In *Effetti personali*, in contrast, it is Valentina's
mother who belongs to that generation. Thus the feminism of that period is
presented ironically, through the eyes of a daughter who, when she could not be
left with her grandmother, had had to accompany her mother to demonstrations
and consciousness-raising workshops. The mother, abandoned by her husband
in the 'golden age' of the movement, 'quando dai tronchi colava solidarietà
femminile e dai rami cadevano gli slogan più spavaldi' (*Effetti personali*, p. 19)
('when female solidarity flowed down the trunks of the trees and the boldest
slogans dropped from the branches'), is shown to have derived great support
from feminism; but Valentina, representing her mother as existing in a hippy-
skirted time-warp, makes fun of her enthusiastic adoption of a completely
different personality, and of every 'alternative' possible:

> quando papà ci ha lasciate è proprio successo questo: si è fatta la permanente
> afro e dopo aveva un'altra vita. O un'altra anima, se vogliamo chiamarla così, È
> andata a cambiarla dalla sua amica parrucchiera. (*Effetti personali*, p. 20)

> when Daddy left us what happened was this: she got herself an Afro hairdo and
> after that she had a different life. Or a different soul, if we want to call it that.
> She went and changed it at her friend the hairdresser's.

> Tu, mamma, hai preso tutto in blocco: femminismo, astrologia, yoga,
> psicanalisi, erboristeria, politica, agopuntura, medicina omeopatica, Herman
> Hesse, Kamasutra, macrobiotica, cucina cinese. È' un mescolone che a te ha
> fatto bene; in me, invece, deve essere avvenuto una specie di ingorgo. (*Effetti
> personali*, p. 83)

> You took everything *en bloc*, Mummy: feminism, astrology, yoga, psychoa-
> nalysis, herbalism, politics, acupuncture, homeopathic medicine, Hermann
> Hesse, the Kama Sutra, wholefoods, Chinese cookery. It's a mixture which did
> you good; but in me there must have been some sort of blockage.

As the last part of this quotation indicates, Valentina presents herself as
reacting against such perceived excesses. Nevertheless, as a result of her adventures and her relationship with Ante, she finds that instead of being totally
absorbed in her emotional life she can now, like Riccardo, 'avere tante cose per
la testa' (*Effetti personali*, p. 83) ('have lots of things in her head') in such a way
that each of them limits the importance of the others. Not only does this
resemble the position achieved by Paola at the end of *Piazza*, but it is also,
despite the lack of feminist theory, likened to her mother's experience:

Non è buffo che io abbia dovuto viaggiare per tremila chilometri, sedurre un
poeta, mettermi forse nei guai con il controspionaggio d'oltrecortina, entrare
in una vasca piena di schiuma alla melissa per provare finalmente anch'io questa
sensazione che tu, mamma, insieme alle tue compagne, conosci da vent'anni?
(*Effetti personali*, p. 83)

Isn't it strange that I should have had to travel three thousand kilometres,
seduce a poet, perhaps get myself in trouble with communist counter-espion-
age, and get into a lemon balm bubble bath before being able to feel what you
and your friends, Mummy, have felt for twenty years?

Despite the differences between their characters, Valentina's mother is supportive of her daughter's venture. The warmth and tenderness of this mother-
daughter relationship is strikingly different from those depicted in earlier books.
The fact that the mother now belongs to a lower class and a younger generation
suggests that the distance from autobiography which Duranti has now achieved
is responsible for this.

There are other senses too in which Valentina's mother, Riccardo and Ante
represent extremes between which Valentina seeks a middle way. The mother's
tolerant approach to all kinds of behaviour is contrasted both with Ante's rigid
Marxism and with the firm moralism of the extracts from the writings of the
Fathers of the Church which are used as epigraphs to the chapters. Riccardo,
who had exploited these works as source-material for the books which he writes
to a formula – this is another case of Duranti satirizing the literary world –
epitomizes Western society's concern with material gain; while Ante seems,
until the end of the novel, to embody a view of the self according to which
possessions are unimportant. Valentina is unable, ultimately, to accede to this
view and remain with him. In the final passage, addressed now to him, she
recognizes that her dream of a 'terza scelta' ('third choice') is an illusion, as
elusive as Milos Jarco himself, but she realizes that she must act 'come se il giusto
equilibrio fosse un'ipotesi realizzabile' (*Effetti personali*, p. 166) ('as though the
happy medium could be achieved'). The final position, as in *Lieto fine*, is one of
irony: 'nel punto esatto dove l'ultima illusione è caduta, lì comincia la
commedia' (*Effetti personali*, p. 167) ('at the very point where the final illusion is
destroyed, comedy begins').

The narrative technique used in *Effetti personali* illustrates Duranti's aims
particularly well. The tape-recorder device enables her consistently to use the
language of conversation with the narrative being predominantly in the present
tense; while even the first, retrospective chapter uses the perfect tense, rather
than the more literary past definite. The effective and well-crafted combination
of serious moral and social issues with an entertaining plot, narrated in readily
accessible language, gives the novel wide appeal.

The cover illustration of Duranti's most recent novel, *Ultima stesura* (1991), a
fifteenth-century French miniature, shows a painter painting her own selfportrait, while looking at herself in the mirror. This evokes the book's themes

very effectively: having drawn on her life as a source of her art, especially in her earliest works, Duranti now, as a more self-conscious literary artist, takes the complex relationship between life and art, and the intermingling of truth and fiction, as her actual subject. The book is explicitly a meta-narrative, as the narrator-protagonist is a woman writer who writes about her own earlier work; but the *mise-en-abîme* structure, and the self-reflexive game of mirrors, are even more complex. Not only can a character in the narrator's fiction be a narrator in its own right (p. 160), but also, and even more importantly, Duranti, as the creator of the whole, is writing and reflecting about her own act of writing.

The narrator-protagonist, Teodora Francia,whose career bears certain striking resemblances with that of her creator, while not being an exact copy of it, collects together eight of her short stories, dating from her beginnings as a writer to the present. She sets them into context in her life, evoking in each case, always in present-tense narrative, the moment when it was given its final, determining shape. Whether or not the stories are set in her own world, whether they are told by a female or a male narrator, and whether the main character resembles her or is her complete opposite, the interaction between her experience and her writing clearly emerges. Deep resonances link her life to her fiction, by parallelism or contrast, and her writing itself affects her life. For instance, her first story, begun as a celebration of life after she had left her husband for her lover, ends with the defeat of the life-affirming character, in a conclusion which betrays Teodora's own repressed grief at her enforced separation from her son and her lover's opposition to her writing.

Themes already present in Duranti's novels are explored from new angles. For instance, the difficult quest for identity, and for the true self, is evoked through the various names by which the narrator is known in the course of her life. The name which she chooses to use for her writing is intended to symbolize the combination of 'writing' and 'living', combining as it does her own baptismal name with the surname of her second husband, as, indeed, the name 'Francesca Duranti' does. The same themes are also explored through the episodes in which, during her second marriage, Teodora constantly looks at herself in the mirror on putting away her writing and going to greet her returning husband. Duranti's concern about the woman writer's difficulties in combining 'living' and 'writing' is now extended to those of any writer. Both activities are essential, but they are incompatible: in reflecting on her past Teodora finds that she has needed to live as well as to write, to be involved with others as well as to be self-sufficient, to be an actor as well as an observer. But (like Aldo in *Lieto fine* who finally gives up his telescope and his narration to take part in the play-acting) she cannot do both at once, and (again like Aldo) whichever activity she is engaged in she longs for the other. By the end of the novel the idea that deep personal suffering can produce art helps her to accept her own isolation.

The novel is very cleverly constructed, with what at first seem casual background details finally fitting together to tell Teodora's own story. References are also made along the way to many aspects of the writer's craft, from the techniques of good storytelling to the use of the tools of writing – the pen in the earliest story, then the typewriter, and then the computer: such comments can be used, with due care, to analyse the author's own earlier writings.

Francesca Duranti's earlier books can also perhaps be illuminated by the teasing coincidences which sometimes occur between them and the imagined life or works of her near-namesake. For instance, the use of Garrone as Teodora's maiden name emphasizes the element of self-representation in Duranti's Fabrizio Garrone in *La casa*; whilst the names of Teodora's first husband, Carlo, her second, Marco Francia, and her daughter, Eloisa, coincide with those of Paola's husbands and daughter in *Piazza*. Teodora, unlike Paola, has a son by her first marriage; but his name Nicola, echoes that of Lavinia's son in *Lieto fine* who, for different reasons, is also separated from his mother. Personal experience, it would seem, remains a potent force in Duranti's writing, but it has been increasingly distanced both by being blended with fiction and through the literary game of mirrors. Teodora defiantly declares in the course of her seventh story, where the narrator of the story and the overall narrator coincide, that her creative energies are by no means exhausted. Neither, it would seem, are those of her creator. She may, like Teodora, have lost her initial spontaneity, but she still possesses the ability to surprise, stimulate and entertain with ever more ingenious narrative structures.

BIBLIOGRAPHY

Works

La Bambina (Milan: La Tartaruga, 1976); reprinted (Milan: Rizzoli, 1985 edition cited); edited by F. M. Masini (Florence: Sansoni, 1986).
Piazza mia bella piazza (Milan: La Tartaruga, 1978).
La casa sul lago della luna (Milan: Rizzoli, 1984). Translated by Stephen Saltarelli as *The House on Moon Lake* (London: Collins, 1987).
Lieto fine (Milan: Rizzoli, 1987).
Effetti personali (Milan: Rizzoli, 1988).
Ultima stesura (Milan: Rizzoli, 1991).

Chapter 8

Rosetta Loy
The Paradox of the Past

SHARON WOOD

Rosetta Loy's first novel, *La bicicletta*, appeared in 1974; the latest, *Le strade di polvere* (her only work so far to be translated into English) dates from 1987. Three other books appeared in the intervening years; and Loy's work reflects the changing sense of female identity felt and described by women writers in Italy during this period. Between the 1970s and 1980s much women's writing moved away from an overtly feminist stance which took the real lives of women as material for short stories and novels. This production of the 1970s was the feminist equivalent of 'littérature engagée', in that by exploring areas of experience previously ignored or suppressed by literature, it aimed to challenge both the political and moral status quo. Between the 1970s and the 1980s, there was a changing sense of female identity in Italian women writers, a shifting relationship between self and text, and an increasing reluctance to see narrative and fiction as a suitable forum for the social and political questions raised by the turmoil of the late 1960s and early 1970s. In the work of Rosetta Loy we can see these parallel trajectories of feminism and the novel as they mirror themselves in each other: the divide between fiction which attempts to change the world and fiction which would create an alternative reality. Rosetta Loy's writing provides a fascinating example of the way in which the social, moral, political, and also sexual content of narrative of the 1970s gave way to an art which is more self-consciously fictive: the feminist also becomes a modernist.

Rosetta Loy was one of many writers for whom the discovery of feminism led to a radical transformation in her own life. Born in 1931 of a Roman mother and Piedmontese father into a wealthy family, she married in 1955 and still lives in the same house on the outskirts of Rome where she brought up her four children. She was already in her forties when she embraced the ideals and challenges of feminism in the 1970s, and still regards feminism as a marvellously liberating discovery. She rebelled, if quietly, against the normal expectations of a woman of her social class, but the rebellion was for a long time accompanied by a deep sense of doubt and guilt about her activity as a writer. In this sense she can be compared to any number of women writers for whom the act of writing is simultaneously an affirmation of identity and a refusal to mirror preconceived social images of women's role and behaviour. Like Jane Austen, who used to cover over her written sheets with a piece of blotting paper when someone came into the room, for many years she wrote in secret. Her upper-class, strictly Catholic family found the idea of writing absurd, and the idea of a woman writing preposterous. Not even the Viareggio prize for first novels, won in 1974 with *La bicicletta*, succeeded in persuading them that it was a suitable occupation for a woman. As she noted in a recent interview, 'Non era cosa concepita nella mia famiglia una donna che scrive' ('For my family a woman who writes was inconceivable'). Not until the mid-1970s, after much encouragement from her husband, the publication of her second novel, *La porta dell'acqua*, and the empowering impact feminism had made upon her, could she claim the designation of writer without experiencing a sense of guilt.

It was not writing which Rosetta Loy found difficult, but letting the world know that she wrote, seeking public recognition. Writing was, she says, a 'refuge'; her solitary childhood was marked by acute shyness and a partial deafness which inevitably distorted her commerce with the world. In writing she could herself take on the role of protagonist. Writing served as a guarantee for the subjective, offering a sense of the world centred on the self. It was an escape from, and simultaneously into, her own world; writing became re-writing, as her relations with the world around her were redefined through the process of narration.

In a peculiarly symbiotic relationship between life and text, Loy drew heavily on her own childhood experience in her early work. While large numbers of writers begin more or less overtly with autobiography, and both men and women write about childhood, for Loy, women do so from a different perspective, since their experience of childhood is different.

> L'uomo ha dell'infanzia un ricordo più felice e libero. Il mito dell'infanzia nella letteratura maschile è nostalgico, vincente. Per la donna è invece il simbolo della sua costrizione, del suo sacrificio. Per me, scrivere dell'infanzia è stato dunque parafrasare la condizione di tutta la mia vita, e forse di tutte le donne, almeno quelle della mia generazione. (In interview.)
>
> Men have a freer and happier memory of childhood. The myth of childhood in men's literature is nostalgic, victorious. For women on the other hand it's the symbol of their constraints, of their sacrifices. So for me, to write about childhood has been to paraphrase the condition of the whole of my life, and perhaps that of all women, at least those of the same generation as mine.

Childhood is real but it is also a metaphor; not, as in Elsa Morante's work, a metaphor of hope in a world that has grown up mad, but of a condition from which it is almost impossible to escape: like the innermost figure in a babushka doll which prefigures all future containments and confinements. While Loy's second novel *La porta dell'acqua* recounts a primary childhood trauma of separation and loss which literature may reveal but can never compensate for, the earlier *La bicicletta* (1974) reveals us to be prisoners of our past at the very moment we think we have forgotten or transcended it. This first novel follows the lives of a wealthy, upper-middle class family around the end of the Second World War, closely based on Loy's own family. War itself is not the point here; what concerns Loy is the social and psychological response to dramatic and traumatic circumstances. Surface events – the end of fascism, the occupation of Rome by the Nazis, reprisals against partisans, the ideological influence of communism, and the postwar recovery – are all represented; yet Loy is not content simply to reconstruct political or social history. What interests her is the oblique relationship her characters have with their times. These are not protagonists, makers of history, as Natalia Ginzburg observes in her preface to the first edition:

> I personaggi guardano la realtà come dall'alto d'una finestra o d'una terrazza. Non riescono ad afferrarne che gli echi e i lampi ... Evocati in gruppo, questi esseri trovano difficile non soltanto esistere nel mondo esterno, ma anche esistere individualmente [...] Tutto il racconto è come un sommesso bisbiglio corale dove si alza a tratti una voce più acuta, una più impaziente e ansiosa interrogazione e ricerca di libertà.

> The characters look down on reality as though from a high window or a terrace. They manage to grasp no more of it than its echoes, flashes ... Evoked as a group, these creatures find it difficult not only to exist in the external world, but also to exist individually [...] The whole story is like a low choral whisper where now and again a sharper voice makes itself heard, a more impatient and anxious questioning and search for liberty.

Loy's characters are cut off by the very privileges which their class and wealth bestow upon them. Removed from history and experience, which seems to pass them by, they are only occasionally aware of their imprisoned condition; only occasionally does this awareness surface and lead them to seek to escape. Loy's affectionate yet dispassionate critique centres itself on the 'superficialità dell'ambiente per cui tutto quello che è dietro non conta, non insegna, non esiste' (in interview) ('superficiality of that environment for which everything which lies behind doesn't count, doesn't teach, doesn't exist').

The narrative hinges on four children and their family as they move through adolescence into early adulthood. Details of childhood are piled up, from the scraped knees to the ink-stained fingers, from siblings' squabbles to the first stirrings of sexual interest, in a narrative which, like that of Natalia Ginzburg herself, does not insist on a linear 'story' but is more concerned to re-create, through sensual impressions, a physical existence. But just as the narrative does not follow a highly developed plot, so the characters do not live their lives mindful of past and future. Life is not for them a learning experience: and yet one of the implicit and fundamental notions of the book is that freedom can only come from experience and memory of experience, from a reckoning with both personal and public history. The two girls, Maddalena and Speranza, however, quickly forget the hardships and difficulties of war, which impinge only tangentially on a burgeoning sensual and sexual consciousness.

> Tenere a volte hanno sguardi di pietà per un gatto, una vecchia; altre volte irritano e stupiscono per la loro stolida indifferenza. Il passato non esiste tanto il futuro preme: tedeschi, guerra, SS, che sono a confronto di questa smania di vivere. Di possedere. Il passato le ha appena sfiorate con le sue terrificanti giornate, la loro memoria è breve, chiusa intorno a piccoli fatti. (*La bicicletta*, p. 59)

> Tender sometimes, they can look pityingly at a cat, an old woman; other times their stolid indifference can infuriate and astonish. The past doesn't exist so urgent is the future: Germans, war, SS, what are they compared to this burning desire to live? To possess. The past has barely touched them with its terrifying days, their memory is short, closed around little things.

Yet for one of these girls at least it is not so much the past as the future that is a prison. Maddalena grows up the cool embodiment, the well-groomed carica-ture almost, of the expectation her class has of her sex. She meets a young ambitious lawyer who fits her idea of the male as escort of good family and better prospects; already her future is no longer her own, but already written in the social code and reflected in the mind of her conformist, colourless fiancé. The name of the other sister, Speranza (Hope), is belied by her later appalling experience in bearing a dead child.

The one member of the family who cultivates a memory of the past is fascinated by the horror of the atrocities committed. Giovanni lives and experi-ences the past differently, seeking knowledge, becoming almost obsessed. Loy says, referring to Giovanni, that 'Quella che vive il passato in modo particolare sono io. Per me il passato è sempre qualcosa che continua a essere.' (in interview) ('I'm the one who lives the past in a particular way. For me the past is always something which continues to be'). The moment when Giovanni sits in an empty cinema watching a documentary about the Belsen victims stands as testimony to the public and collective act of forgetting which has already taken place (the recent historical works Giovanni orders from the librarian are covered in dust: 'Not much call for that kind of thing'), while simultaneously underlin-ing the fragility of the re-established order. Even as he reads about the concen-tration camps, Giovanni is well aware of the precarious and yet extraordinary nature of the present which would seek to wipe out the past:

> Una bocca come una voragine vuole inghiottirlo, lui ha sempre sofferto di vertigini. Eppure è tutto finito, i Cattivi sono stati puniti e Vendetta è stata fatta, ogni cosa è tornata nell'ordine: i bambini saltano a corda nelle strade e gli uomini tornano a casa la sera, io sono qua tranquillo nell'ombra e le sorelle siedono sui gradini a sbucciare una noce, mangio l'uva e rido della mamma che imita le zie. La cuoca coglie l'insalata con le forbici e un calabrone blu si posa pesante sulla corolla di una petunia. (*La bicicletta*, p. 66)

A mouth like an abyss wants to swallow him up, he's always suffered from dizzy spells. And yet it's all over, the Baddies have been punished, Revenge has been taken, order has been restored: the children skip in the streets and men go home at nights, I'm sitting here peacefully in the shade and my sisters sit on the steps shelling nuts, I'm eating grapes and laughing at mother who is doing a take-off of the aunts. The cook's cutting lettuce with the scissors and a bumble-bee lands heavily on the corolla of a petunia.

Giovanni's intense consciousness of the situation is marked by a momentary reversion to a first-person narrative as Loy slides in and out of the minds of her characters, revealing them not through their actions, nor even their thoughts, but through their sensations. It is a form of fiction which declines to follow the path of an omniscient and detached narrator. The act of narrating aligns and fuses itself with different characters in turn to focus less on how they are seen than on how they see.

Giovanni, too, suffers the attrition of the everyday, a process of forgetting, as the compelling power of the present reasserts itself. He abandons his plans to join Simon Wiesenthal in his hunt for Nazi criminals, and little by little he loses contact not only with the past, but also with those people who represent his own personal history. He becomes a wealthy, bored, and somewhat uneasy wanderer in search of adventure, of fleeting human contact.

Clearly to cling on to the past is to renounce the present and to renounce living. With each slippage of the past, something is lost, both for the individual and the society in which she or he lives. This is the contradiction which Rosetta Loy explores in her work. The political point is made with reference to the German chancellor Adenauer, much admired by the father. It is a point leavened with humour as the family butler Adone, slightly deaf, believes his own praises are being sung. This episode again recalls the work of Natalia Ginzburg in the author's ability constantly to change both points of view and tone within the space of a few brief sentences. Loy's is a style which is associative, rejecting linear narrative logic in favour of a cluster of connected memories and sensations:

'Pare [...] che in Germania ci sia già una prodigiosa ripresa, - dice il padre, - grande uomo Adenauer'. Adone si ferma con il piatto in mano, ha udito il suo nome. Deve essere un po' duro di orecchi, bisogna fare attenzione quando guida. Per questo forse il padre gli siede sempre accanto e dice: attenzione un camion, attenzione un ciclista, un carro di buoi, suonano dietro, unendo insieme i sensi di questo Adone che non conosce Adenauer e immagina il suo nome pronunciato con tanta lode. Ma Adenauer è riuscito a fare un mucchietto dei peccati commessi dai suoi connazionali, Giovanni non osa dirlo al padre che tanto stima il vecchio che si comunica ogni mattina. Ma allora tutti i morti, le torture, i bambini che disegnavano alberi e pane, il venerando statista se li nasconde sotto la camicia, in quello stomaco dove scende l'ostia. (*La bicicletta*, p. 74)

'It seems [...] that there is already an extraordinary revival in Germany', says the father, 'great man, that Adenauer.' Adone stops, a plate in his hand, he's heard his name. He must be a bit hard of hearing, you have to be careful when he is driving. Perhaps that's why father always sits next to him and says: watch out, there's a lorry, watch out, there's a cyclist, an ox and cart, they're sounding their horn behind us, co-ordinating the senses of this Adone who does not know Adenauer and imagines his name being spoken in such praise. But Adenauer has managed to make a tidy little pile of the crimes committed by his countrymen, Giovanni does not dare say that to father who has so much respect for the old man who takes Communion every morning. And so all the dead, the torture, the children who drew pictures of trees and bread, the venerable statesman hides them under his shirt, in that stomach into which the host descends.

Giovanni's high moral principle is incapable of extending itself to his immediate personal and sexual affairs, however, and there is considerable irony in his relationship with Piera, a lower-class woman with whom his older brother Michele has already had an affair. Michele's plans to send Piera to college and give her an education meet with his parents' astonished disapproval and the relationship is abandoned. Michele goes on to be a successful engineer who makes a 'good' marriage. But his increasing unhappiness is marked ever more eloquently by the barriers he imposes between himself and his family, his harshness with the men who work for him, his betrayal of his wife, and his silence.

Piera is also abandoned by Giovanni, pregnant this time; the mention of her name at the dinner-table a few months after her abortion and departure for Turin causes not even a ripple of emotion; Piera has become like an unrecognised character on a distant stage. Loy is highly critical of the hypocrisy of her own class; this failure of memory, the failure to connect, is a personal and social catastrophe, and is here revealed as a failure of language. Whilst in Natalia Ginzburg's *Lessico famigliare* it is language, the common store of stories and memories, which provides the semantics of individual lives and gives meaning to the family as an entity, for Loy language becomes an instrument of isolation and alienation: the set phrases of convention become the devalued currency of the wealthy:

'C'è una lettera per te'. 'Questo te lo manda la mamma, ti aspetta mercoledì'. 'Adone, ma cosa lo suoni a fare il gong se siamo già tutti qui, pensare ragazzo, qualche volta devi anche pensare'. 'Che freddo fa stasera ...' Le frasi si intrecciano passando da uno all'altro con i grissini il vino rosso e il sale. Parole rituali che si depositano come una patina sugli oggetti (la brocca di ceramica, la fruttiera di Via Valadier), sui fiori e la frutta le pagode cinesi dei parati rappezzati con cura da chi conosce il valore del danaro. (*La bicicletta*, p. 122)

'There's a letter for you'. 'This is from mother, she's expecting you Wednesday'. 'Adone, why on earth are you sounding the gong when we're all here? Think boy, sometimes you have to think as well'. 'It's really cold this evening ...' The sentences interweave, passing from one to the other together with the bread sticks, the red wine and the salt. Ritual words which deposit themselves as a veneer on objects (the ceramic jug, the fruit bowl from Via Valadier), on the flowers and the fruit, the Chinese pagodas of the walls carefully papered by people who know the value of money.

Loy's work addresses a paradoxical situation: the need to recall the past, the urgent imperative of memory, and simultaneously the impossibility of wiping out the past, which continually resurfaces like so much flotsam and jetsam. 'Come tornare indietro, come riafferrare il bambino che correva lungo la strada di campagna con la camicia gonfia di noci ...' (*La bicicletta*, p. 151) ('How can you go back, how can you recapture the small boy running along the country road, his shirt stuffed full of nuts ...') is counterbalanced by the second question, 'Come censurare la memoria; brani navigano simili a lastre di ghiaccio, cozzano, si deformano ...' (p. 157) ('How can you censure memory; fragments float like sheets of ice, crash into each other, become deformed'). Loy's concern with the past is not simple reconstruction, for such a project is impossible. History in this first novel is not seen through the eyes of its characters; rather, it resonates through their experience, in more or less recognized ways. Memory is unreliable, and too many interests are at stake for the past to be represented other than through the desires and wishes of the present. Hence, her rejection of classical forms of narrative construction in favour of an allusive and associative yet tightly controlled style which renders the past not as objective fact but as subjective memory and experience. Her method of writing piles up fragment on tiny fragment of detail, as she places before us images, colours, tastes, smells. This is not nostalgia, but a critical account of a specific relationship with the past, as experienced by a particular class. The restless nature of the narrative with its shifts, turns and changes of direction provides a correlative to the restlessness and imprisonment of her characters as they struggle to come to terms with their condition. The acquisition of identity for Loy's characters bears a high cost indeed.

La porta dell'acqua appeared two years later, in 1976. During the mid-1970s Loy wrote cultural journalism for *Noi donne*, the journal of the UDI, the Union of Italian Women. These were the years when feminism in Italy was at its peak and achieving its most notable political victories: fascist family law, for example, was finally discarded in favour of allowing couples to divorce. Much writing by women at this point took the form of confessional, autobiographical work, with women literally writing their own lives. Whilst Loy's first two books, *La bicicletta* (1974) and *La porta dell'acqua* (1976), contain much autobiographical material, they do not follow patterns of feminist confessional fiction which saw the written celebration of women's lives, struggles, and sexuality as a correlative to political militancy: it is only in the 1980s, in *L'estate di Letuché*, that Loy takes an adult woman as her protagonist. Yet in these early works, Loy shares on a deeper level the obsession with identity and questions of subjectivity foregrounded by feminism and women's fiction in the 1960s and 1970s. The title of this second work is taken from a poem by Lorca in the *Divan del*

Tamarit, called 'Gacela de la raiz amarga', 'Poem of the Bitter Root':

> There is a bitter root
> And a world of a thousand terraces.
>
> Not even the smallest hand
> Breaches the door of the water.

The bitter root is what lies at the heart of every individual life and social experience, the inevitable and incurable sense of pain and loss which accompanies the process of living. For Loy it is 'l'impossibilità dell'infanzia di comunicare – perchè non esiste una porta dell'acqua, non esiste un linguaggio comune fra il bambino e l'adulto' (in interview) ('the impossibility for childhood to communicate – because there is no such thing as a door of water, there is no common language between child and adult'). While *La bicicletta* took us into the lives of adolescents, *La porta dell'acqua* takes us further and more deeply into the mind of its seven-year-old narrator. Childhood is viewed neither elegiacally nor nostalgically, but as a moment of separation and trauma which offers a bleak blueprint for the future. The child fails to grasp the ways of the world not simply through undeveloped intellectual power, but because the world is not accessible to rational understanding.

The standard and rigidly Catholic education of the daughter of wealthy parents is described – convent schooling, piano lessons, servants and governess. Yet this apparent privilege (Loy describes her own life as 'easy and fortunate, on the surface') conceals a ritual whose aim is to subdue and repress, where fear is the other side of devotion. Privilege becomes sadistic imposition and constraint, as in the music lesson:

> Mi dava il tempo e il suggerimento delle note illuminata da un sorriso costante ma la bocca che si apriva sulla bella dentatura compatta aveva qualcosa di crudele. Quando sbagliavo una luce di trionfo si levava suo malgrado dalla salda corona di incisivi e canini e con slancio irrefrenabile mi schiacciava la mano sulla tastiera. (*La porta dell'acqua*, p. 42)

> Illuminated by a constant smile she would beat time and tell me the notes but there was something cruel in the mouth which opened onto her compact beautiful teeth. When I made a mistake, despite herself a triumphant light rose up from her solid crown of incisors and canines and with an unstoppable rush she would crush my fingers on the keyboard.

The religious education imparted by the nuns similarly centres on a sadistic sense of pain and guilt, with an undercurrent of irony which is humorous and simultaneously distances the reader from the account:

> Madre Gregoria diceva che gli ebrei avevano crocefisso Gesù e poi avevano gridato che quel sangue innocente ricadesse pure su di loro e sui loro figli. Il viso rubicondo circondato dai raggi inamidati della cuffietta esprimeva pena e rammarico per tanta stoltezza. Poveri bambini ebrei che non avevano suore

che potevano insegnare loro a dire 'voiture' o 'parapluie' né potevano mangiare i fragoloni che Suor Lucilla innaffiava lasciando colare l'acqua giù per il pendio mentre il vento sollevava la grande sottana scura. Non aspettavano loro la fumata bianca per gridare giubilanti 'Habemus papam, habemus papam...' (*La porta dell'acqua*, p. 18)

Mother Gregoria used to say that the Jews had crucified Christ and then shouted for that innocent blood to fall on them and their children too. The ruddy face circled by the starched rays of her coif expressed pain and grief at such foolishness. Poor Jewish children who had no Sisters to teach them how to say 'voiture' or 'parapluie', who couldn't eat the enormous strawberries which Sister Lucilla watered by pouring water down the slope while the wind lifted her dark habit. They could never wait for the white smoke to cry out joyfully 'Habemus papam, habemus papam...'

Yet *La porta dell'acqua* is far more than just another book about the repressive absurdity of an over-strict religious education. The narrative is a contemplation of the devastating consequences of early experience, a re-creation of the calamity of childhood. The narrator has not yet learned the conventional parameters which all children eventually learn to call time and space; she has neither absorbed the sequential logic of cause and effect nor learned to subordinate the senses to reason. Reality is not at this stage equivalent to the life of the mind. Every detail, sound, sight, and smell is enlarged by the concentrated attention of the narrative, magnified to fill the whole of the child's horizon, and no facet of sensory experience is taken for granted or dismissed. Each moment is complete in its own pleasure or pain, and since time is not lived as a sequence of largely predictable events, no future moment can be guaranteed. As she waits for her governess to return from her weekly afternoon off, the child is convinced she will never return, and despairs: the rationalist notions of probability, cause and effect, action and consequence, are irrelevant to the desire of the small child.

Her sense of reality is intimately bound up with her sense of oneness with the mother figure, who in this novel is not her own natural mother but the German governess Anne Marie. Consciousness is not ontological but relational: space and time are marked off not by clocks and objects but by the presence or absence of Anne Marie, by her approach or her withdrawal. As she wakes the girl imagines the governess coming in to her bedroom:

Chiusi gli occhi la vedevo e la sentivo in una unica sensazione: asciutta come il mercurio, ma morbida, aderente. Lei immensa io piccola, lei senza peso. Avanzava verso di me in un crescendo che aveva del sublime. Mi copriva, mi inglobava senza lasciare vuoti o spiragli. (*La porta dell'acqua*, p. 3)

Having shut my eyes I saw her and felt her in one single sensation; dry as mercury, but soft and clinging. She is immense, I am small, she is weightless. She came towards me in a crescendo which had something of the sublime. She covered me, enclosed me, leaving no spaces or cracks.

Whilst the 'real' Anne Marie is volatile and treacherous, as liable to punish as to gratify, the narrator holds an image of her which suggests the pre-linguistic bliss described by Jacques Lacan, the time of perfect happiness, the psychological stage prior to entry into language and into the symbolic order, with the accompanying division of the self into self and other. The beloved image of Anne Marie stands as a miraculous guarantee against the threat of loss and emptiness; her embrace offers completion and plenitude.

There is however a story, or perhaps a history, which brutally intrudes into this illusion of timelessness, oneness and bliss. The German governess reads out an instructive tale in which a little girl by name of Paulinchen disobeys her mother and plays with matches; the house catches fire and she is burnt to death. In *The Uses of Enchantment*, Bruno Bettelheim discusses forms of fairy tales and children's stories which act as teaching narratives, not in a narrow moral sense but in ways which reassure the child of the normality of what they are experiencing, and promise a happy ending. In listening to the story of Paulinchen our narrator fails to draw the required moral conclusion, and comes to the much bleaker existential conclusion that logic and justice do not exist at all:

> Come sopportare l'idea di una punizione così atroce per la piccola curiosità di una bambina lasciata sola in casa? Perchè non era intervenuto l'angelo Custode, dov'era? Dove era Gesù Bambino che in camiciola si affaccia ai tabernacoli e vede e sa tutto? Dov'erano Anne Marie, la mamma, papà, Italia e Letizia? Sfogliavo indietro il libro e il cattivo Friedrich che strappava le ali alle mosche era lì rincalzato nel suo letto mentre Paulinchen correva con le vesti in fiamme [...] Paulinchen era forse ebrea? [...] Nello strazio della sua irrimediabile condanna andava in frantumi ogni possibile logica. Battevo con fracasso sul pavimento, la sorte di Paulinchen era inaccettabile, dava nausea e vertigine. (*La porta dell'acqua*, p. 11)

> How could you bear the idea of such an atrocious punishment for the little curiosity of a girl left alone at home? Why hadn't her Guardian Angel intervened, where was he? Where was the Infant Jesus who appears in the tabernacle in his long shirt and sees and knows everything? Where were Anne Marie, mummy, daddy, Italia and Letizia? I flipped back through the book and naughty Friedrich who pulled the wings off flies was there tucked up in bed while Paulinchen fled with her dress on fire [...] Was Paulinchen Jewish maybe? [...] Every possible logic was shattered in the anguish of her irremediable sentence. I thrashed furiously on the floor, Paulinchen's fate was unacceptable, it made you sick and giddy.

The narrator is betrayed by the story as she is later betrayed by the departure of Anne Marie. The logic of dependency and higher authority is smashed, and with her compulsive demand to hear the story again and again, the narrator seems to rehearse and internalize the mechanism by which mothers and daughters, real or symbolic, are irredeemably doomed to separation and schism; the daughter is inevitably betrayed and cast off by the person most loved. The 'crudeltà delle parole', the cruelty of words, is displaced by the cruelty of real and equally irrational loss, just as children's play is preparation for adult activity. Anne Marie leaves; the sense of plenitude is lost, the charmed circle of lover and beloved is broken, as Anne Marie no longer reflects back to her the desired image:

> Nello specchio dove ci riflettevamo abbracciate vedevo i suoi occhi rinnovare e prolungare un sorriso dove si concentravano, inafferrabili, le immagini di una felicità che trascurando la mia pena e la mia stanchezza, il ritardo, escludevano ogni mia partecipazione. Ero rimasta a guardarla muta, sgomenta. (*La porta dell'acqua*, p. 73)

> In the mirror where we could see our reflections hugging each other I could see her eyes renewing and prolonging a smile in which were concentrated the elusive images of a happiness which, unmindful of my grief and tiredness, the late hour, excluded all possibility of my participation. I stayed there looking at her, silent, dismayed.

Six years passed between the appearance of *La porta dell'acqua* and *L'estate di Letuché*, years of further intense and dramatic change in Italy. Whilst social unrest was less pronounced and a period of increasing 'depoliticization' had begun, there was still much terrorist activity, including the kidnapping and assassination of Aldo Moro. Writing at a time when Italy was taking political decisions with far-reaching consequences, Loy offers in this novel an oblique reading of three different moments of Italian history which she interweaves and intertwines in a narrative form which redefines the relationship between abstract time and concrete event, and which questions the possibility of rescuing history from anything other than myth. The 'present' of the novel is set at the time of the assassination of John F. Kennedy and of Rudi Dutchke, of student riots and of the Russian tanks rolling into Prague. Into this world of the 1960s, Loy inserts episodes from the Resistance and the pre-war period in a structure which questions the possibility or desirability of bringing the past into the present, of seeing the past as anything other than detritus lapping around our feet.

Loy herself says of this novel that it is her least accomplished, the most discontinuous, the most revealing of her struggle with new subject-matter and different narrative forms. The protagonist, a professional, married woman with a small son, falls in love and leaves her husband. She follows her lover to Milan, becomes involved with his friends, and in seeking to know him better delves into his past and that of his circle of friends. Whilst past episodes thus come to light, they cannot finally define the people she now finds herself involved with, and the suicide of her lover's friend Carlo remains an impenetrable enigma to protagonist and reader alike.

The protagonist's profession as an art restorer is itself an icon of the ambivalence of her position and purpose, which is to act in the present to reconstruct an authentic image of a product from the past, to recreate an object or moment from history. This recreation of the past in the present implies a continuity of experience and value; objects continue to circulate, to be exchanged in a process which is a material line across the smooth dimension of time. Personal memory is seen to be unreliable, insufficiently linear, liable to slips, gaps and exaggerations: the passage of time cancels some areas of experience, highlights others. Memory, as a cognitive process firmly based on the present, is incapable of contemplating the past, of seizing it. For Antonio on the contrary, the *déraciné* intellectual the protagonist falls in love with, the past is literally *created* by the present in a reversal of the conventional sequence of things and in contradiction to codified history. The central dialectic of the novel is outlined in a dialogue between the first-person narrator and Antonio in an exchange which lies literally and philosophically at the heart of the novel:

> 'Tu fantastichi troppo' dice 'nella vita non ci sono storie, ma solo momenti. E quei momenti là si dissolvono, spariscono, capisci? Di loro non resta che quello che hanno prodotto, che può essere una sonata di Beethoven ma anche niente, o invece sangue, morte. Ma quel momento là non c'è più ... Anche la memoria è un momento [...] Tu credi di ricordare, invece stai solo inventando'.
>
> 'Non è di memoria che parlo, ma di qualcosa di diverso, chiamiamola conoscenza. Ed è proprio attraverso certi elementi sempre simili che puoi arrivare a capire, e quindi a sapere [...]'
>
> 'Io non ho nessun interesse alle ricostruzioni, anzi, in un certo senso mi fanno orrore. È come mettere le mani in mezzo ai cadaveri.' (*L'estate di Letuché*, p. 85)

> 'You imagine too much,' he says, 'in life there are no histories, only moments. And those moments dissolve and disappear, don't you see? All that is left of them is what they have produced, which might be a Beethoven sonata, yet it might be nothing, or blood, or death. But that moment itself no longer exists ... Memory is a moment too [...] You think you are remembering, but you are only inventing'.
>
> 'It's not memory I'm talking about, but something different, call it knowledge. It is through certain elements which are always the same that you can come to understand, and so to know [...]'
>
> 'I have not the slightest interest in reconstructions, in fact I find them appalling in a way. It's like sticking your hand in among dead bodies.'

The protagonist seeks in both her profession and her personal life an intellectual grasp of the past, a re-evocation of experience which will transcend the merely material. Loy herself comments on her protagonist that:

> Cerca i collegamenti. È una che vuole vedere la storia nella sua globalità, come se il passato e il presente fossero un tessuto che uno guarda. Il suo desiderio di ricuperare il passato è anche il desiderio di avere una visione globale. (In interview.)

> She seeks connections. She is someone who wants to see history in its globality, as if past and present were a tissue to be looked at. Her desire to recuperate the past is also a desire to have a global vision.

This is a desire which Loy herself shares. Yet she also acknowledges that 'il passato è finzione, perchè non può mai essere esattamente quello che è. Io razionalmente lo penso' (in interview) ('the past is fiction, because it can never be exactly what it is. Rationally that's what I think'). It is this contradiction, this tension, which gives this work its central impetus.

Whilst the act of love offers moments of fusion which seem to go beyond the immediate physical circumstance, the sense of continuity offered is an illusion, a myth. Love may give the illusion of an instant which can be infinitely expanded, but it then becomes not so much history as fantasy. The human body is unable to sustain its mythic status, by which Loy means the abolition of, the escape from the deadening, destructive progression of time, into the archetypal, almost mathematical pattern of the universe:

> Ogni istante è come se dovessimo giungere al punto, al centro di quel misterioso disegno dove si diramano perfette le linee dell'esistenza.
> Ma il disegno sfugge, è sfuggito anche quel giorno, il punto si è allontanato e si è confuso [...] Adesso è finita, un'operazione rapida, indolore, il balenare di un lampo (forse il riflesso dell'orologio?), è arrivato a separare, tagliare, dividere. A rimettere ordine nel disordine, la ragione al posto del fantastico. Un lampo, e l'animale mitico è adesso solo una pelle vuota nel letto. (*L'estate di Letuché*, p. 56)

> Every instant is as if we were about to reach the point, the centre of that mysterious design from which the lines of existence spread out perfectly.
> But the design escapes us, it slipped away that day too, the point grew distant and confused [...] Now it's finished, a rapid, painless operation, a flash of light (a reflection of a watch perhaps?) come to separate, cut, divide. To restore order to disorder, put reason in place of the fanciful. A flash, and the mythic animal is now no more than an empty skin lying in the bed.

The narrator/protagonist seeks to restore the past through knowledge, through what Antonio sees as an intrusive appropriation of another person's experience. Knowledge of the past becomes a form of possession which for Antonio and his friend Carlo can be only fetishistic. The narrator seeks information about Antonio's father, a weak-willed fascist shot by Resistance fighters, about his past and present relationship with his friends Carlo and Alessandra, and about the figures who appear in a forgotten painting discovered at Antonio's house in the country. It seems that for Loy it is through the suggestion of objects that different strands of experience, past and present, can connect in an almost mystical, symbolic overlaying of images; these are moments when, as she puts it in words which might have come from Calvino, 'i piani si intersecano, le immagini si sovrappongono l'una sull'altra' (in interview) ('levels cross each other, images are superimposed one on to the other'). Whilst the geometrical rhetoric of crossing lines and planes may superficially resemble Calvino, Loy is in fact light years from his theories on the combinations of objects and figures as constitutive of a basic set of narrative possibilities. For Loy the superimposition and recurrence of images or objects offers the only continuity that can exist. Objects have the power to confer meaning, and even identity. Antonio has taken over the country-house of his friend Carlo: for the protagonist, it is almost as if he has *become* Carlo.

The recurring object which provides a kind of Ariadne's thread through the novel, connecting the discourse on a metaphorical level, is fruit, or rather apples, the symbolic fruit *par excellence*. They are mentioned repeatedly: the apples which the narrator's husband Paolo ate in the belief they contained a rejuvenating substance and which she disliked (a reversal perhaps of the story of Eve and her path to knowledge), the apple trees at Malimbrosia, the Pomeranian apples of the camp sergeant where Antonio was held prisoner during the war, Esther's apple jam. The apples recur as a motif, a reflection of a notion of continuity that has nothing to do with linear time, which resides in objects, and is metaphorical rather than realistic.

The effort to repair the past as if it were some worn object, to restore 'il gioco disfatto dal tempo' ('the game undone by time'), to restore memory and fix some moment of the past, is the urge which similarly underlies the collection of short stories, *All'insaputa della notte* (1984). What the stories have in common is nothing other than the fact that they all take place on the day that, unknown to the characters themselves, the Second World War broke out. To restore the past, unmediated by the present and in its entirety, is of course an enterprise which is always and already doomed to failure, as Loy herself says in the Introduction to the work:

> Quel giorno si è staccato dagli altri e come una mongolfiera è rimasto sospeso in aria, aspetta ancora una risposta [...] Il tempo ci sta spezzando in due: noi gli siamo in realtà superiori ma lui è più furbo [...] Questi nove racconti sono il modestissimo tentativo di eludere la sua mobilità. Di appuntarlo, di fermarlo nell'istante prima della grande notte. Ma si possono acchiappare delle farfalle e appuntarle sul cartone mentre volano, ancora vive? (*All'insaputa della notte*, p. 9)

> That day has separated itself from other days and like a balloon it has remained suspended in the air, still waiting for an answer [...] Time is splitting us in two: we are in reality above it, but time is cleverer [...] These nine stories are a very modest attempt to evade its mobility. To pin it down, to stop it at the moment before the great night. But is it possible to catch butterflies and pin them onto cardboard while they are flying, still alive?

Rosetta Loy's latest novel, *Le strade di polvere*, is her first work to have been translated into English. The novel is neither autobiographical nor concerned with childhood or the psychological development and trauma of individual contact with the world; nonetheless it is still very much concerned with the experience of time. The experimental language and syntax of earlier novels give way to a novel which, on the surface at least, follows more traditional narrative forms and structures, and indeed locates itself firmly in the nineteenth century with its references to Napoleon, Marengo, and public and civil struggles of the age. Yet this paradoxical novel, for all that it is set in the nineteenth century, is not in any sense a 'historical novel', in that it does not claim to be a fictionalized or imaginative account of a real set of circumstances. It tells the story, but not the history, of a family, and is much more than a family 'saga'. The characters of the novel are a family of agricultural workers in Piedmont, the land of Rosetta Loy's father and where she spent a large part of her own childhood. The book's dust-jacket describes it as a book about 'love, war, children, death. The time of desires which burn themselves up, of dances, of seasons, of youth, the cruel and magic moment of all that leaves no trace of itself'. In conversation Loy desecribes the genesis of the novel as a particular house in Piedmont much loved by her; once again, it is objects which provide the only guarantee of continuous existence through time. Loy describes her own work as:

> Un momento del tempo, visto attraverso una casa, ossia l'unica cosa reale, vera, concreta, tangibile. Il resto nasce da questa casa. Anche per quello ho mescolato quell'elemento fantastico, perchè la casa mi sembrava quasi magica. (In interview.)

> A moment of time, seen through a house, in other words the only thing which is real, true, concrete, tangible. Everything else arises out of this house. That's also why I mixed in the element of fantasy, because the house seemed to me almost magical.

This novel, whilst full of more or less clear and oblique references to the events of the past century (and Sacarlott, one of the principal characters, is a survivor of a number of its battles), seems to root itself in a kind of eternal present, where time is circular rather than linear, where death is not an end to things, where identity changes along with a person's name, where there are no clear boundaries or marked limits. With its view of time which appears to be monumental rather than progressive, the novel allies itself much more closely to the sweeping imagination of writers like Gabriel García Márquez (much admired by Loy) or Günther Grass than to most of Loy's contemporaries in Italy. While Loy employs the language of realism, the surface texture is consistently heightened by narrative strategies which turn the realistic form back onto itself and turn the linear into the circular, the progressive into the labyrinthine.

Identity in this novel is not a matter of temporality nor even of names, for these change along with the transformation of character as the result of experience, by the passage of time. The romantically disappointed Matelda becomes the needlework artist La Fantina who weaves her own story into her work; the object of her frustrated love, Giuseppe, is better known as the romantic musician Giai; Pietro, known more affectionately as Pidrèn, later becomes the tough, war-bitten Sacarlott; and, in the most grotesque change of all, the repressed Bastianina becomes Sister Gertrude Rosalia, known as the 'Magna Munja', the 'Great Nun'. For Sacarlott, a name cannot contain an existence, which must be constantly re-invented: not, as in existentialist thinking, because in the absence of a greater authority the individual must assume, minute by minute, responsibility for his or her being, but because there are no guaranteed causal connections between moments. Nothing will undermine 'la sua incrollabile convinzione che l'unico modo di salvarsi l'anima sia dimenticare quello che è stato' (*Le strade di polvere*, p. 25) ('his unshakeable conviction that the only way to save one's soul is to forget what has been').

Yet forgetting is hard: in his dying moment Sacarlott sits bolt upright in bed in horror, overcome with fear of the Cossacks encountered during the Napoleonic campaigns in Russia. Sacarlott is finally undone by what has been omitted or suppressed in his narrative; for Loy, the connecting threads of time continue to work even if we are unaware of them, or even if we would snap them off: the past continually returns to us. Similarly Sacarlott's sons, Luìs and Gavriel, are drawn to each other despite different temperaments, inclinations, and years of separation. When Luìs cheerfully abandons college and returns to the Piedmont farm, he finds his brother initially wary but fascinated:

> Ma quei fili che partivano dalla medesima stanza, dalle medesime canzoni della Gonda, dagli stessi odori e gli stessi suoni, gli stessi sapori, lo stesso tremore infantile alla voce del Sacarlott, avevano continuato invisibili il loro percorso, inavvertiti e ignorati anche da chi li aveva un tempo tenuti stretti fra le dita. (*Le strade di polvere*, p. 67)

> But those threads that started out from the same room, from Gonda's same old songs, from the same smells and sounds, the same childish trembling at Sacarlott's voice, had invisibly continued their route, unnoticed and ignored even by those who had once held them tight in their fingers.

Life is seen not as linear history but as variations on repeating patterns which take the form of circles or labyrinths. Existence does not end with death; Maria's first husband Giuseppe, known as Giai, continues after death to make his presence felt, as well as his feelings for his sister-in-law Matelda, by the mournful sound of his violin in the house and around the well; the spirit of the Gran Masten returns to give heart to his son who is struggling against a flood which is reminiscent of scenes such as the opening of Fogazzaro's *Piccolo mondo antico*. This is a world where it is the supernatural, the magic almost, which gives meaning: Marletteira, consecrated to the Virgin, has prophetic dreams to compensate for what she misses of more earthly pleasure, Matelda is credited with visionary gifts, and events are quickly turned into myth and legend. The young boy Gioacchino's fall from the roof is an apotheosis of the transforming power of myth:

> Era volato giù senza un grido. Lentamente, ondeggiando, i capelli fini e lisci che fluttuavano nell'aria, le ali della giacchetta marrone. Così lo avevano visto la Fantina e lo Scarvé venuto a chiedere i soldi per la riparazione del tetto. Non era un corpo che cadeva avevano detto, era una piuma che volava e volava e

non la finiva mai come se quel fienile fosse stato più alto della torre di San Giorgio. Volava senza peso, bianco come la cera. (*Le strade di polvere*, p. 56)

He had flown down without a cry. Slowly, floating, his fine, smooth hair fluttering in the air, his short brown jacket like wings. This is how Fantina saw him, and Scarvé, who had come to ask for money to mend the roof. It wasn't a body falling, they had said, but a feather that flew and flew and seemed never to stop as if that hayloft had been higher than the tower of San Giorgio. He flew without weight, white as wax.

This is comparable to the scene of the assumption of Remedios, in Márquez's *One Hundred Years of Solitude*. Other moments recall the South American writer too, in the intensity of images which express simultaneously themselves, as well as a series of relationships in the world, and an emotional and intellectual response. Art, the creation of images, has the ambiguous power to both move and to destroy, and the artists in this novel are women. Bastianina's paintings earn her respect but also fear; the priest's cassock embroidered by the skilful Matelda, a whole narrative of local life, belief, and despair, almost burns his back with its startling brightness, and the voice of Rosetta del Fracin in church scandalizes as it enchants.

On his return from the wars Sacarlott's body was covered in scars: 'ognuna aveva un nome, ricordavano sulla sua pelle foreste e fiumi, campi e bivacchi' (*Le strade di polvere*, p. 21), ('and each scar had a name, recalled on his skin forests and rivers, fields and bivouacs'). This episode recalls in its turn Herbert Truczinski in Günther Grass's novel *The Tin Drum*; Truczinski's own back is a mass of weals, each of them a self-contained and complete narrative. Here again, as also in Franz Kafka's short story, 'In the Penal Colony', history is literally written into flesh, to be read and decoded. History is no abstract concept for Loy, but a cyclical recurrence of events which inscribe themselves into the material body of individual lives. Whilst Loy does not share the passionate political commitment of Márquez or Grass, and whilst her view of time, identity and narrative functions on a psychological and local rather than epic level, in this latest novel she shares something of their ability to transform the real.

In *Le strade di polvere* considerations of time and identity are set free from the constraints and conventions of 'real' time, and emerge into a narrative space which no longer situates itself at a specific juncture of self and history. With the adoption of a narrative technique which recalls the structure and formation of nineteenth-century narrative even while it undermines the beliefs about the world which informed them, Loy is not being ironic. The reversion to more traditional narrative forms suggests a perception that the novel is inadequate or insufficient for investigating the phenomenological relationship of self to the world or that such an investigation is no longer pertinent. Much Italian writing of the 1980s stresses the ludic qualities of narrative in a move away from the view of fiction as an essentially 'realistic' reflection and critique of the social context; Loy's move away from more experimental strategies and syntax, adopted to cut open the babushka doll to reveal the figures hiding inside, paradoxically underlines her attention to surface form, in a text in which the story becomes paramount.

Loy is a writer surprised by her own success, which after all came only with her latest novel, *Le strade di polvere*. She continues to be an intensely personal writer, even though the autobiographical element of her work is now, she says, 'hidden'. It is Loy's own struggle with the dialectic of the past, on the one hand, as harsh reality, and on the other, as a more or less nostalgic fiction, which pervades all her work, whatever its setting. She is a writer who has struggled through to a style and a form of fiction unique in recent Italian literature, one which connects her work on the level of narrative to European and South American writers, even while her texts recount stories and experiences which are quintessentially Italian.

BIBLIOGRAPHY

Works

La bicicletta (Turin: Einaudi, 1974).
La porta dell'acqua (Turin: Einaudi 1976).
L'estate di Letuchè (Milan: Rizzoli, 1982).
All'insaputa della notte (Milan: Garzanti, 1984).
Le strade di polvere (Turin: Einaudi, 1987). Translated by William Weaver as *The Dust Roads of Monferrato*, (London: Fontana, 1991).

Interview

Unpublished interview with Rosetta Loy by Sharon Wood, Rome, January 1991.

Chapter 9

Giuliana Morandini
Outer and Inner Frontiers

ELVIO GUAGNINI

Giuliana Morandini is a writer who cannot readily be categorized as belonging to any particular literary movement, even though her thematic and artistic interests clearly reflect contemporary concerns and issues. A possible reason for her independence is that she has remained faithful to a precise set of related ideological preoccupations rather than pursuing formal innovation or succumbing to the dictates of literary fashion. The serious nature of her interests is confirmed by her dual vocation as a novelist and as a critic and essayist. In this latter guise, Morandini has principally focused on the culture of *Mitteleuropa*, on Triestine literature, on the relationship between literature and psychoanalysis, and on women's writing. Her most significant contributions in this area are her investigation into women's mental hospitals (*... e allora mi hanno rinchiusa*, 1977), in which patients recount their experiences; an anthology of late nineteenth- and early twentieth-century Italian women's fiction (*La voce che è in lei*, 1980); and a collection of writings on Triestine culture (*Da te lontano*, 1989).

However, the true measure of Morandini's standing as a writer is provided by her three novels: *I cristalli di Vienna* (1978), *Caffè Specchi* (1983), and *Angelo a Berlino* (1987), for which she was awarded, respectively, the Premio Prato Letteratura, the Premio Viareggio, and the Premio Selezione Campiello.

Morandini's first novel, *I cristalli di Vienna*, as is evident from its title, is structured around the interplay between metaphorical and realistic elements (the latter enriched with autobiographical allusions). The central image of crystal glass with its reflections and refractions varying with the intensity of the incoming light, and with the delicacy and fragility of its beauty, seems to allude both to the heroine's spiritual predicament and to the novel's historical situation: an image which suggests both nostalgia for a lost world and the devastation and upheaval caused by the violence of war. The title also evokes Vienna, the city where the heroine conjures up memories of her childhood; the city which produced those crystal glasses; a city of mythical enchantment; the city of Biedermeier but equally the city whose cathedral decorations evoke the precarious grotesque grandeur of history:

Pinnacoli, fregi, sculture, colonne, si erano schiusi da parti insensati. Gronde muschiose ghignavano con bocche deformi. Neri, grigi, bianchi calcinati screziavano le pietre corrose. L'orgia di immagini aveva i riflessi dei rettili quando si sollevano dal letargo e intrecciano accoppiamenti crudeli. Sgomenti, trionfi, oscenità premevano nello scatto delle guglie e degli archi. Le decorazioni attorcigliate sembravano sul punto di riprendere a strisciare, la gloria della costruzione poteva franare d'improvviso nelle schegge'della propria storia. Profeti, scheletri, santi, animali composti da un mosaico di orrori ripetevano il grido di genealogie malate. Su tutto le mani della morte. Urlavano invocazioni e bestemmie, e si piegavano solo al rigore di una parola che possedeva i nervi delle pietre e assolveva ogni gesto, anche se alzato sulla natura e sulla storia. Nell'ordine fiammeggiante si respirava ogni violenza, si incidevano assassini. (*I cristalli di Vienna*, pp. 159–60)

Pinnacles, friezes, sculptures, columns had sprung forth, crazily engendered. Mossy eaves leered through misshapen mouths. Black, grey and white incrustations bespeckled the eroding stones. The orgy of images shimmered like reptiles stirring from slumber to entwine in cruel embraces. Terrors, triumphs, obscenities teemed in the surge of the spires and arches. The coiled ornaments seemed about to slither into motion, the splendour of the building might suddenly fragment into the splinters of its own history. Prophets, skeletons, saints, animals – a mosaic of horrors – echoed the cry of diseased lineages. On everything the hands of death. Oaths and invocations rang out, only silenced by the power of a word which bewitched the nerves of the stones and absolved every gesture, even those made against nature and history. In the fiery order, every kind of violence was inhaled, murders were engraved.

The novel tells the story of a visit to Vienna by Elsa, a young actress, whose difficult and complicated wartime childhood there is relived in the book. But the account of the trip to Vienna only serves as a frame – albeit an important one – in which a crucial formative experience is reconsidered. The journey across Friuli toward Vienna and the conversation in German with a stranger travelling in the same compartment introduce the novel's real journey of discovery. This begins at Elsa's family home near Udine and with her childhood games, and moves out toward the complex relationships within her family, her own feelings, and the peculiar domestic voyeurism she liked to perform from a hidden vantage-point overlooking the dining-room, the hub of domestic life:

Giocare a rimpiattino, trovare un posto dove osservare e trattenere il respiro, isolarsi per tenere gli occhi chiusi e fantasticare e mangiare qualcosa di tutto suo, erano le sue occcupazioni preferite. Gioiva di poter avventurarsi nel mondo e vederlo e imparare a conoscerlo senza cadere lei stessa nella trappola d'essere guardata dagli altri. Le piaceva, come appunto nel caso della sala da pranzo, vedere da un posto scuro le cose e le persone in luce. (*I cristalli di Vienna*, p. 22)

Playing hide-and-seek, finding a place where she could watch and hold her breath, secluding herself so she could keep her eyes shut and dream and eat something all her own: these were her favourite past-times. She loved being able to venture through the world and see it and get to know it without herself

falling into the trap of being observed by anyone else. And, as was just the case
with the dining-room, she liked to see, from a dark place, people and things in
the light.

It is from this vantage point that the child, who is both rational and fanciful, bold
and capricious, timid and proud, possessed – at one and the same time – of a
delicate sensibility and all the ferocity of a potential avenger, witnesses a
macabre, half-orgiastic, half-mystical rite conducted by the high-ranking German officers who have partly requisitioned her home. This ceremony takes
place during an important dinner, where the table is set with priceless, looted
crockery and a precious set of family glasses (the 'Vienna crystals'), kept hidden
until that moment, but which the Germans have insisted on using for their
singular *soirée*. The rite revolves around Iudith, a Jewish girl, who, while still
being prepared for the grim erotic ceremony, is killed in an air-raid which
destroys part of the house. Both the Germans and reality as a whole take on a
radically different complexion for the child after she is repeatedly assailed by the
'fever of evil', first as a result of the events of the evening and the air-raid, and
then as a consequence of further acts of violence: 'la violenza che scomponeva il
mondo spezzettava la sua intimità, dilatava le sue incertezze, la confondeva sino
a farla sentire perduta' ('the violence that was devastating the world shattered her
privacy, magnified her uncertainties, bewildered her until she felt entirely lost').
Thus a Nazi reprisal – the execution of five hostages – comes to symbolize for
Elsa a cruelty 'che rimaneva a sostegno di un'ambizione fallita' (*I cristalli*, p. 118)
('that propped up a failed ambition'). It represents yet another encounter with
death and suffering, with a callous indifference which the end of the war cannot
erase, and which contact with nature only serves to bolster:

> Gli uccelli beccavano sicuri gli insetti, i ragni tessevano lenti e implacabili, gli
> animali cercavano prede e il ronzio della natura pareva a volte un'enorme
> trappola. (*I cristalli di Vienna*, p. 145)

> Birds pecked relentlessly at insects, spiders slowly and unfalteringly wove their
> webs, animals hunted for prey and at times the hum of nature seemed one huge
> snare.

Changes in her own nature, the unavoidable physiological processes of
puberty, likewise signal the end of an era and the biological submission to a
woman's role.

> Altre ferite dovevano in seguito incidere in lei distanze più nette, alimentare
> insicurezza e impaccio, farle pesare nello scorrere dell'esistenza una costrizione
> tenace. Tuttavia quel sangue così scuro e così pronto a coagularsi con quello di
> Iudith, del ragazzo tedesco, dei cinque uomini sulla piazza, rimase per Elsa uno
> dei segni che il tempo può appannare ma che nel fondo di ogni emozione con
> prepotenza riaffiorano. (*I cristalli di Vienna*, p. 152)

> Further wounds were to carve out ever greater tracts within her, stoke her
> awkwardness and insecurity, make her feel an implacable constraint bearing

down upon her as her life progressed. Yet, that blood of hers, so dark and so ready to clot with that of Iudith, of the German boy, of the five men in the square, remained, for Elsa, one of those marks time can efface but which re-emerge with all their force at the bottom of every emotion.

And her encounters in Vienna, her journey's end, provide another opportunity to look back and achieve an understanding of her childhood traumas, re-evoked in nightmare visions which are portrayed in a sombre yet vivid expressionistic style pervaded by a sense of solitude and fear. In these pages where, in Giulio Cattaneo's words, the narrative 'is entrusted to the heroine's gaze' and to her 'slow recognition', Antonio Porta is quite right to claim that 'childhood and pre-adolescent sexuality' emerge as the 'hidden themes of the novel'. But this concern does not exhaust the meaning of a text which explores the mechanisms behind a complex discovery of reality, and of the 'ambiguous relationships that govern the grown-up world'. *I cristalli di Vienna* ultimately affirms the courage required to get to the bottom of life, to be, as Francesco Paolo Memmo puts it, 'always, and in whatever situation, an eye-witness to one's own history and that of others'. Morandini herself described the difficult process behind the writing of this novel:

> Le parole scivolavano indolenzite, fermavano queste improvvise infiammazioni della memoria. Come nel sogno ci si riconosce in diverse figure, così mi riusciva difficile sapere se il mio occhio era incollato allo spioncino del nascondiglio o se cercava l'alba con gli occhi dei fucilati. L'infanzia inquieta e la città mitteleuropea del silenzio, che sembrava più Mal Strana che Vienna, stringevano eventi della storia e vicende intime negli stessi nodi. Con questo dolore ma anche con questa consapevolezza ho ripercorso l'antica ferita. (*La Stampa*)

> Words slid along painfully, fixed each sudden kindling of memory. As in a dream where you recognize yourself in different figures at the same time, I found it hard to make out whether my eye was glued against the peephole of Elsa's hiding-place or if it was watching out for the dawn like the eyes of the condemned hostages. The troubled childhood and the central-European city which seemed more like Mala Strana than Vienna, bound historical events and personal memories together in the same knot. With this pain but also this awareness, I reopened the old wound.

The novel is characterized by the embedding of different points of view and perspectives, a device which Enrico Ghidetti sees as contrasting 'analytical and evocative tones' with 'sudden fevered lyrical flights', 'childhood memory' with 'adult understanding', thereby creating a tension which ensures 'the authentic feel of a confession'. It is this tension, furthermore, which is the source of the novel's vivid and articulate style, a style which is ideally suited to a work which contrasts the lively sensibility of the child with the calm restrained lucidity of the adult.

Morandini's second novel, *Caffè Specchi*, has prompted more than one critic to feel that 'we are entitled to ask ourselves whether the heroine's personal baggage might not conceal, beneath a double bottom, autobiographical truths'. But it is quite clear that, as Enrico Ghidetti goes on to point out, 'compared to Elsa in *I cristalli di Vienna*, right from the start the heroine seems rarified as if the author did not seek her out directly but via an illusory game of mirrors'. Once again, Morandini has chosen a suggestively evocative title. A Caffè Specchi actually exists in Trieste, and the heroine frequents the city's cafés where events and conversations central to the plot take place. However, the idea of mirrors can also allude to the heroine's nature, to a view of reality, and to its representation in the novel. The plot as such is fairly slender, so that it almost seems to be, in Giovanni Giudici's words, 'up to the readers themselves, if they so wish, to piece episodes together into a coherent *fabula*; or else surrender to them as if time and space did not exist, live off them and let them reflect insoluble anxieties'.

The heroine, Katharina Pollaczek, a young woman of Slav origin brought up in Trieste, returns to the city in order to apply for custody of her son Friedrich, from whom she has become separated after her mentally-disturbed husband had deserted her. The narrative charts her wanderings through the streets of Trieste (never explicitly named but clearly recognizable), her encounters with enigmatic characters, and her accidental involvement in events which deeply disturb her (for instance, her arrival at the scene of the murder of a young Serbian woman). She is equally disturbed by the volatile, unstable atmosphere of the decaying, once-great trading centre, which nevertheless still exerts a fascination through its racial and linguistic mix, through its atmosphere of expectation and timelessness. The narrative itself is left suspended, its conclusion left untold. Yet, in the final chapter we find Katharina far away from the ambiguous and somewhat sinister environment of *Mitteleuropa*, across the sea, in Algeria, in a new world, as indecipherable as the old one, but where, perhaps, a new freedom may be achieved.

From one point of view, the novel seems to reiterate the most hackneyed, canonical themes of Mitteleuropean literature, typical of the voguish nostalgia for this tradition apparent in the early 1980s. On the other hand, its ostentatiously flaunted repertoire of traditional themes and settings is reworked in a novel fashion, as if to test whether these can still serve to explore problems of identity and an enigmatic, crisis-ridden universe. The novel is not a pretext for Katharina to take us on a guided tour of Mitteleuropean common-places, a trip around a museum-city. Thus, traditional *topoi* are highlighted expressionistically, serving as emblems of a manifold, mysterious reality – symbols both of past splendour and of present decay. They are the signs of a city whose tangled knot of historical problems is almost inextricable, given the disparity and indecipherability of its individual strands, a place where even monuments 'are isolated' and have 'an artificial layout' (p. 54). Perhaps only a world such as that created by

Morandini – variegated and picturesque, enigmatic and ever-changing, where all kinds of unexpected meetings take place and different languages are spoken – could provide the setting for *Caffè Specchi*, which, rather than explore a place, explores a character out to discover both her own past and her present nature. The people, the places, the weather, the encounters Katharina has in the city are like so many fragments of her own life-story and of the identity she wishes to recover. However, precisely because all she has are fragments, pieces of a jigsaw that life and history have scattered far and wide, she has difficulty recomposing them, an operation which at least in the society in which she finds herself, is impossible. For it is a society which, like its history, is as multi-layered and impenetrable as the white-washed walls of Katharina's hotel room:

> La camera d'albergo era stata solo ripulita, non aveva conosciuto pittori ma imbianchini frettolosi. Sì, tinta su tinta fa risparmiare colore, si usa dire. E la tinta si ispessisce sempre più. Le tinte sono come la storia. Si scrive sopra, su tutto, righe nere coprono i fatti ... und Gott stehe uns bei. Si sgretolano gli stucchi e le pareti si staccano, farà parte dell'inevitabile. Importa salvare le apparenze, si dà una pulitura sommaria. Quanto si mostra non è quello che è, come nei migliori assassinii, il volto di chi li ordina non si conosce, perché nulla si trasformi. (*Caffè Specchi*, p. 9)

> The hotel room had only been redaubed, it had never seen a real decorator, just hurried whitewashers. Yes, coat upon coat saves on colour, they say. And the dye grows ever thicker. Its layers are like history. You write on top of it, all over it, black lines cover up the facts ... und Gott stehe uns bei. Plaster crumbles, walls fall apart, it's all part of the inevitable. But appearances have got to be kept up, another coat hastily applied. Nothing is quite how it seems, like in all the best murders, and you never see the face of whoever has them carried out – so that nothing ever changes.

Similarly, places and situations are symbolic, as indeed is the landscape.

> Nel cielo gonfio e teso al limite, solchi scuri, vene di stagno e piombo, percorrevano la volta violacea, disegnavano in tutte le direzioni i diagrammi della bufera. Le nubi si dividevano in una mappa governata da campi magnetici [...] La bora si avvicinava, caricava il paesaggio con potenza. Non la si vedeva; la si riconosceva dalle case, dai tetti dove entrava da padrona [...] Si mascherava da strega folle d'orgasmo mentre puliva e ripuliva la piazza del mercato. Il selciato luccicava come calvizie e le raffiche lasciavano dietro la loro rabbia un vuoto bianco. (*Caffè Specchi*, pp. 12–13)

> In the taut, swollen sky, dark furrows, veins of tin and lead, crossed the violet panoply, tracing the chart of the storm in all directions. Clouds split into a map governed by magnetic fields. [...] The tempest was approaching, charging at the landscape with all its might. It could not be seen but could be sensed from the houses, from the rooftops of which it took possession [...] Disguised as an orgiastic witch, time and time again it swept the market-place. The paving shimmered like a bald head and the squalls left a white void in the wake of their fury.

The book abounds with such evocative passages; and Morandini's love of imagery enables her to capture inner landscapes, and attempt an impossible rejoining of the various and conflicting moments of past and present. Such images are ubiquitous – even in the café, the observation of a drop of milk on the table seems to turn this into a hospital furnishing or a mortuary slab:

> La goccia di latte versato sul marmo si era divisa. Due gocce candide come pupille la guardavano dal piano verde, e la mano dell'uomo in camice si alzò puntando il dito, gridava il suo nome, gli occhi non erano raggi di luna ma lame. (*Caffè Specchi,* p. 15)

> The drop of milk spilt on the marble had split into two. Two candid drops watched her like pupils from the green surface, and the white-coated man raised his hand pointing his finger and shouted out her name; his eyes were not moon-beams but blades.

Katharina's eyes which are 'too bright', her extreme sensitivity to light, and her fear of blindness are all emblematic of a hypersensitive inner vision, a state of anguish and fear which leads her to see, in the fragmentation and decay of the outer world, the parallels with her own crisis. In this respect, *Caffè Specchi* is not just another book constructed out of modish, canonical components, but an uncomfortable novel, rich in suspense and only occasionally touched by moments of irony which almost seem designed to highlight the artificiality of the settings within which Katharina moves. Far from presenting a nostalgically embroidered vision of the past, the text closes with a comparison of different cultures, the old world and the new, one at its twilight, the other at its dawning and waiting to be discovered.

To some extent, *Angelo a Berlino* returns to and expands upon the themes of the two earlier novels. The book tells the story of a young woman, Erika Kunze von Bassewitz, who moves from East to West Berlin with a study grant received almost by chance (though nothing, the novel constantly reminds us, ever happens by chance) in order to conduct research in two areas. The first concerns the layout of Berlin, the original town-plan, the policies of the elector of Brandenburg, Friedrich Wilhelm, and the architectural choices of Karl Friedrich Schinkel. The second involves the fate of scores by Brahms and by Beethoven bizarrely split into vocal parts on one side and instrumental ones on the other between the two halves of the city: a symbol of its division and a spur to, and portent of, its reconciliation and reunification.

Erika, too, comes from a divided family and a divided region, Mecklenburg. Her mother Sophie, an ex-pianist, has had severe mental problems. Her family, of aristocratic stock, has been forced to leave its home and estates, since they were in an area which, after the war, was transferred to Poland. Erika and her sister Ulrike, in fact, have had a Polish nanny; and it is in Polish that Ulrike records her passionate affairs in diaries whose powerful erotic charge disturbs

Erika, bringing her face to face with the problem of love and sex. Exile from land and property lies at the root of another trauma: the loss of contact with nature and, at the same time, with a natural way of life. The psychological inhibitions which condition Erika's behaviour arise from her physically divided family, from her mother's mysterious love-life and illness, and from the death of Ulrike, gunned down on the border after making love to a Soviet soldier. Erika, at first, eschews all emotional and sexual contact, then gives herself over entirely to the discovery of her own identity, to an exploration of family history, and to the arduous task of piecing together broken fragments of a lost whole. At the same time, the story of Erika's personal search is accompanied by the novel's complementary investigation of Berlin and of Germany.

With this combination of subject-matter, Giuliana Morandini takes up themes already examined in important works by German writers such as Uwe Johnson and Christa Wolf. But Mario Spinella has rightly pointed out that, where in books like *Mutmassungen über Jakob* and *Der geteilte Himmel*, 'the wound appeared more immediate, the cut still fresh', Morandini lends her novel 'the dense texture of memory, binding past and present into a tight knot of implications'. Morandini's treatment of the city is also personal. 'For Erika,' in the words of Massimo de Angelis, 'or indeed for any German, Berlin cannot be unknown. It is *the* city, *home*,' and, as such, Erika's tale represents a 'gradual homecoming, a return to the past [...] and, via the past, the piecing back together of an identity, both personal and historical'. Berlin, moreover, in the author's own words 'è un luogo di nevralgica attualità per la coscienza d'Europa, e più per la nostra coscienza di moderni' (*Il Gazzettino*) ('is a nerve centre for European consciousness and, even more so, for the consciousness of modern man'). It is an emblematic microcosm of Europe in other respects too: an amalgam of devastation and the will to rebuild, of rubble and grandeur, however tarnished by war and history, where the indigenous population rubs shoulders with immigrants of every kind, and where a new mass culture is steadily taking over, provoking alienation, rejection, abnormal and unhealthy growth, strange hybrids and interbreeding.

If the city is one of the novel's central themes, the others are the angel of the title and the border. So who or what is this emblematic 'angel'? On the most literal level, it is the statue of an angel on a bridge over the Elbe at Dresden, a city completely destroyed by Allied bombing during the Second World War. It is also, however, Walter Benjamin's 'angel of history' from *Geschichtes-philosophische Thesen* (1940) which is recalled in the novel's epigraph:

> The angel of history keeps his face turned towards the past. Where we see a chain of events, he sees a single catastrophe relentlessly piling ruin upon ruin and heaping them at his feet. He would dearly like to halt it, waken the dead, put the fragments back together. But a wind-storm is raging from heaven, is caught up on his wings and is so strong that he can no longer fold them. This

storm is driving him inexorably towards the future, to which his back is turned, while, before him, the pile of ruins rises ever further into the sky. What we call progress is this storm.

It is a symbol, then, of a complex, dramatic view of history. But the angel is also Erika herself, who by crossing the border and recomposing traces of her own identity, sets out to reconstruct a devastated reality.

The book's interest in the border is explored with a clear awareness of what a border can actually represent – a wound, a laceration, a trauma – as is quite clear from its opening pages:

> Era sempre una strana emozione passare una frontiera. Da bambina provava un certo eccitamento quando la sballottavano da un paese all'altro. Attraversava il confine a piedi, attenta alla differenza vaga tra un terreno e l'altro. Ora, passare il confine significava provare quanto la città stesse vivendo la divisione, una ferita che non rimarginava [...] Qualche piccola pianta cercava di crescere tra due pietre, accanto a una finestra murata alla meglio con mattoni e sassi accumulati. Le pietre erano servite di appoggio a una mitragliatrice e la casa di fronte, rimasta dall'altra parte, era butterata dalle raffiche; una faccia inguaribile, per un vaiolo preso in gioventù, quando il tessuto è delicato e l'infezione lascia fori più grandi. (*Angelo a Berlino*, pp. 5–6)

> Passing over a border was always a strange feeling. As a child, she had felt a certain thrill whenever she had been jolted from one country to the next. She used to cross the frontier on foot, alert to the vague difference between one terrain and the other. Now passing over the frontier meant sensing how sharply the city felt its own division, a wound that would not heal [...] A few tiny plants were striving to grow between two lumps of rock, next to a window haphazardly walled up with piles of bricks and stones. The lumps of rock had been used as a machine-gun rest and the house opposite, left on the other side, was pockmarked with bullets; an incurable face, devastated by a childhood attack, when the skin is delicate and the pox leaves deeper scars.

The border is also the place where Ulrike and the Soviet soldier, Ghiori, make love, a further symbolic, enigmatic event in the novel. Ghiori represents another culture – the peasant world of the East which war has summoned forth – and violently grafted on to an urban society with a different system of ideas and a different way of life. In the erotic quest which costs Ulrike her life, she braves death almost out of sheer curiosity to learn what it means to make contact with this alien world. Thus, as Massimo De Angelis says, Russia 'is constantly there in the background, it is the chapter that has yet to be written, in the same way as the rediscovery of a German identity cannot be separated from its relationship with Europe and, to a great extent, with Russia itself. Otherwise fear will never be overcome'. In the novel, the border *is* a wound cutting through the heart of the city, a scar traced by its tragic history. At the same time, the border is the city: a complex organism whose past Erika is able to relive thanks to an elderly scholar who specializes in archaeology and town-planning. She has been sent to him to receive supervision in her research, but reaches him only after experiencing the contradictions and mysteries the city has to offer. Among her most significant encounters are those with an enigmatic young Turkish woman for whom Erika feels a powerful, even physical, attraction, and with a general's widow, xenophobic and bitterly opposed to the changes which have transformed her city, who manically defends her own identity by constantly and obsessively moving and rearranging furniture. The meeting with Leopold, the elderly scholar, also turns out to be highly significant, as Erika gradually learns of his relationship with her mother, and of the times Ulrike, too, visited him.

This multi-layered novel is marked by constant changes of scene, shifts of perspective, the magnification of details, and the intersection of different levels. These formal characteristics correspond to Morandini's intricate interweaving of family and individual case-histories, of past and present, and of different atmospheres and settings: interiors and exteriors, childhood landscapes and metaphorical transformations, emblematic and symbolic places – like the abattoir with its reminders of recent tragedies – and equally symbolic meeting-places where different cultures and ways of life come into contact: the bar with its bizarre puppet-show and its Turkish immigrants where Erika strives once again to disentangle the mysteries in which she is enmeshed.

Erika reacts with extreme sensitivity not only to the smells, noises and bodies which surround her, but also to the various aspects of the city and its history. Although she is a mass of conditioned responses and psychological problems waiting to be resolved, she is still capable of perceiving and interpreting reality with great lucidity. Her observations and conversations give rise to penetrating reflections on themes which, within the overall economy of the novel, acquire a wider significance. Thus, she comments on architecture's relationship to history and politics, on the notion of history as an idea and as truth, on the meaning of museums, on harmony and discord in life, on beauty and its torment, and on the social function of art. The following passage is typical of this aspect of the novel:

> 'Quell'edificio – le disse d'un tratto il direttore – l'ha costruito Gropius. È pieno della bellezza del Rinascimento e della ragione del nostro secolo ... Poco più in là – aggiunse – si torturavano delle persone che avevano il torto di parlare ... Un inferno di voci dietro la casa rossa e oro'. (*Angelo a Berlino*, p. 117)

> 'That building,' the director said to her all of a sudden, 'was built by Gropius. It's full of the beauty of the Renaissance and the rationality of our century ... A little further that way,' he added, 'they used to torture people who'd committed the crime of talking ... . An inferno of voices behind the red and gold house'.

In the divided and devastated city, Erika acts out her neuroses, phobias and repressed desires, and thereby comes to know the various layers of her personality. Despite a declared interest in psychoanalysis, Giuliana Morandini makes sparing use of technical terms in presenting her heroine's psychological drama. Psychoanalytic notions may underpin the narrative at many points, but they are always translated into action, so as not to weigh down the story with the language of theory.

Overall, the novel is an account of a discovery of the ways of the world: a discovery of how historical wounds may be healed, of how mass culture, for all its vulgarity, may represent an opportunity for contact and integration. And it also becomes the discovery of how eclecticism, kitsch, the architecturally heterogeneous may all be signs of vitality, of an urge to grow and explore – like the energy shown by the young people in a co-operative engaged in a strange and inventive reconstruction of war-damaged buildings along the frontier. Erika's encounter with this group and her love for Thomas – the architect who has given up his personal academic research to take part in a project which pushes back boundaries in every sense of the term – reveals to her that preserving one's own identity must not undermine one's efforts to live in the world and bear witness to the meeting of different peoples, tastes and generations.

The city comes to symbolize this complex attempt to piece life back together with the most varied of materials; an attempt which, by suggesting that the world is still inhabitable, is attractive in its very precariousness. From this perspective, Morandini may be seen to be both sifting through precious archaeological discoveries and bringing to light the vulgar and trivial charm of the everyday. She can be said to be drawing up a balance sheet both of the old and exhausted generations and of the new and young ones waiting to see things with their own eyes. The city, described in a rich variety of stylistic registers, is the point at which the debris and the raw materials of history are compacted together. It is a crossroads where different worlds converge, and where there is no turning back, no way to shake off the dust of history and war. It is a place where the museum, which preserves and legitimizes history, is at odds with the city, which transforms everything that comes into its sphere of influence. Thus, books, as Thomas puts it, 'pretendono di assegnare un posto alle cose' ('presume to assign things a place'), in contrast to the city streets which 'le mostrano come sono' ('show them as they are').

Like her other novels, *Angelo a Berlino* goes beyond its immediate subject-matter and setting. It deals with the dissolution of the past, with the need to remember with clarity, with the sheer precariousness of the present, and with the relationship between mass culture and historical memory. It ponders, finally, like Morandini's other books on the courage needed to overcome the pain of living; that same courage which conquers, in both the inner and outer worlds, new prospects for life and freedom.

Translated by Paul Barnaby

BIBLIOGRAPHY

Works

... *e allora mi hanno rinchiusa* (Milan: Bompiani, 1977; 1985).
I cristalli di Vienna (Milan: Bompiani, 1978; 1989). Translated by Blossom S.
  Kirchenbaum as *Blood Stains* (St Paul, Minnesota: New Rivers Press, 1987), not
  cited.
La voce che è in lei. Antologia della narrativa italiana tra '800 e '900 (Milan: Bompiani,
  1980).
Caffè Specchi (Milan: Bompiani, 1983).
Angelo a Berlino (Milan: Bompiani, 1987).
Da te lontano. Cultura triestina tra '700 e '900 (Trieste: Edizioni Dedolibri, 1989).
Since this chapter was completed, Morandini has published a fourth novel, *Sogno a
  Herrenberg* (Milan: Bompiani, 1991).

Reviews

Cattaneo, G., in *La Repubblica*, 30 June 1978.
Porta, A., in *Corriere della Sera*, 9 July 1978.
Memmo, F. P., in *Paese Sera*, 16 July 1978.
Ghidetti, E., in *Rinascita*, 21 July 1978, and 16 September 1983.
Giudici, G., in *L'Espresso*, 17 April 1983.
Giovanardi, S., in *La Repubblica*, 15 April 1987.
De Angelis, M., in *Rinascita*, 25 April 1987.
Spinella, M., in *Alfabeta*, 101, November 1987.

Interviews

La Stampa, 21 July 1978.
Il Gazzettino, 25 March 1987.

Chapter 10

Roberto Pazzi
Dialogues of History and Fantasy

PHILIP COOKE

After many years of relative obscurity as a little-known, but well-respected poet, Roberto Pazzi took the Italian literary world by storm in 1985 when he published his first prose work, *Cercando l'imperatore*. Since then, Pazzi has written another four novels, *La principessa e il drago* (1986), *La malattia del tempo* (1987), *Vangelo di Giuda* (1989), and most recently, *La stanza sull'acqua* (1991).

Pazzi's novels have attracted critical attention for their imaginative and captivating stories, for their bold experimentation in structure and style, and for their interesting blend of literature and philosophy. They have appealed to widely differing sections of the reading public; *Vangelo di Giuda* was highly praised by high-brow critics, but also won the Grinzane-Cavour prize, whose selection jury is made up entirely of students.

The success of his prose works has meant that Pazzi has, by and large, stopped producing poetry. His long years of poetical apprenticeship have, nonetheless left their mark on his writing. His prose often reads like poetry, and with a little imagination it is frequently possible to divide sentences in his narrative writing into free verse. Furthermore, occasional phrases and even whole sentences drawn from his earlier poems reappear in his novels. For example, the phrase 'l'esperienza anteriore' (p. 67) ('the anterior experience') which appears in his second novel, *La principessa e il drago*, is the title of his first published collection of verse. It is almost as if Pazzi is trying to rewrite or rework his poetic experience in a different form.

As a result of this reworking, there are many thematic similarities between his poetry and his prose. Both corpora deal extensively with time, history and memory and tend to depict individuals as solitary and impenetrable. However, it would be wrong to assume that Pazzi has undergone little or no change in his outlook, that he is simply rehashing tired old ideas. Pazzi has progressed, and his work has consistently moved in new and interesting directions. Unlike his poetry, his prose work demonstrates a growing interest in philosophy. After *Cercando l'imperatore* which contains a critique of existentialism, Pazzi makes a conscious attempt in *La principessa e il drago* and *La malattia del tempo* to expound a pessimistic philosophy derived from, amongst others, Schopenhauer, Nietzsche and Polybius. However, this attempt to fuse disciplines has, I think, led him into a number of problems, for, whilst he is a gifted and highly talented storyteller, it is far from certain whether he is as strong a philosopher. Pazzi's third novel, *La malattia del tempo*, best demonstrates his strengths and weaknesses.

Set in the near future, *La malattia del tempo* describes the conquests of Aiku, a Mongol warrior, who, armed with a selection of nuclear and chemical weapons, soon manages to dominate half the world. When his army reaches the shores of the Po at Ferrara, he puts a stop to the slaughter and calls a congress at Vienna. Gradually the whole world begins to slip back in time to the date of the first congress of Vienna, 1815. Unconcerned by this strange time-warp, Aiku marries an Austrian princess, only to find himself stranded on an island during his honeymoon when supplies of fossil fuels dry up. Meanwhile Halley, the President of America's chief adviser, sets out into the desert in his car. There he meets his ancestor Edmund Halley, the discoverer of the famous comet, and realizes that he will become the next Aiku, accompanied by an army of blindly faithful soldiers who will follow him on yet another conquest of the world.

The novel's ending underlines the main thesis of the work – the cyclical nature of history, the sickness of time. Yet, while *La malattia del tempo* tells a fascinating story, its central philosophical argument, that history is repetitive, though one shared by an alarmingly large number of intellectuals, is as unoriginal as it is unpersuasive. We simply have to look at the fantastic improvements in medical science over the last hundred or so years to show that we are not just going round in circles. Although Pazzi would, perhaps, not himself admit to flaws in his world view, he is, however, refreshingly aware of the problems of this kind of writing. His fourth novel, *Vangelo di Giuda*, is a sustained critique of the potential of literature as philosophy, and his most recent work, *La stanza sull'acqua* is almost aphilosophical. Whilst all his novels are worth reading, I shall deal primarily with *Cercando l'imperatore* and *Vangelo di Giuda*, as it is in these novels that Pazzi most convincingly combines his various skills.

The plot of *Cercando l'imperatore* is inspired by one of the major turning points in twentieth-century history – the Russian Revolution of 1917 and the subsequent collapse of the Tsarist order. In the book, Tsar Nicholas and his family are imprisoned in a requisitioned house at Ekaterinburg. As the novel develops, so Nicholas becomes more withdrawn and pensive. His wife tries to encourage him to fight back, but he views his imminent demise with detachment and resignation. In fact, he is more concerned with ridding the house of the forces of darkness which have entered in the shape of the ghost of the dead monk Rasputin, now exercising a demonic influence on his daughter Tatiana Romanov. Using a poisoned pomegranate, Tatiana kills herself and the rest of the family before the Bolshevik gaolers can perform the murders themselves. Meanwhile, the Preobrajensky regiment, led by the charismatic Prince

Ypsilanti, search for their Tsar across the Siberian plain. The soldiers gradually perish from disease and madness. A malevolent force toys with them, deliberately foiling their attempts to communicate with the real world in Moscow. Under the leadership of the silent Mongol Kaigiar, half of the regiment mutinies and sets off into the 'taiga', a dark, unexplored forest. When after two years of marching, a few surviving faithful soldiers reach Toboisk, the city where they mistakenly expected to find the Tsar imprisoned, Ypsilanti who had long suspected the futility of their mission, takes his own life.

Despite the wealth of historical detail, *Cercando l'imperatore* is clearly not a historical novel. Pazzi leads the reader through a mysterious, ethereal world in which realism gives way to fantasy. This development can best be traced in the novel's short, but carefully constructed opening chapter. We begin by learning that the telegraph in the small, remote town of Vachitino has not been working for some time. This apparently insignificant detail assumes great importance when the Preobrajensky arrive hoping to telegraph Moscow following rumours of unrest there. All of this is described in a conventionally realistic fashion, as though we are reading an accurate historical account. Indeed, historians of the Russian Revolution and ensuing civil war have consistently argued that one of the reasons for the eventual White, anti-Bolshevik defeat was their inability to communicate effectively with their forces. However, doubts as to the nature of the novel's initial realism begin to surface when we are given the background to the regiment's long march. The soldiers had learnt about the revolutionary upheavals in St Petersburg from a group of mysterious, wandering Jews who vanished 'come venissero dal nulla' (*Cercando l'imperatore*, p. 9) ('as if they had never existed'). One of the officers had begun to wonder whether his soldiers had simply dreamed about the Jews, and from then on a strange fever had spread through the regiment. At this point, the novel appears to be slipping from realism to surrealism. The rapidly decaying relationship between the novel and its apparent historical setting then dissolves completely, when at the end of the chapter, Boris the cobbler, a character drawn more from the world of fable than from history, emerges from his workshop with a replica pair of the Tsar's boots. The following day, as if by magic, following the departure of the regiment, the telegraph starts to work again. In the space of a few pages, Pazzi has subtly turned his novel from realism into sheer fantasy.

One of the book's most striking characteristics is the fashion in which the changing fortunes of the regiment and events at Ekaterinburg are described in alternating chapters. This structure is a highly effective means of portraying the novel's parallel tragedies. Themes and ideas in the Preobrajensky chapters shed greater meaning on the Romanov chapters and vice versa. Nicholas and Ypsilanti both spend a good deal of time deep in thought musing about past events as their lives collapse around them; the Romanovs and the Preobrajensky are gripped by the same delirium; Rasputin is parallelled with the silent Mongol

Kaigiar; and the vast desert across which the soldiers wander functions in contrast to the prison in which the Romanovs are confined. Subtle chapter interplay is frequently created by the appearance of similar themes or ideas occurring in the minds of the protagonists of each half of the narrative. Unable to communicate by conventional means, it is almost as if parapsychological methods take over. At the end of Chapter 3, Ypsilanti proposes a shooting expedition but is told by his orderly that as it is the birds' nesting season this would be an infraction of nature. Ypsilanti agrees: 'Già, Alioscia, hai proprio ragione, bisogna lasciarla fare la natura, non turbarla, ne abbiamo goduti anche troppi di strappi alla sua legge, di *miracoli*' (*Cercando l'imperatore*, p. 38, my italics) ('You're right, Alyosha, you're right. We must leave nature alone, not disturb her, we've flouted enough of her laws, we've enjoyed enough of her *miracles*'). Immediately afterwards, in the following chapter, we find Nicholas looking: 'alle finestre di casa Ipatiev sul viale d'accesso, là nella direzione lontana degli *spari*, se mai accadesse qualcosa, se mai un *miracolo* potesse avvenire, (*Cercando l'imperatore*, p. 39, my italics) ('out from one of the windows in Ipatiev's house onto the driveway, the side away from the *shooting* in case something might happen, a *miracle* might occur').

At another point, Nicholas and Ypsilanti both independently remember an incident when they had discovered an ancient statue. And throughout the novel the Tsarevitch, Alexei, talks to the birds which, it turns out, are the souls of the dead soldiers, 'transferred' to Ekaterinburg by a process of metempsychosis. Interestingly, Pazzi has revealed to me that the original version of the novel dealt solely with the story of Nicholas and his family, and was entitled *Nicola e Dio*. It was only at a relatively late stage that he decided to weave in the story of the Preobrajensky. The novel shows few signs of its initial single-story design, and Pazzi's success in carrying off this complex editing process is, in many ways, remarkable. There are, however, occasional stylistic indications which reveal the different stages in the evolution of both the work and the writer. The style of the Romanov chapters is, like his earlier poetry, relatively simple:

> Ecco ora gli veniva in mente che non aveva mai viaggiato, perché non era mai stato lo sconosciuto che si rivela poco a poco, per come offre una sigaretta, o accavalla le gambe, o chiude il finestrino ... No, lui era sempre stato dappertutto già subito il massimo che un uomo potesse essere, accecante: lo Zar. Non aveva lasciato che la fioca luce di fuori entrasse, che gli occhi dei compagni di viaggio si abituassero al suo volto in penombra, mentre il treno penetrava la notte, e solo qualche improvviso lampione di una stazione in corsa lo sfiorasse senza scoprirlo mai tutto. Che sapeva in fondo del viaggio? (*Cercando l'imperatore*, p. 103)

> But now, he remembered he had never travelled, he had never been the stranger who gradually reveals himself by the way he offers a cigarette, crosses his legs, gets up to close the train window ... wherever he had gone, he had been immediately, blindingly, the greatest a man could be, the Tsar. He had

not let the faint light from outside reach him, he had not let the eyes of his companions grow used to his face in the semidarkness, while the train cut through the night, and only the occasional station light ran across his features without revealing him completely. What did he know of journeys, in the end?

In the Preobrajensky chapters, on the other hand, Pazzi frequently appears to be experimenting, seeking out the extremes of expressivity in language. The descriptions of the power of nature, particularly in the early stages of the book are conceived in a wantonly excessive 'grand style', in a deliberate formal search for linguistic totality:

> Un giorno la terra s'era spaccata cominciando a vomitare tutti i suoi umori segreti. L'acqua e il fango avevano dapprima paralizzato la marcia. La primavera era scoppiata violentemente e improvvisa come una febbre ... s'era dovuta imbrigliare la terra impazzita che in pochi giorni aveva trasformato i ghiacci immobili in laghi insidiosi ... Ormai l'estate, la breve e feroce estate siberiana, restituiva a tutti quei corpi giovani un languido desiderio di riposo, una sete di piacere e di sonno più devastante della fatica invernale. (*Cercando l'imperatore*, p. 37)

> Then one day, the frozen earth split, spewing out its secret humours, and water and mud first paralysed the column of marching men. Spring burst as violently and suddenly as a fever ... they had to bridle the insane land that in a few days had transformed a static world of ice into snaring quicksands ... And now summer, the short harsh Siberian summer, gave to those young bodies a sluggish desire for rest, a thirst for pleasure and for sleep that was more devastating than the weariness of winter.

Nature is one of the leading characters of *Cercando l'imperatore*, moving and participating organically in the general development of the tale. Elemental forces accompany the soldiers throughout their difficult journey. Frequently, nature hinders their progress, or deceives them into thinking that they have made some headway. Only when the soldiers enter the forest does it appear to offer some respite:

> Qualcuno dei più lesti, come il georgiano Ignatic, s'era lasciato tentare ed era riuscito a salire sulla cima di un albero altissimo. Giunto lassù Ignatic era talmente colpito da quello che vedeva da dimenticarsi della caccia.
> Dovunque volgesse lo sguardo compariva una distesa di erba di tutte le tonalità contro il cielo più azzurro che avesse mai visto. Quelle cime non erano tutte uguali: alcune, più ardite e orgogliose, parevano voler pungere il cielo e contentarsi a stento di quell'altezza, rinviando a una prossima primavera il sogno di elevarsi fino alle nuvole. Altre macchie, più rotonde e accoglienti, parevano preoccupate di fornire appoggi e nascondigli, gonfie della vita dei nidi e dei covili sotto le radici. S'indovinava che erano vecchissimi alberi, più antichi di quelli più aguzzi, forse avevano già raggiunto i primati celesti che i più giovani ancora sognavano e se n'erano dimenticati, lasciandosi invadere da tutte le viti che ospitavano. Lassù Ignatic pensava che davvero le ore, i mesi, gli anni dovevano essere tutte uguali e non avrebbe avuto senso contarli. Alcuni uccelli dall'ampia apertura d'ali si calavano su un punto là in fondo con la

velocità dei predatori: un acuto strido lo avvertiva che una vita doveva essere
sacrificata a un'altra secondo la legge più antica della terra, quella del più forte.
(*Cercando l'imperatore*, pp. 95-6)

Some of the more athletic, like Ignatic the Georgian, had been tempted and
had climbed the top of the tallest tree. When he reached the top he was so
struck by what he saw he forgot the hunt.

Wherever he turned his gaze there was a vast expanse of different greens
against a sky of the most intense blue he had ever seen. The tops were not level:
some braver, prouder, seemed to want to burst through the sky, hardly content
with their height, merely pausing until the following spring in their dream of
touching the clouds. Other areas of the forest were more rounded, more
welcoming, seemed more concerned to furnish perches and hiding places; they
were bursting with the life to be found in the nests and in the burrows under the
tree roots. They were obviously older trees, more ancient than the ones whose
tips pointed brazenly to the sky; perhaps they had reached those blue heights
the younger ones aspired to and had forgotten about them, letting themselves
be absorbed by the lives they sheltered. Up there, Ignatic thought that, really,
hours, days, years, were all the same and there was no sense in counting them.
Some broad-winged birds in the distance plunged with the speed of predators,
and a high strident call told them that one life had been sacrificed for another
according to the oldest law on earth, the law of the strongest.

The depiction of nature as a force outside the control of the human race, points
to Pazzi's principal philosophical interest in the book: whether we are, as the
existentialists argue, able to shape our own destiny, and by extension history, or
whether we are simply the unfortunate victims of fate. The novel, and in
particular its treatment of the regiment's drama, makes it clear that Pazzi's
outlook on this matter is deeply pessimistic. From the very start, the
Preobrajensky function on another, separate plane of existence, almost as if they
have ceased to be and have become ghosts. Their aura of mystery is heightened
when we find that they leave 'un segno di passi e di ruote che, poco dopo,
pareva sparire come per incanto. Come se nessuno fosse passato da quelle parti'
(*Cercando l'imperatore*, p. 31) ('footprints and wheel tracks that seemed to
disappear immediately, as if a spell had been cast, as if no one had passed by
there'). Despite their heroic efforts, they do not appear to get very far, and
having covered five hundred versts, senior officers do not feel they have got any
closer to Tobolsk. The fact that the regiment no longer has a Tsar to serve means
that the soldiers' actions are effectively useless and pointless: their lives are now
over. The significance of the title is thus explained: their search is an allegory of
the individual's futile attempt to hold onto the self as history passes it by.

This existential tension is revealed most forcefully in the book's treatment of
Ypsilanti. Our first encounter with him establishes him as a hero of almost
Homeric stature, as a great leader of men and a devoted servant to the Tsar. He
becomes obsessed with the breakdown in communications and feels that his
regiment must set out on the march in order to perpetuate their earthly

existence. As the march continues, so Ypsilanti becomes more and more withdrawn and pensive. His life, and the lives of his soldiers, seem gradually but inexorably to be slipping away. One evening he listens to his troops as they prepare to settle down for the night. The soldiers are clearly enthused by the prospect of reaching and saving the Tsar, but Ypsilanti knows full well that their mission is hopeless. As conditions worsen, and rumours of mutiny begin to reach him, he is confronted with the ravings of the infantryman Ostov who accuses him of being evil and responsible for a violation of nature. In his madness, Ostov has realized that the regiment is not fighting a logistical or geographical enemy, but a powerful metaphysical force. Yet, instead of ordering the soldier to be shot for insubordination, Ypsilanti orders his large mirror to be brought from his tent, having learnt that the demented man had spent a good deal of time staring at a small mirror before going to bed. The mirror is a recurring symbol in Pazzi's fiction, and functions as a vehicle for the discovery of the self. Ostov slowly begins to undress before the large mirror and when he is completely naked he disappears into the forest never to be seen again. The whole scene is narrated with great skill and intensity:

> Il folle allora, visto apparire quel grande specchio ritto fra lui e il reggimento, resosi conto che i soldati s'erano un po' allontanati e non l'inseguivano più, parve incuriosirsi, abbassando lentamente il fucile senza tuttavia abbandonarlo. Fatti alcuni passi, venne a trovarsi proprio davanti allo specchio che rifletteva leggermente inclinata verso il terreno la sua immagine intera sullo sfondo dei primi alberi della tajga. Non ne aveva mai visto uno così grande, fino a quel momento aveva conosciuto solo il proprio viso in un frammento di specchio non più grande di un palmo. Ora pareva spaventato e affascinato dalla scoperta del suo corpo, come se gli rimandasse uno sconosciuto.
>
> Muoveva le gambe, le braccia, e si toccava come cercasse di penetrare dentro quell'immagine troppo vasta da riconoscere solo con gli occhi. Pareva che volesse aiutarsi con le mani, non riuscendo ad esplorarsi solo con la vista. A un tratto, con uno strano sorriso, cominciò lentamente a spogliarsi, senza tuttavia allontanare troppo l'arma da sé. I vestiti cadevano lentamente. Prima la giacca, poi il berretto, poi la cintura, poi le scarpe, poi i pantaloni. Rimase nudo. Ora sorrideva ad occhi socchiusi, si chinava a raccogliere la camicia e se la strusciava addosso sussurrando parole incomprensibili ... Fece per voltarsi lentamente abbandonando specchio e fucile, con un passo leggero eppure candenzato.
>
> A Ypsilanti non appariva più uno dei suoi soldati, uno degli uomini che l'avevano seguito e obbedito in tante fatiche, ma un animale libero di correre sotto il sole, appartenente ad un altro mondo. Il capitano Karel vicino al suo plotone fece un segno di puntare e si voltò al principe Ypsilanti in attesa dell'ordine. Ma il principe, con un gesto di infinita lentezza, abbassò la mano guantata facendo segno di abbassare l'arma, rimanendo a fissare l'uomo che s'allontanava finché non sparì nella tajga. (*Cercando l'imperatore*, pp. 61–2)

He gently lowered his rifle without letting go of it, took a few steps and was in front of his reflection, tilted slightly toward the ground, with a full backdrop of the first trees of the taiga: he had never seen such a big mirror; up to that moment he had merely known his face in a fragment barely the size of the palm of his hand. Now he seemed frightened and fascinated by the discovery of his body, as of that of a stranger.

He moved his legs, his arms, touched himself, as if to enter into that image too vast to be taken in by the eyes alone. The clothes fell to the ground slowly, first the jacket, then the beret, the belt, the shoes, the trousers, until he was naked. He smiled with half-closed eyes, bending to pick up the shirt, rubbing it against his skin, whispering incomprehensible words ... he turned slowly, abandoning mirror and rifle, and moved with measured light steps.

To Ypsilanti he no longer seemed one of his soldiers, one of the men who had followed him and obeyed him through so much; he was an animal free to run under the sun, a creature of another world. Captain Karel, next to his platoon of riflemen, made the sign to take aim and turned to Ypsilanti waiting for the order. But the prince, with an incalculably slow gesture, lowered his gloved hand in a signal not to shoot, and remained watching the man until he had disappeared into the taiga.

What Ostov has seen is the terrible reality of his empty self, he has found that at the very heart of things there is nothing there. His earthly being now an empty shell, his disappearance into the forest is a final gesture of escape from the world, a flight into a region untouched by history.

The Ostov episode affects Ypsilanti deeply. He decides to split the regiment even before the impending mutiny takes place. The last act of his existence will be to die serving the old order that is crumbling around him. His suicide before the domes of Tobolsk is the only perfectly free act left open to him.

The novel is, to say the least, gloomy. The ending, though, does promise some relief. The pomegranate that Tatiana uses to save the Romanovs from their historically grizzly shooting, bludgeoning and immersion in acid, is a classical symbol of birth and regeneration, and the birds that have flocked to the house with the dead soldiers' souls inside them launch themselves 'come furie contro i Rossi a colpi di becco, a graffi di artigli, a voli in picchiata sulle loro teste, mirando agli occhi, alla bocca, alle mani' (*Cercando l'imperatore*, p. 175) ('like the Furies against the Reds with their beaks, their claws, diving at the top of their heads, aiming for eyes, mouths, hands').

Pazzi's fourth novel, *Vangelo di Giuda*, is by far his most sophisticated and ambitious work. Considerably longer than anything else that he has written, it is Pazzi's philosophical and literary 'summa'. As a result, the intellectual breadth of the book is both impressive and daunting. Pazzi deals with Western philosophy from Plato to Derrida, with Western literature from Homer and Virgil through to Dante and Eco, and, as if this was not enough, he also rewrites the early history of the Christian Church.

The plot is complex. Cornelia, the daughter of the executed Roman poet Cornelio Gallo, has learnt his works off by heart following the government destruction of the original manuscripts. She arrives on the island of Capri determined to recite to the Emperor Tiberius her disgraced father's entire opus.

Despite his initial hesitancy, Tiberius accepts Cornelia's proposal and in a series of lengthy night-time sessions listens to her 'readings'. These sessions culminate in the recital of Gallo's masterpiece, a poem recounting the life of the prophet Jeshua. Tiberius warms to the story of Jeshua and determines to hamper the spread of a gospel written by Judas, which he learns threatens to alter Jeshua's original message. In order to do this, Tiberius commands that a series of false gospels be put into circulation which offer a series of alternative stories to the one told by Judas. Numerous ingenious twists subsequently occur concerning the authenticity of both Gallo's and Judas' accounts of Jeshua's life; and Tiberius' plans collapse. The false gospels which he spreads to protect Jeshua will eventually become the basis of Christianity and lead to the downfall of the Roman Empire. Into this main story, Pazzi weaves a series of connected sub-plots dealing, variously, with the incestuous love affair between Caligula and Drusilla, the mutiny of the once-faithful Hispana regiment, and the story of the Jewish widower Giaro, and his daughter Ester.

Critical reaction to *Vangelo di Giuda* has been, predictably, mixed. The book angered *L'Osservatore Romano*, the official mouthpiece of the Vatican, which was outraged by Pazzi's depiction of the false nature of the synoptic Gospels. These criticisms appeared shortly after the explosion of the Rushdie affair; fortunately, however, they did not lead to the persecution of the Italian author, nor were death threats made against him. Indeed, other bonds seem to unite Rushdie and Pazzi. Both writers possess the same imaginative sense, are interested in the problems of good and evil and of the divided self, and share a common belief in the disorder and chaos of the universe. Gibreel Farishta's reflection in the *Satanic Verses* that 'the doctors had been wrong to treat him for schizophrenia, the splitting was not in him but in the universe' is one with which Pazzi would readily agree. Other, less tendentious reviewers have praised the book for its dazzling ambition, but as yet no single critical approach has managed to establish just what it is about. Yet, while it is not at all easy to link the many thematic girders around which the book is built, it does, I think, have a substantial unity: *Vangelo di Giuda* is a critique of literature as philosophy, and of the written word as a source of truth. Pazzi questions the contribution that literature (including the literature that he writes) can make to the human quest for knowledge and happiness. In particular, the two main characters in the book, Tiberius and Cornelia, are depicted as being so obsessed with literature that their lives are dominated by it.

Although Capri's appeal as an island paradise far from Rome is a factor in Tiberius's decision to move there, its chief attraction lies in its being the reputed dwelling place of the Sirens, whose story, as recounted in the *Odyssey*, the Emperor has read again and again. Odysseus' fascination with the Sirens' song has been interpreted as symbolically representing the human quest for know-ledge, even if its acquisition is a painful process. Tiberius is not·then searching for a peaceful life on the island, but for knowledge; his behaviour is guided by his reading. Yet, as his astrologer, Trasillo ironically reflects 'le Sirene non c'erano più sull'isola; solo nella poesia di Omero ancora ammaliavano col loro canto' (*Vangelo di Giuda*, p. 36) ('the sirens were no longer on the island; only in Homer's poetry could they still enchant with their song'). True knowledge in a real world outside of Homer's poetry is therefore unattainable, and Tiberius can only pretend to search for it. Thus, Trasillo recalls how, shortly after their arrival from Ostia, the emperor had gone to the rocks and covered his ears with his hands to muffle the intensity of the Sirens' non-existent song, a gesture repeated by all his obsequious courtiers except one, who refusing to act out the pretence, was sent to perish in a far-flung corner of the Empire.

This unfortunate courtier is not the only person to suffer from Tiberius' obsession with literature. He decides to populate eternity with numerous members of his senate so he will not experience the same sense of boredom that Achilles did, when, in Hades, he had been moved to envy the life of the last pig farmer on earth. Bad luck for the senators in question, but at least Tiberius will have someone to talk to amongst the shades. Tiberius' problem, Pazzi suggests, is that he is unable to separate literature from life. He attempts to understand himself and the world through literature, but only ends up causing misery and suffering for himself and for others. When he is made aware by Ester, who accompanies her father Giaro on a diplomatic mission to Capri, that he is leading a 'non-life', a life in a dream, he believes that to escape from this condition he must search for and destroy Judas' gospel. Instead, as Cornelia reflects, what he really needs to search for is the 'amore sepolto dentro di lui' (*Vangelo di Giuda*, p. 173) ('love buried deep inside him') which, of course, is what he does not do. Obsessed with a written text, he fails to lead his own life. Again, it is literature, or in this case a gospel, which provides an obstacle to his happiness.

When Cornelia arrives in Capri, Tiberius believes she is one of the mythological Parcae 'venuta e recidere il filo della sua esistenza' (*Vangelo di Giuda*, p. 28) ('come to cut the thread of his existence'). His initial reaction is, therefore, to consider her as a figure from literature, rather than as a real person. She soon reveals her true identity but the question as to whether she really exists is quickly raised. Having spent her lifetime learning the poetry of her persecuted father, she is now pure memory, unaffected by the ageing process: 'Cornelia, invece d'invecchiare, era stata risucchiata indietro nel tempo, ringiovanendo ad ogni poema che imparava' (*Vangelo di Giuda*, p. 39) ('Cornelia, instead of growing older, had been sucked back in time, growing younger with every poem that she learnt'). In 'becoming' her father's poems she has achieved immortality, but lost her self: 'Io ho passato anni a ripetere migliaia di versi che furono giornate, notti, della vita di mio padre, non ho più vissuto la mia e ora sono solo memoria' (*Vangelo di Giuda*, p. 32) ('I have spent years repeating thousands of lines that were the days and nights of my father's life. I have not lived my life, and I am now just memory'). Pazzi seems to be suggesting that the more literature you read, or – in his case – write, the less chance you have of living in the full sense of the word. Literature is thus placed in opposition to Life. Hence, the search for immortality through writing which has been the driving force behind many of the major figures in world literature (including, I suspect, Pazzi himself), is seen as deeply misguided.

The negative effect that Cornelia's immersion in literature has had on her life is further illustrated when her love affair with the librarian Egisto is recounted in the terms of a highly artificial literary cliché, strikingly similar to the way in which Paolo and Francesca fall in love in *Inferno V*: 'Ed era stato leggendo della passione per Citeride che poco a poco s'era rivelata la loro' (p. 44) ('As they read of his [Cornelio's] passion for Cytheris so gradually their own revealed itself'). Yet, whereas Paolo and Francesca are murdered by her jealous husband and are eternally damned for their 'literary' lust, Cornelia immediately questions the authenticity of her own passion, believing that it is literature, rather than real mutual emotion that has brought them together: 'Sono dannata a vivere all'ombra di mio padre anche l'amore per te Egisto' (*Vangelo di Giuda*, p. 44) ('Even in my love for you Egisto, I am condemned to live in my father's shadow'). Egisto attempts to persuade her otherwise: 'Non è vero, non siamo di papiro, né di pergamena. Quando sei entrata nella biblioteca tu mi desideravi come t'ho subito desiderato io' (*Vangelo di Giuda*, p. 44) ('It's not true, Cornelia, we are not parchment or papyrus. When you first came into the library you desired me just as I desired you'); but her concern to carry out her martyr's mission coupled with her doubts as to the true reason for her emotion, means that she renounces her own literature-generated love and continues to learn her father's poems. As such, Cornelia's choice, as distinct to that made by Paolo and Francesca is to reject a life in literature, by putting literature in what is perhaps its proper place, in the mind and not in life. Indeed, it is when Cornelia finally finishes reciting her poems to Tiberius that she decides to depart with Giaro, and become a mother to Ester. Her face grows older so as to reflect her true age, and she returns to a normal existence.

Pazzi seems to be suggesting that love and literature are incompatible. Logically then, love untouched by literature, should lead to more satisfactory relationships. However, an analysis of some of the other relationships in the book suggests otherwise. Tiberius' youthful love for Vipsania is thwarted by Augustus, who forces him instead to marry his crabby daughter Giulia. An Assyrian dancer collapses and dies moments before she was to make love with a praetorian guard. A soldier in the Hispana regiment hears that his beloved, the daughter of the disgraced senator Sejano, was raped before being strangled by her executioner. Bedicca, a native living near the regiment's camp, hears of the death of her lover Lucio Libone at the hands of the cohort commander Quinto Bruto, and plans revenge. Together with her associates, she tears the soldiers of

Quinto's cohort limb from limb and reserves a special punishment for her lover's murderer. In the centre of a field of destruction, carnage and mutilated limbs stands the commander's eyeless head, placed on a pike above his severed hands and genitals, 'orrendo trofeo delle sacerdotesse della luna' (*Vangelo di Giuda*, p. 185) ('a horrendous trophy of the high-priestesses of the moon'). Caligula and Drusilla briefly find happiness in their incestuous relationship, but it is clear that it cannot last for long. In order to prevent the spread of rumours concerning Caligula's strange sexual practices, Drusilla poisons herself. Even without the interference of literature, Pazzi implies that successful human relationships are impossible.

During the account of Cornelia's problematic love affair, an important passage describes Egisto's belief in the capacity of the written word to find all the answers:

> Anche Egisto conosceva la magica felicità di scorrere nelle grammatiche le regole invisibili della vita, il disegno sotteso allo scheletro del mondo, fatto di parole che evocano sogni diversi a seconda di come si coniughino verbi, aggettivi, sostantivi, di come si pronuncino accenti, spiriti, dittonghi. (*Vangelo di Giuda* p. 44)

> Egisto too knew the magic feeling of finding in grammar books life's invisible rules, the underlying design of the structure of the world, made of words which evoke diverse dreams according to the way verbs, adjectives and nouns inflect, and accents, spirits and diphthongs are pronounced.

Egisto's reported thoughts are reminiscent of the structuralist movement's claims to be able to discover, through linguistics, the deep inherent 'structures' of the universe. In particular, the geometric expression 'sotteso' (subtended) seems drawn directly from the structuralist vocabulary. Shortly after this scene, Egisto disappears from Cornelia's life, and although not described in the novel, the great library of Alexandria was, as is well known, subsequently destroyed. Pazzi implies that in our modern post-structuralist era, confidence in the discovery of transcendental absolutes via language is, as the French philosopher Jacques Derrida argues, no longer possible; linguistics and other ordered conceptual frameworks are no longer relevant in a disordered world. Egisto and his library are therefore symbols of a knowledge which is no longer attainable. Umberto Eco makes a similar point in *Il nome della rosa*, in which another librarian and his library, which goes up in flames at the end of the book, function as symbols of the grand, but doomed, structuralist project.

Despite these general reservations concerning the effectiveness of language to convey meaning, Pazzi underlines throughout the book the superiority of the spoken as opposed to the written word. For him, orally transmitted culture is to be valued above all attempts to transfer the living word onto paper. Written culture, and by extension the culture that he himself produces, only fossilizes and perverts the original messages of the speaker. It is for this reason that

Cornelia wishes to recite her father's poems to Tiberius rather than copy them out onto parchment. She believes that her father's poetry will live for ever in Tiberius' immortal soul. As Cornelia explains to Tiberius, the same ideas were held by Jeshua:

> Il potere di una parola è nella coscienza di chi la ascolta molto più che nel papiro che la preserva. Jeshua voleva che le pagine fossero le anime in ascolto come è ora la tua mente … I secoli avrebbero distrutto un papiro, mai l'anima. (*Vangelo di Giuda*, p. 115)

> The power of a word is derived more from the consciousness of the person that hears it than from the papyrus that preserves it. Jeshua wished that his pages were the souls that listened to him, just as your mind is now … Time would destroy papyrus, but never the soul.

Taking the argument a stage further, both Gallo and Jeshua believe that the written word can be misused by interest groups and turned into an instrument of power. For this reason, Gallo criticizes Virgil's *Aeneid* for its praise of the *pax romana*, and Jeshua expressly forbids his followers to write down his teachings. Yet despite this prohibition, Judas transcribes Jeshua's words in the hope that they might help to create an anti-Roman separatist movement. The process of transferring speech to writing is, however, not a simple one:

> Giuda ogni notte faticava non poco a tradurre la spoglia profondità di Jeshua nel suo greco, come se i suoni di quella voce fuggissero dai caratteri impuri di quella lingua in cui non aveva mai parlato; provò allora in aramaico, ma ancora più acuta ebbe la sensazione di non riuscire a tradurre la verità di quell'uomo in segni scritti. (*Vangelo di Giuda*, pp. 113–14)

> Every night Judas struggled to translate the depths of Jeshua's simple words into Greek, as if the sounds of that voice fled from the impure characters of that language in which he had never spoken; he tried Aramaic instead, but then he was even more conscious of his inability to translate the truth of that man into written signs.

There is then in the novel a consistent questioning of literature and of the written word in general. Most of these ideas are filtered through the central character of Tiberius. It is he, more than any other character in the novel who is obsessed with a search for knowledge and the idea of a vision of truth. Tiberius initially turns to mysticism and astrology in order to satisfy his thirst for the 'absolute'. A similar shift of outlook is evident in Margaret Yourcenar's *Memoirs of the Emperor Hadrian*, a work and a writer Pazzi greatly admires. Yet, though Hadrian in Yourcenar's work wistfully reflects that when the philosophers have nothing more to tell us 'it is excusable to turn to the random twitter of birds, or toward the distant mechanism of the stars' and proceeds to embrace such speculative systems, Tiberius is quick to realize their poverty. As such, Pazzi would appear to have reached an even more negative standpoint than the one he held at the time of writing *Cercando l'imperatore* where Tatiana's 'rescue' of the

Romanovs demonstrated a certain faith in the power of mysticism. Further evidence of a greater pessimism in the novel is the fact that in the story of the distant ninth Hispana regiment, a clear reminiscence of the Preobrajensky in the earlier novel, the soldiers no longer search for their Emperor in order to save him, but to kill him.

After Tiberius has listened attentively to Cornelia's recitations which replace his astrologer's meaningless drivel, he soon finds himself feeling sympathy for Jeshua's teachings. When he hears from Cornelia that Jeshua has been crucified in the name of the Roman Empire, he is therefore more than a little upset. Furthermore, the idea that Jeshua's teachings will be misused and twisted in Judas' gospel disturbs him deeply. One night he is struck by the image of a circle of light on his desk and finds what he thinks is the solution to his problem, the creation of a whole set of false gospels to run counter to the perverted message of the one written by Judas, and thus prevent the fruition of his plan. At this point the novel begins to get extremely convoluted. What Pazzi attempts to do is make his narrative deliberately difficult to follow, so that his readers experience the same sense of elation and delusion that Tiberius feels. The bewildered reader becomes Tiberius, straining to understand but ultimately getting nowhere. For this reason, it would be pointless to attempt to explain the logic behind Tiberius' various actions, the numerous about-turns caused by oscillations between truth and lies. It is simply enough to realize that whatever Tiberius does, he gets it all wrong because, in order to exact revenge against the Roman Empire that had condemned him to death, Cornelio Gallo had deliberately twisted the truth in his poem. He had lied about Jeshua's crucifixion in order to trick Tiberius into creating the gospels. Tiberius' knowledge of the content of Judas' gospel is itself based on a falsehood, a lie invented by the would-be visionary poet. His discovery is not then a discovery at all. He has not found the answer which will prevent the propagation of a false picture of his and Jeshua's life. Instead, he unconsciously causes the 'false' story of Jeshua's crucifixion to be spread through the gospels and this eventually leads to the consolidation of Christianity and the fall of the Roman Empire.

Tiberius' abject failure is cruelly highlighted by Pazzi in his use of metaphors and images from the closing stages of Dante's *Paradiso*, when the medieval poet, having reached the end of his journey, studies the circle in which Christ's face appears. His desire to know reaches a cosmic level and he is struck by a 'fulgore' (compare Pazzi's 'folgorato' = 'struck' juxtaposed with the image of the circle) and discovers the hidden message of the Word. A similar moment of supreme wisdom is not available to Tiberius, nor, Pazzi implies, is it available to us. It is only in his final moments that the dying Emperor finally begins to understand. Caligula arrives, bearing the original, 'authentic' manuscript of Judas' gospel which describes Jeshua wandering through Egypt, rather than suffering the pain of crucifixion. Yet even with this knowledge, he still does not grasp the exact truth. As his death agony overwhelms him he suspects the worthy Cornelia, 'l'ignara artefice della vendetta del visionario poeta' (*Vangelo di Giuda*, p. 227) ('the unknowing artifice of the visionary poet's vendetta'), and not her father, as the true author of the subterfuge.

What is the message of the book? The fact that its title is the same as Judas' misrepresentation and paper-based ossification of Christ's message, thrown into a brazier by Caligula at the end of the story, indicates a possible, pessimistic line of interpretation. I prefer, however, to see this ending as an act of liberation for Pazzi himself. It is, in a sense, a preparation for the more hopeful novel, *La stanza sull'acqua*, and ultimately a decision to turn away from the negative philosophy which has for too long pinned him to the more shadowy corners of existence.

BIBLIOGRAPHY

Works

Fiction

Cercando l'imperatore (Genova: Marietti 1985; new edition Milan: Garzanti, 1988). Translated by Margaret J. Fitzgerald as *Searching for the Emperor* (London: Deutsch, 1989).
La principessa e il drago (Milan: Garzanti, 1986). Translated by Margaret J. Fitzgerald as *The Princess and the Dragon* (London: Deutsch, 1990).
La malattia del tempo (Genova; Marietti, 1987). Translated by Vivien Sinott as *Adrift in Time* (London: Deutsch, 1991).
Vangelo di Giuda (Milan: Garzanti, 1989).
La stanza sull'acqua (Milan: Garzanti, 1991).

Poetry

L'esperienza anteriore (Milan: I dispari, 1973).
Versi occidentali (Quarto d'Altino: Rebellato, 1976).
Il re, le parole (Manduria: Lacaita, 1980).
Calma di vento (Milan: Garzanti, 1987).

Chapter 11

Fabrizia Ramondino
The Muse of Memory

JONATHAN USHER

Fabrizia Ramondino's two novels written in the 1980s, both dealing with a decadent middle class forced to rub shoulders with the lower orders of Naples and its environs, have earned praise for their elegant yet lyrical use of language. Ramondino's is an original voice, with thought-provoking contributions not only to the portrayal of female consciousness, but also to the perception of time and memory. Her work from the beginning and the end of the decade offers radically different technical treatments of these constant themes.

Her first novel, *Althénopis* (1981) is a partially first-person re-evocation of a series of lost worlds which are presented to us via a fascinating pot-pourri of unbridled poetic suggestion and conscientious, almost academic regard for authenticity.

The core of the book relates, in a series of loosely-linked chapters, the odyssey of a young girl (the narrating voice) through Naples and its environs in the closing stages of the war and the immediate *dopoguerra* (postwar years), as she and her middle-class family, down on their luck and soon to be fatherless, are passed on from one set of eccentric relatives to another. In the epilogue, the narrator returns to Naples, years later as an adult, to be present during her mother's last illness.

The title, *Althénopis,* is explained in a footnote of playful folk-etymological discussion:

> Il nome della mia città natale. In origine il suo nome significava 'occhio di vergine'. Ma pare che i tedeschi, durante l'occupazione, trovandola così imbruttita rispetto alle descrizioni di Mozart ... le mutarono il nome in Althénopis, che starebbe appunto a significare 'occhio di vecchia' ...
> (*Althénopis*, p. 10)

> The name of my native city. Originally its name meant 'maiden's eye'. But it seems that the Germans, during the Occupation, finding it so decrepit compared with Mozart's descriptions ... changed its name to Althénopis, as if to mean 'hag's eye'

This apparently gratuitous digression on the title's meaning encapsulates the narrative situation of the novel, but in a characteristically ironic way, for Ramondino is attempting with the eyes of an older woman to see Naples with the fresh, girlish eyes of her former self.

The novel engenders some contradictory sensations. On the one hand, the very rootlessness of the young girl is translated by the narrative voice into a tremendous celebration of place, just as the constantly shifting tableau of relatives, who accept the girl out of obligation and sufferance, provides an overwhelmingly claustrophobic feeling of family. At the same time, the constant attention to detail, the obsessive, almost amorous respect for the *paraphernalia* of place, epoch and family circle, bring an almost mythic dimension to nostalgia.

Leaving aside the exoticism of wartime Campania, the lost world Ramondino evokes is one we are all inevitably exiled from: the knowing 'innocence' of childhood; the emotional topography of places from our past which survive unchanged only in memory; those instances in the constant physiological and psychological flux of extended families when our individual sense of belonging or exclusion is established for ever; in short, the world that constitutes our personal mythology. These topics are of course commonplaces of fiction, and set Ramondino squarely in the magico-nostalgic tradition of writers such as Elsa Morante. Ramondino's own writerly fascination with memory fiction, and her debt to previous masters, is playfully signalled in a passage in *Althénopis* where the narrator tells of an uncle's fixation with the complete Gallimard edition of Proust's *À la recherche du temps perdu*.

The literary exploitation of personal memory is fraught with difficulties and requires special gifts and a high degree of discipline. When authors delve into their past, should they squeeze their grown-up personae into the child-sized clothes of yesterday, or should they shrink themselves to infant dimensions, still shrouded in outsize adult garments? Clearly the choice of the narrating voice is crucial.

In *Althénopis* Ramondino opts for a variable voice. First-person and third-person narration are interwoven in a complex tissue, where the status of the narrator is constantly changing. Whilst the book echoes with the names and eccentricities of countless down-at-heel aunts and degenerate uncles and cousins, the narrator-figure and her immediate family are never named (except for the long-dead father, mentioned in passing towards the end of the second section), and only perfunctorily described, as if taken for granted. This anonymity paradoxically encourages the reader to assume an autobiographical identity between the author and the narrator, much as close friends often feel no need to call each other by name.

However, this able mimicry of the environment of first-person narration should not be confused with autobiography, even though much personal experience has clearly leaked into the novel. Rather, the 'I' narrator has a twofold function: first of all as a 'point of view', a sentient witness, a surrogate for the reader to identify with; and secondly as an opportunistic 'frame' for the series of tableaux which make up the bulk of the novel. The focus is on the world surrounding the 'I' figure, rather than on the character herself. Much of this re-evocation of ambience acquires its own autonomy, both narratively and syntactically (starting with the splendidly observed raffish grandmother in the opening chapter), and many of the instances of first-person usage are couched in a betrayingly collective 'we'.

Intermittently, however, the 'I' narrator ceases to be an enabling fiction and claims our attention as a protagonist, as when she describes the effect of sun and sand on her skin, or the womb-like experience of crawling into stale sheets impregnated with her own smell. These autobiographical epiphanies are short-lived, however, and Ramondino quickly reverts to defining her narrator by defining her environment.

The tension between these two elements, the *material* remembered and the *act* of remembering (or between autobiographical experience and fictional impulse) surfaces explicitly in a series of footnotes, such as when the young girl has fallen in with the band of kids who taunt the village idiot, encouraging him to urinate in front of them: '"Dai, piscia!", gli chiedevamo. Lui si tirava fuori la parte – così lo chiamavamo noi bambini – e la sollevava per fare il getto più alto' ...' (*Althénopis*, p. 27) ('"Go on, piss!", we'd ask him. He'd pull out his *parte* – that's what we kids called it – and lift it up to get the highest possible squirt ...'). The footnote to the word *parte* states:

> Rivivere tutti i fatti raccontati in questa storia mi è costata molta fatica. Rivedere poi il testo per adeguarlo alla memoria e al lettore ha richiesto un certo lavoro. Qui ad esempio nella prima stesura avevo scritto 'cazzo'. Si trattava di un pigro indulgere alla moda, segnale anche di una certa senilità di pensiero, e oltre tutto di una grave improprietà di linguaggio, perché allora questa parte del corpo, come molte altre cose, non aveva per noi un nome. Veniva infatti chiamata 'il fatto' 'il coso', o 'chisto' o 'chillo'. Infine era proprio 'la parte' o 'o piezzo', almeno per noi bambine, mentre il resto era il corpo. Parte quindi non del corpo del ragazzo, ma di un corpo cosmico e misterioso. A questa 'parte' era associata quindi una numinosità che non può essere resa da termini come 'pene', o 'cazzo', il primo per gli ovvi limiti delle scienze esatte, il secondo perché, come tutto il linguaggio osceno, riduce la numinosità a sola forza bassa ed infera, mentre l'ambiguita è una caratteristica essenziale del numinoso. (*Althénopis*, p. 27)

> Reliving all the incidents related in this story has cost me a great deal of effort. Revising the text, subsequently, to adapt it to memory and the reader, required a fair bit of work. Here, for example, in the first draft I had written '*cazzo*' [prick]. It was nothing more than a lazy concession to being trendy, a sign of being mentally past-it, and most of all it was a major inaccuracy of language, because at that time this particular part of the body, like many other things, just didn't have a name. It got called '*il fatto*' [business], '*il coso*' [thingummy], or '*chisto*' [this] or '*chillo*' [that]. Finally it was indeed '*la parte*' [the part] or '*o piezzo*' [the piece], at least for us girls, whilst the rest was just the body. So it

was not part of the boy's body, but rather of a mysterious cosmic body. This 'part' was invested with a supernatural aura which terms like 'penis' and 'prick' just cannot convey, the first because of the obvious limitations of scientific language, the second because, like all obscene expressions, it reduces the supernatural to a vulgar lower force, whilst ambiguity is one of the essential characteristics of the supernatural.

The footnotes, like the occasional episodes where the first-person narration is authentically self-centred, serve to demonstrate that the almost magical illusion of *temps perdu* is just that: an illusion fabricated by imaginative effort and controlled by a severe conception of mnemonic propriety. We only become aware of the magic when the spell is broken, when the lyrical flow of the narrator is interrupted by the disembodied voice of the writer of footnotes.

If the first-person stance is primarily a device for stringing together the external definitions of the narrator's identity, then the abrupt change to third-person narration in the epilogue should come as no surprise. With the severing of the umbilical cord by leaving Naples, the narrator can now indulge in *self-definition*. Just as, in the first part of the novel, the ambient world was introduced by first-person triggering, so now the inner world of the narrator is finally realized by third-person analysis and description. The apparent disembodiment of the narrating voice is accompanied by the capitalization of many of the key words: Daughter; Mother; Family; Widowhood, as if they can be dealt with, and emptied of their power to hurt, by a generic objectivity.

This last section of the book, where the narrator recounts the painful coming to terms with her relationship to her mother, is all the more harrowing because of the desperate, almost clinical detachment of the writing, which paradoxically conveys far more explicit detail about the character's anguish than the coy use of the first person earlier in the book.

This switch of voice is indicative of a second area of memory writing where choices have to be made, namely in the organization of the material. Whereas autobiography superimposes an external structure on the free range of subjective recollection, fiction can adopt a wide range of organizational strategies which need not respect chronological, developmental or topographical constraints. *Althénopis* is constructed in three major sections, two of which correspond to the succession of temporary family refuges, whilst the third relates the 'home'-coming of the narrator. These sections, as units, are indeed in their proper chronological sequence. However, within these sections, the chapters seem like randomly chosen sketches, sometimes of people, sometimes of places.

Even here, the apparently loose structure turns out to be highly organized. The initial impression is of somebody opening an old, haphazardly-stocked family album, with loose snapshots falling out, commenting spontaneously on the photos as they slip to the floor. Like the non-naming of the narrator, this disregard for accurate sequence ably mimics a familiarity between narrator and reader, prompting a belief that we do not need to ask certain questions.

The succession of portraits of people and places adhere to the underlying dictates of a 'grammar of memory' in an admirably faithful way, with little concession to narratively tempting, but psychologically external tidying processes. The grandmother, with her baroque mixture of piety and a 'past', actually dies at the end of the first chapter, but almost immediately revives to lend ambiguous spice to the subsequent chapters. The grandmother is a memory talisman, a key to unlocking the childhood of the narrator.

From a narrative point of view, the grandmother, the subject of the first portrait, acts as a point of departure for a host of ancillary descriptions, which in their turn become subjects in their own right in later chapters. At the same time, what may be the main focus of one chapter will become a minor or altered focus in a later section. It is a subliminal, almost Ariostesque *'entrelacement'*, with constant cross-reference to stories, places and people.

Beyond these associative and combinatory structures, there are longer-term literary designs which become evident only on closer reading. The description of the grandmother's decline, into childishness then death, which occupies the first chapter, neatly anticipates the same fate of the narrator's mother in the final chapter. Both are accompanied by signs of frustrated or damaged sexuality: the grandmother's toilette includes mysterious unguents for treating venereal disease, the legacy of a strained relationship with her husband; the mother in her final agony begins to masturbate, much to the discomfiture of her prim relatives.

The same mother-grandmother parallelism can be seen in the demeaning power struggles both have to undergo when their traditional housekeeping roles are compromised by age or poverty. The grandmother's spendthrift cooking binges are the delight of the grandchildren, but when their joylessly practical mother arrives, supplanting grandmaternal authority, the old lady is reduced to subterfuge and guerilla tactics, making late-night sorties into the darkened kitchen. Later in the book, when the family are the reluctant guests of grander relatives in Naples, the mother resorts to similarly secret meals for her children, using a primus in a bedroom corner.

Sometimes these parallels are variations on a theme: the novel contains a series of male homecomings, eagerly awaited by the largely female population of Ramondino's universe. The grandmother awaits the return of a prisoner-of-war nephew she dotes on; the narrator looks forward to the infrequent visits of her father; a run-down single mother, living on the edge of town, patiently watches for the arrival of her lover with his cheap-jack gifts and travel-stained socks; the narrator's paternal grandfather makes periodic trips home to his wife from Rome, where he is involved in high-level freemasonry.

Each of these fleeting male appearances is doomed to disappoint: the nephew does not reciprocate the grandmother's exclusive passion; within hours of his arrival, the father reveals himself to be a sullen intruder; the travel-stained lover slumps down alone with his *limonata* and a fag; the freemason only returns to get his rank underwear washed, his stay in Rome revealed as a pathetically sordid amorous adventure.

The few males who remain permanent residents of Ramondino's Althénopis are a strange gallery of misfits who survive because their eccentricities allow them to occupy precarious ecological niches in an otherwise all-female society. Some, like the fastidious zio Alceste, are able to maintain the androgynous privileges of childhood, substituting the attentions of a doting, domineering mother for the complications of an adult sexual relationship. Others survive by being failures, gaining by pity the acceptance they would never have earned by respect. Still others try, with mixed success, to gain attention by classic southern-male ostentation, like zio Chinchino with his vulgar display of generosity and consumption.

The only males to gain unstinting respect from the narrator are those who have renounced social insertion for the sake of unsociable and often obsolescent trades: an artisan who makes small masterpieces out of salvaged tin cans; a charcoal-burner conscious that he is the last repository of a dying rural craft; an itinerant greengrocer who takes pride in disposing his lettuces on his cart with humour and elegance. Their manifest dignity only serves to emphasize the sorry mess the other males spread around them, a mess symbolized by the tell-tale droplets of urine left on the toilet-seat, and the sudsy ring of grime they leave on the bathtub.

These studies in disappointment, like the references to urine, punctuate the novel with an apparently artless symmetry, inexorably restating from generation to generation the same shortcomings and the same misplaced aspirations. Indeed, one could almost say that being let down by men is not only the eternal feminine condition but also, paradoxically, the very source of female identity.

Forced to live from their own emotional reserves, the women adopt survival strategies which gradually come to characterize them: the grandmother takes refuge in a highly sensual cult of saints; the mother takes refuge in an isolating migraine; a young housewife, making up for some unspoken shortcoming in her marriage, indulges in periodic bouts of pathological sexual licence.

Another level of organization concerns the movement from place to place, portrait to portrait, and chapter to chapter. Here too, sophisticated narrative procedures lie beneath the surface anarchy. Take place, for instance: one of the strongest memory stimuli, and something Ramondino is especially sensitive to. Place can jog the memory, but it can also provide a thread of continuity, joining chapters together.

The first chapter opens with a description of the grandmother pyrotechni-cally, almost psychedelically traversing the minuscule sun-baked piazza of Santa Maria del Mare as if she were some prima donna crossing a floodlit stage. The second chapter deals with the stage itself, that is to say the piazza and its bit-part actors. The third chapter opens with one of the houses which overlooks the

piazza like some theatre balcony, and the fourth starts with the paths and alleys
which lead off from the piazza. Similar progressions can be found with the
sequence of kitchen scenes later, where the secret life of 'below-stairs' offers its
compensations to children denied contact with adults of their own class.

There is an interesting psychological progression in the ordering of places
and people, which corresponds to the increasing social maturity of the narrating
persona. The child's attention is initially focused exclusively on the figure of her
grandmother, and then, gaining confidence and autonomy, the girl takes in the
surroundings in the form of the piazza, only to be brought back to the puzzled
exploration of home and family by the momentous arrival of her mother, who
usurps the grandmother's hitherto privileged domestic reign. After a period of
adjustment, the child becomes bolder, and strikes out on her own, annexing the
lanes, the lemon-groves, the roof-tops and seashore as a no-go area for adults.

In this first period of psychological adjustment, almost anything and anybody
the narrator comes into contact with – pigshit and prickly pears, grandmothers
and pregnant vagrants – have a kind of awesome supernatural quality, which
Ramondino calls 'numinosity'. This pre-rational phase is characterized by
unconscious intensity of concentration: when the narrator sees, hears, feels or
tastes, that sensation fills her being to the exclusion of all else. Ramondino's
verbal evocation of this stage of development is absolutely masterful, and attains
a lyrical beauty, as when describing a waterside fishing community:

> Gli uomini non fumavano Nazionali, ma estraevano le sigarette da brillanti e
> colorate scatole di cartone; spirali di fumo ondose e profumate si alzavano oltre
> i loro capelli neri e ricciuti, quando si stendevano con le gambe allargate a
> riposare sulla spiaggia. Perfino le piante erano diverse, crescevano piú piccole,
> ma con colori e odori piú intensi, in vasi formati da barattoli – per noi invece
> erano consueti solo i vasi di creta, le pentole bucate, gli orinali bianchi listati di
> blu –; e il basilico era piú pungente, piú rosso e piú fitto il geranio; intensissimo
> poi era il profumo del geranio, che ci lasciava col fiato mozzo. Mancava invece
> la dolcezza delle rose, quasi i petali non sopportassero il vento marino; sui
> piccoli appezzamenti, che c'erano dietro le case, dove la terra era grigia,
> mescolata alla sabbia, crescevano piccoli pomodori leggermente pelosi, che noi
> raccoglievamo furtivi per gustarne l'acre concentrazione che ci scoppiava in
> bocca; e piú piccoli erano i capperi, e piú dolci e meno acquosi i fichi.
> (*Althénopis*, p. 79)

The menfolk didn't smoke Nazionali, but produced cigarettes from shiny,
brightly coloured cardboard packets; sinuous fragrant spirals of smoke rose
above their black curly hair as they lay with their legs apart, resting on the
beach. Even the plants were different, they grew to a smaller size, but with
intenser colours and scents, in pots made from tin cans – we were used to
earthenware pots, leaky saucepans, blue-lined white potties – ; and the basil
was more pungent, and the geraniums were redder and more luxuriant; the
scent of the carnations was overpowering, taking our breath away. What was
missing was the sweetness of roses, almost as if the petals couldn't stand the sea
breeze; in the minute allotments behind the houses, where the earth was grey,

mixed with sand, there grew little, slightly furry tomatoes, which we used to steal so as to taste the bitter concentration that burst in our mouths; and the capers were smaller, and the figs sweeter and less watery.

The translation can provide some of the flavour of the imagery, but cannot reproduce the rhythmic, hypnotic accumulation of the phrases, with their repeated comparatives and poetically inspired inversions of word-order

As the narrator's experience grows broader, and her social and intellectual maturity develops, so the evocations become less exclusive. Objects and people are examined not so much for their secret essence, as they had been in the child's 'numinous' phase, but rather for clues as to their interaction. Thus the country-side and beach, quintessential to the toddler, gradually cease to dominate the narrator's imagination. Domestic interiors now merit glorious, almost archaeo-logical inventories, but only to illustrate the changes in the fortunes of the families inhabiting them, or to reveal the slow stratification of generations, each careless of the values of the last. Portraits of people now succeed each other with an almost casual frequency, as if overshadowed by décors which exert the grim fascination of the scene of a crime.

Such material minutiae cruelly catalogue the gradual fading of the stamp of personality which had given rise to a particular décor. Just as, at a personal level, the book records the slow decline of both the grandmother and the mother, so the mute agony of decaying, once proud furniture, and the rusty retirement of impractical kitchen gadgets of yesteryear, chronicle the more generalized de-scent of an upper-middle class family, encumbered by inappropriate cultural heirlooms and nostalgia for better times, toward the anxious margins of the proletariat.

The passion for inventory reaches its climax in the last section, appropriately called *Bestelle dein Haus* ('put your house in order'). The review of the lounge, the bathroom, the dining-room, and their accumulated detritus, is almost a substitute interrogation of a past whose inhabitants have long since departed. Each object commented on is an icon of memory, a clue to the dynamics of relationships, personalities and sensations, which the narrator has no other material means of resurrecting. Here is a passage where the narrator contrasts present décor with past lifestyle:

> Poi vennero le altre camere da pranzo – aperti gli scantinati a liberare i mobili acquistati nella stagione della giocondità coniugale e della floridezza economica – sistemate sempre accanto al Salotto, negli appartamenti di città. E siccome la Rappresentanza della famiglia in città costava assai più che in campagna, più rozza e meno nutriente diventava la qualità dei cibi: con alterigia l'esile fruttiera di cristallo accoglieva l'umile uva fragola, la pera bacata; sulle generose e larghe lame di acciaio dei coltelli mai si rifrangeva il festoso riflesso dei vini; gli argenti esposti sulle mensole non conservavano nemmeno più la memoria dei rostbeef stesi su letti di puré da un lato e di piselli tenerissimi dall'altro, delle maionesi, dei polli arrosto inghirlandati di patatine novelle, delle salse alla besciamella,

delle torte, delle mandorle salate e dei pistacchi, ma parevano funebri doni di
tombe regali. Un'indigenza particolare emanava da quella camera da pranzo:
quella di chi continuamente si raffronta a un passato piú fastoso.

'Perché non mangiamo in cucina?' proponeva una delle figlie con giovanile
spregio delle usanze familiari. (*Althénopis*, p. 246)

Then came other dining-rooms – the cellars would be flung open to free
furniture bought during the season of marital bliss and economic prosperity –
dining-rooms which were always next to the Sitting-Room, in the city flats.
Since Keeping-Up-Appearances cost a great deal more in the city than in the
country, food became that much less refined and nutritious: with stubborn
pride the delicate cut-glass fruit-bowl now played host to humble, cheap
grapes and wormy pears. No more did the substantial, broad knife-blades
reflect the festive hue of wines: the silverware set out on the shelves retained
not even a distant memory of joints of roast beef lying on twin beds of purée
and peas, of mayonnaises, of roast chickens garlanded with new potatoes, of
bechamel sauces, of cakes, salted almonds and pistacchios – now the silverware
looked like funerary offerings from some royal tomb. A particular poverty
emanated from that dining-room: the poverty of those who continually
compare their present state with a richer past.

'Why don't we eat in the kitchen?' suggested one of the daughters with a
youthful disregard for family tradition.

As this itemized review proceeds, the narrator becomes more and more aware of
the personality and presence of her mother, or rather Mother, and realizes how
shockingly far her own identity as Daughter is bound up with that of her
mother. The last chapter plays with the paradox of the narrator's true birth as a
woman being dependent on the death of her mother, as if death were an act of
involuntary childbirth. This is the culmination of a long process of tragic
compensation which sees the narrator's adulthood confirmed at the cost of her
mother's regression into childhood.

This final dénouement, both of the affective tangle between mother and
daughter, and of the obstacles to an uncomplicated relationship between the
narrator and her memory of the past, arouses suspicions about the ordering of
the sections of the book, despite their apparent chronological sequence. The
last section is in many respects the *first* stage in the recuperation of memory,
and acts as a postscripted preamble to the real childhood sections inaugurated
by the portrait of the grandmother. Thus, just as there was a strong cyclical
sense in the repetition of the same family dramas from generation to generation, so, ultimately, the novel itself is based on a loop structure, ending with its
beginning.

If *Althénopis* tries to grasp reality by means of extension, encompassing a
broad sweep from earliest childhood to an adulthood conferred only on the
death of one's parents, Ramondino's second novel, *Un giorno e mezzo* (1988),
squeezes as much experience as it can into a period of thirty-six hours during a
weekend in September 1969. Pretty well every mental and bodily function and

dysfunction makes its appearance, along with a bewildering gamut of intellectual and emotional states. Like a kaleidoscope whose outer dimensions give no clue to the visual infinities within, *Un giorno e mezzo* packs a stunning variety of sensations into its deliberately confused microcosm: the author effortlessly transports the reader from the deathbed ramblings of an alcoholic to a child's pleasure in making mud pies and messing with rabbit droppings.

This major difference of narrative economy, with its emphasis on concentration rather than extension, explains why the single narrating voice of *Althénopis* has been replaced by three main voices, plus a series of cameos where minor characters supply the focalization. The representation of the weekend is achieved by intertwining the experiences of the three main characters – two young women with problems, and one old man with failing health. The setting is a crumbling villa in Naples which has been subdivided and sublet to a bewildering menagerie of tenants, ranging from doctors working on night shift at the local hospital, to agriculture students from remote rural provinces. Pervading everything is the sense of crisis as the Student Movement of May 1968 begins to run out of steam.

The Villa Amore, with its ramshackle alterations, its genteel and not so genteel poverty, its threatened disappearance under the pre-stressed concrete of the building boom, provides a mini-history of what has happened to a certain kind of Mezzogiorno. The original aristocratic estate had been ably misappropriated by an early nineteenth-century factor, one Gaetano Amore, whose descendants had obtained a title through helping the Piedmontese army crush brigandage. With social promotion, the *arriviste* Amore family gradually begins to manifest the same lack of vigour, the same tendency to decline as genuine blue-blooded stock. By the time Ramondino provides her weekend portrait, only the memories and habits, but none of the substance, remain from this period of opulence. The villa is an empty shell recolonized by ever stranger life-forms.

Apart from this symbolic value, the Villa Amore is conceived and treated almost as a theatrical stage, ready with its myriad exits, entrances, balconies and pergolas, to host some bittersweet comedy, Neapolitan style. Indeed, one of the minor characters, an activist who untypically believes in action and not words, exclaims: 'Questa non è una casa, ma un teatro!' (*Un giorno e mezzo*, p. 120) ('This is not a house. It's a theatre!'). As with a stage, none of the action takes place more than a few yards from the villa (there is a bar just down the street), and there is a constant oscillation between outdoor scenes in the neglected terraces and gardens, and indoor scenes in a variety of locales ranging from grand frescoed salons mutilated with makeshift mezzanines, to mean bedsits in converted stables.

The same kind of oscillation takes place with the point of view: almost every chapter is seen from one of the three main characters' standpoint, allowing not only a kind of mutual enhancement (we see what characters think, and what others think of them), but also a tremendous chronological density: in effect, the day and a half of experience is multiplied by three, with some events shared and some private. Again, like the villa itself, this ploy is eminently theatrical, with the illusion of the whole of human experience (conception and death included) concentrated into an arbitrarily reduced time scale.

The novel begins with the dyspeptic insomnia of Don Giulio Amore, one of the decrepit, down-at-heel descendants of the original Don Gaetano. Drinking whisky to mask the pain of a heart condition, he falls into a reverie about his past sex-life, a reverie interrupted by the arrival of a seamstress who has come to sew some drapes for him. Trying to translate dreams into reality, he makes a groping attempt to seduce her, which ends in the ignominy of *ejaculatio praecox*. In his shame, he visits the local bar for more whisky, mortifies himself clumsily in a bramble-filled gap-site, and returns reluctantly to his bedsit. There, he indulges in a hollow camaraderie of sexual innuendo with his doctor neighbour, asleep on his feet after an arduous shift at the hospital: the badinage concerns their 'conquests' that night. Each knows that the other is maintaining a front of male bravado, but is reluctant to puncture the pretence, perhaps out of a strange sense of delicacy.

This first chapter is a wonderfully sensitive account of the process of unwilling accommodation to old age. Ramondino's reconstruction of the 'thought'-processes and physiological indignities of a clapped-out sexual predator would be impressive even from the pen of a male writer. What is striking about the portrayal is that Don Giulio Amore, for all his faults and prejudices, is treated in a fundamentally sympathetic way: from the decrepit facade of his pointless existence he exudes a strange kind of charm.

If the first chapter catalogues a universal, timeless predicament, then the second takes us swiftly into the mêlée of ephemeral passions of 1968–9. The reader is drawn into a meeting of left-wing militants as, wreathed in cigarette smoke, they joust for supremacy with competing quotations from Lenin and Rosa Luxemburg. The atmosphere, with political rivalries masking what are really the politics of unstated sexual jealousy, is recreated with devastating authenticity. But what is truly remarkable about this chapter is Ramondino's ear for language, perhaps the result of her sociological experience recording interviews for an earlier book. She resurrects, in all its mesmeric sterility, the jargon of the time. The dialogue teeters convincingly on a knife-edge between formalized dialectic, procedural wrangles and barbed allusions. Long quotations, from genuine contemporary pamphlets or perhaps able forgeries, are incorporated in the narrative.

The first response of the reader to this strange 'newspeak' is one of mixed embarrassment and amusement. Did they really speak like that? They really did, of course, and Ramondino's purpose in representing it is not parodic: it is more a punctilious respect for period, like the loving catalogues of furniture in *Althénopis*. The effect of this language, after the whisky-soaked ramblings of Don Giulio in the first chapter, is to pull the reader into a very precise historical situation, only to reveal that the underlying dynamic of the characters is not historically determined at all, but is merely a younger, temporarily disguised stage of the same erotic rat-race.

Here is a sample, where Ramondino gets not just the vocabulary right ('irrelevant' and 'denim jacket' are masterfully resurrected), but also reproduces that wonderful, acidulous mixture of selfless idealism, self-importance and low procedural skulduggery.

> 'La questione che affronterò oggi,' esordì Dario, 'non è epistemologica, ma politico-linguistica. Mentre Lenin dové combattere su due fronti, da un lato contro il populismo, dall'altro contro il revisionismo della dottrina marxista, a noi spetta un terzo compito, quello di demistificare il linguaggio rivoluzionario mutuato dal leninismo per ingannare le masse.'
>
> 'Scusa,' intervenne precipitosamente Michele, 'prima di proseguire dovresti avvertire i compagni che l'ordine del giorno è stato cambiato. Stasera dovevamo discutere i documenti berlinesi per il controcorso. Forse non hai avuto tempo di leggerli?
>
> Dario lo fissò sorpreso per l'interruzione.
>
> 'Certo che li ho letti, ma mi sono parsi così irrilevanti che me n'ero dimenticato. Trattano di asili antiautoritari e di comuni, questioni a mio avviso piccolo-borghesi.' E con tono secco precisò: 'La rivoluzione non la fanno i bambini; quanto alle comuni, non vogliamo certo creare i falansteri fourieriani, altri sono i nostri compiti strategici.'
>
> Hutta si alzò in piedi di scatto, parandosi davanti a Dario. Per il caldo si era tolta la giacca di jeans ed era rimasta in maglietta, una maglietta nera e scollata che aderiva al petto abbondante e le scopriva le braccia. Dario, colpito, la fissava, come se prima non l'avesse mai vista. Ma subito lo sguardo si spense e chiese con freddezza: 'Volevi dire qualcosa?' (*Un giorno e mezzo*, pp. 19–20)

'The issue I'm going to deal with today,' Dario began, 'is not epistemological, but politico-linguistic. Whilst Lenin had to fight on two fronts at once, on the one hand against populism, on the other against revisionism of Marxist doctrine, we have yet a third task, that of demystifying revolutionary language, borrowed from Leninism merely to fool the masses.'

'Excuse me,' Michele interrupted, 'before going on, you should warn the comrades that the order of the agenda has been changed. Today we were to have discussed the Berlin papers for the *controcorso*. Perhaps you didn't get time to read them?'

Dario looked hard at him, surprised by the interruption. 'Of course I read them, but they seemed so irrelevant that I just forgot about them. They're all about anti-authoritarian nurseries and communes, petit-bourgeois stuff in my view.' And he added, cuttingly, 'Kids don't make revolutions; and as for communes, surely we're not into Fourier-style *phalanstères*: we've got other business, strategic business to attend to.'

Hutta suddenly rose to her feet, facing Dario squarely. In the heat she had taken off her denim jacket, and underneath she was wearing a distinctly low-cut teeshirt which emphasized her generous breasts, and left her arms bare. Dario stared at her in amazement, as if he had never seen her before. But then the stare faded away, and he asked coldly, 'Did you want to say something?'

The so-called revolutionaries' unwillingness to talk about nurseries forms part of a subtle sub-text in *Un giorno e mezzo,* where Ramondino exposes the 'decoupling' of the sexual and political revolutions of 1968. In the chapters which follow, we see this ill-assorted community from the viewpoints of two women, both in their late twenties or early thirties, each with relationship problems, each involved in the political turmoil of the time, but each with a very different way of coping, or not coping, with the private and public demands made upon them. Erminia, Don Giulio's immediate neighbour, is a primary-school teacher whose emotional life has come unstuck after a long affair with a political activist, followed by a failed suicide attempt.

At school, her teaching, which had been innovative and anti-disciplinarian, had been successful as long as she had reserves of energy and optimism. Now that her life is a mess, she no longer has the charisma to motivate her pupils, and it will be only a matter of time before her class becomes unmanageable. Such apparently 'background' detail, however casually presented, is of course hugely significant: Ramondino is mapping the *terra incognita* where ideals and psycho-sexual needs compete, and schools, with their constant pressure of primary human emotions, were to become a trying environment for ideological crusaders.

When the novel takes on Erminia's voice, she is beginning to worry that she might be pregnant. At the famous political meeting she forms a casual liaison with a left-wing Greek student, and her insecurity about this new relationship, and her worries about her late period, will lead to a devastating attack of migraine which will cause the next political meeting to be cancelled.

Throughout the novel, Erminia is looking for some kind of role, a feeling of being needed, even though she is too embroiled in her own crisis to become a competent carer for others. She acts on impulse as a surrogate mother to her best friend's daughter, taking her on holiday, but in fact she needs to be mothered herself, pouring out her troubles and generally seeking attention. Even her migraine is interpreted, by those less well-disposed towards her, as an attempt to capture everyone's attention.

Her best friend, Costanza, is a cousin of Don Giulio. She lives with her daughter on a precarious private income, whilst pursuing a career as a painter. She is not maternal by instinct, and finds coping with the child mentally and physically exhausting. Her emotional life, too, is unsatisfactory. After living in France for a couple of years, she got involved with Corduras, a clandestine worker for the Algerian independence movement. Forced to return when things got too hot for her in France, she had come back to Naples and had gone to live with her old art-teacher. After the birth of their child, the art-teacher had suffered a severe nervous breakdown, leaving Costanza to fend for herself.

Costanza suffers from having actually created the kind of obligations and involvements which Erminia unrealistically craves. In addition to her daughter and the father of her child, she also has to look after her bedridden mother, and keep an eye on the frail Don Giulio. As if this were not enough, she takes a protective interest in a street urchin she has 'inherited' from a friend.

In a way, the two women provide complementary portraits of the stress of trying to fulfil two roles – on the one hand being autonomous individuals, irrespective of sex, and on the other, being women in a society which is undergoing a profound but incomplete metamorphosis in terms of sex- and age-hierarchies. For all their brave talk about equality, many of the male student activists are heavily contaminated with southern *machismo,* and for all the emphasis on the 'new generation' of 1968, both women are critically just a little too old to take part unreservedly. Both drink too much as a result, and abuse their health with irregular eating and sleeping patterns. Neither is really capable of either accepting their lot, or doing something concrete to change the world.

Central to the dilemma of both female characters is the question of children. Whilst Ramondino's first book is a child's-eye view, a celebration of childhood from within, with little regard for what it is like to be a parent, *Un giorno e mezzo* has some telling passages where adults try to come to terms, half bemused and half aghast, with the strange, alien presence called children. The myths of parental bonding, or even of the general likeability and innocence of children, are cruelly exposed. Here is a passage by which any adult who has had to compete with the night-time hyperactivity of offspring will immediately recognize that Ramondino's writing rings true. Costanza has just put her daughter down for the night, but at the cost of letting her crawl into her own grown-up bed.

> Urlò nel sonno. Pio Pia ebbe un soprassalto, si mise a sedere spalancando gli occhi; rassicurata dalla presenza della madre al suo fianco e dal silenzio, si riadagiò sul guanciale. Costanza non le poggiava accanto il capo, ma riversa sul fianco aveva i capelli e le braccia penzoloni, finché scivolando insensibilmente, si trovò all'improvviso in terra. Pio Pia, che per tutta la notte aveva combattuto con il corpo della madre, finalmente aveva vinto la guerra e giaceva ora al centro del letto, con le braccia aperte.
>
> Stesi allora in terra i due cuscini, nel timore che la bambina a sua volta cascasse, Costanza scavalcò la ringhiera della culla e vi si accoccolò riaddormentandosi subito. (*Un giorno e mezzo*, p. 33)

> [Costanza] screamed in her sleep. Pio Pia shuddered and began to sit up, her eyes wide open; reassured by the presence of her mother at her side, and by the silence, she lay back down on the pillow. Costanza didn't dare put her head down on the same pillow, but, turning on one side, allowed her hair and arms to dangle over the side of the bed, until, slipping imperceptibly, she found herself all of a sudden on the floor. Pio Pia, who all night had fought against her

mother's body, had finally won the war, and now lay at the centre of the bed, with her arms splayed out.

Putting out two cushions on the floor, in case the child should fall in her turn, Costanza climbed over the railings of the child's cot, curled up and fell asleep at once.

Apart from the honesty of this passage, what is interesting is Ramondino's restatement of that ambiguous interchangeability, already seen in *Althénopis,* between adult and child. Not only do they symbolically swap beds, but the child is revealed as forceful as well as wilful: able, by a ruthless pursuit of what it wants, to manipulate more complicated, less secure adults. The adult, in turn, envies the child's success, and returns to infantile behaviour to try to obtain from others what cannot be got by adult interchange. The poetic, almost lyrical treatment of such episodes takes away nothing from the bleak judgement Ramondino passes.

Erminia and Costanza are the two faces of childcare: Erminia displays the ingenuous assumption that children are fulfilling, fun, and grateful for every gesture; Costanza resents the fact that they are parasites, sucking from the parent vital and unreplenishable reserves of energy and freedom. Neither woman feels complete: one needs responsibility, the other needs freedom. Both are disappointed.

As a deliberate contrast to these passive portraits, Ramondino indirectly provides the reader with the image of a woman who has chosen, at great personal cost, the active solution. I say indirectly, because most of the information about her is provided by interior monologues and recollections filtered through Erminia and Costanza. Irene's idealism is expressed in deeds, not words: she teaches in an unofficial slum school, she rejects all coquetry, she is discreet about her own problems (to the point of not informing her friends when she is admitted to hospital), she keeps her emotional life (which runs with a subterranean force: here, Ramondino's evocation of Irene's hidden passion is beautifully controlled) subordinate to her civic commitment. Her death, which leaves both Costanza and the urchin she has adopted grieving, is an emblem of the demise of a certain kind of practical socialism. It is a far cry from Erminia's politically inspired 'non-authoritarian' schoolteaching with its narcissistic search for approval.

A similar kind of balancing can be seen in the male characters, most of whom, to use a phrase current at the time, could be accused of indulging in 'intellectual masturbation'. Corduras, with his mysterious medical missions to countries freeing themselves from colonial repression, is an uncomfortable reminder that commitment must translate itself into action. The contrast with the other militant from outside the incestuous Neapolitan *gruppuscolo* is all too clear: Walter Scott Palumbo belongs to an intellectual tradition that has no time for either the byzantine word-games and relativism of the Neapolitans, or for the morally secure but dialectically hazy politics of Irene and Corduras. Whereas Corduras, arriving tired and hungry after a long journey, will discreetly lay out the corpse of Don Giulio to spare his friends the anguish of discovery, Palumbo (whose light reading is cruelly revealed as Brecht) unfeelingly dismisses Erminia's hospitalization for suspected poisoning as 'una giornata persa in chiacchiere e psicodrammi' (*Un giorno e mezzo*, p. 169) ('part of a day wasted in gossip and psychodrama').

These contrasts and symmetries, it seems to me, are not constructed for ideological motives, even though Ramondino demonstrates a masterly imaginative command of political discourse and thought-processes, and does have views on the values and non-values of the period. Her main interest is in exploring the interface between external commitment (whether to people, ideas or a vocation) and the inner, biological realities of identity. Hers is a poetics of stress in all its forms. The contrastive portraits allow the author to examine and compare the varied adaptive mechanisms of her characters as they try to reconcile the demands made on them. The 'psychodramas' of the Villa Amore are a microcosm of the crisis of values caused by the loss of direction of the student movement, and, in a more diffuse way, the crisis of Naples and the South, caught in a time-warp between antiquated and modern (that is, northern European) patterns of existence.

The 'parallel divergences' of the characters' responses also serve a structural purpose. The novel is a welter of sensations, from menstruation to migraine, heartburn to wet dreams. Time sequences are equally bewildering, as is the use of narrating voice. By providing recognizable overarching patterns, Ramondino tempts the reader to organize classifications and 'make sense' of this experiential avalanche. As the reader pursues this imaginative reconstruction, all kinds of other links begin to surface, as in a game of recognition. By putting two and two together, the reader can deduce that Jorgos, Erminia's new boyfriend, is the same Greek student Palumbo mentions as gathering information on fascists in the engineering faculty. What increases our appetite for intrigue is that Palumbo also says that the Greek is the present boyfriend of his own sister (p. 130). One is left wondering whether the characters are truly ignorant of these crucial relationships, or whether there is a tacit assumption that some things are just not talked about, because jealousy is 'uncool'.

Such ironies are easily created in a work with a multiple point of view and a non-linear time structure. The apparent anarchy of 'who belongs to whom?' resolves itself in a casual, almost lazy way. The effect of this gradual improvement in the reader's orientation, the coming together of scattered information into a coherent picture, is a clever simulacrum of the arrival of an outsider into a close-knit group. The reader, too, feels he has just got off the train at the *stazione centrale,* and has been deposited, uncomprehendingly, in the rabbit-warren of the Villa Amore. Ramondino creates the absolute certainty that the life of the villa has been going on before your arrival, and will continue inexorably after you have left. But with life spilling out at each end, how does Ramondino manage closure?

   The characters who open and close the novel seem at first to have little in common: one, Don Giulio, is old, with a faded aristocratic elegance, the other, the young urchin Pietro, has no graces at all. But behind these differences lies a substantially similar situation. The chapters can be read almost as transpositions of each other. Both characters are restless, both are in quest of somebody to talk to, both leave their suffocating sleeping quarters to wander around the side-streets, both make their way instinctively to the gardens of the Villa Amore. Even Don Giulio's sexual dysfunction, the *ejaculatio praecox,* is paralleled by the nocturnal emission of Pietro's wet dream. This parallelism is made all the more striking by the divergence between age and youth, superannuated seediness and primal innocence, and creates a kind of loop structure, a sensation of cyclicality similar to the mother–daughter dualism of *Althénopis.*

   Even the title, *Un giorno e mezzo,* with its pun on Mezzogiorno, contributes to this sense of infinity, for it goes twelve hours beyond the Aristotelian unities, initiating, then abandoning, the reader into yet another incomplete psychodrama in the Villa Amore.

   To sum up, then, the essence of Ramondino's writing is a tension between a delight for detail and an underlying ambition for universals. It is the capture of a wider, more permanent reality by the poetic recreation of ephemera – momentary physiological sensations, fleeting feelings, 'dated' verbal expressions, long-vanished petty worries and so on, which combine emblematically. It is a fragile art based on the risky accumulation of apparently random 'collectibles', which constitute an aromatic, alchemically distilled essence of period. The reason Ramondino pulls it off is that the apparently undisciplined indulgence in recollection is always accompanied by strict narrative and linguistic control. Narratively, she works in short sections, which are often relatively unconnected. Each section is therefore almost a new beginning, a mini-novel which requires its own dose of figurative and evocative density. In this way, the memorabilia are essential to the action(s), and never seem like clutter as they would in a novel articulated in longer narrative units.

   An example of such underlying economy occurs in *Althénopis* where the narrator's cruel eye for detail, which scrutinizes tile by tile zio Alceste's patho-logically spotless bathroom, is accompanied by an equally cruel nose which detects the ammoniac ferment of urine. This hygienic paradox, lovingly, and one might think excessively indulged in by Ramondino, turns out to be a crucial anticipatory metaphor for Alceste's unresolved life choices. In its strange way, far from appearing as padding, the bathroom Baedecker allows Ramondino to take narrative short-cuts, to define Alceste in all his essence(s) by his ablutions.

   For all the effectiveness of such a technique, the author is clearly aware of the risks: just when lyrical effusion is beginning to get the upper hand, she will cut short with a brutal remark that unmasks the commemorative illusion (and simultaneously demonstrates how we, as readers, have been carried away in our turn). Again, in *Althénopis,* after a wonderful passage on the inhibitions and half-truths associated with money, the narrator cuts in with: 'Solo la merda quindi era merda. Donde l'importanza del cesso, come luogo di verità, di pura realtà, non brutale né ideale' (p. 244) ('Only shit could be counted on to be shit. Whence the importance of the lavatory, as a place of truth, of pure reality, neither brutal nor idealized') Likewise, linguistically, even in the throes of recollective enthusiasm, marvelling at every object in the crazy attic of memory, the writer shows an iron grip not only on lexical propriety, but also on prosody, producing a powerful medium whose balanced periods and rhythmic cadences are proof of the labours of a real poet.

BIBLIOGRAPHY

Works

Napoli: i disoccupati organizzati (Milan: Feltrinelli, 1977).
Althénopis (Turin: Einaudi, 1981).
Storie di patio (Turin: Einaudi, 1983).
Taccuino tedesco (Rome: La Tartaruga, 1987).
Un giorno e mezzo (Turin: Einaudi, 1988).
Dadapolis (Turin: Einaudi, 1989).

Chapter 12

Francesca Sanvitale
Investigating the Self and the World

ANN HALLAMORE CAESAR

Francesca Sanvitale is the author of three novels – *Il cuore borghese* (1972), *Madre e figlia* (1980) and *L'uomo del parco* (1984), and a collection of short stories called *La realtà è un dono*, which appeared in 1987. The protagonists of the three novels and of the title story to *La realtà è un dono* are women, and in each case the narrative concerns itself with a retrospective, but not chronological, account of a substantial slice of its heroine's past. Although the stories are about different protagonists with their own names and identities, the reader is often reminded that their emotions and experiences have a common origin in their author. One noticeable characteristic of the writing that emphasizes the intimacy of the relationship between author and character is the consistency with which Sanvitale handles the passing of time. For those who read her books in sequence, each narrative ends at the point at which fictional time and real time correspond. So *Il cuore borghese* which, despite its publication date, was begun in 1962 and took six years to complete, concerns itself with Italy in the 1950s, *Madre e figlia* focuses on the years from the 1930s onwards and closes in 1978, while *L'uomo del parco* covers the period between 1962 and 1982. In keeping with this practice, the title story of *La realtà è un dono* refers to the thirteen years up to 1987 and was itself written between 1981 and 1987. This chronological progression has encouraged at least one critic to read the three novels as a trilogy, a chronicle of postwar Italy, but in practice the narrative structure of each of Sanvitale's works is extremely complex because it is determined by the vagaries of the protagonist's mind as she maps her own history, in an effort to reach some kind of understanding of the present.

The link between fictional time and the time of writing on the one hand and between author and character on the other, lies in the single chronology shared by the different protagonists, so that their age at any given point is loosely consistent with the passing of real time. They share a birth–date of around 1930. So Irma, the protagonist of Sanvitale's most recent work, is, at fifty–six, the oldest of her four principal female characters. (Sanvitale herself was born in 1928.) As we shall later see, these very precise references to time passing, the remorseless process of ageing that makes it visible to each and every one of us, and the ever-evolving and deeply problematic perception of the real that accompanies it, is central to all Sanvitale's work. Her writings never lose sight of Italy's recent past, from the invasion of Abyssinia to the kidnapping and murder of Aldo Moro, but as her recent collection of stories illustrates so effectively, what determines our lives for most of us are the smallest and apparently most insignificant phenomena. Hidden from the watchful observer, only the attentive protagonist may trace that moment of transition in an effort to come to terms with the present; and even that can only be achieved retrospectively, long after the event.

In marked contrast to the often painful intimacy which develops as the protagonist searches through her past, Sanvitale herself is sparing with the details of her own life. Born in Milan in 1928, she later moved to Florence where she lived for some twenty years before moving to Rome. Alongside her literary work, she also writes articles on contemporary life, culture, and politics. Her novels, in particular *Madre e figlia*, draw, as I have suggested, considerably from her own past, but the significance of this rests not in the detail but in the experiential basis that lies at the heart of her writing and reminds us of the lived connection between author and text.

Sanvitale's most recent heroine, Irma, is preceded by Giulia in *L'uomo del parco*, who in turn was successor to Sonia in *Madre e figlia*, and before her Olympia in the less successful *Il cuore borghese*. The three women are quite distinct, each with her own life and preoccupations, but they share with Irma a hunger for self-knowledge that must be satisfied if they are to cope with life in the present. The essential condition of each of these women is solitude, even though in *Madre e figlia*, the first novel I shall discuss, Sonia knows that she will only reach some kind of equilibrium once she has explored her own life in relationship to her now dead mother's.

The *Madre e figlia* of the title refer to Signora Marianna (unmarried despite the form of address) and Sonia her daughter, but it also reminds us that mothers are always already daughters. It refers in other words to the condition of each woman as mother *and* daughter, which can occur contemporaneously as much as sequentially, as the author points out in an essay called *Maternità* written in 1981, and included in a collection of Sanvitale's essays, *Mettendo a fuoco*, published in 1988, where, speaking in her own voice, she writes:

> Madri e figli. In me, come in ogni donna convivono le due figure. Nell'essere figlie e nell'essere madri [...] Così si alterna la nostra vita di donne, nella debolezza di chi chiede e nella forza di chi accoglie e produce. Nell'essere figlie e nell'essere madri. (*Mettendo a fuoco*, p. 9)

> Mothers and children. In me, as in every woman the two figures coexist. In being daughters and in being mothers [...] In this way our lives as women alternate, between the weakness of one who demands and the strength of one who gathers in and produces. In being daughters and in being mothers.

In the novel the central relationship between mother and daughter is contained between Marianna's memories of life as the youngest child of doting parents and Sonia's experiences of motherhood.

Sonia is born in 1930 when her illegitimacy is still a mark of shame. Her birth is the result of a liaison between her mother and a married army officer for whom her mother leaves the comfort and security of a once aristocratic family, now on the decline. The 'bell'ufficiale' ('handsome officer') of Sonia's imagination makes fleeting visits and gives them material support, albeit sparingly and reluctantly. Mother and daughter live in semi-clandestinity, moving between Milan, Florence and Rome, from apartment to rented room, from hotel to pension according to the fluctuations in their allowance – a vagabond existence determined by their understanding that they are being pursued from place to place by the 'bell'ufficiale's' jealous and pistol-brandishing wife. Only many years later when Sonia herself is a middle-aged mother does she learn that the vindictive wife was an invention of her father's to keep them at a distance after he had become involved in another extra-marital relationship. Mother and daughter's history is recounted by Sonia, even where Marianna is the protagonist, she is always represented through her daughter. So the maternal voice is suppressed and the narrative remains adamantly silent on what Marianna thinks of her daughter. The act of writing, we learn, takes place four years after Marianna's death when Sonia is still unable to free herself of her mother's presence and of her own corrosive guilt. By writing about her, Sonia can return her to life ('e via via che scrivo proprio a mia madre chiedo scusà' (*Madre e figlia*, p. 3): 'and gradually as I write it is precisely of my mother that I ask for forgiveness'), protect her ('si ferma sorpresa e non capisce la mia preoccupazione; sono io, come ho sempre fatto che la difendo' (p. 3): 'she stops surprised and she does not understand my concern; it is I, as I have always done, who defends her'), and change the otherwise irrevocable: 'Io l'ho mantenuta come uno stupido marito [...] Adesso se potessi render viva la ragazza che è stata, sarei pronta [...] a fare qualunque cosa' (p. 4) ('I have supported her like a stupid husband [...] If now I could bring back to life the girl she once was, I would be ready [...] to do anything').

The mixture of love and self-abnegation, rage and hatred that informs Sonia's relationship to her mother continues to overwhelm her four years after Marianna's death. Rage when, having taken over from her father as provider for her mother, she watches helplessly as her mother scuppers all the plans and hard work that have gone into trying to ameliorate their condition, by secretly taking out loans which have to be repaid with accumulated interest. On discovering the existence of one loan which is so steep she doubts if she will ever be able to pay it off Sonia finds herself threatening to kill her mother. Like her father before her, Sonia, an adult woman, resorts to running away from home, but she fails where her father succeeded because the two women are brought together

once again by a common biology. In the next episode we learn that Marianna
has joined her daughter in Rome to nurse her through the after effects of a
miscarriage. Sonia's miscarriages, abortion and confinements, Marianna's breast
cancer and suspected tumour ensure that mother and daughter remain tied to
each other. For Sonia the female body tightens the emotional bonds that bind
her life to her mother's.

How far are we being offered in this study of mother and daughter a
relationship that is remarkable for its atypicality, and how far does it reproduce
features of other mother–daughter narratives? It is a characteristic of traditional
narratives of growing-up that maturity and selfhood are reached through a
process of differentiation and separation, as the child gradually breaks free of the
parental hold and asserts his or her autonomy. Maturity here is defined in terms
of self-sufficiency, autonomy and separation. It was when women writers of the
1920s (writers such as Colette and Woolf) explored in autobiography and in
fiction their troubled relationships with their mothers, and this only after the
death of the mother, that we find a different preoccupation with the maternal
figure, riddled with ambivalence and a desire both to connect and separate.
More recently, since the 1970s, at the time Sanvitale was working on *Madre e
figlia*, women's writing has often taken the form of a 'sustained quest for the
mother' which has been accompanied by the death or elimination of fathers and
brothers. It is within this tradition that Sanvitale's own novel fits and an
interesting comparative study could be made, for example, between *Madre e
figlia*, Marguerite Duras' *L'amant* (1984) and Christa Wolf's *Kindsheitsmuster*
(1976) as narratives of mother–daughter relationships.

Looking beyond literary narrative, these representations of the fraught and
guilt-ridden nature of the mother–daughter relationship are endorsed by recent
psychoanalytic case-studies. Melanie Klein, whose work has enjoyed a considerable revival of interest in the last few years in Italy as in other countries, also
addresses, from the standpoint of her own case-studies, the intensity and
ambivalence of a daughter's feelings for her mother, such as Sonia experiences in
Madre e figlia. In her writing, Klein, like Sanvitale, remains silent on the subject
of maternal emotion, choosing instead to focus on the formation of the child's
identity in relationship to her mother. In her influential essay 'Love, Guilt and
Reparation' of 1937, she argues that the child will always feel deeply conflictual
emotions towards her mother, and will continue to experience throughout her
life a characteristically intense mixture of violent hatred and idealizing love.
(The intensity of that ambivalence is fuelled in *Madre e figlia* by Sonia's awareness
that she will never escape her mother.) More recently, the emphasis on
connection rather than separation has itself become the subject of analysis in
Nancy Chodorow's study of motherhood, *The Reproduction of Mothering. Psychoanalysis and the Sociology of Gender* (1978). Here she argues, contentiously but
persuasively, that where boys develop a sense of a self that is separate and

distinct, girls define and experience themselves as continuous with others; an attribute that is consequent upon their preoedipal attachment to their mother. It is this sense of connectedness and the accompanying fluidity of the self that is so marked a characteristic of Sanvitale's heroines and also of her own relationship to them as their author.

At a formal level the elision of narrator and protagonist is registered in *Madre e figlia* by the manipulation of narrative voice. Although the narrative is mostly in the third person, there are occasions when, by switching to the first person, the distinction between protagonist and narrator is removed. The implication that they have a common identity is later confirmed when we learn that Sonia often writes about herself in the third person when she is searching for self-understanding: 'Un mese prima che la madre morisse, scrisse una pagina perché voleva capire ciò che sentiva. Come si fa spesso trasferì il breve racconto in terza persona.' (*Madre e figlia*, p. 207) ('A month before her mother died, she wrote a page because she wanted to understand what she felt. As often happens she switched the short narration to the third person.') The novel opens in the first person as the narrator conjures up moments from her mother's childhood. Memories that belong to the dead woman have now become part of her daughter's inheritance. But success or otherwise in overcoming the 'rigido vetro' ('the sheet of glass') that separates the living from the dead, Sonia from Marianna, depends also on the interlocutor, the reader who in turn will inherit those memories. So narrator and reader, mother and daughter slide in and out of each other, interact in such a way as to create a sense of continuity in and beyond the narrative itself.

Within the novel Sanvitale usually intervenes in her own voice when she wants to link the narrative to the process of writing and discuss some of the problems it raises. The story of the lives of mother and daughter is determined by Sonia's memory of events, for almost all the characters are dead at the time of writing. The narrative itself is episodic and fragmentary. Blocks of time are dredged up from the past so that the narrative can infuse them with life, but what rises to the mind's surface is often not easily or honestly transferable to the public domain. One problem in particular which is aired here and will be explored further in *L'uomo del parco* is the nature of the relationship that exists between individual lives and public events. Sanvitale is too politically committed as a writer to believe that historical processes and social change do not, of themselves, have profound consequences for those who live through them, but the problem remains of how to represent that interaction without distorting or betraying the integrity of her protagonists.

> È un'angoscia che si ripete quando, per un'immagine o un richiamo mentale o una coincidenza fortuita o per fatti di cui vengo a conoscenza, mi trovo a confrontare la parola storia con la vita di Sonia e di persone di cui ho incrociato i destini. (*Madre e figlia*, p. 73)

It is a source of anguish that recurs each time when, because of an image or a mental recall or a chance coincidence or because of facts that come to my attention, I find myself comparing the word history with Sonia's life and the lives of people whose destinies I have crossed.

Sanvitale spins her narrative like a spider's web, her characters enmeshed and imprisoned in its delicate threads, but somehow, at the same time, she has to relate the circumstances of their lives to those of the real, historical world to which the fiction refers, a world of facts – of dates and public events – a reality that can be looked up and confirmed in public records and books. What Sanvitale does is make the reader party to her struggle to reconcile the inner world of memory and the outer world of history.

Con umiltà, ma anche in modo ignobile, vado cercando di rendere più salda con artifici la ragnatela ondeggiante. Sfoglio libri, accetto fatti, non discuto su ciò che la carta stampata mi propone. Non avendo altri riferimenti, do per scontato che lì, a casaccio, sta la realtà di cui mi voglio impossessare. Con queste cordicelle imprigiono Sonia e Marianna, mi convinco che intorno a loro crescono solidi puntelli. (*Madre e figlia*, pp. 57–8)

With humility, but also ignobly, I go on searching for devices to secure the undulating web. I leaf through books, I accept facts, I don't argue over what the printed page tells me. Having no other references, I assume as given that there, at random, lies the reality that I want to take possession of. With these fine threads I imprison Sonia and Marianna and persuade myself that firm supports are growing up around them.

The task threatens to be insurmountable. Her head, she claims, is incapable of holding the sequence of events, its logic escapes her because her mind cannot *know* what happened in the past except where it has touched on her life, and then she can only know it as she experienced it – a very partial, shaky knowledge indeed. For all the difficulties it presents, and for all her reservations about the undertaking, what is such a striking feature of Sanvitale's writing is the way she excels in recreating an aura of the past, not as background or detail or indeed 'facts', but as a critical part of her protagonists' lives and formation. The tensions produced by her resistance to narratives whose authority does not derive from first-hand experience, together with her awareness that the subjective voice can only speak with authority of what she has experienced (memory is a form of experience too) are pervasive in Sanvitale's next novel *L'uomo del parco*.

The complex structure of *L'uomo del parco* reflects the struggle of its protagonist, Giulia, to reconcile layers of memory and life, selfhood and history that overwhelm her. The stakes are now higher than in *Madre e figlia*, for Giulia's grasp of contemporary life is in jeopardy and with it her sanity. The narrative covers the period in Giulia's life that began in November 1962 and ends in 1982, almost contemporary with the author's completion of the novel.

However, instead of a unilinear narrative, time is presented in layers, an archaeology of the mind. The first and longest section, 'La città incantata' ('The bewitched city'), takes the reader through Giulia's mind into the phantasmagoric city that she inhabits, part Rome, an archaeological city which carries its 2,000 years so that they are visible to the human eye, and part Leningrad, a city, in contrast, dreamed up and developed by just one mind, so that 'standoci dentro sembra di vivere all'interno di un'altra mente, di un altro sogno' (*L'uomo del parco*, p. 9) (being inside it, one seems to be living within another mind, another dream'). The city is frozen, held in the grip of an exceptional cold that takes it beyond time into Giulia's hallucinatory vision of her life lived 'in un tempo senza confini' ('a time without limits'), where dreams spill over into waking hours and where the difference between the two levels of consciousness has been abolished. She wanders the city's parks and on one such occasion meets a man on a park-bench. Their meetings become regular (although Giulia has no explanation for their regularity). She begins to talk about her past, and in particular her parents and their desire for each other before she was born and began to hate them. Her history is contained in a large trunk in her room. With her eyes shut, she thrusts both hands into the trunk and pulls out from the confusion of objects, letters and photographs heaped inside, something to show the man in the park. For the reader, who is also trapped in the protagonist's terrifying consciousness, the thaw brings a gradual process of re-entry into a more attenuated, less painful reality. Gradually the man on the bench materializes into an independent presence with a name, Tommaso, and a history of his own that includes the woman he lives with and their child. The 'gran gelo' ('great freeze') yields to the 'notti bianche' ('white nights') of high summer, Leningrad to Rome, the phantasmagoric to the real.

The next section 'Dopo molti anni' disconcerts the reader by opening on a desultory conversation between Tommaso and Giulia, from which we learn that it is now 1982, six years after the events described in the previous section. In Tommaso's absence (his personal and professional commitments keep him very occupied so his visits to Giulia are infrequent), Giulia begins to reminisce about her past; about journeys she has made, about her parents, and then, in logical progression, given the nature of the relationship, about her husband. This leads into the section 'Antefatto' ('The story up till now') and episodes in her life from 1962 onwards. Opening with her visit to the police station, escorted by her husband, where she has to put in an appearance to make a statement about her failed suicide attempt, it closes with a first-person account of an August spent alone by the sea after the previous summer (which we deduce was the one at the end of the first section) had been spent in Rome. The narrative concludes with 'Epilogo in terrazza' ('Epilogue on the terrace'), which takes us from Giulia's observations of urban life immediately after Aldo Moro's kidnapping, and subsequent murder, in 1978 to the present, 1982.

The discontinuities of chronology and register ensure that the novel is not easy to assimilate. A further disquieting aspect is that the progression from the phantasmagoric city of the mind, in the opening section, to the Rome of today, at the end, is not as unproblematic, or as reassuring, as my summary implies. Giulia's return to a recognizable reality is accompanied by her heightened awareness of the unreality that seems to lie at the heart of much contemporary life, epitomized at the end of the novel through the more filmic aspects of life in Rome in the days and weeks following Moro's kidnapping (the road blocks, the random police searches, the arsenal of heavy weaponry, the constant helicopter surveillances). Giulia thus comes to realize that the significance of this deluded pretence of total control is that it is a response to the fear that has taken hold. It signifies 'we are safe because we are protected!'. What she thought in her alienated state, her 'time of unreality', her mind projected outwards on the world around her, she now learns *was* already there. So the journey from the 'inner' world of a mind breaking down to the 'outer' world of urban life, from the 'unreal' to the 'real', unravels these sets of opposites to reveal that they create difference where difference does not exist. By now Giulia is only too well aware that what she took to be her 'illness' is part of contemporary life with its own existence and history. The events associated with Moro's kidnapping are seen as another stage in an urban reality that has, since 1970, become increasingly frightening, even in terms of personal safety – where once doors were left unlocked, dogs, private security firms and safety locks vainly try to keep homes secure. Meanwhile a bicycle ride near the coast takes her into a landscape of debris, squalor and waste. In an essay on Pier Paolo Pasolini, Sanvitale explained that what she admires so much about him is that he is one of the very few Italian writers who has made his own existential anguish correspond with an analysis of Western democratic structures. Not only does her own writing share that ambition, but she, like him, describes contemporary life through the environment it produces. Giulia's bicycle ride leads her into a non-landscape such as the one where Pasolini found his death.

> Questa seconda forma del tempo nella quale Pasolini era entrato – la nostra in cui viviamo – non conteneva più paesaggi. Non forme ma teatro. In una luce che non è luce la vita è ridotta a demente presenza. Pasolini è morto, appunto, non in un paesaggio o ambiente da lui descritto, da noi vissuto ma nella cancellazione, vuota di senso teatrale, di quel paesaggio. (*Mettendo a fuoco*, p. 76)

> This second form of time that Pasolini had entered – ours in which we live – no longer contained landscapes. Not forms but theatre. In a light that is not light life is reduced to demented presence. Pasolini died, precisely, not in a landscape or environment described by him, lived by us, but in the erasure, devoid of any theatrical meaning, of that landscape.

As with Pasolini, Sanvitale's vision of contemporary life is often expressed through environment. Her narratives always carry a very strong sense of place;

above all cityscapes (the cities of her own life, Milan, Florence and, with an extraordinary intensity of its own, Rome), but as she draws closer to the present so these spaces have given way to the much more contained space of the home as the only environment where one can feel safe.

It would be a mistake to see Sanvitale's protagonists engaged purely in the pursuit of self-understanding, of some kind of stability which would allow them to get on with the business of living. The object of the quest is no less than reality itself, but it can only be apprehended in relation to the self who lives it. Reality changes, it is continually reforming and has the unfortunate habit of fragmenting into many realities as soon as it is approached. It can only be understood retrospectively; this calls for a doubling back, a re-viewing of one's past in the light of the present. *L'uomo del parco* is full of images of circularity, the most dominant being the image of the labyrinth at Epidauros. Travelling through Greece with her son, Giulia becomes increasingly fascinated by the idea of reaching a centre, a revelation. What the labyrinth ensures is that in order to reach that centre, one has to double back on oneself continually: 'per raggiungere il centro bisognava fare almeno tre volte un giro completo e tornare sempre sui propri passi' (*L'uomo del parco*, p. 109) ('to reach the centre one had to make a complete circle at least three times and retrace one's steps every time'). She learns from a book about labyrinths that the word derives from the Minoan for 'casa della doppia ascia' ('the house of the double axe') signifying 'per metafora un percorso difficile che protegge nel suo punto centrale qualcosa d'importante, sconosciuto, sacro e pieno di poteri' (*L'uomo del parco*, p. 115) ('a metaphor for a difficult journey that at its central point protects something important, unknown, sacred and endowed with magical powers'). On learning subsequently that there was no truth whatsoever in this etymological 'fact', far from regretting the demise of her own satisfying theories on the subject, she celebrates the freeing of reality from a retrospectively constructed logic and its return to a situation in which it can only be partially understood.

> Il mondo dei simboli tornava ad essere solo un artistico sogno del reale e stava sopra ad esso come un arabesco, una semplificazione da bambini di ciò che è difficilissimo da comprendere perché troppo complesso. (*L'uomo del parco*, p. 120)

> The world of symbols went back to being no more than an artistic dream of the real which it overlay like an arabesque, a childish simplification of what is extremely difficult to understand because it is too complicated.

In a witty, self-deprecatory *excursus* Sanvitale offers a pertinent reminder that reality and symbol are two completely different entities, and, in the words taken from George Bateson's book on *Mind and Nature* in her essay on Margaret Thatcher and the Falklands war: 'The map is *not* the territory, and the name is *not* the thing named', she reminds us of the dangers incurred by forgetting this simple truth. In adopting the labyrinth to make her point, she has of course chosen one of the most potent symbols of the human condition for many modern writers – Kafka, Robbe-Grillet, Borges and Calvino to name just a few. And by moving backwards and forwards between fascination for the labyrinth as object and then as metaphor, Sanvitale can safely disregard her own warnings about mistaking symbol for reality. Furthermore, perhaps unwittingly, in choosing Greece and the Minoan civilization to make her point, she has turned to a very similar reference to the one Freud used, when, in his essay 'Female sexuality', which appeared in 1931, he finally recognized the importance of the pre-oedipal mother-daughter bond, comparing it to 'the discovery, in another field, of the Minoan-Mycenean civilization behind the civilization of Greece'.

Since the publication of *L'uomo del parco* two more books have appeared: the collection of stories entitled *La realtà è un dono*, (1987), and, more recently, a collection of articles, *Mettendo a fuoco. Pagine di letteratura e realtà*, which appeared in 1988. The presence of the word 'reality' in their titles indicates Sanvitale's continuing search for an understanding of reality's enigmas. Her essays show her to be a challenging and provocative polemicist who uses the form to discuss contemporary life from a cultural and socio-political standpoint. The 'irrealtà' ('unreality') that she sees as its dominant characteristic is attributed to the contempt for history that has developed in Italy since 1945, when history itself, she claims, opted for fable by dividing into two blocks – fascism and resistance. Sanvitale's pessimism, however, lifts a little when she turns to women. Feminism is for her the one truly radical movement and, as women slowly and painfully acquire consciousness of themselves, there is the possibility that the process of disassociation of the private self from the public may be reversed.

Sanvitale's hopes for a future society have no part though in her stories which are concerned with the physiological and psychological damage caused when a protagonist is catapulted out of a familiar reality. Self and reality are shown to have much the same kind of mutually affirmative relationship as self and first name usually enjoy. However odd or unsuitable for the person it identifies a name may at first appear to be, after a while the two become inseparable, and it is impossible to imagine that individual with any other name. It has become a part of their identity. So it is with reality. A sense of self is confirmed by the life it is embedded in: by friends and family, work and home. The process moves in two directions; we draw on our environment for our sense of identity, and, as a result, that reality is confirmed by virtue of our being part of it. So indistinguishable are they that reality is described by Sanvitale as fitting 'come una pelle' ('like a skin'). One example of this process at work which draws on a male protagonist is 'Cena del primo dell'anno con ospiti di riguardo'. Here a successful, but snobbish and complacent author spends a few days over New Year in town away from his entourage of friends and without his wife Marina to protect him.

He accepts an invitation to a party, where he assumes other guests are going to be suitably impressed by his presence. Instead he finds that he is in the midst of another coterie that has formed around another personality, who is far too creative to have ever actually written a word. This brief and relatively harmless excursion into a different environment has devastating physical and psychological consequences. After making good his escape, he collapses in a nearby doorway:

> Aspettai nel buio colando lacrime e asciugandomi gli occhi. Mi ero allontanato da Marina ed ecco avevo perso il senso della realtà e di me stesso. [...] In fondo era anche una burla: non avevo un centro, ero sempre stato un insieme sconnesso, il mio io in frantumi era tenuto da una colla di cui non avevo la scorta. Immaginavo di dover ritirare i pezzi del mio corpo sparsi qua e là e la mia fantasia così si concentrava su un braccio lontanissimo e galleggiante nell'aria, su un piede o su un ginocchio che nel buio si allontanava verso le scale. Li raccoglievo, li riportavo verso il mio fianco che aspettava, mutilo di tutto. (*La realtà è un dono*, p. 148)

> I waited in the dark dripping tears and drying my eyes. I had gone away from Marina and the result was that I had lost my sense of reality and my sense of self [...] Deep down it was also a joke: I had no centre, I had always been a disconnected whole, my fragmented self was held together by a glue for which I had no supplies. I imagined that I had to gather up the bits of my body that were scattered here and there and in this way my imagination concentrated on an arm that was a long, long way off and floating in the air, on a foot or on a knee that in the darkness moved off towards the stairs. I gathered them up, I brought them back to my bereft, expectant, trunk.

Rest, a change of diet and medicines are prescribed, and these appear to deal with the problem; but the protagonist knows that he can never again return to being 'himself'.

What the title story, 'La realtà è un dono' adds to the others in the collection is the protagonist's observation that our identity is not only put into jeopardy by the world around us, but is itself also victim of inexorable, and inescapable, physiological processes from within. Irma realizes that although nothing at all has changed in the composition of her body, what it expresses is now another reality: 'al posto di un corpo molto sessuale, c'era una donna magra e un po' curva alle spalle, il seno pesava verso il basso come un ingombro' (*La realtà è un dono*, p. 211) ('in place of a very sexual body, there was a thin woman, a little round-shouldered with breasts hanging down like a burden'). Although most of the protagonists of these stories are middle-aged, with old age beckoning (and often capable of detecting the marks in everybody around them save themselves), Irma has far more insight than her fictional predecessors in the same volume. She is more honest with herself and therefore manages to make connections where others cannot see them. Irma like all Sanvitale's heroines is deeply aware of the physiological dimension to our sense of self and reality – we are what our bodies permit us to be.

The story is long, almost novella length. It refers to a period of some thirteen years in the life of its protagonist and was itself written over six years. By Sanvitale's standards the structure is straightforward. It opens with Irma sitting on her balcony, which overlooks the Tiber, meditating on her past, before returning in flashback to what she has singled out as the decisive moment in her life some thirteen years earlier whilst on a brief, and as it turns out nightmarish, holiday in Vienna. The city of her dreams, of Brahms and Rilke, does not of course live up to expectation – days without work or domestic duties to shape them soon lose their rhythm and purpose, but worse is to come. One evening on her way to the opera she shuts her finger in the taxi-door and finds herself spending a hallucinatory evening in hospital and, the next day, engaged in a fortuitous sexual encounter with a man who, like her, has his mind on other things. On her return to Rome Irma falls ill, but when she resumes her work as laboratory technician she exercises the same conscientious, careful efficiency and colleagues notice nothing amiss. Something, however, has changed even though it appears to be no more than a few barely perceptible modifications in her life-style. She finds herself walking aimlessly around the city-centre, she goes to the cinema on her own and has an affair or two.

> Proprio per una segreta concatenazione di fatti, curiosità non dette, impulsi non scatenati, ed anelli concentrici era cresciuta una richiesta di vita mai vissuta che l'aveva spinta a caso verso la novità. (*La realtà è un dono*, p. 262)

> Precisely because of a secret chain of events, unspoken questions, pent-up drives, wheels within wheels, a demand for life never lived took hold within her and pushed her haphazardly towards the new.

What has happened is that a trickle of reality has entered an existence that has always before been so controlled as not to admit inner modifications. But there is a price to pay, and a high one at that: the onset of old age. Sitting on her balcony many years later, Irma's understanding of the role that journey has had in her life is facilitated by a book that she is struggling to read on catastrophe theory, lent to her by a former colleague at the laboratory. Developing from work done in the field of mathematics, what catastrophe or chaos theory postulates is that the slightest or most insignificant of causal changes can have undreamed of consequences for the universe. It means that prediction is impossible without a total knowledge of the state of a system at any given moment. The theory becomes startlingly relevant to Irma when she applies it to her own life and realizes that the slight variation in life-style introduced by her trip to Vienna has resulted in far-reaching and unexpected psychological and even physiological changes. Her insight though can neither change reality nor make it more acceptable. It most certainly does not imply that she has come any closer to understanding what this reality is. Far from it; the story and the book end by turning the affirmative title 'La realtà è un dono' into two interrogatives, 'ma la realtà, che cos'è la realtà? forse un dono?' ('but reality, what is reality? a gift perhaps?').

The men in Sanvitale's novels lack the qualities we find in her female characters. They are remote figures, often mediated through the consciousness of the female protagonist, who ensures that they will attract little sympathy. The more powerful they are in relationship to the protagonist the more dehumanized they are presented as being. Giulia's husband Pietro is described as part vampire, part tyrant: 'Nello sguardo gli leggevo desiderio di tortura, furibonda sete di distruzione' ('I could read in his eyes the desire to torture, a furious thirst for destruction'); whereas Sonia's morally reprehensible father is always referred to as the 'bell'ufficiale' – a wooden puppet who has not realized that the Duce, not the King, now pulls his strings. No more agents of their lives than the women protagonists, they are none the less presented as less susceptible to the troubling discontinuities that exist between experience, time, and reality, because they are so adept at separating present from past, reason from emotion. Julius, a character in *Il cuore borghese* is such a man; he has repressed memory because of its painful associations, and now the only question he asks of the world around him, and then only if it gets into his line of vision, is 'a che serve?' ('what use is it?'). His mistress Olympia is body where he is pure mind: 'il corpo è Olympia e lui la mente deformata e cresciuta a dismisura' ('The body is Olympia and he the deformed mind, grown out of all proportion'). Julius is a perverse presence in the novel, but even Tommaso of *L'uomo del parco*, who is decidedly more sympathetic than many of his predecessors, none the less shares with them an unproblematic approach to the real. Tiredness makes him begin to think that those around him are unreal, leaving his certainty in himself untouched. When he enters a strange environment, he 'controllava la realtà, ne faceva l'inventario' ('he controlled reality, he drew up an inventory of it'). Tommaso's solidity and lack of self-doubt may startle the reader who might reasonably have assumed from the first part of the book that Tommaso only existed in Giulia's hallucinating consciousness.

What makes the two sexes so different in Sanvitale's mind? There are of course circumstantial differences. Her women protagonists are described in the context of their private life at home; their workplace, if they have one, is seen as being of so little significance that the reader is often unaware of what they do. Married life seems to be a recipe for disaster. Men do not appear to make good husbands, and marriage brings out the worst in them on a Richter scale that stretches between indifference and cruelty. The only relationship between the sexes that brings happiness is a non-sexual friendship between the woman protagonist and a younger man who listens without making demands – a *confidant*. In *Madre e figlia*, Sonia finds happiness in her conversations with the young doctor treating her mother; Giulia in *L'uomo del parco* finds the same peace in her relationship with the otherwise committed Tommaso (who is also a doctor). Quite apart from her husband's failings, marriage itself drives Giulia to try suicide instead, for she feels she cannot continue with a life so lacking in content; a shortfall in reality, summed up by her as an existençe 'lacerata dall'incoscienza, dalla mancanza di realtà' ('racked by insensibility, by the absence of the real'). Later her friendship with Tommaso leads her to live his reality, unable to establish her own, she 'continuava a confondere sé e lui' ('continued to confuse herself with him'). There is a moment in 'La città incantata' section when she finds a pipe in the trunk of memories, lights it and begins to smoke – it reminds her of the man in the park. Curiously, she finds that her relationship to reality changes as mind and body close up and project a single identity.

> Lo sguardo usciva lento dagli occhi e non si proiettava più prensile verso le cose che non si potevano' prendere, ma stava bene arcuato dentro alle palpebre e aspettava che gli oggetti della realtà venissero a tiro. Emetteva fumo e respiro come se il corpo fosse un prezioso polmone meccanico. (*L'uomo del parco*, p. 23)

> Her gaze emerged slowly from her eyes, no longer reaching for the things it could not seize hold of, but staying taut behind her eyelids waiting for the objects of reality to come within range. She breathed out smoke and air as though her body were a precious mechanical lung.

Luigi Baldacci commented in his introduction to *Il cuore borghese* that Sanvitale's writing is the work of a moralist, but of a moralist who is not a philosopher, because she is 'troppo calata nella biologia del suo personaggio' ('too steeped in the biology of her characters'). But it is this biology which Sanvitale so unswervingly demonstrates must be our starting-point in our apprehension of the real. She rejects the Cartesian view of a self sustained by thought with no interaction between body and self.

Sanvitale in this respect makes uncomfortable reading. She is unsparing in her descriptions of the humiliations and pain that bodies bring. Bodies that have no consideration for the women who inhabit them; bodies that have aged, bodies that continue to have sexual desire when it seems faintly indecent. In *Madre e figlia*, the narrative moves directly from Sonia's abortion to her mother's mastectomy, and then to Sonia's miscarriage at six months and her mother's tumour. In 'La realtà è un dono', Irma charts the physiological changes that herald the start of old age.

> Il caos delle cellule, di cui era stata recipiente e teatro, a poco a poco si era acquietato ed era apparsa la curvatura del mondo che la circondava. Non riconduceva più niente a sé però, nel momento in cui la sua rigida struttura cristallina si era spezzata, il corpo e il viso, con una trasformazione che le parve vicina alla magìa, erano diventati vecchi. La vita era stata impressa in una rete di segni e di cabale sulla sua pelle e sulla sua carne. Il corpo non voleva più il piacere e se nè stava dimenticando. (*La realtà è un dono*, p. 276)

> The chaos of the cells of which she had been both recipient and theatre, had slowly quietened down and the curvature of the world about her had

appeared. She no longer brought anything back to herself however, in the very moment that her rigid crystalline structure had snapped, her face and her body had grown old with a transformation that seemed to her close to magic. Life had been imprinted on her skin and on her body in a network of cabbalistic signs. The body no longer wanted pleasure and was slowly forgetting all about it.

Processes of ageing determine other people's perception of Irma, but by way of compensation they reduce and intensify her own field of perception.

Chronologically Sanvitale's three novels and her collection of stories have taken the reader from postwar Italy to the present day. Each book is self-contained with its own story to tell, but it is noticeable how the women protagonists have themselves aged with the passing of time, in step with their author, leaving us now on the brink of old age. Past experiences, and sometimes decades in her protagonists' lives are evoked without ever losing sight of the processes of recall or re-experience. In the same way as time is never treated as a moment, but always as a process, similarly writing itself is an activity which is not tied to the single moment – a stable vantage-point which can oversee the landscape of the past – but a continuing process which itself is susceptible to changes incurred by the passing of time. In Sanvitale's words: 'i due fondamenti del fatto letteratura: la memoria e il tempo' (*Mettendo a fuoco*, p. 117) ('Time is one of the two fundamentals of the literary act, the other being memory').

In May 1986 Sanvitale addressed a group of writers from Italy, Russia and America on the subject of 'Lo scrittore e il limite della coscienza'. She opened with a rejection of impersonal discourse and 'la strada obbligata della riflessione oggettiva' ('the compulsory route of objective reflection') in favour of narratives in which the writer is always 'all'indagine dell'io e del mondo' ('investigating the self and the world'); only once one has the courage to live one's own subjectivity can one write. Literature, she argues, must resist the compart-mentalization of experience and repression that lies at the root of our behaviour as social beings. Her position is wholly at odds with post-modern culture, which she describes in terms of a shipwreck where literature is just one of the fragments of the detritus that bobs along on the surface. In this post-modern age, the writer is neither friend nor foe, just irrelevant, while writing occupies a position 'nella non-memoria, nella non-coscienza, nella non-vita' ('in non-memory, non-consciousness, non-life'). There have been other prophets of doom before her – Adorno and Horkheimer to name just two – but Sanvitale insists that the present is different because the ship has gone down. Reverting to the language and the imagery of the body, literature

> non ha più il suo liquido amniotico, che era appunto il fattore tempo e il fattore memoria, dal quale sorgeva il suo valore. (*Mettendo a fuoco*, p. 119)

> no longer has its amniotic fluid, the time factor and the memory factor from which its value came.

Sanvitale's insistence on the visceral link between living and writing, author and text, the importance given to a female subjectivity which connects where others may wish to fragment, leads back to the search for reality. This, however, is a search which carries its risks, for in the absence of demarcation between the self and the world, our sense of reality can be hallucinatory, phantasmagoric, a frontier state where real and unreal are indistinguishable.

The writing is remarkable with its obsessive, tormented representation of her women protagonists who exist on the borderlines of the real but are fighting back all the time, resisting the inchoate state of non-difference that will otherwise be their destiny. The surreal, hallucinatory quality of some of her writing links her to Elsa Morante and to Anna Maria Ortese, while her valorization of individual memory to confer self-knowledge and with it a sense of identity brings to mind Natalia Ginzburg and Anna Banti. Where Sanvitale stands alone is in the magnitude of her undertaking; the urgent need to find a new experiential relationship to reality before it is too late and the detritus bobbing on the surface of the sea finally sinks under its own dead weight.

BIBLIOGRAPHY

Works

Il cuore borghese (Florence: Vallecchi, 1972; Milan: Mondadori, 1986).
Madre e figlia (Turin: Einaudi, 1980; Milan: Mondadori, 1986).
L'uomo del parco (Milan: Mondadori, 1984; reprinted 1987).
La realtà è un dono (Milan: Mondadori, 1987).
Mettendo a fuoco. Pagine di letteratura e realtà (Rome: Gremese, 1988).
Since this chapter was completed, Sanvitale has published a new novel Verso Paola
    (Turin: Einaudi, 1991).

Chapter 13

Antonio Tabucchi
Splinters of Existence

ANNA LAURA LEPSCHY

The art of Tabucchi has often been defined as minimalist. Barilli ('Spino e Anastasia', p. 29) takes Bret Easton Ellis' phrase 'less than zero' and applies it to the splinters of existence which Tabucchi puts before us, and which disintegrate as they are presented. Like most writers of the 1980s Tabucchi belongs to no group or movement, but in his individualistic approach gives pre-eminence to the art of narration, letting this bestow unity to the fragmentation of experience. The intellectual quest, which may be expressed as travel to foreign lands, or as a journey of the mind, allows Tabucchi to create realities which prove ephemeral, enigmatic and uncertain.

An original and idiosyncratic writer, Tabucchi is difficult to place within literary traditions. The Italian 'magic realism' of the 1920s, important for his development, finds echoes in his work. Some of Enrico Pea's and Massimo Bontempelli's narratives, opened almost at random, seem to have a family resemblance to Tabucchi's work, in their stylistic movements and tones as well as in some of their themes. But Tabucchi is free of the somewhat parochial elements of these authors and goes beyond the boundaries of national traditions. Other authors he admires can often be glimpsed in his writings: Conrad, Henry James, Borges, Márquez, and above all Pirandello and his own Pessoa, whom, as a specialist in Portuguese literature, he has brought to the attention of the Italian public with his essays and translations. The title he has given to one collection of Pessoa's writings 'Una sola moltitudine' could be extended to Tabucchi's characters: they too are ambiguous, a multitude of personalities within one person – Pirandello's 'uno, nessuno e centomila', Pessoa's heteronyms (see Tabucchi, Un baule pieno di gente, pp. 42–53).

Tabucchi's first two novels, Piazza d'Italia (1975) and Il piccolo naviglio (1978), stand together in his oeuvre for their similar technique, both having a picaresque quality and an exuberant variety of styles and expressionistic details, which, whilst appearing to give only the outer shell, create instead disoriented, questing figures, who briefly make contact with each other and then revert to isolation. In Piazza d'Italia, three generations from Borgo in the Tuscan maremma are followed in their rebellions against the state; in the period which spans Italian history from Unification to post Second World War, from Garibaldini to communists, they are all in conflict with their masters. The main characters with their symbolic names recalling Risorgimento figures and places, Garibaldo, Quarto, Volturno, leave their village, freely or constrained, to join wars in Europe, in Africa, and seek their fortunes in the Americas. Their world in Borgo is dominated by family life, with a sequence of notable women: Esperia, consumed with love for the sea, Asmara, the partisan, who saves the villagers from massacre, Anita, who becomes a nun and refuses to see anyone for the fifty-six remaining years of her life; around them revolves another group of eccentrics: the fortune-teller Zelmira, the nihilist puppeteer Apostolo Zeno, the free-thinking priest Don Milvio, who ends his days burrowing like a mole underground, musing on the failure of the Church.

Cesare Segre described the novel in the blurb as 'una favola popolare così raffinata da rendere inavvertibili le sue arditezze' ('a popular fable of such sophistication as to conceal its bolder features'). The narrative is presented in a cyclical form opening with the epilogue containing the death of Garibaldo, with which the narrative also ends. The material is organized in brief sections, from a paragraph to a couple of pages, with programmatic titles like 'C'è speranza nell'Argentina' ('There's hope in Argentina') or 'L'infallibilità del papa non è più un dogma' ('The infallibility of the Pope is no longer a dogma'). These sections are inserted into three 'tempi', perceived as the changing images in a film sequence. The popular storyteller's style is often in the mode of Verga: 'Gavure era gobbissimo, perché aveva avuto le Febbri ... Quando venivano le Febbri era meglio che Dio se li prendesse con sé. Ma Gavure, nonostante i febbroni era campato' (*Piazza d'Italia*, p. 47) ('Gavure was bent double, because he'd caught the Fevers ... when the Fevers came it was best if God carried one off. But Gavure, despite raging fevers, had survived'). Juxtaposed are passages of overt sophistication: 'Passavano estati languide, acquose, di nostalgie affogate nel rosso dei cocomeri e sogni addormentati nell'afa dei pomeriggi' (*Piazza d'Italia*, pp. 63–4) ('They spent languid, watery summers, with nostalgia drowning in the redness of water melons and dreams asleep in the sultriness of the afternoons'). There are also memorable surrealist effects, like Plinio's gesture – he flings his amputated foot at St Peter's in Rome and sends a postcard back to his Esterina: 'Ho preso a calci Pio IX. Rispettosi saluti tuo Plinio' (*Piazza d'Italia*, p. 15) ('I've given Pius IX a good kicking. My respects, Plinio').

The unexpectedness and success of this novel lies in these juxtapositions, in the broken sequence, with themes which disappear and reappear, in the characters depicted from the outside, but carrying an inner world which motivates their action, public and private, and always idiosyncratic.

As in *Piazza d'Italia*, in *Il piccolo naviglio* private events are interlaced with public, or, as Capitano Sesto would put it, 'storie' ('stories') with 'Storia'

('History'), by which he and his family are variously affected: fascism, the 1948 elections, the postwar building boom, communism, and so on. This novel too has a cyclical structure, opening and closing with Capitano Sesto's metaphorical launching of 'il piccolo naviglio' ('the little ship'), the story he will finally write after the many voyages of his imagination (we may recall that the epigraph of the novel is Montale's 'arremba su la strinata proda le navi di cartone' ('bring the paper boats on to the scorched shore') from the *Ossi di seppia*).

The popular element is also an essential component of *Il piccolo naviglio*. The very presence of three successive protagonists called Sesto creates a strange mythical continuity, where ostensibly the same individual experiences innumerable vicissitudes across the generations. There are also touches of the fairytale, as in the description of the twins, Maria and Anna: 'si affacciarono alla finestra, come nella favola fanno le figlie dei mugnai che sposano i figli del re ... e vennero pellegrini dai paesi più lontani solo per vedere le due fanciulle' (*Il piccolo naviglio*, p. 49) ('they appeared at the window, as in fairy stories millers' daughters do, who marry kings' sons ... and travellers came from distant lands just to see the two maidens').

Transformations of names had been a minor feature in *Piazza d'Italia*: Volturno refused to come to terms with the world and inverted everything, not only accounts but also names, calling Garibaldo Odlabirag and Anita Atina, the latter sticking 'perché bello e facile' (*Piazza d'Italia*, p. 21) ('because it was attractive and easy'). Gastone Vuretti was so overcome by his first day at school that he only managed to stutter the first syllables of his name and was consequently always known as Gavure. In *Il piccolo naviglio* changes of name are a major theme right from the first chapter, which refers to 'Leonida (o Leonido)' (*Il piccolo naviglio*, p. 11) ('Leonida (or Leonido)'), later explained by Argia's conviction that a rough, masculine man like her husband could not be called by a name with a feminine ending. Sesto (the second) is also endowed with a different name at birth. He is the son of the identical twins Maria and Anna, who both appeared as pregnant after only one was seduced. Together they give birth to a boy whom they nevertheless call Marianna, and who is later referred to as 'Sesto detto Marianna' ('Sesto known as Marianna'). The character who is most affected by these changes of name, which often reflect the scarce respect afforded to individual identity, is Capitano Sesto himself. When he acquires a stepfather he is transformed into Alcide (in homage to Alcide De Gasperi, the Christian Democrat statesman), whereupon the bereft child promptly invents a companion, his faithful dog Sesto. His original name is restored to him on the birth of a brother on whom in turn is bestowed the name Alcide.

Another feature along with changes of name, which superficially depersonalizes the character, but which in fact has the opposite result, showing how humanity tenaciously survives efforts to suppress it, is animal imagery and metaphor. Argia is minuscule, she is like a mouse. Her daughter-in-law

Addolorata who writes pleading letters, is a clam: 'le parole verticali di una cozza addolorata supplicavano che le fosse fatto rivedere il piccolo Sesto prima che le sue valve si chiudessero per sempre' (*Il piccolo naviglio*, p. 125) ('the vertical words of a grieving clam begged that she should be allowed to see little Sesto again before her valves closed forever').

Sesto's companion Ivana, called Rosa (Luxemburg), is driven to suicide by the police. When he is subsequently tried, he vents his outrage against the establishment: policemen, lawyers and judges are all seen as animals, this time very different from 'the mouse' and 'the clam' – they are donkeys, gorillas and mastiffs, braying and snarling in turn. When Sesto is finally released from the mental hospital to which he had been relegated after his outburst ('dichiaro inoltre di esser stato giudicato da un gorilla e da un equino travestiti da giudici' (*Il piccolo naviglio*, p. 183): 'I also declare I was tried by a gorilla and by a donkey dressed up as judges'), he makes his way to the village of his birth and collects information from the 'vecchissima cozza' ('the ancient clam'). Now he is ready to set sail, to tell his tale.

In this second novel Tabucchi's narrative has become more complex and the world it creates has greater intricacy and richness, both in its psychology and its social involvement. As his narrative moves into the 1980s, the social and political elements belonging to the reality of Italy will be minimized, giving way to a more metaphysical view of life conveyed in nuances which in their turn will take the place of former expressionistic strokes.

The reversals which Volturno practised in *Piazza d'Italia* become the leitmotif of the collection of short stories *Il gioco del rovescio* (1981; quotations from the second edition with additions, 1988), with the title taken from the opening story. The 'rovescio' here is no longer a manifestation of rebellion against the world, an attempt to transform reality, it is the acknowledgement that things are very often the opposite of what they seem, or rather, as Tabucchi says in the introduction, all the stories are linked by the realization that 'una certa cosa che era "così" era invece anche in un altro modo' (*Il gioco del rovescio*, p. 5) ('a certain thing that was "so" was also different'), thus offering the reader the possibility of multiple interpretations. The story 'Il gioco del rovescio' is pervaded with different examples of 'reverse', beginning with the image of Velasquez' *Las Meninas*, which the narrator's friend Maria do Carmo had defined as a 'gioco del rovescio' ('game of reversals'), and ending with the same image, after her death, with the narrator's belief that she is now able to see the reverse of the picture (concerning *Las Meninas* and the *mise-en-abîme*, see Foucault, *Les mots et les choses*, pp. 19–31). The narrator recalls Maria do Carmo's admiration for Pessoa and his understanding of life's 'game of reversals', whilst her widower claims that she had played the game her whole life, which casts doubt on her republican past and her political involvement, and makes her reality disintegrate for the narrator.

This story has a geometrical structure, with past and present appearing in alternating sections. It opens with the present, with the news which reached the narrator in Madrid of Maria do Carmo's death; it passes to his memories of her, then to his train journey from Madrid to Lisbon and regularly back and forth, until it settles in the present in the meeting with her widower. The note that Maria do Carmo left for the narrator bore the single word SEVER, which he reverses both to its Portuguese *revés* (reversal) and to its French *rêves* (dreams), which are linked in his mind through the image of another self watching himself from the outside, as if in a dream. The story closes with the narrator in a dream, trying to join Maria do Carmo, now aware of the reverse of *Las Meninas*, in the central point of the picture: ' ... m'incamminai verso quel punto. E in quel momento mi trovai in un altro sogno' (*Il gioco del rovescio*, p. 24) ('I set off towards that point. And at that moment I found myself in another dream'; for the importance of dreams in Tabucchi, see Lepschy, 'Filling the Gaps').

Pessoa's presence is significant not only in the case of the short story 'Il gioco del rovescio', but for the collection as a whole. Other writers and literary works form the substance of a number of late stories: 'Il piccolo Gatsby' is populated with characters of the 1930s, who have their equivalents in the narrative of Fitzgerald; Dino Campana ('Dino artista') is the protagonist of 'Vagabondaggio', and Pindar of 'Una giornata a Olimpia'.

The reversal may be based on personality, as in 'Lettera da Casablanca'. This is the homely letter a transvestite called Giosefine sends the sister he has not seen since childhood. It is a story of memories like 'Il gioco del rovescio'. As an enigmatic picture had an important role in the latter, so music and songs create the nostalgic atmosphere of 'Lettera da Casablanca', from the waltzes and songs of their mother's after-dinner entertainment to the cabaret of Giosefine's night club. Also based on the reversal of personality, this time with a touch of mystery, is 'Teatro', where the narrator's host in Mozambique, Sir Wilfred Cotton, who entertains him with solo scenes from Shakespeare, is discovered after his death to have been a great Shakespearean actor who had disappeared without a trace. The narrator learns the reasons for this disappearance, but will not disclose them to us: 'Erano motivi generosi e nobili, forse patetici. Non sarebbero stati male in una commedia di Shakespeare' (*Il gioco del rovescio*, p. 55) ('They were generous, noble reasons, perhaps full of pathos. They would not have been out of place in a Shakespeare play'). Mystery, generated from a wonderfully evoked long childhood summer, also pervades 'I pomeriggi del sabato', where an absent father (possibly dead) is glimpsed cycling past the house every Saturday afternoon by his small daughter.

In 'Dolores Ibarruri versa lacrime amare', one of the most subtly constructed and effective stories of the collection, there is a double twist. The libertarian Rodolfo, who had fought with the International Brigades, had reproached la Pasionaria for her orthodoxy, warning her that she would eventually weep bitter tears. At the end of his life, tormented by Khrushchev's revelations, he receives a note, ostensibly from la Pasionaria herself, with the message of the title. This is interwoven with the story of his much loved son, sender of the note, who in the last paragraph turns out to have been murdered for political (presumably terrorist) activities.

This gives an idea of the variety which the theme of reversal assumes in Tabucchi. To this main theme can be added a sub-theme of travel, when characters are outside their normal surroundings and are presented as more isolated and impressionable. Travel may be part of the plot, as in 'Il gioco del rovescio', or relived in the memory of the narrator as in 'Lettera da Casablanca', or it may lead to an encounter in a foreign country, as in 'Teatro'. Another sub-theme is that of memory, often related to death or the presentiment of death: the narrator and the widower remember Maria do Carmo in 'Il gioco', Giosefine, before his operation, recalls his childhood in 'Lettera da Casablanca', and in 'Dolores Ibarruri' the twice-bereaved mother re-evokes family life when her son was a little boy.

Variety of tone is achieved in these stories by the creation of contrasting narrative voices. The most intellectual, in the first story, is also – the author tells us – the most autobiographical, with the narrator being a young academic who divides his time between Italy and the libraries of Madrid and Lisbon. The narrators of the other stories are further removed from Tabucchi, many of them being women. There is the young woman social worker of 'Voci', full of resourceful competence in her professional life and illusions in her private life. The use of 'voices' is one of the most original stylistic features of the collection. In this particular story we have the voice of the narrator interweaving with the voice of her telephone caller, all reported by her, sometimes as direct speech, sometimes as indirect, and sometimes as indirect free. There is the distraught mother in 'Dolores Ibarruri', talking to a journalist, rambling about the past, trying to understand her tragedy. Similar in style is the letter of the transvestite Giosefine reminiscing before his operation. Most striking of all, perhaps, is the young boy of 'I pomeriggi del sabato', who conveys how the monotonous family routine is transformed by the explosive effect of his sister's reported sightings; here we have another notable example of filtered voices, creating a polyphonic effect.

In Tabucchi's next two narratives, *Donna di Porto Pim e altre storie* (1983) and *Notturno indiano* (1984), what had only been a sub-theme of *Il gioco del rovescio*, namely travel, comes to the fore. In the preface to *Donna di Porto Pim* Tabucchi talks of his predilection for travel accounts, which have the advantage of offering 'un *altrove* teorico e plausibile al nostro *dove* imprescindibile e massiccio' (*Donna di Porto Pim*, p. 9) ('an *elsewhere*, at once theoretical and plausible, to our inescapable, unyielding *here*'), clarifying however, that although he had been to the Azores, much of the volume is fictional. Equally in *Notturno indiano*, although the book opens with the addresses of the places mentioned in the text,

Tabucchi offers this list that it may give the illusion of casting light 'a questo Notturno in cui si cerca un'Ombra' (*Notturno indiano*, p. 13) ('on this Nocturne in which one seeks a Shadow'), or that it may allow 'l'irragionevole congettura che un qualche amante di percorsi incongrui potesse un giorno utilizzarlo come guida' (p. 13) ('the unreasonable supposition that some lover of incongruous itineraries might one day use it as a guide').

The protagonist of many of the stories in *Donna di Porto Pim* is the whale, and the book closes with 'Post Scriptum, una balena vede gli uomini' ('Postscript. A Whale's View of Man'), a 'reverse' tale, or, as Tabucchi says, a tale which is both inspired by 'un mio vecchio vizio di spiare le cose dall'altra parte' (*Donna di Porto Pim,* p. 11) ('a bad habit of mine of spying on things from the other side'), and by the poetry of Carlos Drummond de Andrade (another author Tabucchi has translated). 'E come sono poco rotondi, senza le maestosità delle forme compiute e sufficienti, ma con una piccola testa mobile nella quale pare si concentri tutta la loro strana vita' (*Donna di Porto Pim*, p. 89) ('Not rounded at all, lacking the majesty of our complete and self-sufficient forms, with little, moving heads where all their strange life seems to be concentrated'): these are men seen by the whale, with a process of Shklovskian estrangement, as Ravazzoli ('Viaggi tangenziali e storie ribattute', p. 32) points out. Elsewhere it is the whales which are almost mythical creatures, whose fascination is parallel to the fascination of the traditional way of life of the Azores: both seize the narrator's imagination as phenomena in the process of extinction. Alongside the whale there are few notable humans, as in the last story, the one which gives the collection its title. Here Tabucchi uses the device of a narrator who tells a tale so that his listener may record it: 'scrivi che questa è la vera storia di Lucas Eduino, che uccise con l'arpione la donna che aveva creduta sua, a Porto Pim' (*Donna di Porto Pim*, p. 87) ('write that this is the true story of Lucas Eduino, who killed the woman he'd thought was his, with a harpoon, in Porto Pim'), concludes the narrator at the end of a powerful, incisive account of his betrayal at the hands of the woman who had enticed him away from his life as a whaler, to sing for the clients in her tavern.

The night, which is so important for Lucas Eduino, dominates in *Notturno indiano* both as bringer of dreams and of insomnia. The epigraph of the book is Maurice Blanchot's maxim: 'le persone che dormono male sembrano essere più o meno colpevoli: che cosa fanno? Rendono la notte presente' ('those who sleep badly seem to a greater or lesser degree guilty: what do they do? They make the night present'). In his search for Xavier Janata Pinto, the narrator's encounters are mostly nocturnal, in the penumbra of hotels, from seedy to luxury, in the night rounds of a hospital with cockroaches crunching under foot, in the night crossing by ferry with the disjointed conversation common to travellers, in an after-dinner discussion with a gnostic member of the Theosophical Society, which keeps returning to the poetry and sayings of another gnostic, Pessoa, in a meeting with a tiny, monkey-like prophet during a stop-over on a night bus-ride to Goa, in a conversation with a Portuguese Jesuit and with Tommy the postman, who is gradually working through the Philadelphia telephone direc-tory, sending postcards home. These are the outward stages of the search. They are characterized by sharp, concrete descriptions and by a succession of dialogues which instead are psychologically elusive and enigmatic.

With dreams and stories, or stories that may be dreams, the search for Xavier becomes a reverse search: it is not the narrator who is looking for Xavier, but Xavier, perhaps his heteronym, who is looking for him. Roux, Rouxinol, the narrator's nickname, becomes fused with Xavier's image of himself as a noctur-nal bird. Roux asks for Mr Nightingale in the last hotel, and, at the news that he has left, adopts his tastes and habits, telling his dining companion that in the book he is writing 'io sarei uno che si è perso in India' (*Notturno indiano*, p. 77) ('I am someone who has lost his way in India') and outlining the story of Xavier – his story – up to the present. The search is over. Seeker and sought have become one, or a double, neither of whom wants to continue: 'ora che mi ha trovato non ha più voglia di trovarmi … e anch'io non ho più voglia di esser trovato' (*Notturno indiano*, p. 80) ('Now that he has found me he no longer has any desire to find me – and I have no desire to be found either'). The story ends as the narrator plans the end of the story.

Of these two 'travel' books, *Donna di Porto Pim* is more like a mosaic, with the various components indeed creating in the reader's mind 'un *altrove* teorico e plausibile' ('an imaginary and credible *elsewhere*'). With his penetrating, unemphatic style Tabucchi presents a strange but credible world whose charac-ters are vulnerable and yet powerful. *Notturno indiano* is the more satisfying book: to these qualities are added the elements of a continuous narrative which allows Tabucchi to create a natural link between the disparate encounters, each one a perfect sketch, which the search for Xavier brings together to form this nocturnal view of India – not only in the traditional sense that he is the source of focalization, but because the search, in its gradual transformation, gives an unexpected meaning to his journey. These further implications are touched on in 'La frase che segue è falsa. La frase che precede è vera' (in *I volatili del Beato Angelico*), which is a fictitious exchange of four letters between Tabucchi and Xavier Janata Monroy, his acquaintance at the Theosophical Society, who reads more into *Notturno indiano* than Tabucchi is prepared to accept, insisting that it is pervaded with Hindu philosophy. Tabucchi acknowledges that 'i libri sono quasi sempre più grandi di noi' (*I volatili del Beato Angelico*, p. 48) ('books are almost always bigger than ourselves'), but modestly claims that his correspond-ent's interpretation is based on an 'equivoco', ('misunderstanding'), and to prove his predilection for 'equivoci', he sends him a copy of his latest book.

'I treni che vanno a Madras', one of the stories in the collection *Piccoli equivoci senza importanza* (1985) picks up the theme of *Notturno indiano*, with the narrator on a night train from Bombay to Madras, hinting that the victim of a nazi doctor may have taken his revenge on his persecutor, now living in India as an Argentinian citizen. This story was incorporated into the film version of *Notturno indiano*, directed by Alain Corneau (see Scrivano, 'L'orizzonte narrativo di Antonio Tabucchi', p. 10).

The reader frequently has to integrate and interpret in the course of these stories, but sometimes the mystery persists and clarification is inopportune: 'Malintesi, incertezze, comprensioni tardive, inutili rimpianti, ricordi forse ingannevoli, errori sciocchi e irrimediabili' (*Piccoli equivoci senza importanza*, p. 7) ('Misunderstandings, uncertainties, belated understandings, useless regrets, unreliable memories, foolish and irreparable mistakes'). What counts is the elusiveness of relationships, a past which resurfaces unexpectedly, chance events and their irreversible effects, reactions at a tangent to their cause, and what Ravazzoli calls 'paesaggi della psiche e stati d'animo dell'ambiente' ('Antonio Tabucchi', p. 77: 'landscapes of the psyche and states of mind of the setting'). Unlike *Il gioco del rovescio,* most of the narrators in *Piccoli equivoci* are male, some of them a transformation of the author, which Ravazzoli characterizes as belonging to 'heterobiography' (p. 77); these include 'I treni' already mentioned, and, also in the first person, the story of the title and 'Rebus', 'Gli incanti', 'Any where out of the world', and, in the third person, 'Rancore e nuvole'. The other stories, which Ravazzoli situates within 'autofinzione' ('autofiction'), have women as narrators in the first person: 'Aspettando l'inverno' and 'Stanze', or men very remote from the author: 'Isole', 'Cambio di mano' (both in the third person), and 'Cinema', which has a hidden narrator. This division, which Ravazzoli herself considers tentative and flexible, has to my mind the merit of distinguishing between the more intellectualizing narrators and the meditative but instinctive ones.

The treatment of time, which has been a complex feature of Tabucchi's work, from *Il piccolo naviglio* with Sestos spanning the generations, to *Il gioco del rovescio* with its interplay of past and present, and to *Notturno indiano*, where the past catches up with the present, is again memorable in *Piccoli equivoci*. The eponymous story shifts between past and present: the narrator's recollection of his student life with Leo and Federico and with Maddalena, whom they are all three in love with, is interspersed with the present of the trial, in which Federico is the judge and Leo is the accused. The phrases they jokingly used in their youth: 'un piccolo equivoco senza importanza, un piccolo equivoco senza rimedio' ('a little misunderstanding of no importance, a little misunderstanding that can't be corrected'), acquire a sense of irony and of finality as Leo is about to be sentenced for presumed terrorist activities. As students they had acted, Maddalena a magnificent Antigone to Federico's Creon; now they are all incapable of abandoning the parts they have been assigned – the adolescent play-acting of their choice has become the adult role-playing of necessity: 'ormai le parti erano assegnate e era impossibile non recitarle' (*Piccoli equivoci*, p. 16) ('the roles had been allotted and it was impossible not to play them').

In 'Rebus' there is a temporal organization dependent on an opening dream-sequence, which prepares the reader for an unresolved outcome. We are left with the same mystery as the narrator: why did the driver of another car try to kill Miriam and the narrator on the rally? Why was the Bugatti Royale elephant replaced? Were Miriam and her husband really intent on killing each other? Where did they both disappear to? The tale ends with a comment about narration and dreams: 'Ma a lei perché interessano le storie altrui? Anche lei deve essere incapace a riempire i vuoti fra le cose. Non le sono sufficienti i suoi propri sogni?' (*Piccoli equivoci*, p. 46) ('But why are you interested in other people's stories? You too must be unable to fill in the gaps. Can't you be satisfied with your own dreams?'). Dreams and storytelling both supply the links which escape our reason, both fill the gaps left by everyday reality. This reminds one of the comment by Borges (*Doctor Brodie's Report*, p. 13): 'writing is nothing more than a guided dream'.

The languid Riviera of the rich is the setting for 'Rebus', Lisbon cafés at nightfall are the location of the Baudelairean 'Any where out of the world'. The narrator is a young language teacher; he discovers in the local paper the message (reminiscent of the newspaper advert in 'Rebus': 'Lost elephant looking for 1927 Bugatti') which gives the title to the story. This leads his thoughts back to a relationship, a triangle, the desire to escape from the spleen of Paris to a white marble city on water, a planned reunion after the insertion of the newspaper message, tragedy and guilt. As in 'Rebus' we share in the suspense and mystery; in this case the identification of narrator and reader is aided by the transforma-tion of 'I' into 'you', which also allows the narrator to stand aside and observe himself. The switch is neatly engineered by means of a transitional impersonal 'you':

> e anche questo mi dà il senso di una libertà bella e superflua, come quando hai pensato a lungo di fare una certa cosa e finalmente ci sei riuscito. E ora che fare? Niente, non far niente. Siediti in quel caffè al tavolino ... apri il giornale, l'hai comprato per pura apatia'. (*Piccoli equivoci senza importanza*, p. 72)

> This too gave me a feeling of splendid and superfluous freedom, just as when you've wanted for ages to do something and finally you've done it. And what was to be done now? Nothing, just nothing. Sit down at a table in that café ... open the newspaper, which you bought quite indifferently'.

'Cambio di mano' also has elements of a detective story, this time set in the New York of wealthy criminals, where the protagonist has to find his contact at a performance of *Rigoletto*, at the words 'Sparafucil mi nomino' ('Sparafucil is my name'). Stylistically as well as episodically this is a very fast-moving story, with a dialogue technique that fits the speed, and which Tabucchi perfects in this collection. Here is an example:

Presero un tavolo discreto. Cameriere tolga tutte queste candele, ne basta una, desideriamo luce bassa. Facciamo pazzie? D'accordo. Allora ostriche per cominciare, lo champagne non molto gelato, come ti chiami? Non ha importanza. Io mi chiamo Franklin, come ti chiami? Chiamami come ti pare. Perfetto. Cometipare è un bel nome, ma sembra più un cognome, ma se vuoi così, Cometipare. (*Piccoli equivoci senza importanza*, p. 127)

They chose an inconspicuous table. Waiter take away all those candles, one's enough, we want subdued light. Shall we go overboard? Yes let's. Then oysters to begin with, and champagne, not too cold, what's your name? It doesn't matter. I'm called Franklin, what about you? Call me what you like. Perfect. Whatyoulike is a lovely name, more like a surname, but whatever you say, Whatyoulike.

Mystery and dreams are the substance of 'Gli incanti'. It has echoes of 'I pomeriggi del sabato', with a narrator who is a young boy on a long summer holiday, a little girl (this time a cousin), an absent father and a cat. The mystery here does not involve an apparition, but an evil power precipitating various disasters, for which the children's diet of melodramatic stories and films makes them particularly receptive. The kitten – Beelzebub's cat, the unwelcome gift of a suspect stepfather – is blamed. To counteract this malevolence, Clelia casts her own spells. She is a magnificently characterized child, with a squinting eye that starts rotating wildly in moments of stress. The sense of tension and foreboding which the children experience is conveyed by the narrator as he filters Clelia's reactions, contrasting with the surface normality of the adults. At the same time he dreams of the wartime political execution of his uncle at the hands of the usurper, his step-uncle, and above all he invents an escape route for himself by dreaming that his own absent father (dead? missing?) will take him away in a red Aprilia bought specially for the occasion. With the narrator a child, the emphasis is more on the present, but there is also a shift in time with memories of peaceful summers before the appearance of the step-uncle: 'Le nostre fughe nella pineta, le scorribande fra i cespugli, il mare che si scorgeva dalle dune: tutto finito, lo sentivo' (*Piccli equivoci*, p. 49) ('Our flights into the pinewoods, our sorties among the bushes, the sea glimpsed from the dunes: all gone, I knew it'). The dreams too, recalling figures who have disappeared, are indicative of the coexistence of past and present.

Tabucchi explores the relationships of the young and the old with their families. In 'Isole' a pensioner who had worked on the ferries all his life rejects his sophisticated daughter's offer of a home in a letter stylistically reminiscent of Giosefine's informal tone in 'Lettera da Casablanca', with the excuse that he wants to rear chinchillas. There are two stories in which the theme of the solitude of old age leads to an unexpected ending. In 'Aspetta l'inverno' the illustrious writer's widow, after presiding over manifestations of reverence and respect, on her return home from the funeral starts methodically burning her husband's manuscripts, uttering the words 'Povero stupido – povero caro stupido' (*Piccoli equivoci*, p. 27) ('Poor fool, poor dear fool'). The resentment expressed by a woman who has lived in the shadow of a great man is explored again in 'Stanze', where the elderly sister of a seriously ill famous academic, goes over their relationship, with memories sparked off by family photographs, and admits to herself, after a lifetime of devotion, that what she now feels is hatred. Her gesture at the end, when she prepares an injection to ease her brother's pain, is open to another interpretation. Hatred of one sibling toward another is the theme too of a one-act play, 'Il tempo stringe', in *I dialoghi mancati*, (1988).

Resentment is also the theme of 'Rancore e nuvole', this time in the part of a self-made man, a professor of Iberian literature, who uses his long-suffering wife and his reactionary teacher as stepping stones in a successful career, where he is however unable to forget the past and feels vindictive toward everyone in his profession. Some elements are effective: the scholar's discovery of Portugal and his reaction to his favourite author, Machado, whose Juan de Mairena articles he particularly appreciates for their 'capacità di assumere maschere' and their 'sottigliezza pseudonimica' (*Piccoli equivoci*, p. 92) ('capacity to wear masks', 'subtle ability to assume various roles'). But the protagonist's pettiness is such that it destroys the reader's empathy.

The first story, 'Piccoli equivoci', had role-playing in the past and in the present as a component. This prevails in the last story, 'Cinema', which in many ways is reminiscent of Pirandello's *Questa sera si recita a soggetto*, with its fusing of actors and characters, and of his *Sei personaggi*, with its repetition of identical dialogue. Pirandello dominates in the recent 'Il signor Pirandello è desiderato al telefono', a one act play in blank verse in *I dialoghi mancati*. As Tabucchi explains in the preface, the dialogue is occasioned by a meeting Pessoa and Pirandello – two kindred spirits – might have had, but never did. The setting of the play is a Portuguese psychiatric hospital in 1935 with a small group of patients as the audience for an actor who has been sent to amuse them, in the role of Pessoa, or, as he says: 'sono Pessoa che finge di essere un attore/che stasera interpreta Fernando Pessoa' (*I dialoghi mancati*, p. 16) ('I am Pessoa pretending to be an actor / who tonight is playing the part of Fernando Pessoa'). The thread running through the play is the desire to ring Pirandello on the part of the actor/Pessoa, who switches continuously from one role to the other. When he is Pessoa, Tabucchi gives him paraphrases of some of the real poet's lines, like 'Peripezie ne ho avute molte / tutte dentro di me, beninteso' (*I dialoghi mancati*, p. 17) ('Adventures I have had many / all within me, naturally'), and his answer on love: 'Potrei dirvi che è l'essenziale, / e che il sesso è solo un accidente' (p. 21) ('I could tell you that it is the essence / and that sex is only accidental') (see Pessoa, *Il poeta è un fingitore*, pp. 52, 33). The inmates participate, echoing in chorus the words Pirandello is made to utter. When the telephone actually rings on stage it is Pessoa who answers, only to be brusquely transformed into the actor again by the producer at the other end, who tells him his time is up.

The metaphorical search, which is a thread running through Tabucchi's narrative, whether it is a search to fill the gaps existing between disparate elements, or a search 'alla rovescia', as for Xavier, becomes the subject of *Il filo dell'orizzonte* (1986), an elusive and open-ended detective story. This work (again brief and incisive, like all his novels) is in some ways reminiscent of *Notturno indiano*: the search appears at first to be a real one, leading the enquirer from clue to clue, involving meetings with a series of otherwise unconnected individuals, and in the course of the pursuit the seeker takes the place of the sought, so that the discovery of another becomes the discovery of the self.

The setting for the inquiry is Spino's home town, an unnamed Genoa, with its crumbling historical centre, its port, its hills, its cafés. But in his various encounters, as he tries to piece together the few clues he has about the 'Carlo Nobodi', or the Kid (as he prefers to call him, being an *aficionado* of old films), who has been shot presumably by the police, and had ended up in the morgue where Spino works, parts of Genoa and its surroundings, hitherto unknown to him, are visited. A novelty too are the people he meets. From them and from the photo found on the body, Spino reconstructs something of the Kid's character and life. His careful perusal of an enlargement of the photo ('l'ingrandimento-traccia alla *Blow-up*' ('the enlargement-clue as in *Blow-up*') as Stefano Tani, ('Il filo del silenzio', p. 176) calls it) yields his most exciting clue. This is part of the title of the newspaper held by the father and reflected in a jug of water, the word 'Sur'. Argentina, guesses Spino, and his guess is later confirmed. The importance of this photo (another aspect of which will be mentioned later) recalls other photos in the work of Tabucchi: they may be a link with the past, like the parents' photo in 'I pomeriggi del sabato', the series in 'Stanza' and Dolores' photo in 'Cambio di mano', or they may be a pointer to the future like the protagonist's photo in Sparafucile's handbag, again in 'Cambio'. They may also be a warning not to take images out of context as at the end of *Notturno indiano*: 'Méfiez-vous des morceaux choisis' (pp. 77, 81) ('Beware of selected pieces').

Films too are prominent in the work of Tabucchi, often representing an alternative reality, as in 'Gli incanti', 'Any where out of the world', and 'Dolores Ibarruri'. They are an intrinsic element of *Il filo dell'orizzonte*. Sara, who shares Spino's love for old films, identifies herself with their heroines, whether they be Myrna Loy or Virginia Mayo, to create a romantic life full of exotic journeys that Spino denies her. For Sara, films lead to day-dreaming, while Spino sees their correspondences with the life that surrounds him. The inhabitants of the morgue become Mae West, Marcelino Pan y Vino as well as the Kid; when he is near a vast flight of steps in the cemetery he thinks of *Battleship Potemkin*, and even feels he is being filmed. Anna Longoni ('Antonio Tabucchi', p. 139; see also Tani, 'Il filo del silenzio', p. 139; Morabito, 'Antonio Tabucchi', p. 143) in her review of this novel, relates the striking use of the perfect tense throughout the book to a film technique, with a narrator describing image after image the events of a film, which are momentarily present for us, and very quickly become past.

The more Spino is urged to drop his investigation, the more insistent he becomes, wanting to discover not who shot the Kid and why, but who the Kid was, to give him an identity. It is Sara who first voices what must have already been in Spino's mind, when she sees the victim's photo in the paper: 'Con la barba e venti anni di meno potresti essere tu' (*Il filo dell'orizzonte*, pp. 31–2) ('Grow a beard and lose twenty years and it could be you'). Later, when Spino is looking at the photo found on the Kid, which also contained a dog, his memory stirred and 'non per finzione, ma reale dentro di lui, una voce infantile chiama distintamente "Biscotto! Biscotto!"' (*Il filo*, p. 58) ('Not inventing, but really hearing it in his mind, a child's voice distinctly calls "Biscuit! Biscuit!"'). When another acquaintance, the jazz pianist Peppe Harpo, asks him 'Ma chi è lui per te?' ('But what is he to you?'), Spino replies: 'E tu ... tu chi sei per te? Lo sai che se un giorno tu volessi saperlo dovresti cercarti in giro, ricostruirti, frugare in vecchi cassetti, recuperare testimonianze di altri, impronte disseminate qua e là e perdute?' (*Il filo,* p. 80) ('And you ... what are you to yourself? Do you realize that if you wanted to find that out one day you'd have to look for yourself all over the place, reconstruct yourself, rummage around in old drawers, get hold of evidence from other people, clues scattered here and there and lost?'). In an interview for *L'Espresso* (p. 188) Tabucchi mentions the Shakespearean phrase which Spino makes his own: 'Piange, chi era Ecuba per lui?' ('What's Hecuba to him, or he to Hecuba, that he should weep for her?' *Hamlet*, II, 2). It is his thoughts on Hecuba that lead to Spino's dream within a dream and a return to childhood innocence. At the last appointment he is sure no one will be there, and here the investigation ends, in laughter, with the partial discovery of the Kid and of himself.

Tabucchi wrote a postscript to the novel – some of which may refer to himself and/or Spino: 'Ho comunque notato che più s'invecchia più si tende a ridere da soli' (*Il filo*, p. 107) ('All the same I observed that the older one gets the more one tends to laugh to oneself'). As for the name Spino, he says, some may think it is short for Spinoza.

> Spinoza, sia detto per inciso, era sefardita, e come molti della sua gente il filo dell'orizzonte se lo portava dentro gli occhi. Il filo dell'orizzonte di fatto è un luogo geometrico che si sposta mentre noi ci spostiamo. Vorrei molto che per sortilegio il mio personaggio lo avesse raggiunto, perché anche lui lo aveva negli occhi. (*Il filo dell'orizzonte*, p. 107)

> Spinoza, let me say in parenthesis, was a Sephardic Jew, and like many of his people carried the horizon within him in his eyes. The horizon is in fact a geometrical locus, which moves as we move. I wish that by magic my character had reached it, since he too had it in his eyes.

The horizon that shifts as we shift is indicative of Tabucchi's narrative world, of a world which has a visible reality but which is unattainable, eluding our grasp every time we try to approach it. In *I volatili del beato Angelico* (1987), the introduction explains the 'fractalian' nature of these pieces: 'come schegge alla deriva sopravvissute a un tutto che non è mai stato' (*I volatili del Beato Angelico*, p. 9) ('like drifting splinters survivors of some whole that never was'). In the eponymous first story the 'filo dell'orizzonte' belongs to the world of this 'tutto che non è mai stato', the world of the imagination of Fra Angelico, who communes with the winged creatures of his fantasy. We have already had an example of Tabucchi's 'spiccata passione per la pittura' ('marked passion for painting') as he put it in an interview for *Panorama*, in the relevance given to *Las Meninas*. 'I volatili' is a brilliantly written account of how Fra Giovanni da Fiesole (Fra Angelico) was led to depict in his pictures the three-winged creatures that came to rest in his convent, visible to him alone. In his description of these fantastic beings, Tabucchi uses the focalization of Fra Angelico, who combines the prosaic with a sense of mystery: one of the creatures has 'delle braccine giallastre come quelle dei polli spennati' (*I volatili*, p. 12) ('small yellowish arms like a plucked chicken's') and communicates with the monk by means of the multicoloured plumage of its wings; another is 'quell'esserucolo rotondeggiante con la coda imprendibile come una fiamma' (*I volatili*, p. 20) ('that little round creature, tail elusive as a flame'). This gift for expressing visual invention verbally becomes a complex form of ecphrasis in 'La traduzione', where the narrator is describing a picture in a gallery to a blind friend.

Other 'splinters' in this volume also relate to earlier themes, as we have seen in the letters linked to *Notturno indiano*. The fable 'Una giornata a Olimpia' is picked up by 'Lettera di Calipso ninfa, a Odisseo re di Itaca', but the classics do not seem to inspire Tabucchi's best work: Calipso's envy of mortality and fear of the eternal leaves too little to the imagination. Fables from a later tradition have instead a gripping effectiveness as 'L'amore di Don Pedro', where the king to avenge himself of the murder of his lover, proclaims a coronation, exhuming her body and riding in state with her crowned corpse dressed as a bride by his side. The academic story, of which we already had an example in 'Rancore e nuvole', is picked up again in 'Le persone felici', but here too the relationship of a scholar and his young assistant, his lover, does not rise above parody. Other recurring themes are those of the destruction of manuscripts ('Storia di una storia che non c'è') and suicide ('Ultimo invito').

In the already cited 'Il signor Pirandello è desiderato al telefono' both Pessoa and Pirandello refer to their impending deaths, Pessoa's in 1935 and Pirandello's in 1936; the former knows because he has consulted his horoscope, and as for Pirandello, 'lo so chi glielo ha detto, / che è stata Madama Pace, perché ogni domenica mattina / lui riceve i suoi personaggi' (*I dialoghi mancati*, p. 42) ('I know who told him, / it was Madama Pace, because every Sunday morning /

he is at home to his characters'). Presages of death, soothsayers' predictions, visions of the future post-factum, are themes variously developed by Tabucchi to give an outward pattern to existence, as in two letters included in the section 'Passato composto', the letter of Don Sebastiano de Aviz, the sixteenth-century king of Portugal to Goya, and that of Mademoiselle Lenormand, an early nineteenth-century fortune-teller, to Dolores Ibarruri, la Pasionaria.

In the introduction to *I volatili*, Tabucchi associates 'Passato composto' with 'Gli archivi a Macao' as 'eccentriche a se stesse, profughe dall'idea che le pensò' (*I volatili*, p. 9) ('eccentric to themselves, refugees from the idea that thought them up'). 'Gli archivi di Macao' in my opinion, together with 'I volatili', is the most impressive of the collection; it is related to the two letters I have cited from 'Passato composto' for its temporal conflation, albeit in this case more complex. After an opening in which the narrator tells of a surgeon's refusal to operate on his father's pharingeal carcinoma until after an important medical congress, we find the narrator on a flight to Hong Kong, bound for Macao and its archives. A bump of the plane takes him back to his thirteenth birthday, when he is riding on the back of his father's scooter and as his father's scarf slips off it reveals 'una ferita orrenda che ti squarciava il collo da parte a parte ... ma tu non sapevi di avere quella ferita e sorridevi ignaro' (*I volatili*, p. 73) ('a horrible wound that gashed your neck from side to side ... but you did not know you had that wound and you smiled unaware'). Over this image of thirty years earlier is superimposed the tragic, recent one. To this double image is added another: the thirteen-year-old narrator on the back of the scooter is on his way to Macao, explaining to his father that he is going to research on Camilo Pessanha, who wrote the line 'Sono fiorite per sbaglio le rose selvatiche' ('The wild roses have blossomed in error'). To which comes the benign query: 'ti pare che abbia un senso?' (*I volatili*, p. 75) ('Does it really make sense?'). The line of poetry? Research? Life? But all this turns out to be a letter, not as in the case of Goya and la Pasionaria, to a public figure of the future, but to the dead father, or 'alla tua traccia che hai lasciato dentro di me' (*I volatili*, p. 74) ('to the trace you have left in me'), to the narrator himself.

In the six short stories, written over the course of the last five years, which make up his most recent collection *L'angelo nero* (1991), with its Montalian echo which takes us back to *Il piccolo naviglio*, Tabucchi picks up some of the political concerns of his early novels. In an interview for *La Stampa*, he reveals how in recent years he has been disturbed by the revisionist view of history: 'Questa correzione della storia che si tende a fare in una società opulenta, cinica e totalmente impermeabile alle questioni morali mi dà un senso di repulsione ... Credo che il fascismo sia stata una grande ferita storica che non si è ancora rimarginata' ('This correction of history which is frequently produced by a rich, cynical society, totally insensitive to moral questions, is repellent to me ... I think that fascism is a great historical wound which has not yet healed').

In 'Capodanno' the theme of fascism in Italy emerges most openly: the small boy who is living in a fantasy world with the Vernian Captain Nemo is haunted by the reality of his 'heroic' father's execution by the partisans; 'Notte, mare o distanza' introduces the Portugal of the late 1960s and the police harrassment of students; "Staccia buratta' analyses the behaviour of a promoter of Céline. Other stories present different aspects of contemporary malaise. In 'Il battere d'ali d'una farfalla a New York può provocare un tifone a Pechino?' a Signor Farfalla's hypothetical account of his crime becomes the confession of a *pentito* (a criminal turned state witness), and another confession, of an artistic kind, is woven into the most Montalian of the stories, 'La trota che guizza fra le pietre mi ricorda la tua vita', where the poet who is about to betray his work seeks a form of absolution.

In the interview for *La Stampa*, quoted above, Tabucchi questions the importance critics give to his style:

> 'Quanto alla diversità di scrittura, nonostante quello che dicono alcuni critici sullo stile, a me non interessa ... Credo che la mia sia una scrittura molto di anima e non di mente, dettata dalle circostanze, dai luoghi, dalle stagioni. A me interessano la storia e la psicologia dei personaggi, non la scorza' (*La Stampa*, 2 March 1991)

> As to diversity in writing, in spite of what some critics say about style, it is of no interest to me ... I feel that my writing comes from the soul and not from the mind, dictated by circumstances, places, seasons. I am interested in the story and the psychology of the characters, not in the shell.

Nevertheless one of the characteristics of this collection is the variety in the narrating voice. 'Voci portate da qualcosa, impossibile dire cosa' is addressed to a 'you' narrator whose technique for telling stories is mentally to extract sections of conversations overheard and to piece together the verbal mosaics to form a narrative. In 'Notte, mare o distanza' there are two levels of narration: the outer narrator describes the methods of the inner narrator who is responsible for choices in the plot and for alternative outcomes; whilst in 'Staccia buratta' there is the problem of the starting-point of a narrative.

In his introductory note Tabucchi talks of his black angels, whose wings are not covered in feathers but in bristly hair. These evil presences haunt the stories: the most clearly defined is the 'guardian angel' of 'Staccia buratta': it has the face of an aged child and dark furry wings. They also take other forms, sometimes that of a fish, as in 'Notte, mare o distanza' where a 'cernia pingue, lustra, oleosa' (*L'angelo nero*, p. 39) ('fat, shining, greasy grouper') is inserted by the inner narrator into the plot, first making its appearance in the police car, and then growing in size and importance as the story closes and two of the characters disappear astride its back: 'immaginò bizzarramente che salissero le scale a cavalcioni di quella cernia moribonda' (*L'angelo nero*, p. 48) ('he had the bizarre fantasy that they went up the stairs astride that expiring grouper'). In

'Capodanno', which has echoes of Tabucchi's earlier 'Gli incanti', a dead fish is one of the anonymous gifts sent to the mother to remind her of her fascist husband's watery end; the story closes with the child preparing to cultivate poison in a rotten fish. The book's final words are: 'il pesce rosso doveva essere completamente putrefatto' (*L'angelo nero*, p. 152) ('the goldfish must have rotted completely'). This theme of evil which had made its appearance in *Piccoli equivoci* permeates the whole of *L'angelo nero*. Tabucchi explains its importance in terms of a private and public malaise, as well as of his greater awareness in his maturity of the shadowy aspects of existence: '*L'angelo nero* è nato da quel luogo doloroso e privilegiato, per guardare il mondo, che è l'esperienza del malessere' (*L'angelo nero*, p. 3) ('*L'angelo nero* came from that painful and privileged lookout on the world, which is the experience of ill-being').

The two worlds which Tabucchi had so far created, one with his fables *Piazza d'Italia* and *Il piccolo naviglio*, in which the sharp, expressionistic strokes of the outer form conceal an unspoken inner existence, the other, in which ambiguities and reversals are presented as splinters of existence, have now been enriched by his latest work, *L'angelo nero*, where elements of the two worlds merge: the greater political commitment of the early novels is injected into enigmatic fragments, all now imbued with a powerful sense of discord and evil. Further developments can be expected from an author who is only in mid-career.

BIBLIOGRAPHY

Main Works

Piazza d'Italia (Milan: Bompiani, 1975).
Il piccolo naviglio (Milan: Mondadori, 1978).
Il gioco del rovescio (Milan: Saggiatore, 1981; Milan: Feltrinelli, 1985).
Donna di Porto Pim e altre storie (Palermo: Sellerio, 1983. Translated by Tim Parks in
     Vanishing Point (London: Chatto and Windus, 1991) as *The Woman of Porto Pim*.
Notturno indiano (Palermo: Sellerio, 1984). Translated by Tim Parks as *Indian Nocturne*
     (London: Chatto and Windus, 1988).
Piccoli equivoci senza importanza (Milan: Feltrinelli, 1985). Translated by Frances Frenaye
     as *Little Misunderstandings of No Importance* (London: Chatto and Windus, 1987).
Il filo dell'orizzonte (Milan: Feltrinelli, 1986). Translated by Tim Parks as *Vanishing Point*
     (London: Chatto and Windus, 1991).
I volatili del Beato Angelico (Palermo: Sellerio, 1987). Translated by Tim Parks in
     Vanishing Point (London: Chatto and Windus, 1991 as *The Flying Creatures of Fra
     Angelico*.
I dialoghi mancati (Milan: Feltrinelli, 1988).
L'angelo nero (Milan: Feltrinelli, 1991).
I have used the English translations, sometimes with modifications, in the text of my
     chapter. Since this chapter was completed Tabucchi has published two new books:
     Requiem (Milan: Feltrinelli, 1992) and *Sogni di sogni* (Palermo: Sellerio, 1992).

Critical Works

Barilli, R., 'Spino e Anastasia', *Alfabeta* 95 (1987), 29

Barilli, R., 'Tabucchi, Fortunato, Barbaro', *Alfabeta* 109 (1987) , 12

Borges, J. L., *Doctor Brodie's Report* (Harmondsworth: Penguin, 1970).

Caesar, M., 'Italian Fiction in the Nineteen-Eighties', in Smyth, E. J. (ed.),
   Postmodernism and Contemporary Fiction (London: Batsford, 1991), pp. 74–89.

De Michelis, C., *Fiori di carta. La nuova narrativa italiana* (Milan: Bompiani, 1990), pp.
   196–8.

Foucault, M., *Les mots et les choses* (Paris: Gallimard, 1966).

Lepschy, A. L., 'Filling the Gaps: Dreams in the Narrative Fiction of Antonio
   Tabucchi', *Romance Studies*, 18 (1991), 55–64.

Longoni, A., 'Antonio Tabucchi, *Il filo dell'orizzonte*', *Autografo* 4 (1987), 137–40

Morabito, P., 'Antonio Tabucchi, *Il filo dell'orizzonte*', *Il Verri* 8:7 (1988), 141–3.

Nava, M., 'Ritratto di Antonio Tabucchi. Le metamorfosi di uno scrittore', *Corriere
   della Sera*, 19 March 1988, 3.

Pellegrini, E., 'Su alcuni libri di narrativa "impura"', *Il Ponte* 49 (1988), 246–55.

Pessoa, F., *Il poeta è un fingitore. Duecento citazioni scelte da Antonio Tabucchi* (Milan,
   Feltrinelli, 1988).

Ravazzoli, F., 'Viaggi tangenziali e storie ribattute: l'insonnia narrativa di Tabucchi',
   Autografo 2 (1985), 23–37.

Ravazzoli, F., 'Antonio Tabucchi, *Piccoli equivoci senza importanza*', *Autografo* 3 (1986),
   76–9.

Scrivano, R., 'L'orizzonte narrativo di Antonio Tabucchi', *Il banco di lettura* 6 (1990),
   10–14.

Tabucchi, A., *Un baule pieno di gente. Scritti su Fernando Pessoa*, (Milan: Feltrinelli,
   1990).

Tani, S., 'Il filo del silenzio', *Il Ponte* 43:6 (1987), 174–7.

Interviews

Marcoaldi, F., *L'Espresso*, 19 October 1986, 187–92.

Cherchi, G., *Panorama*, 2 September 1990, 93.

Lombardi, P. D., *La Stampa*, 2 March 1991, 3.

Chapter 14

Pier Vittorio Tondelli
The Calm After the Storm

DIEGO ZANCANI

Pier Vittorio Tondelli fits the image of a young 1980s writer almost perfectly. Born in 1955, his first book appeared in 1980. He is interested in youth culture, contemporary music, jazz and American novels of the 1960s. He has a penchant and a very good ear for the language of teenagers and a flair for 'speaking in writing' which is one of the features of contemporary narrative texts. He is, by his own admission, not a critic nor a literary pundit, nor is he interested in ideologies. His personal 'voice' may indeed show some insecurity. Although it is loud and occasionally foul-mouthed, it has a distinct residue of tender, even lyrical, undertones. He has inherited some of the traits of American 'beat' novels; two of his favourite authors are Jack Kerouac and James Baldwin and he has a tendency to be inspired by 'On the Road' stories. His frequent reference to a 'young Holden' also points to the importance of J. D. Salinger's novel *The Catcher in the Rye* (known in Italy as *Il giovane Holden*). The language that some of Tondelli's characters use is similar to the witty blend of 'sardonic hyperbole ("It was the last game of the year, and you were expected to commit suicide or something if old Pencey didn't win") and inspired invective' used by the young Holden Caulfield (see Curtis, 'How to Invent Teenagers'). Salinger's novel, published in 1951, 'was in the vanguard of what became the teenage rebel movement' (Curtis), and Tondelli's first book had some similarities to this American-inspired prose. His early work seems to embody some of the so-called postmodern attitude to certainties, to a heroic past, which are treated with scepticism or irony. The effect on the reader is more shocking than aesthetic. Nevertheless, even if the label postmodern had a precise meaning, to categorize Tondelli as such would be an oversimplification. His characters may seem lonely, derelict figures, but they have a yearning for dialogue, and are set in a carnivalesque atmosphere. Such features inevitably recall Mikhail Bakhtin's studies of the novel and the semiotic work by Julia Kristeva. I do not wish to imply that Tondelli read, at an early date, either of these authors, although he does mention in some of his works the lectures given by an Italian professor who had worked on carnival and folk literature (Piero Camporesi).

In other contemporary writers, like Aldo Busi, there seems to be a tension between the picaresque, almost surreal elements in the life of sophisticated urban society, and the myths of a rural past. Tondelli is not in the least interested in the agricultural reality of the generation before him. For example, references to traditional food, which is so important in the region he comes from – Emilia-Romagna – are incidental and frequently ironical. The rejection of the past is of course compulsory in generational storytelling. In some of the *Altri libertini* stories, the characters also deny the future. To an older generation some of Tondelli's works may seem to be lacking in depth or seriousness. This, which may itself be a superficial observation, could be said of most activities inspired or influenced by carnival, which was an extremely serious business.

Pier Vittorio Tondelli is a writer liked by the young, who have responded to the colloquial style of his early works, recognizing in it many of the elements of their own everyday speech, including obscenities, ironies, obscurities and suspended sentences. They also recognized in Tondelli's early writing an attempt to replace abstractions, ideologies and theorizations with straightforward emotions. The latter are expressed in a direct, almost physical, corporeal way. This effectively becomes the language of his first book *Altri libertini*, published in 1980, when the author was twenty-five years of age. An older, academic, generation may be obsessed with meaning and interpretation rather than with an immediate response to and acceptance of the work of art or artefact as an experience. This is no way to approach Tondelli. The 'erotics of art' advocated by Susan Sontag, for contemporary works, 'in place of a hermeneutics' may be more appropriate. The six stories that make up *Altri libertini* contain distant references to violence. This is reminiscent of Pasolini's use of violent themes and language. But the distance between the two is vast. The realistic representation of his characters is only one of the aspects of Tondelli's narrative. His first published book is partly a generational 'novel', partly *on the road*. As in most 1980s narrative, dialect is absent in Tondelli's works (except for one or two short phrases) and his models are more American than Italian. In this sense his work represents one aspect of what historians have defined as the 'Americanization' of Italy (Lanaro, *L'Italia nuova*). In the first story of *Altri libertini* nearly all the personal names have an American ring to them (Johnny, Molly, Giusy). The stories themselves do not appear to have a common core or development. They are heterogeneous, although one of the unifying features is provided by the youth of the characters who have a strong individualistic quality. The stories are set in the late 1970s. Of the main preoccupations in Italy at that time only one seems to be treated in a prominent way and in the first person: drug abuse; the other, political terrorism, is not mentioned. The material, like the language, is loose, the opening sentence of the book expresses a cold, impersonal, and somewhat futile sense of life. This is exemplified by swearing at the unpleasant season and its weather conditions. There are no certainties in this world and who knows what values are, who needs values?

> Sono giorni ormai che piove e fa freddo e la burrasca ghiacciata costringe le notti ai tavoli del Posto Ristoro, luce sciatta e livida, neon ammuffiti, odore di ferrovia, polvere gialla rossiccia che si deposita lenta sui vetri, sugli sgabelli e nell'aria di svacco pubblico che respiriamo annoiati, maledetto inverno, davvero maledette notti alla stazione [...] (*Altri libertini*, p. 1)

> It's been cold and raining now for days. The freezing storm forces us to spend the nights at the tables of the Posto Ristoro; bare and livid light, mouldering neons, smell of railways, reddish-yellow dust that collects slowly on windows, stools and in the air of public no-hope that we languidly breathe. Damned winter, truly damned nights at the station...

One may wonder who are the 'we' referred to in this first sentence. It is a descriptive sentence. There is a traditional use of style with a prevalence of nouns over verbs, the so-called nominal style. The author carefully chooses an almost literary vocabulary (with connotations going back to classical and medieval imagery centering around the word 'burrasca', 'sea-storm') which contrasts with the colloquial phrase 'aria di svacco pubblico', representing the sense of boredom and dissatisfaction shared by the young. The narrator, in a supposedly 'physical writing', tends to be elusive, and in the early stories of *Altri libertini* the self, the 'I', is substituted by an undefined and choral 'we'. The individual exists only as part of a group, the group of outcasts, young junkies, drifters, the old prostitute of the *Posto Ristoro*. This is a railway snack bar, but in Italian it has connotations of 'restoring to health, refreshing' which contrast with the rather hopeless position in life of the outcasts. They, in their extreme precariousness still form something apparently cohesive, the 'society' shaped by the weather, by the seasons of the year and, above all, by the night. They are, to use a common term, favoured by Tondelli, 'the fauna' of the Posto Ristoro, and such animalesque references are frequent in his works. Like animals some of his characters act solely by instinct. But one of their motivating forces is pleasure rather than food, even the self-destructive temporary pleasure of narcotics. The first episode ends at dawn, after Giusy and others have obtained their fix or other gratification or individual pleasure, the only existing standard: 'Giusy si avvia barcollando verso casa. Quasi mattino. La prossima notte tornerà al Posto Ristoro come sempre oppure se ne andrà via dalla città e da tutti e il Bibo lo lascerà' (*Altri libertini*, p. 34) ('Giusy staggered off towards home. Nearly morning. The next night he will return to the Posto Ristoro as always, or he will go away from the city and from everyone and he will leave Bibo'). Giusy is a nocturnal animal who will go back to the Snack Bar, with its limited, claustrophobic, violent fauna. His choices, like those of his friends, are limited; either go back to the bar as usual, or leave the town, friends and all.

It is striking that in experimental, nocturnal writing of this kind the pseudo-Aristotelian unity of time and place is respected. This shows the underlying stability and relatively traditional framework of these stories. The suppressed theatrical elements suggested in 'Posto Ristoro' emerge more clearly in the second episode which even in its title 'Mimi e istrioni', clearly refers to popular theatre. Although the Italian title is in the masculine, the story is written from a feminine perspective. The main characters are three girls, and a young gay transvestite, Benny. The group is despised by the middle-class population of Reggio Emilia because its members are considered as sexually loose, immoral, degenerate outcasts. They of course seem to have a great time. They seem driven by pranks and jokes and are full of vitality, as befits a group of well-fed, independent teenagers. The author effectively mimics their language and mannerisms. Comic effects are created in a jocular, expressive, exaggerated use of language, in which even traditional childish rhymes (like the one about Epifanìa) are exploited, as exemplified on the local radio station: 'si vanvera soprattutto delle nostre povere eroine Cinderella e Joan-of-arc oppure Alice o la Virginiawolf o quella sfigata poveraccia dell'Epifanìa che ogni anno tutte le feste gliele fanno portar via.' (*Altri libertini*, p. 41) ('We chat about our poor heroines, Cinderella and Joan-of-arc or Alice or Virginiawolf or poor unlucky Epiphany, who is made to carry off all those celebrations every year').

Unlike the first episode in which there is no change in the junkies' stultifying and dangerous, albeit colourful, everyday reality, in 'Mimi e istrioni', the characters are more conscious of ideological issues. They are more involved in political debate, there is reference to collective consciousness and 'public' versus 'private' discussion. They participate in a deeply ironic way in local radio broadcasts. But this is only one small part of the scene on which they act, which is wider and more open (the streets, the square) than in the previous episode (the inside of the Snack Bar, a disused rail coach, the railway lavatory).

The girls rebel against bourgeois normality, against the close mentality of the small town. Their actions seem to have an impact on the middle-aged population who label them as 'the garbage of Reggio' in one of Tondelli's rare outbursts of dialect.

After the sense of purposelessness, of drifting and of pure fun which emanates from the beginning of this episode, there is a change in tone. In the spring the girls participate in a theatre group which helps them to raise their awareness of feminist issues. They pursue a personal search for an identity which will become clear after the summer, after the holidays which the three girls and their gay friend will spend in different parts of the Mediterranean, Greece, Spain, Turkey: 'Ma quando ci si ritrova a settembre si capisce che qualcosa di nuovo è purtroppo arrivato. E non sarà mai più come prima'. (*Altri libertini*, p. 63) ('But when we come back in September, you can tell that something new has, regrettably arrived. And it will never be like before again'). In fact Benny, the ex-transvestite, turns up with a beard and a pretty girlfriend, stating: 'Insomma care mie il tempo dello svaccamento è terminato' (*Altri liberini*, p. 64) ('My dear, the time for drifting is over'). 'Svaccamento' is connected to 'svacco' in the previous episode and points to a clear change in attitude. There is a contrast between the carefree attitudes that the young girls show at the beginning of the story and the sense of crisis at the end. At the end there is the realization that the change from the perfect sense of fun of youth to a more mature attitude cannot be made without some penalty. This realization leads one of the girls to attempt suicide and the episode ends with her friends too rejecting their futile past as the two of them meet in a hospital corridor:

> e ci abbracciamo forte e diciamo forza forza che gliela fa, ma c'è quasi nausea per quegli anni sbandati e quel passato che vorremmo anche noi rigettare assieme alla Nanni, quel pomeriggio vuoto di febbraio. (*Altri libertini*, p. 65)

> and we hug each other and say come on, come on, she's going to make it, but we're almost sick over those aimless years, and that past which we, like Nanni, would like to reject on that empty February afternoon.

There is no judgement of the actions of the characters on the part of the narrator, but the purely instinctive, animalesque attitude which we noticed in the first episode and partly in the opening of 'Mimi e istrioni' is now accompanied by more reflective moods which can be seen in the following episode as well.

The third episode, is entitled, perhaps paradigmatically, 'Viaggio' ('Journey/Trip') and is narrated in the first person. The main story is clearly set in 1974, whilst its preamble in which the narrator's friend fantasizes about a possible trip to Bombay to buy drugs is set at a later date. In 1974 the visit to Brussels 'cheaper than Paris, more provincial and more Northern' (*Altri libertini*, p. 69) 'Ci serve per smaltire l'esame di maturità e i sonnolenti anni dell'apprendistato' ('Was necessary to us to recover from our "A level" exams and the sleepy years of our apprenticeship').

'Viaggio' is written partly as a diary and it is the first episode set abroad in Belgium, Holland and Britain. In Brussels a group of students from various countries are decorating a small hospital; they sleep in the basement. This is simply an account of how young people meet and relate to each other, through smoking pot, talking, having a party. 'Viaggio' represents a point of comparison with the Italian provincial atmosphere that was prevalent in the previous two episodes. After Brussels and Amsterdam, the story moves to Bologna, with its university life in the background. Occasionally the experimental, though somewhat predictable nature, of the narrative emerges: for example, in the following list, one of many used by the author, especially when he is trying to escape a narrative impasse:

> Molto spesso cuciniamo in casa soprattutto uova. Uova bollite, strapazzate, incamiciate, fritte, sott'olio, sotto spirito, in salamoia, in naftalina, affumicate, alla piastra, in omelette, a fette, a dadi, a taglioline, all'occhio di bue, alla coque,

brinate, gelate, bollenti, alla crema, gratinate, affogate e ripiene. (*Altri libertini*, p. 92)

Very often we cook at home, mostly eggs. Boiled, scrambled, poached, fried, stored in oil, pickled in spirits, in brine, in moth-balls, smoked, grilled in omelettes, sliced, diced, in strips, à la coque, chilled, frozen, boiling, with cream, au gratin, poached and stuffed.

This kind of apparently gratuitous listing which borders on nonsense and on pure oral pleasure, has a long tradition in popular literature, especially in the region of Italy Tondelli comes from. It was used in the sixteenth century by Giulio Cesare Croce, in poetry which was set to music and sung at street corners. We find it in particular in compositions relating to or written during carnival, and this remote connection with folk literature seems to confirm Tondelli's interest in narrative akin to the carnivalesque. In the 'trip' episode the process of growing up is underlined: Gigi, the protagonist's friend, has stopped injecting out of poverty and love: 'eppoi si cresce, questo è innegabile, si cresce, perdio quanto siamo cambiati dall'estate di Amsterdam e non siamo più bambini che si sentono offesi.' (*Altri libertini*, p. 95) ('And then you grow up, this cannot be denied, you grow up, by God how we have changed since the summer in Amsterdam and we aren't children any more who feel offended').

Offended by whom? By parents, by society, by adults in general, all categories that were rejected by the 'children' themselves. The emphasis is on change, brought about by growing up, but also by maturing in a more social context. As soon as the story seems to become more 'socially oriented', however, we go back to a more 'private' level. As if some kind of fear had been triggered, a fear of getting involved with a society which was, at any rate, to be rejected. No committed writing, as in the 1960s, seems possible.

We are now in 1976 (p. 102) and the story which has so far oscillated between various narrative possibilities – a travel diary, a generational novel – now becomes a love story. To be more precise it is transformed into a story of homosexual love, which is recounted realistically and sympathetically with a degree of lyricism:

Fino a sera pedaliamo un po' ubriachi quel magnifico quattordici settembre, un caldo primaverile, una luce schietta che quando il sole va giù i mattoni di Bologna avvampano rossi come se la città dovesse da un momento all'altro bruciare e noi restare i soli superstiti scendendo allacciati dai colli verso le macerie sulla nostra bicicletta fiammante. (*Altri libertini*, p. 110)

We pedal until evening, a bit drunk, that magnificent fourteenth of September, a spring warmth, a frank light which when the sun goes down makes the bricks of Bologna flare up red as though the city must burn down any minute, leaving us the only survivors descending from the hills towards the ruins stuck together on our blazing bicycle.

There is a conscious attempt to establish the parity or even the superiority of the 'gay tribe' over the rest of the population, in this case the 'we' refers to homosexuals: 'pensa a te che vali, pensa a noi che siamo la razza più bella che c'è, me lo ha insegnato Dilo questo, ridi, ridici pure su, noi sì che siamo una gran bella tribù' (*Altri libertini*, p. 116) ('Think what you're worth, think about us. Dilo taught me that we are the best race there is. Laugh, feel free to laugh about it, we really are a splendid tribe').

But together with the private love story one gets references to the occupation of the university in Bologna and to riots in Milan in which some of the characters are involved, though they did not intend to. All this, however marginal, shows an interest in the issues which go beyond the individual private story. This broader perspective emerges clearly when the narrator, having been ostracized by the parents of his primary-school pupils on account of his homosexuality, reflects on the state of schooling in Italy in an anarchical longing:

> quando non ci sarà scuola la scuola allora sì che funzionerà e sarà bella finalmente, perché uno si alzerà e andrà al cinema e a fare all'amore ed è questa la scuola, cioè l'esperienza, mica la normalizzazione. (*Altri libertini*, p. 120)

> When school is abolished, then schooling will really work and it will at last be good, because one will get up and go to the cinema and make love, and this is schooling, namely experience, not normalization.

Tondelli returns to the diary form to present the protagonist's crisis. After getting heavily into drugs, he attempts suicide, then goes back home. The episode ends in a circular manner with a reference to the original bet he made with himself, of guessing how many bars there are on a stretch of the Via Emilia. We are in August again, or rather at the end of it. 'Non importa ... Sulla mia terra, semplicemente ciò che sono mi aiuterà a vivere.' (*Altri libertini*, p. 130) ('It doesn't matter ... on my land, simply what I am will help me to live'). The cyclical reference to seasons and months is the nearest one gets to natural phenomena; apart from this the narrator's focus is on the man-made, man-centred; it is as if he himself were something artificial.

Episode number four, called 'Senso contrario' ('Against the flow') is narrated in the first person. It starts with another homosexual encounter, this time between the protagonist and Ruby, a twenty-six -year-old small-time crook who only speaks dialect (though not in the book), and everything seems set for a quiet evening out in the country. But, after a suspense-laden meal at an inn in the mountains nearby, the main character, a rent boy, and Ruby drive back to town. On the way there is a drunken and very 'American' car chase in which a group of vigilantes follows the small Fiat Six hundred driven by Ruby. His name, though American looking, contains a pun on *rubare* 'to steal', and the occupants seem to be worried about the number plate ('ma Ruby tranquillizza, è rubata è rubata niente problemi' (*Altri libertini*, p. 140) ('But Ruby calms them down, it's stolen, it's stolen, no problem').

After the protagonist reaches his home safely, he wakes up at precisely 3.15 a.m. Tondelli reveals that this is a time which has special significance for him with a passing reference to Scott Fitzgerald for whom 'in the real dark night of the soul it is always three o'clock in the morning, day after day'. At this time it is not easy to come to terms with one's existence: 'non riesco a chiudere gli occhi penso e ripenso rumino e rigurgito che sia sul serio fuori?'(*Altri libertini*, p. 142) ('I can't go to sleep and keep thinking over and over again am I really out of my mind?'). He goes home: 'Mi siedo guardo dal finestrino la città perdersi nella periferia la campagna sfilare … Sento come mi fosse improvvisamente cresciuto dentro un vuoto enorme.' (*Altri libertini*, p. 143) ('I sit down and look through the window and watch the city lose itself in the suburbs and the countryside race past … I feel as if a void had suddenly opened up inside me').

These symptoms seem familiar enough and are not much different from traditional growing pains. Although the emptiness around the protagonist is suddenly revealed, it has always existed. The protagonist resorts to drugs, drinking and gregariousness in an attempt to exorcise it. The whole book is marked by anxiety. The existential void cannot be filled by trips, joints, drinks or occasional encounters. Writing, however, may alleviate the sense of emptiness, and it takes on a therapeutic quality.

Episode five bears the title of the book 'Altri libertini', and revolves around students at Bologna university, three girls and two gays. A fascinating young man arrives in their midst and this 'barbarian from Lombardy' has a devastating effect on individuals and on relationships. This is reminiscent of Pasolini's film *Teorema* where a mysterious guest turns out to have great sexual attraction for a whole bourgeois family as well as a religious significance which is certainly lacking in Tondelli's story. The young barbarian happens to be a photographer keen on traditional food and folklore, while the local gay who offers him hospitality loathes all that is regional and national, his tastes being oriental and international. It is a simple, ironic love story with the handsome foreigner at the centre of the desires of the local population. It is the gay who feels most hurt and betrayed at the end. As in other episodes, one particular season of the year brings about change: it is Christmas time, and all the members of the group disband for their winter holidays. All that has happened assumes a rather dreamlike air, the atmosphere of a circus, the circus as used by Fellini, in which, however, love is no more than a party game played in a ring. Tondelli characteristically makes no attempt to judge the behaviour of any of the characters. The ideal 'bellavita' 'good life' is that of 'avere una gratificazione dietro l'altra e non pensare a niente se non ad abbracciarsi e succhiarsi da ogni parte' (*Altri libertini*, p. 162) ('having one gratification after another, thinking of nothing except embracing and sucking each other all over'). They are all, perhaps, puppets, or simply characters in search of an identity.

The most 'reflective' episode of the whole book is the final one entitled

'Autobahn' because it focuses on the basic mood, 'la scoglionatura', a Leopardian type of 'tedium' suitably modernized but far from new. It is true that different generations experience it and question themselves about it. A friend of the narrator calls this dejection *Scoramenti* with a capital *s* and in the plural since it never comes alone. It carries important existential questions even if expressed with an appropriate use of irony, a mock-heroic tone, hyperbole, and long lists:

> Si porta appresso nevralgie d'ossa, brufoletti sulle labbra o nel fondoschiena ma poi i più gravi mali, quelli della vocina; cioè chi sei? cosa fai? dove vai? qual è il tuo posto nel Gran Trojaio? cheffarai? (*Altri libertini*, p. 178)

> He endured his bone neuralgia, little spots on his lips and backside but also more serious ills, the little voices which asked: who are you? what are you doing? where are you going? what's your place in the great cock-up? What'll you do?

Drinking and travelling seem the antidotes to this manic (or is it manic depressive?) mood. The attraction in this case is to the North, the North of Europe, through the nearest motorway to the Austrian border, which starts just a few kilometres from the protagonist's home. The desire, the urge to move away is well expressed in the dialogue with an occasional companion who turns out to be some kind of experimental film-maker: 'Ah, che due maroni questa Italia, io ci ho fame amico mio una gran fame di contrade e sentieroni, di ferrate, di binari, di laghetti, di frontiere e di autostrade, ok?' (*Altri libertini*, p. 189) ('Ah, what a piss-off this Italy, I'm hungry my friend, a great hunger for countries and dirt tracks, railways, railtracks, for ponds, for frontiers and motorways, O.K.?').

It is a naive reaction to Italy perceived as a small provincial country, becoming wealthier and wealthier and representing the more international attitude of the new Europeans. On the other hand, instead of elaborating an individual style, the influence of American models is still strong. They discuss, in an interminable list, all the suitable subjects and approaches to film making (pp. 189-91):

> A morte, a morte! Alla forca! àlla ghigliottina! [...] alla defenestrazione i mafiosi i teoreti, i politologhi, i corsivisti, le penne d'oro, le grandifirme, gli speculatori del grassetto e del filmetto, a morte! a morte! (*Altri libertini*, p. 189)

> Death to them, death to them! To the gallows! To the guillotine! Defenestrate the mafiosi, the theoreticians, the political analysts, the writers of editorials, the grand journalists, the great writers, the speculators in bold type and short films, death! Death to them!

They want a DRUNK CINEMA ('il Rail cinema, il DRUNK, very-drunk, CINEMA, ok?') (*Altri libertini*, p. 191). All that remains of this talk is a liberating and hyperbolic vomiting session (pp. 192–3) and then 'Col naso in aria fiutate il vento, strapazzate le nubi all'orizzonte, forza, è ora di partire, forza tutti insieme incontro all'avventuraaaaa!' (p. 195) ('With your nose in the air, sniff the wind, scatter the clouds on the horizon, come on it's time to go, come on all together

now, let's go for iiii ... t!'). This is the end of the book, and anyone who does
not belong to the same age group feels as if they have trespassed on a teenager's
party. The animal-like quality is also destroyed, but the vitality lingers on.

We can better understand the attitude and the scope of Tondelli's first book
if we examine one of his essays, written as a preface to *Under 25. Giovani Blues*,
an anthology of writing by young people instigated and collected by Tondelli
himself and published in 1986. Here the author hints at the making of his first
book and explains the importance of re-writing. He quotes Peter Bischel
according to whom literature is a kind of game in which one may or may not
participate, but he declares also that in the game of writing 'non è importante
pensare o avere tante idee. È importante buttar giù. L'ispirazione è lavorare. Le
migliori idee vengono scrivendo' (*Under 25. Giovani Blues*, p. 29) ('it isn't
important to think or have lots of ideas. It's important to get things down. Work
inspires. The best ideas come as you write').

There is in Tondelli, like in other writers of the new generation a strong
belief in narrating, which seems to come from a psychological necessity. It is a
statement, it is the nearest thing to action that some of the young achieve. It
resembles a desire to establish one's self in the precariousness of the present. And
a desire to spread it to as many as possible, trying simply to state that a writer is
no longer a special person, that their job only requires the writing bug.

Tondelli's second novel *Pao Pao* (the acronym stands for *Picchetto Armato
Ordinario* 'Ordinary Guard Duty' in the army) follows *Altri libertini* reasonably
closely. It appeared in 1982 and deals with the experiences of the narrator during
his national service in the Italian army. It is partly an investigation of individual
liberty within an authoritarian establishment. It starts with obvious, even banal,
references to a hellish or purgatorial experience (for example, words such as
'bolgia' (*Pao Pao* p. 9), 'sono entrato in purgatorio e non all'inferno' (p. 10) ('I
have entered purgatory and not hell'), 'in questo limbo indefinito' (p. 20) ('in
this undefined limbo')). The protagonist arrives at Orvieto (later called Orviet-
nam) after travelling during the night. Here is a further example of two of his
favourite themes: 'the journey' and the night which can also be mixed in a
metaphorical sense. His animalesque sensitivity has allowed him to 'smell' the
atmosphere of the train, of other soldiers and recruits, and his senses enhance the
feeling of expectation. In his blue holdall bag, together with little personal
souvenirs and a few books by Le Carré he has 'un po' di angoscia', some
anguish. The language is colloquial and relaxed, although some of the mildly
comic effects are created by referring to a more traditional, literary style. Gadda
may be a model, especially at the beginning when the author is recounting the
fact that the only medicine available in the infirmary was aspirin: 'solo aspirine si
potevano fare, per via rettale e per via orale, nel braccio nel culo e nella panza,
solo aspirina, come una barzelletta da caserma' (*Pao Pao* p. 7) ('There was only
aspirin, rectally or orally, in the arm, up the arse or in the belly, only aspirin, like

a barrack room joke'). This young Ulysses starts his search as soon as he gets off the military truck which has taken him from the station to the barracks:

> Ero già del tutto preso dai miei bisogni di diffusione d'amore per le stanze e gli oggetti e le atmosfere, già curiosavo tra gli alberi e i cespugli, già sognavo e fantasticavo e mentre scendevo dal camion, volgevo lo sguardo attorno come un matto, volevo vedere e sapere e digià conoscere. (*Pao Pao*, p. 13)

> I was already completely absorbed by my need to diffuse my love for the rooms, the objects and the atmosphere. I wandered through the trees and bushes, dreaming and fantasizing and as I got off the truck, I stared around me like a madman, I wanted to see and have knowledge and already know.

The use of the imperfect as a verb tense underlines the traditional literary effect, especially if we consider that some phrases have a distinctly nineteenth-century flavour ('già sognavo e fantasticavo' and 'volgevo lo sguardo attorno'). There is fear and desire in a new experience. The long night-journey reminds the narrator of other journeys made by his friends, like the man completely destroyed by drugs which he started taking during his national service. There is a strong desire to resist the basic inhumanity, absurdity, stupidity of life in the barracks, and the desire to understand the processes by which one can acquire knowledge, if not learn, in a strained situation. Details of the initiation into soldiering are provided at length, with some irony and occasional comic effects. The feeling of deprivation of liberty is contrasted with that of freedom represented by a gentleman who happens to walk his dog just outside the barrack window. Although national service is common enough in Italy, it has not been exploited as a source of fiction. And one could claim that this is not fiction either. If living in barracks means a loss of freedom, then falsity, instead of truth and spontaneity, seems the only alternative: 'Potrai fingere, oh questo sì, ma ora sei un soldato e tutto per te è archiviato' (*Pao Pao*, p. 15) ('You could pretend, oh yes, but now you are conscripted, your facts are all listed').

What, one may ask, is 'all listed'? Does becoming a soldier in a non-professional army for a period of twelve months justify such despair? Isn't there a fear that such a strained, and admittedly artificial, situation may reveal, even more than normal life, the weakness of an individual's character? He may already suspect some kind of constitutional feebleness. This seems to be confirmed by the fact that a first rather cursory medical check-up reveals a trivial heart flutter which needs investigating. The protagonist is sent to a military hospital in Rome, another example of surreal alienation, in which the matron (a moustached nun) decrees that the young soldiers should go to bed without supper – at 5 p.m., comments the narrator.

Justification for the writing is provided in a short paragraph in the first few pages of the book – the story is mainly about friendship:

> Questo è il racconto trafelato di come ci siamo incontrati e di tutte le intensità che ci hanno travolto per quei dodici mesi. Voglio molto bene ai miei amici. È

per loro, gli altissimi, che ricordo questa storia che una volta c'era e ora non c'è
più. In onore al glorioso e gayoso 4°/80 che riprendo a raccontare. (*Pao Pao*,
p. 16)

This is the story told breathlessly of how we met and all the intense feelings that
swept over us for those twelve months. I am very fond of my friends. It is for
them, the tall ones, that I remember this story that once upon a time was and
now is no more. In honour of the glorious and gayous 4th division/80 I take
up the tale.

And one can believe him. The difficulty is to find a way of making well-written
private stories, and the diary of everyday life as a soldier, interesting not only to
the protagonist, but to others. This is achieved by recourse to natural curiosity,
rather than to special narrative techniques. The early part of the book is largely
an expansion of a diary, and there is always an element of voyeurism in reading
somebody else's diary, in knowing the details of other people's lives. In the
second half of the book homosexual love stories of various kinds illustrate the
precarious balance achieved by the protagonist/narrator, still formally a soldier
but inserted in a network of personal relationships in Rome. Each one seems to
have an element of creative talent (musical, literary, theatrical); the whole
country seems to have lots of hidden talents, with the implication that, if they
remain within homosexuals, they will not be perpetuated. The homosexual
theme is contrasted with the cliché of an Italian army with a macho, virile,
strong and violent image, scions of a country with a long and glorious history.
There are a few relics of fascist rhetoric. The art of survival celebrated in *Pao Pao*
is composed of evenings out, drinks, joints and camaraderie, all seen as *synchronic*
events. There is no history for these people, as the protagonist recognizes 'nulla
di definitivo' (*Pao Pao*, p. 20), 'nothing final'. The individual drifts in and out of
'stories' like a character in a play. He establishes occasional relationships, has
moments of happiness and depression like everybody else, and there is nothing
more. Italian soldiers are not nationalistic, they have grown up with a much
more international outlook than previous generations. They are more cultivated, or at least some of them are. The narrator talks English to some extremely
ignorant and 'vulgar' American girls in the train, one of whom was born in
Lowell, Massachusetts, Jack Kerouac's birthplace: 'Non conosce i romanzi di
Kerouac, Scott Fitzgerald le dice niente, Norman Mailer meno che meno,
Hemingway, be' questo sì, ha fatto un riassuntino a scuola del Vecchio e il mare.
Basta! basta!' (*Pao Pao*, p. 40) ('She doesn't know the novels of Kerouac, Scott
Fitzgerald means nothing to her, Norman Mailer less than nothing,
Hemingway, well yes, she did a summary at school of The Old Man and the
Sea. That's enough!').

The novel is set in the present and the characters are not concerned with
either the past or the future. It is a 'Macdonald's novel' to be consumed on the
spot, like a pizza and a beer. In some parts it follows the prescriptions for a

'drunk cinema' expressed in the last episode of *Altri libertini*.There is no framework of 'values' or 'beliefs'. The 'structure' can only be studied by exclusive reference to the individual fragments of immediate and extemporary responses to circumstances. This allows us to compare the characters in the novel with actors in the *commedia dell'arte*. The theatrical element is occasionally emphasized. When the protagonist, in the early part of the book, is sent to the military hospital, he manages to escape in the evening by persuading the sentry that he is 'stoned' and he needs his fix. This 'acting' and 'mimetic' tendency is revealed quite frequently and in this sense is paradigmatic of the novel as a whole. It represents an element of immaturity which cannot be resolved, and in this sense makes *Pao Pao*, with its 'funny' title sounding like an Indian cry of war, a less satisfactory work than *Altri libertini*. The detachment of the work of art (Sontag, 'Against Interpretation') is perhaps even less visible than in the best stories of the previous book. One suspects that real names were included in the narrative, for example on p. 37 the surname of Sub-Lieutenant Mariani has been changed from what it was in the first edition. There are, in the novel, certain recurrent themes: a rejection of violence in all its forms and a desire for truth. Lies and betrayals are not allowed, although they might be considered a normal ingredient of love stories. The search, therefore, that we mentioned at the beginning is also for purity, sincerity, intensity and an ideal which is different from that of traditional 'normal' middle classes. And indeed the very idea of normality is abhorrent to the author. To the author the distinction between 'different' and 'normal' should be cancelled. Theories and intellectual reflections are rejected as well: 'non mi frega più tanto di riconoscimenti teorici, anzi, il modo per arrivare al top è forse proprio nel non chieder nulla, lasciare che i corpi si attraggano, e le scintille scocchino senza parole, senza discorsi' (*Pao Pao*, p. 156) ('I don't give a damn any more for theoretical recognition, in fact the way to the top may well lie in asking for nothing, letting the bodies attract, and the sparks fly, without words, without speeches'. The pace of the novel is fast, and if a reader tries to savour it as an *andante* the result can only be strident and out of tempo, if not out of tune. The occasional reflective moments are, however, well written and interesting. During the night, just before going to sleep in the barracks, the narrator is as tense as a cat, in an attempt to come to terms with the alien reality which surrounds him:

> Devo restare in silenzio assoluto e tendere i nervi come un gatto, devo allungare le orecchie e fissare davanti a me un punto impreciso, devo fare lunghi sospiri per raggiungere i bordi di questo mondo incosciente in cui le intimità si allargano e i gesti scattano meccanici e le parole sono soltanto rantolii e mugugni e i corpi troppo paurosamente simili a macchine gettate in manutenzione, a robot impazziti e arrugginiti, a codici disuguali, a doppi tragici delle nostre vite, e ognuno ora sta vivendo la propria storia, risorgendo i fantasmi, sognando situazioni al di fuori del tempo. ... (*Pao Pao,* p. 68)

> I must remain absolutely silent and make my nerves taut like a cat, I must prick
> up my ears and stare in front of me at an undefined point, I must breathe
> deeply to arrive at the edges of this unknown world in which intimacy is
> stretched, and gestures fire off mechanically and words are only mumbles and
> whimpers and bodies too frighteningly like machines thrown into mainte-
> nance, like mad, rusting robots, like dissimilar codes, like tragic doubles of our
> lives, and each one is now living his own story, resurrecting ghosts, dreaming
> situations outside time...

The melancholy appears through the folds of the interior monologue, even in
the imprecision of the language which posits a separation of the bodies (of the
soldiers) and their lives. We should not be looking for coherence in Tondelli's
first two books. Melancholy and despair can easily be followed by *joie de vivre*,
convincingly conveyed by Tondelli's prose. And a naive faith in love and its acts
is partly suggested to the reader through a certain levity of touch. Love is a 'gift
of the gods', but: 'L'amore non è mai là dove lo cerchiamo e vola via da dove lo
crediamo. Proprio per questo e dell'amore e degli dei dobbiamo imparare a fare
senza' (*Pao Pao*, p. 169) ('Love is never where we look for it and flies away from
where we believe it is. That's why we've got to learn to do without love and gods').
In one of his essays Tondelli mentions that literature is no more than a game and
that an author 'writes because he has read'; if so, then 'I read because he has written'.
The book becomes part of the neat tautologies in which no further questions
need to be asked and which attracted Tondelli at the beginning of this narrative.

There is, at the beginning of *Pao Pao*, a reference to the importance of
tautology. The protagonist's brother advised him to reach the barracks early
since it is fundamental to 'iniziare dall'inizio' (*Pao Pao*, p. 9) ('begin from the
beginning'). 'Sublime tautologia' remarks the narrator. In *Rimini* the old German servant 'Hanna, con la sua saggezza tautologica di contadina sveva per cui la
vita è la vita, l'amore è l'amore e il dolore soltanto e semplicemente il dolore'
(*Rimini*, p. 55) ('Hanna with her Swabian tautologic peasant wisdom according
to which life is life, love is love and sorrow only sorrow') represents stability and
wisdom, like the brother in the previous novel, and, although Tondelli does not
show any interest in particular peasant or popular wisdom, he seems to be fond
of relatively simple explanations. But *Rimini* is, at first sight, a rather complex
novel. The reader is struck by a radical change in style with respect to *Altri
libertini* and *Pao Pao*. The language is deliberately literary, even formal at times,
with a considerable amount of verbs in the past historic, a tense which is almost
totally absent in the other two novels. This type of language is reminiscent of
that used in the translation of certain thrillers or in the dubbing of films in Italy,
which always sounds rather artificial. The following passage will illustrate this
procedure:

> [The protagonist, a journalist, and his girlfriend are talking about summer
> holidays. Katy says:]

' ... Avrei pensato a qualcosa per settembre. E tu?'
'Non ho progetti... Vuoi un po'?' [He's eating ham and melon]
'Ho parlato con Ellen stamane. Chiede se per agosto andiamo da lei.
Non ti sembra una buona idea? Poi a settembre partiremo.'
'Da Ellen?'
'A Pantelleria.'
'Il mare mi sembra una buona idea.' (*Rimini*, p. 20)

' ... I've been thinking about something for September. Have you?'
'I don't have any plans ... would you like a little?'
'I spoke with Ellen this morning. She asked whether we would pay her a visit
in August. Doesn't that seem like a lovely idea to you? Then we'll leave in
September.'
'Ellen's?'
'Yes, in Pantelleria'
'The seaside seems like a good idea to me.'

This stridently banal dialogue has snobbish undertones. Ellen and Pantelleria
sound like a parody of a television soap opera and this passage is not the only
piece of this kind in *Rimini*. The novel is made up of different stories all having
this seaside resort as a background. It's a kitsch novel quite suitable for seaside
reading which sold nearly 100,000 copies.

There are in *Rimini* some of the basic themes we have already seen in
Tondelli: a desire for change, separation and loss, expressed by the German
Beatrix. Beatrix searches for her sister Claudia, addicted to drugs, and lost in
Italy. Bruno May, the writer, is looking for the blonde Aelred, the film makers
try to achieve their work of art and Marco Bauer, the protagonist, seeks to fulfil
his own ambition. These are themes of quest and ensuing journey. The theme
of quest in *Rimini* is also cautiously linked to that of a religious search, through
the priest padre Anselme who befriends Bruno. And also by the not-so bizarre
idea that love, whether hetero- or homosexual is part of the music emitted by
Buddhist monks or by pious women reciting a rosary, a kind of universal love
with which viewers of Spielberg's films will be familiar.

Although *Altri libertini* was loosely divided into different episodes, *Pao Pao*
was not, and *Rimini* is orchestrated in such a way as to recall other works of art,
a poem or a particular song. Part One bears as its title 'On a rainy day' and is
subdivided into seven sections. This is followed by an 'Intermezzo' printed in
italics and called 'Pensione Kelly' and Part Two, also subdivided into seven
sections bears as its title 'Rimini', followed by another 'Intermezzo' called
'Hotel Kelly' which comes before Part Three, a short piece called 'Apocalisse,
ora' 'Apocalypse now'. This is the structure as given in the 'contents' list and the
actual novel is also divided into different, but not unrelated 'stories'. It is the first
'ambitious' novel by Tondelli, the first written not as part of a largely autobiographical exercise, but as a conscious, market-oriented product. The young
Tondelli has gone, the novelist is now thirty, and, after hints at change in his

previous works, everything is set for real change. The protagonist of the main 'story' is an ambitious young journalist who is sent by his Milan-based newspaper to edit a special regional insert on the sea coast around Rimini. Marco Bauer is a tough, acute, intelligent journalist who will observe the reality of 'the coast' as well as become involved with it. The novel has a deliberate and attractive erotic theme, the cool and detached journalist is involved with a sensuous, attractive and somewhat outlandish colleague from the local office. It should be stressed perhaps, that it is a female colleague, the only example so-far in Tondelli's novels of heterosexual love, but since it is more a 'storia', an 'affair', albeit intense, and not 'love' it does not count. The stress on homosexual relationships continues in the parallel story in which an anguished writer, Bruno, is trying to come out of a narrative impasse: 'Rimaneva per ore davanti alla macchina da scrivere senza che una sola descrizione si concretizzasse sui tasti. Scrivere diventò un incubo…' (*Rimini*, p. 214) ('He stayed for hours in front of the typewriter without a single description taking shape on the keys. Writing became a nightmare…'). 'Scriveva pagine e pagine, ma nessuna riga degna di entrare in un romanzo. Gettava i fogli in un cassetto su cui era scritto Diario' (*Rimini*, p. 215) ('He wrote pages and pages but not a single line worth putting in a novel. He threw the pages into a drawer marked 'Diary')'.

Altogether *Rimini* is a rather artificial work which tends to become too baroque. The attempt to include a thriller element with the episode of a politician's murder (or was it suicide?) involving local building speculators is too forced to be convincing. But perhaps the whole novel is not to be taken too seriously. What remains at the end is the defeat of the protagonist who thought of himself as God. When his professional investigation proves the 'suicide' of the senator, he realizes that he has actually been used by the criminals.

In a short piece written for a literary magazine (*Panta*, 1) Tondelli sums up the reasons for doing certain things (in this case a visit to the writer Frederick Prokosch's house in Provence):

> È banale dire che in fondo lo scopo di qualsiasi ricerca, per quanto complicata e difficile, è qualcosa che ci sta molto vicino, che è dentro di noi. La freccia dell'arco zen colpisce il centro del bersaglio solo quando trapassa da parte a parte la coscienza di chi l'ha scagliata. Le domande che avrei rivolto a Prokosch potevano rispondere solo a una mia, o nostra, esigenza di sapere e di conoscere.

> It is a banality that the ultimate aim of any search, however complex and difficult, is something that is very close to us, within us. The arrow from the Zen bow hits the bull's eye only when it transfixes the conscience of whoever shot it. The questions I was to present to Prokosch could have answered only my or our need to know and have knowledge.

The last sentence is very similar to the one we found on p. 13 of *Pao Pao*, and maybe the desire to know, and to tell others ('raccontare') is basic to the whole of Tondelli's work.

Published in 1989 *Camere separate* was advertised as the novel of Tondelli's maturity, divided like a musical score and incorporating complex but basic existential themes. But already in *Rimini* we find the following anticipation:

> Certi giorni [Bruno] scriveva pagine e pagine sul sentimento che Aelred aveva fatto esplodere in lui, ed erano pagine che assomigliavano a una partitura musicale, in cui il ritmo del discorso procedeva per poi arrestarsi e continuare su altri toni e altri ritmi fino a riprendere il motivo iniziale. (*Rimini*, pp. 221–2).

> On certain days he [Bruno] wrote pages and pages on the emotions that Aelred had caused to explode within him, and they were pages that bore similarity to a musical score, in which the rhythm of the discussion proceeded then only to stop and continue on other tones and other rhythms until it would again pick up the initial motif.

Some of the imagery in *Camere separate* is familiar, with variations: for example the animal types, mentioned by Tondelli as guests at parties (the fauna), have been substituted by fish:

> alla luce del potente faro, piccoli pesci guizzanti nella consapevolezza della loro agilità, belle aragoste stagionate e ebbre, squali, gamberi rossi, sgargianti pesci tropicali, cetacei, delfini, saraghe… (*Camere separate*, p. 11)

> In the powerful spotlight, little fish, quivering in the knowledge of their agility, elegant lobsters, mature and intoxicated, sharks, red prawns, garish tropical fish, cetaceans, dolphins, sargoes…

He expresses the belief that there are moments in which non-verbal communication can be achieved and be fully satisfactory. There is the implication that such moments will never find adequate expression in writing, even if one tries to write in a direct, concrete, almost 'physical' way: 'Le parole, nella loro sofisticatezza biologica, potrebbero solo confondere un momento che non si esprime attraverso alcun linguaggio se non quello, ficcato nel più profondo della corteccia cerebrale, della lotta per la vita.' (*Camere separate*, p. 21) ('Words, in their biological sophistication, could only confuse a moment which cannot be expressed in any language if not, buried deeply in the cerebral cortex, that of the battle for life.') Physicality and words come together in a bold image, when the narrator seeks to explain how he tried to establish himself as different from his schoolmates: 'forse, nell'uscire da quella classe ginnasiale, … ha desiderato darsi in pasto agli altri offrendo il corpo delle sue parole.' (*Camere separate*, p. 95) ('Maybe, in coming out of that grammar-school class, he wanted to feed himself down to the others, offering the body of his words'). Apart from the identification between 'body' and 'words', made easier in Italian by the typographical meaning of 'corpo' = 'type', 'character', there emerges also a blasphemous reference in a parallel between the writer and Christ who 'offered his body'. It could almost be the result of a meditation on the significance of phrases from the gospels. Indeed the Bible is repeatedly mentioned in this book (pp. 97–8). A religious concern is certainly present in other parts of the novel. On p. 97 he remembers his meditation, his discussions with priests and 'la recita della parola', and again, on p. 98: 'allora Leo avverte in sé la propria vocazione religiosa come qualcosa di irrinunciabile. [...] "You have been bitten by the metaphysical bug" gli aveva detto, un giorno, sorridendo, un amico sacerdote.' ('and then Leo recognizes his religious vocation as something unrenounceable. "You have been bitten by the metaphysical bug" a friend of his, a priest, had said to him, smiling'). Words, the primary objects of a writer are examined, analysed and exorcised in depth and with sincerity. They become autobiographical and address basic, anguished questions: 'Sa di non essere là dove lui si scrive. [...] Ma perché, poi, scrivere? E soprattutto perché pubblicare? (*Camere separate*, p. 93) ('He knows he is not there, where he writes himself down [...] But why, after all, write? and above all, why publish?')

The answer will come on the following page, when, after looking at the objects in his flat, the narrator jokes about 'bed and wardrobe, one book; sofa, kitchen, drinks-cabinet, another book ...' he concludes: 'Vive di parole, letteralmente' (*Camere separate*, p. 94) ('He literally lives on words'). The 'feeding by words' theme returns therefore as a primary concern of this writer. In ancient carnival literature a parallel may be drawn with the figure of the extremely hungry peasant who dreams of eating his own flesh and entrails. This is a novel which, unlike the previous ones, gains on second reading. It has not been understood nor accepted by the literary establishment. It is not in any way, a happy book. It is melancholy, sombre, and always on the edge between life and death. The separation constantly referred to throughout the book characterizes a writer, his choice of this profession and a kind of shame that goes with it. We have peeped into the private love life of the narrator, but we have also observed the mechanisms which make up the book in front of us. The author, faced with the problem of writing, has decided to give us the story of the difficulty of writing, of being and of loving. These turn out to be one and the same thing. The writer has to produce 'words' because they are necessary to his sustenance. It has been done before, maybe more in the cinema than in literature (we are reminded of Fellini and Truffaut in particular), but Tondelli gives us some pleasing digressions and notes from diaries and correspondence. The reader is and remains separate from the author, but reaches a conniving understanding with the narrator.

The difficulty lies in finding a language to express or communicate love to people who cannot be involved with it. In this book the individual self who had been occasionally suppressed or pushed to the margins of the narrative reemerges in a glorious, even a religious context, and contributes to this novel which is intense and sincere.

The figure of Thomas, the narrator's lover, who dies of cancer at the age of twenty-five, is, in some sense, the reason for writing, the Muse, the justification for producing a work of art. Thomas was, in the eyes of others, a 'musicista ben avviato alla carriera di fallito' (*Camere separate*, p. 194) ('a musician well set on a career as a failure'), and yet for the narrator he was the world, the world from which he, because 'different', *diverso*, had to live separate. This world dies and what was already difficult and dark, like writing itself, becomes nearly impossible. It is this struggle that we also witness in Tondelli's book, a book that if he (or the narrator) had a choice, he would prefer us not to read, as hinted on p. 95: when travelling on the Milan underground the author feels the sudden impulse to attack an unknown reader of his novel and shout abuse at him. In order to be able to write, the author has to destroy *the other*. He admits at a certain point that he has become a vulture, that he tears flesh apart. We find strikingly similar images in an essay by Maurice Blanchot entitled 'Literature and the Right to Death': ' ... the act of naming is disquieting and marvellous. A word may give me its meaning, but first it suppresses it. For me to be able to say, "This woman", I must somehow take her flesh-and-blood reality away from her, cause her to be absent, annihilate her' (p. 42). Blanchot's remarks in *The Essential Solitude* also seems appropriate to Tondelli's meditation: 'it seems we have learned something about art when we experience what the word solitude designates ... the same situation can also be described this way: a writer never reads his work. For him, it is the unreadable, a secret, and he cannot remain face to face with it. A secret, because he is separated from it' (pp. 63 ff.).

Everything in this novel underlines the difference, the isolation, the separation, the meaning of the person who cannot have, within human rule, a companion, recognized as husband or wife, the predicament of the homosexual, which represents the separation and the solitude of the writer. Words and phrases mentioning 'separation, separate', abound in the whole book, because even 'what we call art' is a 'realtà separata', and his love itself was called 'camere separate'. Even the interlude represented by a visit to his parents, a pleasant episode in a generally sombre novel, stresses the difference of the narrator. It is a piece of natural, diaristic, prose, with an unmistakable elegiac tone. The recreation of the life of his mother and of his aunts, the realization that the strength of the people of this area of Italy ('un piccolo borgo della bassa padana, con i portici...' (*Camere separate*, p. 107) ('a small town in the Po valley, with porticoes...') lies in the women, not the men, is simple, refreshing, straightforward, and, at the same time, compelling. It is also a revisitation of dark and happy memories, a return to childhood and early adolescence, the rediscovery of the seeds which will lead to his 'différence', to his interest in art and writing.

Tondelli's latest book, published in the autumn of 1990, is a collection of essays, short journalistic pieces and introductions, bearing the title *Un weekend postmoderno*. Some of these pieces are extremely pleasing and some illuminate the rest of Tondelli's production. He reveals himself as a sensitive, and at times mimetic, writer who is trying to get away from the label of 'writer for young people'. He is interested in travel, in different cultures and in the subtle feel of unknown places. He seems to be at his best in some of these.

From the turbulent, sometimes confused and anguished life-situations described in Tondelli's early works, the author has moved to a more reflective and calmer observation of nature, of towns and villages, of other writers, of mundane events: art exhibitions, student gatherings, examinations. He does not like American minimalist writers but he is occasionally attracted by minimalism. Despite his flaws, Tondelli is an interesting writer, truly representative of the 1980s.

Post-scriptum

Shortly before his death, in December 1991, Tondelli returned, like the protagonist of *Camere separate*, to his native town of Correggio near Reggio Emilia in Northern Italy and he may have prepared a sequel to his *Weekend postmoderno*.

BIBLIOGRAPHY

Works

Altri libertini (Milan: Feltrinelli, 1980; paperback, 1987).
Pao Pao (Milan: Feltrinelli, 1982; paperback, 1989).
Dinner Party, 1984.
Rimini (Milan: Bompiani, 1985; paperback, 1987).
Biglietti agli amici, 1986.
Under 25. Giovani Blues, ed. P. V. Tondelli (Bologna: il lavoro editoriale, 1986).
Camere separate, (Milan: Bompiani, 1989).
Un weekend postmoderno (Milan: Bompiani, 1990).

Critical Works

Blanchot, M., *The Gaze of Orpheus* (New York: Station Press, 1981).
Cecchi, O., 'Quel ragazzo del Settanta', *L'Unità*, 17 December 1991, p. 17.
Curtis, Q., 'How to Invent Teenagers in one Easy Novel', *The Independent on Sunday, Sunday Review*, 28 July 1991, p. 22.
L'Espresso, 5 January 1992.
Fano, N., 'I nuovi libertini chiusi nel vuoto dell'incertezza', *L'unità*, 17 December 1991.
Lanaro, S., *L'Italia nuova. Identità e sviluppo* (Turin: Einaudi, 1988).
Panta: I nuovi narratori, 9 (1992): 'Pier Vittorio Tondelli'.
Scott Fitzgerald, 'Handle with care' (March 1936) in *The Crack up*, ed. E. Wilson (New York: New Directions, 1945).
Sontag, S., 'Against Interpretation', in *A Susan Sontag Reader* (Harmondsworth: Penguin, 1964), p. 104.

Chapter 15

Sebastiano Vassalli
Literary Lives

ZYGMUNT G. BARAŃSKI

quello che avevo da dire l'ho sempre detto e – se non mi
tapperanno la bocca con un limone o un fico d'india –
continuerò a parlare

I've always said what I had to say and – if they don't gag me
with a lemon or a prickly pear – I'll carry on speaking
Sebastiano Vassalli, *Arkadia*

It is hard not to recall Vassalli's words about the activity of critics as I begin to assess his literary career: 'Questi fingono di occuparsi di ciò che è il loro esatto contrario perché vogliono insozzarlo. Immeschinirlo. Vogliono ridurre tutto alla loro forma ed anche alla loro misura. Cessi sì, ma nemmeno di quelli alti' (*Belle lettere*, 1991, p. 82) ('These pretend to be concerned with what is their precise opposite because they want to sully it. Cheapen it. They want to reduce everything to their shape and also to their measure. Real shithouses, but not even big ones'). Like his mentor and *alter ego*, the early twentieth-century poet Dino Campana, who, by standing alone, 'ripropone e rinnova [...] ciò che ancora è vivo nella tradizione ottocentesca' (*Opere*, p. xiii) ('reproposes and renews [...] what is still alive in the nineteenth-century tradition'), Vassalli's disgust with the institutionalization of literature is overwhelming. Campana's far from inapposite description of the literary-critical establishment as 'l'industria del cadavere' ('the corpse industry') has become one of the younger writer's key leitmotifs in his recent books. The reasons for Vassalli's repugnance are complex. They involve not just the sense he has of his time and of the 'human condition', but also, and equally significantly, the sense he has of himself. In his work, the culture industry functions both as a metaphor for human pettiness in general and as a microcosm of Italy and its history: 'Noi viviamo da sempre in un paese di confraternite di incappucciati, di mafie; ed è logico che la nostra letteratura sia mafiosa' (*Belle lettere*, 1991, p. 81) ('We have always lived in a country of confraternities, of hooded figures, of mafias; and it's logical that our literature should be mafia-like'). It is the enemy against whom Vassalli has developed his own view of the nature of art and poetry, and against whom, at least since the mid-1970s, he has battled to salvage and revive what is still living in the perennial human need to 'tell stories' (*raccontare*). Finally, it is the source of personal feelings of guilt and frustration: the fact that at the start of his career as a writer he had joined in naive good faith the artistic 'fraternity', and that, paradoxically, however much he might now try to keep his distance from the literary cabals, ultimately, as an author, he cannot but be involved with them. And, in saying this, I am not indulging in facile psychologism; I am repeating Vassalli's own admissions. Especially since 1983 (when in a powerful *j'accuse* – the 'pamphlet' *Arkadia* – he publicly broke with the Italian literary establishment) another feature of Vassalli's most recent production has been a calculated effort to set the record straight about his literary activities, his feelings, his views and his general behaviour.

He has done this in two main ways. First, he has overtly introduced himself into the pages of his three most recent novels. *La notte della cometa* (1984), which 'reconstructs' the 'tragic' life and sordid times of Dino Campana, opens with three chapters which describe the narrator's visit to Marradi, the poet's birthplace. They also contrast Vassalli's careful and sympathetically honest fourteen-year researches into his hero's life with the self-interested 'lies', whether of denigration or celebration, of Campana's earlier biographers, his fellow-citizens, and, naturally, literary historians. Throughout the novel, Vassalli continually underlines the fundamental differences between his own historically sensitive viewpoint and the fabrications of others. (I shall return to the seeming paradox of how a work of 'fiction', in Vassalli's expert hands, can be more accurate and reliable than genres which, customarily, are deemed to enjoy a privileged association with the 'truth'.) In addition, and in a structurally balanced manner which recalls its beginning, *La notte della cometa* closes with three chapters in which the narrator returns to the fore and reflects on what he has learnt not just about Campana but also about poetry, existence in general, and, notably, about himself from the long years of companionship with the older poet. Vassalli's most recent novel, *La chimera* (1990), bears strong organizational similarities to the earlier book. Again it is framed by the author's 'story'; again it is presented as a detailed, even reverential, historical 'reconstruction' ('una storia [...] d'una ragazza che visse tra il 1590 e il 1610 e che si chiamò Antonia' ('a story/history [...] of a girl who lived between 1590 and 1610 and who was called Antonia') – a foundling accused of witchcraft and burnt at the stake – 'e delle persone che furono vive insieme a lei' (*La chimera*, p. 5) ('and of the people who were alive together with her'); and again Vassalli sets his work off, albeit more mutedly than in *La notte della cometa*, against the practices of others – in this instance, of historians who have allowed such a 'clamorous event' to be forgotten (although, rather than against particular groups of individuals, the force of his disappointment is principally turned against the feebleness of communal memory, and especially its twentieth-century variant, which is so selfishly incapable of remembering what is truly important).

These two excellent novels are separated by *L'oro del mondo* (1987), which makes the most telling contribution of the three towards Vassalli's self-presentation. This narratively ambitious work interweaves particularly bleak moments from Italy's generally shoddy participation in the Second World War both with the story of a character called 'Sebastiano Vassalli' growing up somewhat eccentrically during the 1950s, and with the account of his present-day struggles against his father and the literary world of which he has become part. In no other work to date does Vassalli describe as graphically and as humorously as in *L'oro del mondo* the alluringly cloying web of dependence spun by the cultural establishment in order to ensnare even the most independent of writers.

The second significant way in which Vassalli has tried to justify his work and himself is rather more conventional: he has had recourse to genres which traditionally have been associated with the 'confessional' mode. In *Arkadia*, he examines his relationship to the contemporary literary scene in Italy within a framework which depends on recognizable and established critical and historical parameters. His pamphlet provides a chilling report of the machinations of different literary groupings set against the backdrop of selected political events, such as terrorism and 1968 and its aftermath. Vassalli focuses on his colleagues' self-centred posturings and absurd abuses of power which not only marginalize any voice which is not prepared to participate in the latest fashionable fad or to acknowledge the appropriate authorities, but also destroy the very possibility of any 'genuine' poetry actually being produced. So persuasive is Vassalli's argument that, by the end, his decision to 'destroy his home' and 'inhabit the wind' (*Arkadia*, p. 39) represents the only sensible and moral course of action. *Arkadia* makes no effort to conceal its powerful polemical charge – immediately evident from its subtitle, *Carriere, Caratteri, Confraternite degli Impoeti d'Italia* ('Careers, Personalities, Confraternities of the Unpoets of Italy'). It is also openly partial, relies on an effective yet frequently overblown sense of humour, and displays a penchant for apocalypticism. Yet, despite these distorting perspectives, *Arkadia* is not entirely inaccurate in its assessments and descriptions; and it will certainly be of use 'per le tesi di laurea e per gli storici letterari del Duemila' (*Arkadia*, p. 34) ('for the writers of dissertations and for the literary historians of the year 2000 and beyond'). This is a crucial fact: a key feature of all Vassalli's writing is the strong bond which unites it with 'reality'. It is both one of the great strengths of his work and also – as we shall soon see – the source of most of its 'problems', since at the heart of Vassalli's poetics lies the knotty problem of what it is exactly that separates 'fact' from 'fiction', 'living' from 'writing'.

Most recently, Vassalli has chosen the epistolary form to develop his self-reflections further. In 1990, he published two small, highly selective, collections of 'lettere ad amici e conoscenti in cui raccontavo vicende minime, occasioni, opinioni, idee sull'arte, amori e umori, tante cose insomma' ('letters to friends and acquaintances in which I recounted the smallest events, occasions, opinions, ideas on art, love and moods, many things in fact') (*Minima personalia* and *Lettere pisnenghesi*, now collected in *Belle lettere*). In choosing which letters to publish, Vassalli claims that his criteria are simple:

> Seguo solo una mia necessità privata a raccontarmi; e poi anche provo piacere a praticare questa letteratura minima, 'in pantofole': che mi permette di parlare di qualsiasi argomento, dall'etica trascendentale al modo di curare le unghie dei piedi, con quella spensierata leggerezza e direi proprio con quell'assoluta libertà che appartiene appunto al privato e alle opinioni, ed è bandita, giustamente, dalle scritture 'pubbliche'. (Fossi certo che ci saranno, scriverei anche ai posteri!) (*Belle lettere*, 1991, pp. 29–30)

> I only follow a private need to narrate myself; and then I also enjoy pursuing this most minor of literatures, 'in carpetslippers': which allows me to talk about anything, from transcendental ethics to the care of toenails, with that carefree lightness and I would say with that absolute freedom which belongs precisely to what is private and to the realm of opinions, and is banished, justly, from 'public' forms of writing. (If I were certain they'll exist, I would also write to our descendants!)

On one level, Vassalli's *belles lettres* do not really add much to his *œuvre* that is new. We find in them the same caustic wit, the same stylistic confidence in switching between different registers, the same condemnation of all that is false and opportunistic, the same sense of personal isolation and of moral and artistic superiority which mark his other works. On another level, however, they provide vivid new evidence of the suggestively paradoxical nature of Vassalli's artistic and intellectual universe.

Not unreasonably, one might object that the approach which I am taking to analyse Vassalli muddles up life and art. Instead of writing about Vassalli's self-presentation, I should be examining how he textually constructs an image of himself as 'author', a device as old as literature itself, and one which has been especially exploited in recent writing with its obsessively inward-looking metaliterary self-absorption. In fact, doesn't Vassalli himself acknowledge that, in his letters, he is 'narrating himself' (*Belle lettere*, 1991, p. 29)? Isn't his very choice of this genre, despite his protests to the contrary, a quintessentially literary operation, an attempt to establish a link between himself and those writers for whom the letter was still a 'living' option before its demise at the hands of the 'telefono e [...] tutte le altre diavolerie moderne' (*Belle lettere*, 1991, p. 29) ('telephone and [...] all the other modern devilries')? Similarly, doesn't his ironic aside about addressing future generations inevitably recall Petrarch's famous epistle to 'Posterity', an allusion which any Italian secondary-school child would recognize? And to recall Petrarch is surely to raise the ghost of the most exquisitely literary of Western writers, one whose every word was part of an aristocratically elaborate game of self-construction.

All this is quite true (up to a point, at least). And Vassalli himself is more than conscious of the metaliterary implications of what he is doing, hence the inescapable reference to Petrarch; hence, too, his quite unconvincing stress that 'non ho nessun desiderio di resuscitare un genere, quello della letteratura epistolare, che so defunto' (*Belle lettere*, 1991, p. 29) ('I have no desire to revive a genre, that of epistolary literature, which I know to be deceased') given that incontrovertible evidence to the contrary is clearly available in the shape of the book which we are reading. At the same time, what Vassalli is doing is substantially more than just another variation on the post-structuralist and postmodern credos that all writing is simply the result of other writing and is itself resolved as yet more writing (in Italy, this view of literature has gone under the tag of the neo-baroque). On the one hand, all his works reveal that he has an excellent knowledge not just of the literary tradition in general, but also of its specifically modern manifestations (for instance, in *Il neoitaliano. Le parole degli anni ottanta* (1989), a largely parodic cultural 'dictionary' of the key words of the 1980s, Vassalli has much to say about the limitations of contemporary artistic practice; see especially, 'Citazionismo' and 'Neobarocco'). On the other hand, there is no doubt that, even if his own writing is full of 'quotations', these are not to be taken as ends in themselves, never mind as the very essence of art:

> il **citazionismo** è stato l'orizzonte culturale dei banali anni Ottanta: l'"opzione zero" [...] della cultura e del gusto, la trasgressione diventata norma, nella vita e nella società. Nell'arte, il **citazionismo** era il neobarocco: un non-stile che aveva come regola l'eccesso e come trasgressione la 'citazione implicita'. (*Il neoitaliano*, p. 23)

> **quotationism** has been the cultural horizon of the banal Eighties: the 'zero option' [...] of culture and of taste, transgression become norm, in life and in society. In art, **quotationism** was the neo-baroque: a non-style which had excess as its rule and the 'implicit quotation' as its form of transgression.

In no way can Vassalli's letters be reduced to such a lack of writerly and intellectual ambition. However 'literary' they might appear to be on one level, nevertheless, they are always and principally concerned with some sort of 'reality' beyond that of the written word. They deal with matters – the death of acquaintances, the arrival of books, the practices of publishers, the hunting prowess of cats – which have actually occurred, which can be independently and experientially verified. Vassalli, therefore, is quite explicitly shifting the focus of his writing away from the narcissistic, self-indulgent, ultimately vacuous aestheticism of so many of his peers. Instead he is intent on reproposing the age-old question regarding the relationship between writers and the world; he is bent on underlining the necessary contacts between literature and experience, between art and the mundane; most of all, he is highlighting the social dimension of writing, and thus the responsibilities this entails. From this perspective, it is obvious that *citazionismo* is a literary form which refuses to face up to its responsibilities, while, conversely, Vassalli's 'quotations' are necessarily more than ludic decorations. They point not just to the difficulties, the barriers, which impede him in his quest to establish a link with the 'real', but also highlight that he is aware that literature is a self-contained system with its own rules and internal associations. It is precisely the specificities of both life and art which create the tensions between them; and yet, it is also clear that some sort of relationship between them does exist. Indeed, 'quotations' provide a clue to how other writers have tried to deal with the concrete, existential problems which beset them; they, thus, transcend the purely literary, and take on a quasi-historical quality (for instance, in *La notte della cometa*, Vassalli often quotes passages from Campana's writings as if these had the same status as more conventional documentary sources in order to cast light on aspects of his life). In particular, the fact that, as readers, we recognize 'quotations' as such reveals that they are an active force in our lives, that they are part of our world, and that, as a result, they somehow affect the way in which we perceive reality.

The importance of these *Belle lettere* resides in drawing attention to these crucial matters (which I shall deal with in greater depth below). However schematically, Vassalli's letters are emblematic of his whole artistic career. Nowhere else, despite the many, much more substantial genres he has success-fully employed, is the problem of the rapport between fact and fiction, life and invention so starkly posed. At the same time, paradoxically, in no other work are the differences between the two spheres so blurred and yet made so distinct. Only the letter could have allowed Vassalli such freedom, since it is the traditional form both for recording and transmitting the contingencies and minutiae of living (the care of toenails), and for indulging in refined intellectual pursuits (transcendental ethics). Most of all, this genre leaves no doubt that life and art are essentially each a form of 'telling'. What is significant, therefore, are the reasons why one 'quotes', and not the fact of the 'quotation' itself. And these reasons are crucial; they are what divides one writer from another; they are what separates Vassalli from so many of his contemporaries.

Born in 1941, he began his career as a writer by allying himself in 1967 (*Arkadia*, p. 14) with the main politicized avant-garde movement of the time, the *Gruppo 63* or *neo-avanguardia*, which emerged in the 1960s and which continued to maintain a recognizable corporate identity well into the 1970s. Since the mid-1970s, the concept of a 'committed literature' – except, possibly, as regards 'women's writing' – has increasingly begun to fade (there is, at present, some hint of a revival, however, linked to a re-reading of the writings on culture of Walter Benjamin). Thus, in the last decade or so, it has been rare to find authors who, like Vassalli, have been prepared staunchly to continue maintaining a consistent and public belief in literature's inescapable social responsibilities (Fortini, Sanguineti, Sciascia and Volponi are four other eminent names that come to mind in this respect). Inevitably, Vassalli's decision has not been without its consequences. A common feature of postwar Italian 'political art' was the notion of the 'group', the idea of a community of artists working together towards a common aesthetic, ideological and practical end. Naturally, since the late 1970s, given the altered cultural situation, there has been increasingly less interest in pursuing such goals. Thus, as Vassalli himself documents in *Arkadia*, to remain faithful to his beliefs he had to learn to stand alone; he could no longer rely on the support of the group, not least because the group had shown itself incapable of dealing with the changes in reality. In any case, by the early 1980s (though the process of disenchantment had probably begun in the mid-1970s), Vassalli firmly believed that the very idea of producing art 'by committee' was not just absurd, but actively detrimental to the creation of anything of literary value.

This fundamental insight seems to have been stimulated by three major and inter-related factors: first, by his growing familiarity with and understanding of Dino Campana's personal and artistic experiences, in particular the poet's conflicts with the Florentine literary establishment at the beginning of the century; second, by the sense that 'real' art was something rare, perhaps unique; and third, by the realization that many who called themselves artists and intellectuals were not only without talent and sensitivity, but also were simply exploiting literature for their own personal petty ends. In *La notte della cometa*, Vassalli gave narrative shape to these ideas, while making sure that his account of Campana's life and work was accompanied both by a general commentary ón the nature of literature, and by clear parallels with the cultural situation in present-day Italy. A few years later, he reiterated his positions in *L'alcova elettrica* (1986), his partly documentary 'reconstruction' of the events surrounding the two trials in 1914 where Italo Tavolato was charged with obscenity on account of the article in praise of prostitution which he had published in the Florentine avant-garde magazine, *Lacerba*. Where in his earlier book Vassalli had concentrated on Campana, relegating the other intellectuals with whom the poet had come into contact to a secondary position, his attention – to their obvious detriment – was now firmly fixed on them. Vassalli mercilessly dissects the falsity, opportunism, pomposity and stupidity of contemporary Florentine cultural leaders and of their hangers-on. Time and again, Papini, Prezzolini and Soffici are made to damn themselves out of their own mouths and by their own actions; and rarely has Vassalli's humour been so consistently probing as here. Only the solitary shape of Campana who, from time to time, flits before our eyes, represents, once again, a figure of human and artistic integrity. And it is not surprising that, as Vassalli has come to realize ever more clearly the need and advantages of 'cultivating his own garden' – to use the phrase which more and more he has liked to employ to introduce himself on the dustjackets of his books – the character of the 'outsider' should have taken centre stage in all his novels since the mid-1970s.

The ineluctable problem which faces any artist who decides to embrace a 'realist' poetic (and I employ the term here as loosely as possible) is how to bridge the 'gap' between art and life. Furthermore, as regards Vassalli, this is made more complicated by the fact that his commitment takes in both writing – his own and that of others – and society: the two are always one, the one without the other is an impossibility. In simple terms, according to Vassalli, what both share is language and an inherent drive towards narration. As a result the writer, culturally and socially the wordsmith and storyteller *par excellence*, whether she or he wants it or not, is inescapably implicated in the present:

> Le parole sono i mille e mille fili che tengono legato lo scrittore all'epoca in cui vive. Lui può negare la sua epoca, può cercare di astrarsene; ma non può recidere quei fili in modo così definitivo e completo, da arrivare a separarsene davvero. Meglio, quindi, rassegnarsi a fare i conti con il proprio presente e con le sue parole. Anche se si tratta di un presente come quello dei banali anni Ottanta, che ogni giorno si racconta da sé attraverso decine e centinaia di giornali, di radio, di televisioni, di libri: perché anche una simile nebbia, e un tale fumo, se ne individui le parole-chiave, può infine ricomporsi nell'immagine più o meno nitida d'una comunità di persone che s'atteggiano e vestono in un certo modo, che appartengono a un'epoca, che sono un'epoca. Ma sì! Una 'foto di gruppo' […] Come realmente furono (the Eighties), e come io ho cercato di raccontarli in queste pagine. […] Così i tempi, e le parole, ci hanno costretti ad essere. (*Il neoitaliano, Prefazione*)

> Words are the thousands upon thousands of threads which keep a writer tied to the time in which he lives. He can deny his time, he can try to withdraw from it; but he cannot cut those threads in such a decisive and complete manner as to manage actually to detach himself from them. Better, therefore, to resign oneself to come to terms with one's own present and its words. Even if it is a matter of a present like that of the banal Eighties, which every day narrates itself through tens and hundreds of newspapers, radios, televisions, books: because even a similar fog, and such a smokescreen, if you pinpoint its key-words, can finally recompose itself into the more or less clear image of a community of persons who pose and dress in a certain way, who belong to a period, who are a period. Yes, of course! A 'group-photograph' […] As the Eighties actually were, and as I have tried to narrate them in these pages […] The times, and their words, have forced us to be like this.

Existence and writing fuse; reality and words merge. Together they are the forces that shape us: we are their offspring, the bastard children of history and language; and is it any wonder that our memories are full of 'quotations'? In such circumstances, to write is necessarily to deal with life (if not quite to live), and, as a result, writers must be prepared to accept their social and artistic responsibilities. Vassalli has a deadly serious view of writing, and thus his irritation with what he deems to be the frivolities and self-centredness of other artists is comprehensible. As far as he is concerned, they lack that broad ethical vein which so indelibly marks his own work and beliefs. There is no doubt that

Vassalli is a deeply moral writer, resolutely preoccupied with the mess which humanity has permanently made of its time on this planet.

It is not my intention here to assess the ontological validity of Vassalli's perspective on life and art. Ultimately, such an assessment would be quite out of place in a survey of this kind, since, whatever one might think of his ideas, they do clearly 'exist' in his books. What is significant, however, are Vassalli's intellectual and artistic formation, the lines of his development, and the impact of his ideological positions on his work.

For many years Vassalli has made it clear that he now considers as an aberration his time with the avant-garde. Indeed, it is only quite recently that he has begun once more to acknowledge this particular period of his life in the brief biographical notes which accompany his books. Although, on one level – as I have tried to explain – Vassalli's hardline attitude is understandable, it does seem, at least to me, to be unnecessarily harsh, especially as it ends up by presenting a misleading picture of his development. Basically, his position is too reductive. It implies that his artistic career divides into two starkly discrete, self-contained moments. In addition, it has moralistic rather than critical overtones, since it condemns the first period as 'bad' and celebrates the second as 'good'. In fact, a more detached analysis finds it difficult to sustain Vassalli's presentation of his own literary experiences. Thus, not only do important elements of continuity unite his œuvre, but it is also probably better to consider it as having three, rather than two, 'separate' phases.

As far as I know, Vassalli has never explicitly and fully explained what it was that drew him to the *Gruppo 63*; he normally just makes caustic generalizations: 'Anche se vengo dall'avanguardia (maledetta!) e ho pubblicato alcuni libri illeggibili perché credevo che così volessero la storia, i destini umani eccetera. Ma ora faccio libri molto diversi' (*Belle lettere*, 1991, p. 34) ('Even if I come from the (damned) avant-garde and I have published some unreadable books because I believed that history, human destinies, etc. wanted this. But now I write very different books.'). He has come closest to presenting his reasons in a private interview given to an Italian-Canadian scholar, Leonard Sbrocchi (however, now also see the brief measured assessment found in the 'Postfazione' appended to the 1991 reprint of *Manuale di corpo*). From Sbrocchi's summary of this, it transpires that Vassalli feels that he was 'compelled' to join, since the 'neo-avantgarde' represented the sole progressive and artistically experimental force in contemporary Italian letters; one, furthermore, which was sensitive to the works of foreign writers and thinkers (primarily French and German). I would conjecture, however, that another important reason for his decision was the *Gruppo 63*'s fundamental interest, stimulated principally by the Frankfurt School and French structuralist theory (most notably, Althusser and Barthes), in the relationship between art and reality in advanced capitalist societies. Vassalli, as we have seen, has been exploring the same general question throughout his œuvre.

However, this is not simply a matter of broad coincidence. In fact, some of the ways in which the *neo-avanguardia* posed and tried to resolve this problem have had a determining and lasting effect on Vassalli's artistic career. A key axiom of the *Gruppo 63* was the idea that art bore directly on the ways in which people perceived reality, indeed, that language was the major determinant of the way the world was experienced. In line with many Western left-wing thinkers of the time, the *neo-avanguardia* postulated that advanced capitalism ensured social consensus by promoting those discourses which ultimately presented an unproblematic view of its mechanisms. These discourses came together to constitute what was often labelled the 'dominant ideology', the (quasi-) unconscious sense of reality which trapped people into accepting their lives under capitalism as normal. Given the fundamental historical relationship between language, reality and the awareness which individuals have of themselves (a key concept in Vassalli as we have seen – 'The times and their words have forced us to be like this'), the duty of radical avant-garde artists who wanted to bring about political change was to challenge capitalism's homogenized ideological view of the world. Since this was crucially sustained by the ordered system of conventional language and traditional literature, writers had to place discursive disorder, violent experimentation, and a general attack upon all forms of established rationality at the centre of their works, thereby revealing the chaos and contradictions which are capitalism's identity.

For a number of years, Vassalli dutifully followed the example of his older mentors and wrote 'challenging' books which, if not quite 'unreadable', are often not especially easy to comprehend. The most difficult, and probably also the most derivative of the ones I have been able to see, is *Narciso* (1968). This work appears to deconstruct both traditional narrative genres and established views of individuality (which are often at the basis of such genres, individualism – it should also be noted – was considered one of the main bulwarks of capitalism), and replaces these with the chaotic, often undifferentiated, and totalizing flow of the oneiric, of the scatological, of the mythic, of the Jungian 'collective unconscious' (as a student in Milan, Vassalli had written a thesis on art and psychoanalysis). Many of these elements have their origins in Sanguineti's writings (the only figure from the *Gruppo 63* for whom Vassalli has maintained a degree of respect). However, even in *Narciso*, there are already traces of features which will become typical of Vassalli's later writing and which distinguish him from his model. His verbal range and inventiveness, especially at the phonic level, are noteworthy; similarly, his pessimism, his literariness, and a certain poorly-concealed predilection for the concrete, for the 'real', separate him from many of his peers. It is, thus, not really surprising that both *Tempo di màssacro* (1970) and *A a il libro dell'utopia ceramica* (1974; but written between 1969 and 1971) should be much more accessible than *Narciso*. As well as the archetypical, a strong sense of history pervades both books, and both have recognizably coherent logical and 'narrative' structures; in addition, especially in the former, Vassalli's mordant wit is very much in evidence – all characteristics which push his work away from the mainstream of *Gruppo 63* poetics and towards more conventional literary forms.

Vassalli's clearcut abandonment of the avant-garde occurs with the publication in 1976 of *L'arrivo della lozione*, which, together with *Abitare il vento* (1980) and *Mareblù* (1982), constitutes the 'middle' period of his artistic production. All three books are unambiguously 'novels'; although, from Vassalli's earlier phase, they retain the use of short compositional units, a strong plurilingual flavour, a certain tendency towards collage-like forms of organization, and a clear experimental bias – elements which, once again, are also present in his post-*Arkadia* work. At the same time, they could not be more different, and intentionally so, from his earlier writings. History is now to the forefront, and contemporary history at that, as Vassalli explores the ideological and social make-up of Italy in the late 1970s and early 1980s. The stress that he gives his fictional investigations is especially significant in underlining the break with his avantgardism. He turns to the novel, an ideologically compromised form; his books have evident 'realist' ambitions to document the condition of Italy during the *riflusso* (much of the *Gruppo 63*'s polemical ire, it should be remembered, was directed against the perceived conservatism of the neorealists); and, most significantly, rather than challenge the discursive ideological make-up of his readers, Vassalli's aim is both to examine and record the actual discourses which mark the present, and to offer a mental map of their effects on the minds of individuals (this, too, marks an important movement away from his earlier emphasis on the 'collective'). His aim is not to disorientate, but to make his readers recognize themselves and their world in his pages as directly as possible. The shift from the abstractions, whether theoretical or artistic, of the *neo-avanguardia*, with its emphasis on the universalizing and on an art which intervenes at the level of the unconscious, could not be more marked, even if the figures on whom Vassalli concentrates in his three books tend to be exemplary types rather than psychologically independent characters (it is only in his most recent work that such characters emerge). Yet, the transitional status of these novels should also be acknowledged. Thus, the avant-garde's pull towards the archetypical is still discernible in their characterization techniques; as, in general, is its concern with the discursive nature of reality. What Vassalli has done is to give these matters a new emphasis, to present them in a manner which could be appreciated by a more general audience (it has long been one of his most telling accusations against the *Gruppo 63* that they wrote things which could be and, in fact, were only read by fellow-initiates).

Vassalli is a marvellous teller of stories, and it was this great ability which the *neo-avanguardia* suppressed. Hence, probably, a further reason for the irritation which he has continued to feel with this time in his life: it involved a denial of so much of himself. Artistically, *L'arrivo della lozione* is an exhilarating work of liberation, even though the picture it paints of contemporary Italy is decidedly gloomy. It deals with the political, cultural and social environment in which right-wing terrorism can flourish and be institutionally protected. An anonymous journalist-narrator attempts to 'reconstruct' (a narrative strategy, as we have seen, which will become a hallmark of Vassalli's most recent phase) the life of one Benito Chetorni, an emotionally and intellectually backward young Southern petit bourgeois, a 'monster' of egotism and violence, who becomes almost inevitably drawn into the shadowy criminal world of right-wing terror. And yet, for all his monstrousness, Benito is not an entirely unsympathetic character, since, through the course of the book, it becomes increasingly clear that he is a victim not just of his own personality, but also of a violent egocentric father, of an equally violent and stultifying education system, of a hypocritical and superstitious religion, and of a corrupt and amoral social and political system. In order to learn about Benito, who has recently been killed in mysterious circumstances, the journalist interviews a large number of people coming from different backgrounds. In addition, he consults newspaper reports and television programmes. It is this array of official and unofficial voices which permits Vassalli to people his book with a kaleidoscope of different registers and styles, making *L'arrivo della lozione* a most impressive plurilingual work. Television jargon mingles with dialect, religious pomposity with underworld slang, journalese with political sloganizing, ridiculous artificial attempts at using 'standard Italian' with bureaucratese – quite simply, we are assaulted by the discourses of modern Italy. And, if this obsessively self-centred and dishonest babble constitutes its voices, then, the country's corrupt and anarchic condition can come as no surprise. Vassalli employs two main devices to unmask the languages of modern Italy. First, he is constantly nudging them into the realms of the absurd, but an absurd which is only just the other side of 'reality': 'Persone, cose e fatti di questa cronaca non hanno né possono avere riscontro diretto nella realtà. La geografia è "parallela"; il tempo è "prossimo", e basta' (*L'arrivo della lozione*, p. 2) ('Persons, things and events of this chronicle do not have nor can they have any correspondence in reality. The geography is "parallel"; the time is "close" and that's all'). Second, he reveals that their information quotient is negligible, riddled as they are with clichés, lies and self-interest, thereby also raising important questions about the reliability of the sources of our knowledge (I shall return to this point when I look again at Vassalli's final phase). By the end of his researches, the journalist has learned little about Benito, but a lot about Italy, which, in many ways, is the book's true protagonist.

In *L'arrivo della lozione*, Vassalli examines the languages of contemporary Italy from the outside, in a pseudo-objective fashion, an approach which is bolstered by the presence of his journalist-narrator. In his next two books, he dramatically switches tack. Both works are written in the first-person, employing a highly subjective, almost stream-of-consciousness technique, which allows Vassalli to display the thoughts and unconscious of his characters. We are now allowed a glimpse into minds structured by the kinds of discourses he had examined in his previous book. At the same time, on account of their need to develop individual psychologies, both *Abitare il vento* and *Mareblù* are necessarily much less stylistically flamboyant than *L'arrivo della lozione*, although both of them maintain a clear plurilingual patina. Their other main difference from the earlier work is that Vassalli now switches his attention away from the right to focus instead on the Italian left.

The protagonist of *Abitare il vento*, Antonio Cristiano Rigotti, commonly known as Cris, is another petit bourgeois child of the *dopoguerra*, though his roots are Northern (a significant detail, since it implies that, while Vassalli acknowledges regional difference, he also sees the whole of Italy united by a common malaise, a point which is made particularly strongly in the latter part of *L'arrivo della lozione*, where the South comes to stand for the country as a whole). Cris has been in prison for some unspecified left-wing terrorist action, and we follow the last few desperate weeks of his existence as he attempts to escape his past, his environment, and himself. Yet, for all his efforts 'to inhabit the wind', Cris, ironically and tragically, spends most of his time imprisoned indoors guarding a victim of left-wing kidnapping. His final flight into a self-inflicted death thus has an inexorable logic, especially in the light of his increasing mental instability, which Vassalli evokes with great precision and force. Indeed, the last instants of his life represent the only 'sane' moment of calm in the whole book. Cris's only companion and confidant during his tribulations is the Grande Proletario, his penis. That his sole friend should be his sexual organ highlights not only Cris's fundamental selfishness, but also his bleak loneliness and alienation – and it comes as no surprise that, as his psychological condition deteriorates, so he should become impotent (in addition, Cris's obsession with the Grande Proletario and his reification of women permits Vassalli mercilessly to dissect the Italian male sexual psyche and to make some telling points about the relationship between desire and politics in revolutionary youth culture).

Like Benito, Cris too is a monster, but one for whom it is even more difficult not to feel sympathy, since the first-person form allows us to participate in his anguish and breakdown from the inside. We appreciate the frailty of his mental world: a mixture of traditional humanistic education and the clichés of mass and popular culture – he views himself as a knight errant, a cowboy and a super-stud – a set of ideas which leave him quite incapable of dealing with others and with the practicalities of life, especially in a world as selfish and as savage as the one which he inhabits. He is, ultimately, just another victim of postwar Italy, the real 'monster' of the story. And his victim status is enhanced by the novel's prominent metanarrative elements which underline that, although Cris is the book's apparent narrator, he is, in fact, just a textual device, a 'character' at the mercy of his 'author'. Yet, despite the grimness of its subject-matter, *Abitare il vento* is almost certainly Vassalli's funniest book to-date. Cris's conversations with himself and the Grande Proletario and his absurdly naive lucubrations in a mixture of dialect, youth slang and 'standard' Italian, all constantly punctuated by out-of-place – since he is a Northerner – Roman *inzomma*'s and English *oh yes*'s, are great comic inventions as well as bitter indictments of a society which can produce such thinking in someone who, as Vassalli makes clear, is potentially far from stupid. Indeed, much of Cris's sympathetic nature as a character can be traced back to the fact that he makes us laugh. And it is not the least of Vassalli's considerable achievements as a writer that, in the modern Italian prose tradition, he has re-established literary humour as a significant narrative strategy and as a major didactic and pleasurable device.

Mareblù, the most 'symbolic', even 'allegorical', of Vassalli's novels, was written to mark the sixtieth anniversary of the foundation in 1921 of the Italian Communist Party. It is set in a campsite on the Ligurian coast, the Mareblù, which is owned by an opportunistic businessman, is frequented by Northern bourgeois families, and provides work for a sixty-year old Stalinist workman, Augusto Ricci, the book's protagonist. The campsite, which stands for Italy, is the scene and cause of ridiculous class struggles, and the object of petty opportunisms. The novel is both a critique of left-wing ideology (like Guareschi's Don Camillo who converses with the crucifix in his church, Augusto talks to the portraits of the four 'giants of history' – Marx, Lenin, Stalin and Mao – hanging on his bedroom wall), and a reminder of much that is sound in socialist thought; it is both an attack on the PCI's complacency and willingness to compromise, and a memento of its more militant past. As the blurb on the cover of the 1990 revised edition notes, the novel is uncannily prophetic about the problems which the PCI had to face and generally failed to resolve during the 1980s. And yet, despite its intelligence, foresight, and inventiveness, *Mareblù* is the least satisfactory of Vassalli's more conventional books. There is little that redeems Ricci's selfishness and self-pity. There is none of that warmth which can be felt around Cris's sad solitary figure. Augusto's re-working of left-wing ideology in terms of cinematic blockbusters, his rampant misogyny, his drunkenness, his constant betrayal of the credos of socialism, and his bourgeois aspirations create an unpleasant, not to say, repugnant character. In his mind, Ricci transforms everything to serve and legitimate his own egotistical ends; any idea of brotherhood, that most central of socialist tenets, is completely banished from his horizon. He is thus too extreme a figure to serve as a metaphor for the far from unimpressive and often honourable tradition of Italian communism. And this is where *Mareblù*'s weakness resides: it is never quite clear whether it is meant to be making a general statement or whether it is simply the picture of a disturbed psyche. In his previous two books, Vassalli had ensured that such a confusion between their social and individual dimensions did not occur; indeed, much of their efficacy stems precisely from the subtle interplay between these two levels.

One senses, in *Mareblù*, Vassalli's personal bitterness towards the PCI and his resentment at the general bankruptcy of left-wing politics in Italy at the beginning of the 1980s. Although he labels the novel a *commedia all'italiana*, there is, ultimately, little to laugh at as the narrative inexorably proceeds towards the final conflagration and the inevitable alliance and conclusion: 'I proletari e i capitalisti devono lottare fianco a fianco, uniti, per un mondo sostanzialmente simile a quello dove sono vissuti' (*Mareblù*, p. 188) ('Proletarians and capitalists must struggle side by side, united, for a world similar in essence to the one in which they have lived'). In many ways, *Mareblù*'s pessimism looks towards Vassalli's most recent work. Some reviewers have interpreted his increasingly marked blend of bitter humour and existential bleakness as scepticism, if not actually cynicism, charges which I find quite unpersuasive. His perspective, however sardonically pessimistic, is always too honest and too ethical – Vassalli would say too 'realistic' – to merit such reductive categorizations.

In my view, *Mareblù* registered the beginning of a potential crisis in Vassalli's development as a writer (and it is noteworthy that *Arkadia* should have appeared a year after its publication); a crisis, from which he was redeemed by Dino Campana and by an explicit return to what is probably the major font of his inspiration: the investigation of the relationship between literature and life. Significantly, of all his books, *Mareblù* is the one in which this question is most marginal. It lacks almost entirely a metaliterary dimension, the space in which Vassalli normally develops his ideas on art and reality, before launching them into the broader narrative world of his books.

As we have seen, the three novels of his 'middle' period have clear historical and documentary concerns. They also underline the fundamental linguistic bonds which unite the world and the individual, who, in her or his mind, transforms experience into words. Language is not just 'everywhere', it is also 'everything' – life is thus like a book. The many disparate voices in *L'arrivo della lozione* 'narrate' their view of reality; reality answers back as a babel of discourses; Cris and Augusto 'speak' their desires, plans, frustrations and memories; they also immediately transform the present and its events, including their own actions, into language – and it is highly significant that their internal reflections are indistinguishable from the forms of spoken language.

In his last three novels, Vassalli takes these basic premises and develops them in intriguingly new directions. If reality, literature and our minds are all so dependent on language what is it that distinguishes one from the other? In fact, it is clear that both our collective and individual memories are in part structured by literary reminiscences, and that we partly relate to our environment on the basis of the books that we have read (some of Cris's frustration stems from the fact that life does not measure up to what he had learned in his literature classes). Like writing, experience, too, is riddled with 'quotations'. Indeed, the primary sources of our knowledge, whether contemporary or past, are linguistic; and, as a result, like any language-act, they are 'unreliable', since they are the product of writing, with all its mediations and manipulations, and, in addition, are prey to interpretation. As *La chimera* effectively demonstrates, very different conclusions about the Seicento can be reached from not dissimilar documents depending whether you are a nineteenth-century Catholic called Alessandro Manzoni or a late twentieth-century atheist called Sebastiano Vassalli. Our historical sources are always inescapably compromised; what we believe to be 'facts' are nothing of the sort. They are linguistic fabrications whose closest relatives are the inventions of literature. 'Truth' and 'fiction' are one, as Vassalli paradoxically concludes in *La notte della cometa*:

> Io cercavo un personaggio con certi particolari connotati. Il caso me l'ha fatto trovare nella realtà storica e da lì l'ho tirato fuori: con accanimento, con scrupolo, con spirito di verità [...] Ma se anche Dino non fosse esistito io ugualmente avrei scritto questa storia e avrei inventato quest'uomo meraviglioso e 'mostruoso', ne sono assolutamente certo. L'avrei inventato così. (*La notta della cometa*, p. 239)

> I was looking for a character with certain particular traits. Chance made me find him in historical reality and I pulled him out from there: with perseverance, with scrupulous care, with the spirit of truth [...] But even if Dino had never existed I would still have written this story and I would have invented this marvellous and 'monstrous' man, I'm absolutely certain of it. I would have invented him in exactly the same way.

And it is indicative in this context that Vassalli should have used the same information he had gathered on Campana to write a novel and to prepare his 'Introduzione' and 'Cronologia della vita dell'Autore' for his edition of the poet's *Opere*.

What is important is not 'truth', which is impossible, but the 'spirit of truth', which is accessible if one is scrupulously honest. Manzoni, on one level, was 'dishonest' in hiding many of the horrors of the seventeenth century when he wrote *I promessi sposi*; horrors, which *La chimera* graphically reveals. On another level, he was 'honest', since he presented a view of things which conformed to his providential sense of reality. And it is important to appreciate that Vassalli's book is not simply an anti-*Promessi sposi*, but is also an act of homage towards Italy's most famous novel, which, given its standing in Italian culture, continues to be such a living force in the present, thereby stressing once more the literary quality of life. In the same way, *La chimera* is not simply a book about a moment long-lost in time, it is also a statement about the similarities between the past and the present, about the unchangeable face of humanity, and about the origins of contemporary Italy. It is thus perfectly fitting that Vassalli should write his most

explicitly historical novels at the very moment when he calls into doubt the
possibility of history as an objective field of study. Novelists, as long as they
approach their subjects with the proper 'spirit of truth', can actually cast light on
areas which the traditional historian finds difficult to assess on account of the
lack of conventional documentary evidence. Thus, Vassalli fills gaps in
Campana's life, while, in *L'oro del mondo*, he records, for instance, the thoughts
of Italian prisoners of war in Greece and the private conversations between
Victor Emmanuel III and his queen. And there is no doubt that Vassalli's interest
in Italy's twentieth-century history is historical in nature. Once again, he is
trying to establish and understand the logic of the present, as well as to fix Italy's
national characteristics. Thus, it is appropriate that he should also develop his
investigations through more standard means: his book on the early twentieth-
century avant-garde, his 'dictionary' and his *inchiesta*, *Sangue e suolo* (1985), on
the problems of the Alto Adige.

The range of Vassalli's writing is a sign of its seriousness. His permanent
experimentation and switching of direction, especially at the stylistic and
structural level, are marks of his constant effort to find a form which can most
effectively deal with the world. Similarly, his plurilingualism represents a way of
recording the variety of the real. At the same time, both Vassalli's experimentation and his plurilingualism are supremely literary statements. They locate his
work in that broad pluristylistic and 'realist' tradition of committed Italian
writing which has its origins in Dante, its major modern critic in Gianfranco
Contini, and its main twentieth-century literary exponent in Carlo Emilio
Gadda. However much Vassalli might feel alienated, both personally and
artistically, from the contemporary literary scene, his writing provides him with
some reassurance that he is not entirely alone, that there is a long tradition of
Italian authors who have not been prepared to compromise: 'Dante ha scritto *La
Divina Commedia* perchè gli scoppiavano le palle di quelli dello Stilnovo e degli
intellettuali trafficoni dell'epoca [...] non si tratta di un caso isolato, perché tutta
la letteratura italiana si spiega così' (*Belle lettere*, 1991, p. 80) ('Dante wrote the
Divine Comedy because he was totally pissed off with that lot of the Stilnovo and
with the wheeler-dealing intellectuals of his time [...] nor is this an isolated case,
because this is what Italian literature is all about'). Yet, the creative and ethical
onus remains squarely on every artist's individual shoulders. As Vassalli re-
marked to me in conversation, even to write like Gadda now would be absurd.
Each new present speaks and demands its own languages; and it has been
Vassalli's particular success to have found registers which both capture and are
fitting for the 1970s, the 1980s, and now the 1990s.

Finally, however much Vassalli's books might address political and literary
issues, his view of literature cannot be reduced to these. He makes it quite clear
that literature satisfies a deeply spiritual human need and that it helps to make
existence marginally more bearable – hence the 'immorality' of those who

exploit literature for their own selfish ends. Whilst great literature can only be produced by a select few, the drive to 'tell stories' is in all of us; and as long as we do not imagine that we can somehow 'teach' ourselves to 'become' poets or we do not overestimate the value of our chatterings, we can still draw pleasure, solace and instruction from the unique achievements of others. Literature, as Vassalli reminds us time and again, is part of our lives, and, as such, we should show it due respect. It can also help us momentarily counter the bleak realization that 'la vita scorre insensata' (*Belle lettere*, 1991, p. 25) ('life flows by senselessly'). As in Vassalli's own case (and Campana's), literature can provide us with a sense that we are not quite alone.

BIBLIOGRAPHY

Works

Lui (egli) (Florence: Quaderni del Proconsolo, 1965).
Narcisso (Turin: Einaudi, 1968).
Disfaso (Rome: Trevi editore, 1969).
Tempo di màssacro (Turin: Einaudi, 1970).
La poesia oggi (Novara: Ant. Ed., 1971).
Il millennio che muore (Turin: Einaudi, 1972).
A a. Il libro dell'utopia ceramica (Ravenna: Longo, 1974).
L'arrivo della lozione (Turin: Einaudi, 1976).
Brindisi (Bergamo: Edizioni Il Bagatto, 1979).
Belle lettere (with Giovanni Bianchi) (Bergamo: Edizioni Il Bagatto, 1979).
La distanza (Bergamo: Edizioni Il Bagatto, 1980).
Abitare il vento (Turin: Einaudi, 1980).
Mareblù (Milan: Mondadori, 1982; revised edition, 1990).
Vani e servizi with illustrations by Alberto Boschi (Alessandria: Edizioni del Piombino, 1983).
Manuale di corpo (Siena: Quaderni di Barbablù, 1983; reprinted with 'Postfazione', Milan: Leonardo, 1991).
Ombre e destini, with an Introduction by Giovanna Ioli (Naples: Guida editori, 1983).
Arkadia (Bergamo: Edizioni El Bagatt, 1983).
Il finito with illustrations by Michelangelo Pistoletto (Bergamo: Edizioni El Bagatt, 1984).
La notte della cometa (Turin: Einaudi, 1984; paperback edition with some additions 1990). Translated into English by John Gatt as *The Night of the Comet* (Manchester: Carcanet, 1989).
L'antica Pieve di Casalvolone in provincia di Novara (secoli XI–XII) (Bergamo: Edizioni El Bagatt, 1984).
Sangue e suolo (Turin: Einaudi, 1985).
L'alcova elettrica (Turin: Einaudi, 1986).
L'oro del mondo (Turin: Einaudi, 1987).
Marradi (with Attilio Lolini) (Brescia: Edizioni l'Obliquo, 1988).
Dino Campana, *Opere*, edited by Sebastiano Vassalli and Carlo Fini (Milan: TEA, 1989).
Il neoitaliano (Bologna: Zanichelli, 1989).
La chimera (Turin: Einaudi, 1990).
Belle lettere (with Attilio Lolini) (Turin: Einaudi, 1991).
Since completing this chapter Vassalli has published another novel, *Marco e Mattio* (Turin: Einaudi, 1992).

Critical Works

Ioli, G., 'Introduzione', in Vassalli, S., *Ombre e destini* (Naples: Guida editori, 1983), pp. 5–8.

Sbrocchi, L. G., 'Sebastiano Vassalli', in *Dictionary of Literary Bibliography*.

Jones, V. R., 'Intertextual patterning: *I promessi sposi* in *La chimera*', *Italian Studies* 47 (1992), 51–67.

Notes on Editors and Contributors

ZYGMUNT G. BARAŃSKI is Professor of Italian Studies, University of Reading.
LINO PERTILE is Professor of Italian, University of Edinburgh.
MASSIMO BACIGALUPO is Professor of American Literature, University of Genoa.
ANN HALLAMORE CAESAR is Lecturer in Italian, University of Cambridge.
PHILIP COOKE is Lecturer in Italian, University of Strathclyde.
ANNA DOLFI is Professor of Italian, University of Florence.
JOSEPH FARRELL is Lecturer in Italian, University of Strathclyde.
ELVIO GUAGNINI is Professor of Italian, University of Trieste.
PETER HAINSWORTH is Lecturer in Italian, University of Oxford.
ANNA LAURA LEPSCHY is Professor of Italian, University College, London.
ROBERT LUMLEY is Lecturer in Italian, University College, London.
MARTIN MCLAUGHLIN is Lecturer in Italian, University of Oxford.
JONATHAN USHER is Senior Lecturer in Italian, University of Edinburgh.
SHIRLEY W. VINALL is Senior Lecturer in Italian, University of Reading.
SHARON WOOD is Senior Lecturer in Italian, University of Strathclyde.
DIEGO ZANCANI is Reader in Italian, University of Kent.

Index

Adorno, Theodore W., 198
Aleramo, Sibilla, 106–7
Althusser, Louis, 247
Americana, 3
Ariosto, Lodovico, 5, 170
Aristotelian unities, 182, 221
Ashbury, John, 35
Austen, Jane, 122

Bagutta Prize, 3
Bakhtin, Mikhail, 45, 219
Baldacci, Luigi, 197
Baldwin, James, 219
Balestrini, Nanni, 10
Bancarella Prize, 3
Banti, Anna, 199
Barthes, Roland, 43, 69, 247
Bassani, Giorgio, 7, 8, 99
Bateson, George, 192
Beckett, Samuel, 27, 48
Benjamin, Walter, 146, 244
Bettelheim, Bruno, 130
Bischel, Peter, 228
Blanchot, Maurice, 237
Boccaccio, Giovanni, 5, 32
Bompiani, Ginevra, 2
Bontempelli, Massimo, 200
Borges, Jorge Luis, 68, 73, 193, 200, 209
Brook, Peter, 37
Bufalino, Gesualdo, 2, 14, 16, 20–34, 64
Bunyan, John, 73
Busi, Aldo, 2, 14, 35–42, 220

Caesar, Michael, 47
Calvino, Italo, 1–2, 4, 8, 12, 17–18, 44–5, 48,
    75–6, 82, 87–90, 133, 193
Camon, Ferdinando, 4
Campana, Dino, 239–40, 245, 252–6
Campiello Prize, 3, 139
Camporesi, Piero, 219
Capriolo, Paola, 2, 4
Cardella, Lara, 3

Carrol, Lewis, 35, 71, 116
Cassola, Carlo, 7–9, 17
Cattaneo, Giulio, 142
Catullus, 26, 111
Celati, Gianni, 2, 14, 17, 43–58
Céline, Louis-Ferdinand, 43, 216
Chamisso, 112
Char, René, 39
Chiusano, Italo A., 9
Chodorow, Nancy, 187
Christian Democratic Party, 61–2
Colette, 187
Comisso Prize, 75
commedia dell'arte, 231
communism, 9, 62, 202, 252–3
Conrad, Joseph, 90, 200
Consolo, Vincenzo, 2–3, 8, 14, 16, 32, 59–74
contestazione, 10
Contini, Gianfranco, 255
Croce, Giulio Cesare, 224
Curtis, Q., 219

D'Annunzio, Gabriele, 41, 111
Dante Alighieri, 5, 15, 111, 158, 164, 255
D'Arrigo, Stefano, 9
Darwin, Charles, 67
De Andrade, Carlos Drummond, 206
Decadent movement, 110–11
De Carlo, Andrea, 2, 14, 17, 75–88
Del Giudice, Daniele, 2, 14, 17, 89–98
De Roberto, Federico, 64, 66
Derrida, Jacques, 158, 162
Dumas, Alexandre, 63
Duranti, Francesca, 2, 14, 99–120
Duras, Marguerite, 187

Eco, Umberto, 1–4, 9–10, 65, 158, 162
Eliot, Thomas Stearns, 62
Epoca, 39
existentialism, 87, 91, 151, 156, 226, 235, 244,
    253

fascism, 4, 6, 60–1, 127, 133, 193, 202, 215–16, 230
Fellini, Federico, 53, 226, 236
feminism, 9–10, 116–17, 121–2, 127, 139, 187, 193, 222
Fenoglio, Beppe, 76
Fink, Guido, 43–4
Fitzgerald, Scott, 85, 87, 204, 230
Fogazzaro, Antonio, 136
Folengo, Teofilo, 44
Fortini, Franco, 244
Foucault, Michel, 45, 203
Franchini, Antonio, 3
Freud, Sigmund, 193

Gadda, Carlo Emilio, 15–16, 39, 70, 228, 255
Gallo, Cornelio, 158–9, 163–4
Garibaldi, Giuseppe, 60, 64, 66–7
Ghidetti, Enrico, 142
Ghirri, Luigi, 51
Ginzburg, Carlo, 44, 52
Ginzburg, Natalia, 8, 123, 125–6, 199
Giudici, Giovanni, 143
Giuliano, Salvatore, 62–3
Goethe, Johann Wolfgang, 112
Goffman, Irving, 44
Gorgias, 31
Gozzano, Guido, 111, 113
Gramigna, Giuliano, 49–50
Grass, Günther, 135, 137
Greene, Graham, 59
Grinzene-Cavour Prize, 3, 151
Gruppo 63, see neo-avanguardia
Guareschi, Giovanni, 252

Handke, Peter, 90
Hemingway, Ernest, 59, 76, 230
Hesse, Hermann, 117
Homer, 158, 160
Horkheimer, Max, 198
Huxley, Thomas Henry, 67
Hymes, Dell, 44

Il Giorno, 107
Italiana: Antologia dei nuovi narratori, 3

James, Henry, 36, 38–9, 99, 200
Johnson, Uwe, 146
Joyce, James, 15, 44, 63, 70
Jung, Carl Gustav, 248

Kafka, Franz, 31, 87, 90, 116, 137, 193
Kerouac, Jack, 219, 230
Kipling, Rudyard, 61
Klein, Melanie, 187
Kristeva, Julia, 219
Kundera, Milan, 89–90

Lacan, Jacques, 130
Lacerba, 245
Lagorio, Gina, 2
Lampedusa, Giuseppe Tomasi di, 7, 29, 32, 64–5
Lanaro, Silvio, 220
Larkin, Philip, 20
La Stampa, 216
Le Carré, John, 228
Leopardi, Giacomo, 5, 227
L'Espresso, 213
Liala (Liana Negretti), 40–1
Lodoli, Marco, 4
London, Jack, 43
Longoni, Anna, 212
Lorca, Federico Garcia, 127
L'Osservatore Romano, 159
Loy, Rosetta, 2, 18, 121–38
Lukács, Georg, 66

Mack Smith, Denis, 65
Magris, Claudio, 3
Mailer, Norman, 230
Malerba, Luciano, 9
Manganelli, Giorgio, 4
Mann, Thomas, 23
Manzoni, Alessandro, 5–6, 14, 23
Maraini, Dacia, 2, 4
Marcoaldi, F., 47
Márquez, Gabriel García, 135, 137, 200
Mastronardi, Lucio, 8
Melville, Herman, 43, 54
Memmo, Francesco Paolo, 142
Meneghello, Luigi, 3–4, 76
Merleau-Ponty, Maurice, 48
Miller, Henry, 39
minimalism, 17, 27, 51, 238
Montaldi, Danilo, 44, 98
Montale, Eugenio, 5, 37, 40–41, 202, 215–16
Montesquieu, (Charles-Louis de Secondat), 73
Morabito, Piero, 212
Morandini, Giuliana, 2, 139–50
Morante, Elsa, 9, 122, 167, 199
Moravia, Alberto, 1, 8
Morazzoni, Marta, 2
•Moro, Aldo, 131, 185, 190–1
Morselli, Guido, 6, 8–9
Mussolini, Benito, 61
Muzzioli, F., 48

neo-avanguardia (Gruppo 63), 8, 10, 12, 22, 244–5, 247–9, 255
neorealist novel, 7–8, 12, 22, 249
Niemeyer, Oscar, 39
Nietzsche, Friedrich, 152
Noi donne, 127
nouveau roman, 75

Ortese, Anna Maria, 4, 199

Ottieri, Ottiero, 8

Palandri, Enrico, 4
Panorama, 214
Papini, Giovanni, 245
Parazzoli, Ferruccio, 3
Paris, Renzo, 10
Parise, Goffredo, 4, 8
Pascal, Blaise, 69
Pasolini, Pier Paolo, 12, 114, 191, 220
Pavese, Cesare, 8, 85
Pazzi, Roberto, 2, 151–65
Pea, Enrico, 200
Pederiali, Giuseppe, 9
Pessoa, Fernando, 200, 206, 211, 214
Petrarca, Francesco, 5, 242–3
Piccioli, Gian Luigi, 9
Piersanti, Claudio, 4
Pirandello, Luigi, 20, 28, 31, 59–60, 64, 211,
    214
Plato, 158
plurilingualism, 15–16, 249–51, 255
Polybius, 152
Pomilio, T., 55
Porta, Antonio, 9, 142
postmodernism, 15–16, 22, 198, 219, 237, 243
post-structuralism, 22, 243
Prato Prize, 3, 139
Prezzolini, Giuseppe, 245
Prokosch, Frederick, 234
Proust, Marcel, 29, 39, 167

Rabelais, François, 15, 48
Radice, Marco Lombardo, 10
Ramondino, Fabrizia, 2, 18, 166–83
Rapallo Prize, 3
Rasy, Elisabetta, 2, 43
Ravazzoli, F., 208
Ravera, Lidia, 10
Resistance, the, 87, 131, 133, 193
riflusso, 11, 16, 87, 249
Rilke, Rainer Maria, 195
Rimbaud, Jean Arthur, 36, 39
Risorgimento, 32, 64–8, 201
Robbe-Grillet, Alain, 193
Romanticism, 6
Rugarli, Giampaolo, 3–4
Rushdie, Salman, 159
Ruzzante, (Angelo Beolco), 44

Salernitano, Masuccio, 44
Salinger, Jerome D., 61, 219
Sanguineti, Edoardo, 244, 248
Sanvitale, Francesca, 2, 14, 184–99
Sartre, Jean Paul, 67
Sbrocchi, Leonard, 247
Schopenhauer, Arthur, 152
Sciascia, Leonardo, 8, 64–5, 69–70, 73, 244

Scott, Sir Walter, 64
Scrivano, Riccardo, 208
Second World War, 6, 11, 100, 123, 134, 146,
    201, 241
Segre, Cesare, 201
Sgorlon, Carlo, 4
Shakespeare, William, 204, 213
Soffici, Ardengo, 245
Sontag, Susan, 220, 231
Spinella, Mario, 146
Spinoza, Baruch, 213
Stein, Gertrude, 35
Stendhal (Marie-Henri Beyle), 87
Strega Prize, 3
structuralism, 11, 22, 247
Svevo, Italo, 5
Swift, Jonathan, 43

Tabucchi, Antonio, 2, 14, 17, 200–18
Tani, Stefano, 212
Tasso, Torquato, 5
Tavolato, Italo, 245
terrorism, 2, 81, 131, 204–5, 220, 241, 250–1
Togliatti, Palmiro, 67
Tomizza, Fulvio, 4
Tondelli, Pier Vittorio, 2–3, 14, 16, 219–38
Torrealta, L., 52
Truffaut, François, 236
Turnaturi, G., 51
Twain, Mark, 43

Under 25, 3

Vassalli, Sebastiano, 2, 14, 16, 18, 239–57
Verga, Giovanni, 5–6, 31, 60, 65, 201
verismo, 61
Verne, Jules, 216
Viareggio Prize, 3, 122, 139
Virgil, 158, 163
Vittorini, Elio, 3, 67, 70
Volpi, Marisa, 2
Volponi, Paolo, 4, 8, 244

Weill, Simone, 69
West, Rebecca, 53
Wiesenthal, Simon, 125
Wolf, Christa, 146, 187
women's writing, 2, 139, 187
Woolf, Virginia, 187

Yourcenar, Margaret, 163

Zanzotto, Andrea, 20